AN ANTHOLOGY OF ISMAILI LITERATURE

AN ANTHOLOGY OF ISMAILI LITERATURE

A SHIʿI VISION OF ISLAM

EDITED BY
HERMANN LANDOLT, SAMIRA SHEIKH
& KUTUB KASSAM

I.B.Tauris *Publishers*
LONDON • NEW YORK
in association with
The Institute of Ismaili Studies
LONDON

Published in 2008 by I.B.Tauris & Co Ltd
6 Salem Rd, London W2 4BU
175 Fifth Avenue, New York NY 10010
www.ibtauris.com

in association with The Institute of Ismaili Studies
42–44 Grosvenor Gardens, London SW1W OEB
www.iis.ac.uk

In the United States of America and in Canada distributed by
St Martin's Press, 175 Fifth Avenue, New York NY 10010

ISBN 978 1 84511 794 8

A full CIP record for this book is available from the British Library
A full CIP record for this book is available from the Library of Congress

Library of Congress catalog card: available

Typeset in Minion Tra for The Institute of Ismaili Studies
Printed and bound in Great Britain by TJ International Ltd, Padstow, Cornwall

The Institute of Ismaili Studies

The Institute of Ismaili Studies was established in 1977 to promote scholarship and learning on Islam, in the historical as well as contemporary contexts, and a better understanding of its relationship with other societies and faiths.

The Institute's programmes encourage a perspective which is not confined to the theological and religious heritage of Islam, but seeks to explore the relationship of religious ideas to broader dimensions of society and culture. The programmes thus encourage an interdisciplinary approach to the materials of Islamic history and thought. Particular attention is also given to issues of modernity that arise as Muslims seek to relate their heritage to contemporary circumstances.

Within the Islamic tradition, the Institute's programmes promote research on those areas which have, to date, received relatively little attention from scholars. These include the intellectual and literary expressions of Shiʿism in general, and Ismailism in particular.

In the context of Islamic societies, the Institute's programmes are informed by the full range and diversity of cultures in which Islam is practised today, from the Middle East, South and Central Asia, and Africa to the industrialized societies of the West, thus taking into consideration the variety of contexts which shape the ideals, beliefs and practices of the faith.

These objectives are realized through concrete programmes and activities organized and implemented by various departments of the Institute. The Institute also collaborates periodically, on a programme-specific basis, with other institutions of learning in the United Kingdom and abroad.

The Institute's academic and research publications fall into a number of interrelated categories:

1. Occasional papers or essays addressing broad themes of the relationship between religion and society, with special reference to Islam.
2. Monographs exploring specific aspects of Islamic faith and culture, or the contributions of individual Muslim thinkers or writers.
3. Editions or translations of significant primary or secondary texts.
4. Translations of poetic or literary texts which illustrate the rich heritage of

spiritual, devotional and symbolic expressions in Muslim history.
5. Works on Ismaili history and thought, and the relationship of the Ismailis to other traditions, communities and schools of thought in Islam.
6. Proceedings of conferences and seminars sponsored by the Institute.
7. Bibliographical works and catalogues which document manuscripts, printed texts and other source materials.

This book falls into category four listed above.

In facilitating these and other publications, the Institute's sole aim is to encourage original research and analysis of relevant issues. While every effort is made to ensure that the publications are of a high academic standard, there is naturally bound to be a diversity of views, ideas and interpretations. As such, the opinions expressed in these publications must be understood as belonging to their authors alone.

Contents

PART TWO: FAITH AND THOUGHT

I. GOD AND CREATION

II. PROPHETHOOD AND IMAMATE

III. INITIATION, KNOWLEDGE AND MEANING

IV. FAITH AND ETHICS

PART THREE: POETRY

List of Plates

The illustrations in this book are from the collections of the Library of The Institute of Ismaili Studies (IIS), the Bodleian Library at University of Oxford and the British Library, London. Copyright of the illustrations is reserved by the respective libraries.

1. Page from a 19th-century manuscript of the *Iftitāḥ al-daʿwa* (*Commencement of the Mission*) of al-Qāḍī al-Nuʿmān (© IIS MS 1242, f. 33r).

2. Painting of the Fatimid palace at Mahdiyya from a 3rd/11th-century manuscript, the *Kitāb gharāʾib al-funūn wa-mulaḥ al-ʿuyūn* (*Book of Curiosities*) (© The Bodleian Library, MS Arab. c. 90, f. 34a).

3. Page from a 17th-century manuscript of Nāṣir-i Khusraw's *Safar-nāma* (*Book of Travels*) (© British Library Board. All rights reserved. Add. 18418, ff. 76a).

4. Image of a parrot and other birds of prey from a 16th-century manuscript of the *Rasāʾil Ikhwān al-Ṣafāʾ* (*Epistles of the Brethren of Purity*) (© The Bodleian Library, MS Laud Or. 260, f. 146a).

5. Diagram of the cross from Wellspring 32 of Abū Yaʿqūb al-Sijistānī's *Kitāb al-yanābīʿ* (*Book of Wellsprings*), reproduced from a manuscript copied in 1351/1932 (© IIS MS 233, f. 54v).

6. Opening page from an 8th/14th-century manuscript of Nāṣir-i Khusraw's *Wajh-i dīn* (*The Face of Religion*) (© IIS MS 940, f. 3r).

7. Poem from an early 20th-century manuscript of the *Dīwān* of Ibn Hāniʾ al-Andalusī (© IIS MS 1149, f. 50).

8. Poem attributed to Pīr Ṣadr al-Dīn from a 19th-century manuscript of *ginān*s written in Khojkī (© IIS MS KH78).

9. Poem from a 19th-century manuscript of the *Dīwān* of the Persian poet Nizārī Quhistānī (© IIS MS. 904, f. 74).

Foreword

Among the earliest impulses in Muslim literature was that of compiling, collecting and organizing reports of events, persons and their sayings and actions. The onus of being the last among the 'People of the Book' engendered an ethos of preserving and developing what Muslims understood to be their own distinctive narrative in history. This desire for self-definition and articulation was expressed in many forms, one of which can be defined as a process of 'anthologizing' the past. Certainly the collection, preservation and systematization of *ḥadīth* represents one of the earliest expressions of such a process. The collection of biographies and historical accounts as well as the preservation of inherited Arab poetry were others. Perhaps a much more crucial one in the realm of Muslim thought was the collection and translation of the philosophical, scientific and literary heritages of the ancient world, notably from Greek, Persian and Sanskrit. All of this in a larger sense contributed to the consolidation of a 'memory' or more accurately 'memories,' as diverse strands in what was evolving as a pluralistic Muslim society.

This *Anthology of Ismaili Literature* therefore builds on a venerated tradition from the past and an established academic genre in the present. It also brings into focus the dramatic growth of Ismaili Studies that has taken place, particularly in the last few decades to which The Institute of Ismaili Studies has made a major contribution.

As the Shia Ismaili Muslim community commemorates and celebrates the Golden Jubilee, the completion of 50 years of Imamat by the present Imam, His Highness Prince Karim Aga Khan, this Anthology also acts to enable the retrieval and re-creation of their diverse literary heritages. It preserves the multiplicities within the tradition, addresses these heritages within the context of parallel developments among other Muslim schools of thought and stimulates new questions about present and future directions of research. It also acts to further our understanding and knowledge of creative periods in Ismaili history, linking Ismailis to each other but also to other Muslims and more broadly reflecting their contribution to the world's literary and humanistic heritage.

Azim Nanji
Director, The Institute of Ismaili Studies

Preface and Acknowledgements

This anthology was conceived as a way of bringing the literature of Ismaili Muslims to a wider audience. It provides a glimpse into the intellectual life of Ismaili communities down the centuries from texts that were cherished, preserved and copied from one generation to the next. Although these texts originated in the pre-modern period, many of them continue to inspire the lives of Ismailis today.

Most of the translations included in the anthology have been previously published or will appear shortly. Some have been revised from the earlier published version. Unless otherwise indicated, introductions to the extracts have been written by the editors. For the sake of consistency, a uniform system of transliteration has been used throughout the volume. Similarly, some of the subheadings have been changed from those used in the previously published versions. Occasional footnotes have been added or edited to enhance readability. A full bibliography with all citations used in the texts, as well as general works on Ismaili studies, can be found at the end of the volume.

The book is divided into three parts: History and Memoir, Faith and Thought, and Poetry. The organization of each is slightly different. The extracts in Part I are arranged in chronological order. In Part II, greater attention has been devoted to thematic consistency. Part III is organized by language with sections on poetry in Arabic, Persian and the languages of South Asia. Accordingly, one may begin at the beginning or dip into the book and browse at will.

Although a large number of texts have been quoted in the pages that follow, this anthology is by no means a comprehensive survey of the tradition. Many important texts and genres have, regretfully, been left out. Among these are the utterances and writings of the Ismaili imams down the centuries and religious texts of advanced complexity. Nor has it been possible to include extracts from works of modern literature or the significant contributions made by Ismailis in the sciences, such as physics and astronomy. The editors were also constrained by the need to find materials that were already available in English or could be translated within our schedule of publication. Nevertheless, the anthology does offer a broad introduction to the themes and genres of Ismaili literature, suggesting ways to contextualize them. It is our hope that it proves to be a doorway through which readers are drawn toward a fuller exploration of the distinctive qualities and richness of Ismaili literature.

The publication of this anthology would not have been possible without the support of the translators and publishers of the works quoted here, and we are grateful to them for their permission to reprint the selected extracts. We are appreciative in particular of the contributions by Mohammad Adra, S. J. Badakhchani, Hamid Haji, Alice C. Hunsberger, Faquir M. Hunzai, Daryoush Mohammad Poor, Abdeali Qutbuddin and Shafique N. Virani, all of whom prepared new translations especially for this volume. We are also grateful to Dr Farhad Daftary who kindly contributed an essay providing the historical context of Ismaili literature.

The editors would like to thank Alnoor Merchant, Senior Librarian and Keeper of Ismaili Collections at The Institute of Ismaili Studies for providing the images from the Institute's manuscript collections. Sincere thanks are also due to Benoit Junod at The Aga Khan Trust for Culture, Lesley Forbes at the Bodleian Library at Oxford and to the British Library for permission to reproduce the other images of manuscripts in this volume.

Several colleagues at the Institute offered their time and expertise at various stages in the production of this anthology: we would like to acknowledge in particular Nader El-Bizri, Sadrudin Hassam, Shah Hussain, Faquir M. Hunzai and Patricia Salazar. We also gratefully acknowledge the invaluable editorial support of Fayaz S. Alibhai and Nadia Holmes.

Contributors*

MOHAMMAD ADRA is an independent scholar in Islamic and Ismaili studies based in Salamiyya, Syria. He is a graduate of Damascus University, where he studied English language and literature. He has translated into English the *Dīwān* of al-Mu'ayyad fi'l-Dīn al-Shīrāzī, to be published shortly, and is currently translating al-Mu'ayyad's *al-Majālis al-Mu'ayyadiyya*.

S. J. BADAKHCHANI is a Research Associate at The Institute of Ismaili Studies. Formerly Deputy Director of the Central Library at Firdowsi University, he obtained his doctorate in Islamic Philosophy at the University of Oxford in 1989. He has published an edition and English translation of Naṣīr al-Dīn al-Ṭūsī's *Sayr wa sulūk* entitled *Contemplation and Action: The Spiritual Autobiography of a Muslim Scholar* (London, 1998), as well as a new edition and English translation of al-Ṭūsī's *Rawḍa-yi taslīm* entitled *Paradise of Submission: A Medieval Treatise on Ismaili Thought* (London, 2005). He is presently working on a new edition and English translation of three short treatises by al-Ṭūsī, namely, *Aghāz wa anjām* (*The Beginning and the End*), *Tawallā wa tabarrā* (Solidarity and Dissociation) and *Maṭlūb al-mu'minīn* (*Desideratum of the Faithful*).

FARHAD DAFTARY is Associate Director and Head of the Department of Academic Research and Publications at The Institute of Ismaili Studies. He is consulting editor of *Encyclopaedia Iranica* and co-editor of *Encyclopaedia Islamica*, as well as the general editor of the 'Ismaili Heritage Series' and 'Ismaili Texts and Translations Series'. He is the author and editor of several acclaimed books and numerous articles in the field of Ismaili studies. His publications include *The Ismāʿīlīs: Their History and Doctrines* (1990; 2nd ed., 2007), *The Assassin Legends: Myths of the Ismaʿilis* (1994), *A Short History of the Ismailis* (1998) *Ismaili Literature: A Bibliography of Sources and Studies* (2004) and *Ismailis in Medieval Muslim Societies* (2006). His books have been translated into Arabic, Persian, Turkish, Urdu, Gujarati and a number of European languages.

LENN E. GOODMAN is Professor of Philosophy and Andrew W. Mellon Professor in the Humanities at Vanderbilt University. His books include *Islamic Humanism; In Defense of Truth: A Pluralistic Approach*; *Jewish and Islamic Philosophy: Crosspollinations in the Classic Age*; *God of Abraham*; *Avicenna*; *On Justice*, and his Gifford

Lectures, *Love Thy Neighbor as Thyself.* A winner of the American Philosophical Association Baumgardt Memorial Prize and the Gratz Centennial Prize, Goodman has lectured widely in the US and in Israel, Australia, Britain and the Continent. His original translation of 'The Case of the Animals vs Man' appeared in 1978. He is also the translator of Saʿadyā Gaʾōn's Arabic commentary of the Book of Job and Ibn Ṭufayl's *Ḥayy Ibn Yaqzān*. He is now at work on a new book, *God and Evolution*.

HAMID HAJI is a specialist in Fatimid literature. He studied at the Sorbonne and is currently a Research Associate at The Institute of Ismaili Studies. His publications include *Founding the Fatimid State: The Rise of an Early Islamic Empire* (London, 2006), an annotated English translation of al-Qāḍī al-Nuʿmān's *Iftitāḥ al-daʿwa*.

ALICE C. HUNSBERGER has spent two decades studying the works of Nāṣir-i Khusraw. She is editor of *Rhyme and Reason: The Philosophical Poetry of Nasir-i Khusraw* (forthcoming), a volume of articles proceeding from the 2005 eponymous international conference, which will be the first extended study of his poetry both from the point of view of poetic art and philosophical meaning. Her *Nasir Khusraw, The Ruby of Badakhshan: A Portrait of the Persian Poet, Traveller and Philosopher* (London, 2000) has had a second printing in English, and translations into Persian, Tajik, Russian and Arabic. A Visiting Research Fellow at The Institute of Ismaili Studies from 1999–2001, Dr Hunsberger teaches Islamic Studies at Hunter College in New York City.

FAQUIR M. HUNZAI is a Research Associate at The Institute of Ismaili Studies. He obtained Masters degrees in Philosophy, Arabic and Persian languages and literatures from Karachi University and a PhD in Islamic Studies from McGill University, Canada. His publications include *Shimmering Light: An Anthology of Ismaili Poetry* (London, 1996), a new Persian edition and English translation of Nāṣir-i Khusraw's *Gushāyish wa rahāyish* published as *Knowledge and Liberation: A Treatise on Philosophical Theology* (London, 1998), and *The Holy Ahl al-Bayt in the Prophetic Traditions* (Karachi, 2000). He has contributed numerous articles to *Encyclopaedia Iranica* and *Oriente Moderno* amongst others. He is presently working on a critical Persian edition and English translation of Nāṣir-i Khusraw's *magnum opus* on *taʾwīl, Wajh-i dīn*.

SHAINOOL JIWA is Head of the Department of Community Relations at The Institute of Ismaili Studies. A specialist in Fatimid history, she undertook doctoral research at Edinburgh University. Since 2002, she has served as Chief Examiner for Islamic History for the International Baccalaureate Organization. Her annotated translation of al-Maqrīzī's writings on the Fatimid Imam-Caliph al-Muʿizz li-Dīn Allāh is forthcoming and she is at present working on an annotated translation of select sections of the *ʿUyūn al-akhbār* by Idrīs ʿImād al-Dīn.

ARZINA R. LALANI is a Research Associate at The Institute of Ismaili Studies. A specialist in classical Islam with a focus on Shiʿi studies, she is the author of the award-winning work, *Early Shīʿī Thought: The Teachings of Imam Muḥammad al-Bāqir* (London, 2000) with translations in several languages. Her forthcoming publication, *Degrees of Excellence: A Fatimid Treatise on Leadership in Islam* is an edition and translation of Aḥmad al-Naysābūrī's *Kitāb ithbāt al-imāma*. She is a contributor to several encyclopaedias and is a member of the editorial board of *The Qur'an: An Encyclopaedia*. Her current monograph explores *Leadership in Islam: Qur'anic Semantics and Interpretations* from multiple exegeses.

LEONARD LEWISOHN is Lecturer in Persian, Iran Heritage Foundation Fellow in Classical Persian and Sufi Literature at the Institute of Arab and Islamic Studies, University of Exeter. He was formerly a Research Associate at The Institute of Ismaili Studies. He specializes in the study of Persian Sufism and has written widely on the subject. He is the author of *Beyond Faith and Infidelity: The Sufi Poetry and Teachings of Mahmud Shabistari* (London, 1995) and co-editor (with Christopher Shackle) of *ʿAṭṭār and the Persian Sufi Tradition: The Art of Spiritual Flight* (London, 2007).

RICHARD J. MCGREGOR is Assistant Professor of Religious Studies at Vanderbilt University. His area of expertise is in the medieval intellectual and mystical traditions of Islam. He is the author of *Sanctity and Mysticism in Medieval Egypt: The Wafa Sufi Order and the Legacy of Ibn Arabi* (Albany, 2004) which explores the construction and theory of 'sainthood' in Islam. He is co-editor (with A. Sabra) of *The Development of Sufism in Mamluk Egypt* (Cairo, 2006) and is currently at work on a project on visual culture and religious devotion in medieval Cairo. His next major project is a study of aesthetics in the Islamic mystical tradition.

DARYOUSH MOHAMMAD POOR completed a degree in International Relations at the University of Westminster in 2003 before going on to postgraduate studies in International Relations and Contemporary Political Theory, graduating with merit in 2004 from the Centre for the Study of Democracy, University of Westminster. He is currently completing a PhD in International Relations at the University of Westminster. He is an editor and translator at The Institute of Ismaili Studies, where he contributes to the *Encyclopedia Islamica* project and the translation of the Institute's website into Farsi.

ABDEALI QUTBUDDIN is a Visiting Research Fellow at The Institute of Ismaili Studies. A specialist in Fatimid studies, he received his PhD at the University of Manchester, writing a thesis on 'Fatimid Law: Its Sources and its Application in the Dawoodi Bohra Community Today.' He had previously studied at the American University in Cairo for a BA and the School of Oriental and African Studies in London for an MA in Arabic literature. His forthcoming monograph is entitled *Reason and Revelation in Fatimid Thought: The Majālis of al-Mu'ayyad al-Shirāzī.*

NIZARALI J. VIRANI is a physician who has practised in both East Africa and Canada. He received his medical degree from Makerere University in Uganda and completed his residency in internal medicine at the Health Sciences Centre in Winnipeg, Canada. A multiple prize winner in the Gandhi Jayanti essay competitions in East Africa, he served as the editor-in-chief of the periodical *The Elgonian*, and has published short stories in Gujarātī. He is currently finalizing a jointly-prepared work entitled *Journey to the Roof of the World: The Travels of Pir Sabzali in Central Asia.*

SHAFIQUE N. VIRANI is a scholar of Islamic Studies at the University of Toronto. After receiving his PhD from Harvard University, he served on the faculty at Harvard and was later the Head of World Humanities at Zayed University in the UAE. He is the author of *The Ismailis in the Middle Ages: A History of Survival, A Search for Salvation* (Oxford, 2007) and is the recipient of honours from the Middle East Studies Association, the Foundation for Iranian Studies, Harvard University, the University of Toronto, and the government of Iran, which awarded him the International Book of the Year prize.

PAUL E. WALKER is currently Research Associate in Near Eastern Languages at the University of Chicago. He is a historian of ideas with a special interest in Ismaili thought, the subject of many of his books, the most recent of which are *Exploring an Islamic Empire: Fatimid History and its Sources* (London, 2002), *Master of the Age: An Islamic Treatise on the Necessity of the Imamate* (London, 2007), and *Fatimid History and Ismaili Doctrine* (Aldershot, 2008).

* Contributors listed here have translated or revised materials especially for this volume. Contributors whose works have been previously published elsewhere but which also appear in this anthology are noted in the List of Reprinted Works.

List of Reprinted Works

Asani, Ali, S. *Ecstasy and Enlightenment: The Ismaili Devotional Literature of South Asia.* London: I.B. Tauris in association with The Institute of Ismaili Studies, 2002, pp. 161, 165–166.

Esmail, Aziz. *A Scent of Sandalwood: Indo-Ismaili Religious Lyrics (Ginans).* Richmond, Surrey: Curzon in association with The Institute of Ismaili Studies, 2002, pp. 93, 101, 167, 174.

Hodgson, Marshall G. S. *The Order of Assassins: The Struggle of the Early Nizārī Ismāʿīlīs against the Islamic World.* The Hague: Mouton, 1955, Appendix II, pp. 325–328.

Hunzai, Faquir M. and Kutub Kassam (ed. and tr.), *Shimmering Light: An Anthology of Ismaili Poetry.* London: I.B. Tauris in association with The Institute of Ismaili Studies, 1996, pp. 25, 27–28, 44, 89–91.

Ibn al-Haytham, Abū ʿAbd Allāh Jaʿfar b. Aḥmad al-Aswad. *Kitāb al-munāẓarāt*, ed. and tr. Wilferd Madelung and Paul E. Walker as *The Advent of the Fatimids: A Contemporary Shiʿi Witness.* London: I.B. Tauris in association with The Institute of Ismaili Studies, 2000, pp. 65–67, 76–80, 95–97, 166–168.

Idrīs ʿImād al-Dīn, *Tāʾrīkh al-khulafāʾ al-Fāṭimiyyīn biʾl-Maghrib: al-qism al-khāṣṣ min* Kitāb ʿuyūn al-akhbār wa-funūn al-āthār, tr. Shainool Jiwa in *Springs of Knowledge: An Annotated Translation of Idrīs ʿImād al-Dīn's* ʿUyūn al-akhbār wa-funūn al-āthār, vol. 4 (forthcoming).

Ikhwān al-Ṣafāʾ. *Rasāʾil Ikhwān al-Ṣafāʾ*, Epistle 22, tr. Lenn E. Goodman and Richard J. McGregor in *Epistles of the Brethren of Purity* (new critical edition and translation, forthcoming).

Jaʿfar b. Manṣūr al-Yaman, Abuʾl-Qāsim. *Kitāb al-ʿālim waʾl-ghulām*, ed. and tr. James W. Morris as *The Master and the Disciple: An Early Islamic Spiritual Dialogue*, London: I.B. Tauris in association with The Institute of Ismaili Studies, 2001, pp. 116–122, 138–144.

Kassam, Tazim R. *Songs of Wisdom and Circles of Dance: Hymns of the Satpanth Ismāʿīlī Muslim Saint, Pīr Shams.* Albany: SUNY Press, 1995, pp. 183, 232–233.

al-Kirmānī, Ḥamīd al-Dīn Aḥmad b. ʿAbd Allāh. *al-Risāla al-durriyya fī maʿnā al-tawḥīd*, tr. Faquir M. Hunzai as '*al-Risālat al-durriyah*', in Seyyed Hossein Nasr and Mehdi Aminrazavi, ed., *An Anthology of Philosophy in Persia,* Oxford: Oxford University Press, 2001, vol. 2, pp. 192–200. (Revised edition, I.B. Tauris in association with The Institute of Ismaili Studies, forthcoming, 2008).

al-Kirmānī, Ḥamīd al-Dīn Aḥmad b. ʿAbd Allāh. *al-Maṣābīḥ fī ithbāt al-imāma*, ed. and tr. Paul E. Walker as *Master of the Age: An Islamic Treatise on the Necessity of the Imamate*. London: I.B. Tauris in association with The Institute of Ismaili Studies, 2007, pp. 63–69, 71–79.

Lewisohn, Leonard. 'Sufism and Ismāʿīlī Doctrine in the Persian Poetry of Nizārī Quhistānī (645–721/1247–1321),' *Iran: Journal of the British Institute of Persian Studies*, 41 (2003), pp. 229–251; pp. 241, 242.

Meisami, Julie Scott. 'Symbolic Structure in a Poem by Nāṣir-i Khusrau,' *Iran: Journal of the British Institute of Persian Studies*, 31 (1993), pp. 103–117; pp. 110–113.

al-Muʾayyad fi'l-Dīn al-Shīrāzī, *Sīrat al-Muʾayyad fi'l-Dīn*, partial tr. by Joseph E. Lowry as 'The Autobiography of al-Muʾayyad fī al-Dīn Hibat Allāh al-Shīrāzī (ca. 1000–1077),' in Dwight F. Reynolds, ed., *Interpreting the Self: Autobiography in the Arabic Literary Tradition*. Los Angeles, London: University of California Press, 2001, pp. 132–144; pp. 140–143.

Nāṣir-i Khusraw, Ḥakīm Abū Muʿīn. *Gushāyish wa rahāyish,* ed. and tr. Faquir M. Hunzai as *Knowledge and Liberation: A Treatise on Philosophical Theology*. London: I.B. Tauris in association with The Institute of Ismaili Studies, 1998, pp. 41–53.

Nāṣir-i Khusraw, Ḥakīm Abū Muʿīn. *Safar-nāma*; tr. Wheeler M. Thackston, Jr. as *Nasir-i Khusraw's Book of Travels (Safarnama)*, Costa Mesa, CA, 2001, pp. 66–75.

Nāṣir-i Khusraw, Ḥakīm Abū Muʿīn. *Wajh-i dīn*, ed. and tr. Faquir M. Hunzai as *The Face of Religion* (forthcoming).

al-Naysābūrī, Aḥmad b. Ibrāhīm. *Kitāb ithbāt al-imāma*, ed. and tr. Arzina R. Lalani as *Degrees of Excellence: A Fatimid Treatise on Leadership in Islam* (forthcoming).

al-Naysābūrī, Aḥmad b. Ibrāhīm. *al-Risāla al-mūjaza al-kāfiya fī adab al-duʿāt*, ed. Verena Klemm and tr. Paul E. Walker as *A Code of Conduct for Dāʿīs* (forthcoming).

al-Nuʿmān b. Muḥammad, al-Qāḍī Abū Ḥanīfa. *Daʿāʾim al-Islām*, tr. Asaf A. A. Fyzee and revised by Ismail K. Poonawala as *The Pillars of Islam*. New Delhi: Oxford University Press, 2002–2004, vol. 1, pp. 5–17.

al-Nuʿmān b. Muḥammad, al-Qāḍī Abū Ḥanīfa. *Iftitāḥ al-daʿwa wa ibtidāʾ al-dawla*, tr. Hamid Haji as *Founding the Fatimid State: The Rise of an Early Islamic Empire*. London: I.B. Tauris in association with The Institute of Ismaili Studies, 2006, pp. 202–213.

Qutbuddin, Tahera. *al-Muʾayyad al-Shīrāzī and Fatimid* Daʿwa *Poetry: A Case of Commitment in Classical Arabic Literature*. Leiden, Boston: Brill, 2005, pp. 200–208.

Sabzālī Ramzānalī, Pīr, '*Madhya Eshiyā nī rasik vigato*', tr. Nizarali J. Virani and Shafique N. Virani in *Journey to the Roof of the World: The Travels of Pir Sabzali in Central Asia* (forthcoming).

Shackle, Christopher and Zawahir Moir. *Ismaili Hymns from South Asia: An Introduction to the Ginans*. Richmond, Surrey: Curzon, 2000, pp. 96–99.

al-Sijistānī, Abū Yaʿqūb Isḥāq b. Aḥmad. *Kashf al-maḥjūb,* ed. and tr. Hermann Landolt as *Creation and Resurrection: Divine Unity and the Universal Process* (forthcoming); partial tr. Hermann Landolt first published as 'Unveiling of the Hidden,' in Seyyed Hossein Nasr and Mehdi Aminrazavi, ed., *An Anthology of Philosophy in Persia*. Oxford: Oxford University Press, 2001, vol. 2, pp. 71–124, pp. 102–104, 108–116.

al-Sijistānī, Abū Yaʿqūb Isḥāq b. Aḥmad. *Kitāb al-yanābīʿ*, tr. Paul E. Walker as 'The Book of Wellsprings' in his *The Wellsprings of Wisdom*. Salt Lake City: University of Utah Press, 1994, pp. 49–50, 52–54, 91–95, 109–111.

al-Ṭūsī, Naṣīr al-Dīn. *Rawḍa-yi taslīm*, ed. and tr. S. Jalal Badakhchani as *Paradise of Submission: A Medieval Treatise on Ismaili Thought*. London: I.B. Tauris in association with The Institute of Ismaili Studies, 2005, pp. 93–103, 104–117, 109–133.

al-Ṭūsī, Naṣīr al-Dīn. *Sayr wa sulūk*, ed. and tr. S. Jalal Badakhchani as *Contemplation and Action: The Spiritual Autobiography of a Muslim Scholar.* London: I.B. Tauris in association with The Institute of Ismaili Studies. pp. 26–32.

van den Berg, Gabrielle Rachel. *Minstrel Poetry from the Pamir Mountains: A Study on the Songs and Poems of the Ismāʿīlīs of Tajik Badakhshan*. Wiesbaden: Dr Ludwig Reichert Verlag, 2004, pp. 81–82, 229, 278–279, 292–294, 332–333.

Virani, Shafique N. *The Ismailis in the Middle Ages: A History of Survival, A Search for Salvation*. Oxford: Oxford University Press, 2007, pp. 43, 136–137, 173, 174–175, 175–176, 179–180, 181.

List of Abbreviations

The following abbreviations are used for certain frequently cited periodicals and other sources in the Notes and Select Bibliography:

APP	*An Anthology of Philosophy in Persia*: Volume 2, ed. S. H. Nasr with M. Aminrazavi
BSOAS	*Bulletin of the School of Oriental and African Studies*
ER	*Encyclopedia of Religion*
EI2	*The Encyclopaedia of Islam*, New Edition
EI3	*The Encyclopaedia of Islam, Three*
EIR	*Encyclopaedia Iranica*
JA	*Journal Asiatique*
JAOS	*Journal of the American Oriental Society*
JBBRAS	*Journal of the Bombay Branch of the Royal Asiatic Society*
MIHT	F. Daftary (ed.) *Mediaeval Ismaʿili History and Thought*

Ismaili History and Literary Traditions

FARHAD DAFTARY[1]

Representing a major Shiʿi Muslim community, the Ismailis have had a complex history dating back to the formative period of Islam. Currently, the Ismailis, who belong to the Nizārī and Ṭayyibī Mustaʿlian branches, are scattered as religious minorities in more than thirty countries of Asia, the Middle East, Africa, Europe and North America. Numbering several millions, the Ismailis also belong to a diversity of ethnic groups and speak a variety of languages, including Arabic, Persian and Indian languages, as well as a number of lesser known dialects of Central Asia and South Asia, and several European languages.

The Ismailis have produced a relatively substantial and diversified literature, in Arabic, Persian and a number of South Asian languages, on a multiplicity of subjects and religious themes in different periods of their long history. These texts, now preserved in numerous private and public manuscript collections in Yaman, Syria, Persia, Afghanistan, Central Asia, India and northern areas of Pakistan, range from a few historical and biographical treatises of the *sīra* genre, legal compendia and elaborate works on the central Shiʿi doctrine of the imamate to complex esoteric and metaphysical treatises culminating in the gnostic-esoteric *ḥaqāʾiq* system of medieval Ismaili thought with its distinctive cyclical conception of sacred history, cosmology, eschatology and soteriology. From early on, however, a good portion of Ismaili literature related to *taʾwīl* or esoteric and allegorical interpretation of Qurʾanic passages as well as commandments and prohibitions of the Islamic law as interpreted by the Ismailis. Ismaili literature is also rich in religious and devotional poetry.

The bulk of the classical Ismaili literature produced in Fatimid and earlier times was written in Arabic, with the major exception of the writings of Nāṣir-i Khusraw (d. after 462/1072), the Persian poet, *dāʿī*, theologian, philosopher and traveller who is regarded by the Central Asian Ismailis as the founder of their communities. More specifically, the Persian Ismaili literary tradition relates almost exclusively to the Nizārī Ismailis of Persia, Afghanistan, Central Asia and the northern areas of Pakistan. The Nizārīs of these regions have produced and preserved a variety of Persian Ismaili texts written during the Alamūt and subsequent periods of their

1. This chapter is partially based on the author's *The Ismāʿīlīs: Their History and Doctrines* (2nd ed., Cambridge, 2007) and *A Short History of the Ismailis: Traditions of a Muslim Community* (Edinburgh, 1998), where full references are given.

history. The Nizārīs of South Asia have elaborated in Gujarātī and other Indian languages, a distinctive literary tradition in hymn-like devotional poems known as *ginān*s. The *ginān*s have been preserved in writing mainly in the Khojkī script. The Ṭayyibī Mustaʿlians, who in South Asia are designated as Bohras, have preserved in Yaman and India numerous Arabic Ismaili texts of the Fatimid period in addition to producing a significant literature during the Yamani period of their own history. Until the middle of the twentieth century, these Ismaili manuscript sources were by and large not accessible to scholars. As a result, the Ismailis had continued to be studied almost exclusively on the basis of evidence collected or fabricated by their detractors. In modern times, the recovery and study of genuine Ismaili texts on a large scale has provided the basis for a breakthrough in Ismaili studies, a process which continues unabated.

EARLY ISMAILI TRADITIONS

The earliest Ismailis separated from the rest of the Imāmī Shiʿis on the death of Imam Jaʿfar al-Ṣādiq in 148/765. They traced the imamate in the progeny of Ismāʿīl b. Jaʿfar al-Ṣādiq, the eponym of the Ismāʿīliyya. Soon the Ismailis organized a dynamic, revolutionary movement designated by them as *al-daʿwa al-hādiya*, or 'the rightly-guiding mission.' The ultimate aim of this religio-political mission, disseminated by a network of *dāʿī*s or missionaries, was to invite Muslims everywhere to accord their allegiance to the ʿAlid imam recognized by the Ismailis. By the late 3rd/9th century, Ismaili *dāʿī*s were operating in many regions from North Africa and Yaman to Central Asia and Sind on the Indian subcontinent.

The early Ismailis elaborated the basic framework of a system of religious thought which was further developed or modified in the Fatimid period. As only a handful of Ismaili texts have survived from this period, it is not possible to trace the development of early Ismaili thought in any great detail. Central to the early Ismaili system of thought was a fundamental distinction between the exoteric (*ẓāhir*) and the esoteric (*bāṭin*) aspects of the sacred scriptures and religious commandments and prohibitions. Accordingly, the Ismailis held that the Qur'an and other revealed scriptures, and their laws (*sharīʿa*s), had their apparent or literal meaning, the *ẓāhir*, which had to be distinguished from their inner meaning hidden in the *bāṭin*. They further held that the *ẓāhir*, or the religious laws enunciated by the prophets, underwent periodic changes while the *bāṭin*, containing the spiritual truths (*ḥaqāʾiq*), remained immutable and eternal. Indeed, these truths represented the message common to the religions of the Abrahamic tradition, namely, Judaism, Christianity and Islam. However, the truths hidden in the *bāṭin* of these monotheistic religions had been veiled by different exoteric laws or *sharīʿa*s as required by different temporal circumstances. The hidden truths were explained through the methodology of *taʾwīl* or esoteric interpretation, which often relied on the mystical significance of letters and numbers. In every age, however, the esoteric truths would be accessible only to the elite (*khawāṣṣ*) of humankind as distinct from the ordinary people (*ʿawāmm*), who were only capable of perceiving the apparent meaning of the revelations. Consequently, in the era of Islam, the eternal truths of religion could be explained only to those who had been properly initiated into the Ismaili *daʿwa* and as such recognized the teaching authority of the Prophet Muḥammad and, after him, that of his *waṣī*, ʿAlī b. Abī Ṭālib, and the rightful imams who succeeded him; these authorities were the sole possessors of *taʾwīl* in the era of Islam. The centrality of *taʾwīl* for the Ismailis is attested by the fact that a good portion of the literature produced by them during the early and Fatimid times, notably the writings of Jaʿfar b. Manṣūr al-Yaman and al-Qāḍī al-Nuʿmān, is comprised of the *taʾwīl* genre which seeks justification for Ismaili doctrines in Qurʾanic verses.

Initiation into Ismailism, known as *balāgh*, was gradual and took place after the novice had taken an oath of allegiance known as *ʿahd* or *mīthāq*. There were, however, no fixed seven or more stages of initiation as claimed by anti-Ismaili polemicists. The initiates were obliged to keep secret the *bāṭin* imparted to them by a hierarchy (*ḥudūd*) of teachers. Such ideas provided the subject matter of the *Kitāb al-ʿālim waʾl-ghulām*, one of the few surviving early Ismaili texts attributed to Jaʿfar b. Manṣūr al-Yaman. By exalting the *bāṭin* aspects of religion, the Ismailis came to be regarded by the rest of the Muslim community as the most representative of the Shiʿis propounding esotericism in Islam and, hence, their common designation as the Bāṭiniyya. This designation was, however, used in a derogatory sense accusing the Ismailis of generally ignoring the *ẓāhir*, or the *sharīʿa*. The available evidence, including the fragmentary texts of the Ismaili oath of allegiance, clearly show that the early Ismailis were not exempted in any sense from the commandments and prohibitions of Islam. Indeed, early Ismaili teachings accorded equal significance to the *ẓāhir* and the *bāṭin* and their inseparability, ideas that were further elaborated in the Ismaili teachings of the Fatimid period. Such generalized accusations of *ibāḥa* or antinomianism against the Ismailis seem to have been rooted in the polemics of their enemies, who also blamed the entire Ismaili movement for the anti-Islamic views and practices of the Qarmaṭīs, the dissidents who seceded from the early Ismaili community.

The esoteric truths or *ḥaqāʾiq* formed a gnostic system of thought for the early Ismailis, representing a distinct worldview. The two main components of this system, developed by the 280s/890s, were a cyclical history of revelations or prophetic eras and a gnostic cosmological doctrine. The Ismailis applied their cyclical interpretation of time and the religious history of humankind to Judaeo-Christian revelations as well as a number of other pre-Islamic religions such as Zoroastrianism with much appeal to non-Muslims. This conception of religious history, reflecting a variety of influences such as Hellenic, Judaeo-Christian, Gnostic as well as eschatological ideas of the earlier Shiʿis, was developed in terms of the eras of different prophets recognized in the Qurʾan. This cyclical conception was also combined with the Ismaili doctrine of the imamate inherited from the Imāmīs.

ISMAILI TRADITIONS OF THE FATIMID PERIOD

The Fatimid period represents the 'golden age' of Ismailism, when the Ismailis possessed an important state of their own and Ismaili scholarship and literature attained their summit. The foundation of the Fatimid caliphate in 297/909 in North Africa indeed marked the crowning success of the early Ismailis. The religio-political *daʿwa* of the Ismāʿīliyya had finally led to the establishment of a state or *dawla* headed by the Ismaili imam. In line with their universal claims, the Fatimid imam-caliphs did not abandon their *daʿwa* activities on assuming power. They particularly concerned themselves with the affairs of the Ismaili *daʿwa* after transferring the seat of their state to Egypt. The *daʿwa* achieved particular success outside the domains of the Fatimid state, and, as a result, Ismailism outlived the downfall of the Fatimid dynasty and caliphate in 576/1171, also surviving the challenges posed by the Sunni revival of the 5th-6th/11th-12th centuries. Be that as it may, Cairo, founded by the Fatimids upon their conquest of Egypt in 358/969, became the headquarters of a complex hierarchical Ismaili *daʿwa* organization in addition to serving as the capital of the Fatimid state. In Egypt, the Fatimids patronized intellectual activities. They founded libraries and major institutions of learning in Cairo, and the Fatimid capital soon became a flourishing centre of Islamic scholarship, sciences, art and culture, in addition to playing a prominent role in the trade and commerce of the Indian Ocean and the Mediterranean. All in all, the Fatimid period marked not only a glorious age in Ismaili history, but also one of the greatest eras in Egyptian and Islamic histories – a milestone in the development of Islamic civilizations.

It was during this period that the Ismaili *dāʿī*s, who were at the same time the scholars and authors of their community, produced what were to become the classical texts of Ismaili literature dealing with a multitude of exoteric and esoteric subjects, as well as *taʾwīl* which became the hallmark of Ismaili thought. The *dāʿī*s of the Fatimid period elaborated distinctive intellectual traditions. In particular, certain *dāʿī*s of the Iranian lands amalgamated Ismaili theology with Neoplatonism and other philosophical traditions into elegant and complex metaphysical systems of thought as expressed in numerous treatises written in Arabic. Only Nāṣir-i Khusraw, the last major proponent of the Iranian Ismaili school of philosophical theology, produced all of his works in Persian.

With the establishment of the Fatimid state, the need had also arisen for promulgating a legal code, even though Ismailism was never imposed on all Fatimid subjects as their official religion. Ismaili law, which had not existed during the pre-Fatimid, secret phase of Ismailism, was codified during the early Fatimid period as a result of the efforts of al-Qāḍī al-Nuʿmān (d. 363/974), the foremost jurist of the Ismailis. The Fatimid Ismailis now came to possess their own school of religious law or *madhhab*, similarly to the principal Sunni systems of jurisprudence (*fiqh*) and the Jaʿfarī system of the Imāmī (Twelver) Shiʿis. It was during the Fatimid period that Ismailis made major contributions to Islamic theology and philosophy in general and to Shiʿi thought in particular. Modern recovery of their literature clearly attests to the richness and diversity of the literary and intellectual heritage of the Ismailis of Fatimid times.

The Fatimid period is one of the best documented in Islamic history. Many medieval Muslim historians have written about the Fatimid dynasty and state, and there are also memoirs and a multitude of non-literary sources of information on the Fatimids. In the latter category, Fatimid monuments and works of art have been thoroughly studied, and much progress has been made on the scholarly investigations of numismatic, epigraphic and other types of evidence related to the Fatimids. There are also valuable letters, documents and other types of archival materials from Fatimid Egypt, materials which are rarely available for other Muslim dynasties of medieval times. Furthermore, the extensive Ismaili literature of the period, recovered in modern times, contains some historical details in addition to shedding light on various aspects of Ismaili doctrines propagated during this period. As a result of this relative abundance of primary sources, Fatimid history and Ismaili teachings of the Fatimid period represent the best studied and understood areas of research within the entire spectrum of modern Ismaili studies.

As a rare instance of its kind in Ismaili literature, we also have a few historical works written by Ismaili authors from the Fatimid period. These include al-Qāḍī al-Nuʿmān's *Iftitāḥ al-daʿwa* (*Commencement of the Mission*), completed in 346/957, the oldest known historical work in Ismaili literature covering the background to the establishment of the Fatimid state, and Ibn al-Haytham's *Kitāb al-munāẓarāt* on the first year of Fatimid rule in North Africa which was recently brought to light. There are also a number of short treatises on specific Ismaili events, such as the *dāʿī* Aḥmad b. Ibrāhīm al-Naysābūrī's *Istitār al-imām*, dealing with the settlement of the early Ismaili Imam ʿAbd Allāh in Salamiyya, and the later journey of ʿAbd Allāh al-Mahdī, the founder of the Fatimid state, from Syria to North Africa. The Fatimid imam-caliphs are treated in volumes 5–7 of the *ʿUyūn al-akhbār*, written by Idrīs ʿImād al-Dīn b. al-Ḥasan (d. 872/1468), the Ṭayyibī *dāʿī* and historian; this is a comprehensive history of the Ismaili *daʿwa* from its beginnings until the opening phase of the Ṭayyibī *daʿwa* in Yaman and the subsequent demise of the Fatimid dynasty in 567/1171.

Aside from strictly historical sources, Ismailis of the Fatimid period produced a few biographical works of the *sīra* genre with great historical value. Amongst the extant examples in this category, mention may be made of the *Sīra*s of the chamberlain Jaʿfar b. ʿAlī, the courtier Jawdhar (d. ca. 386/996), and the chief *dāʿī* al-Muʾayyad fi'l-Dīn al-Shīrāzī (d. 470/1078). A wide variety of archival documents, such as treatises, letters, decrees and epistles (*sijillāt*) of historical value issued through the Fatimid chancery of state, or *dīwān al-inshā*, such as *al-Sijillāt al-Mustanṣiriyya*, have survived directly or have been preserved in later literary sources, notably in Shihāb al-Dīn Aḥmad b. ʿAlī al-Qalqashandī's (d. 821/1418) encyclopedic *Ṣubḥ al-aʿshā*.

The ground for the establishment of the Fatimid state was meticulously prepared by the *dāʿī* Abū ʿAbd Allāh al-Shīʿī (d. 298/911), who had been active among the

Kutāma Berbers of the Maghrib since 280/893. Meanwhile, after leaving Salamiyya, the Ismaili Imam ʿAbd Allāh al-Mahdī had arrived in Egypt in 291/904, where he spent a year. Subsequently, he was prevented from going to the Maghrib because the Aghlabid rulers of the region had discovered the Ismaili imam's plans and were waiting to arrest him. ʿAbd Allāh al-Mahdī instead headed for the remote town of Sijilmāsa, in southern Morocco, where he lived quietly for four years (292–296/905–909), maintaining his contacts with Abū ʿAbd Allāh al-Shīʿī who had already commenced his conquest of Ifrīqiya with the help of his Kutāma soldier-tribesmen. By 296/908, this Kutāma army had achieved much success, signalling the fall of the Aghlabids. On 1 Rajab 296/25 March 909, Abū ʿAbd Allāh entered Raqqāda, the royal city outside the Aghlabid capital of Qayrawān, from where he governed Ifrīqiya as al-Mahdī's deputy for almost a whole year. In Ramaḍān 296/June 909, he set off at the head of his army for Sijilmāsa to hand over the reins of power to the Ismaili imam himself. ʿAbd Allāh al-Mahdī was acclaimed as caliph in a special ceremony in Sijilmāsa on 7 Dhu'l-Ḥijja 296/27 August 909. With these events the *dawr al-satr* in early Ismailism also ended. ʿAbd Allāh al-Mahdī entered Raqqāda on 20 Rabīʿ II 297/4 January 910 and was immediately acclaimed as caliph there. A unique eyewitness account of the establishment of Fatimid rule is contained in Ibn al-Haytham's *Kitāb al-munāẓarāt*. The Ismaili Shiʿi caliphate of the Fatimids had now officially commenced in Ifrīqiya. The new dynasty was named Fatimid (Fāṭimiyya) after the Prophet's daughter Fāṭima to whom al-Mahdī and his successors traced their ʿAlid ancestry.

The Fatimids did not abandon their Ismaili *daʿwa* on assuming power, as they entertained universal aspirations aiming to extend their rule over the entire Muslim community. However, the first four Fatimid imam-caliphs, ruling from Ifrīqiya (covering today's Tunisia and eastern Algeria), encountered numerous difficulties while consolidating their power with the help of the Kutāma Berbers who were converted to Ismailism and provided the backbone of the Fatimid armies. In particular, they confronted the hostility of the Khārijī Berbers and the Sunni Arab inhabitants of Qayrawān and other cities of Ifrīqiya, in addition to their rivalries and conflicts with the Umayyads of Spain, the Abbasids and the Byzantines. Under these circumstances, the Ismaili *daʿwa* remained rather inactive in North Africa for some time.

Fatimid rule was established firmly in the Maghrib only under al-Muʿizz li-Dīn Allāh (341–365/953–975), who succeeded in transforming the Fatimid caliphate from a regional state into a great empire. He was also the first Fatimid imam-caliph to concern himself significantly with the propagation of the Ismaili *daʿwa* outside the Fatimid dominions, especially after the transference of the seat of the Fatimid state in 362/973 to Egypt, where he founded Cairo as his new capital city. Al-Muʿizz's policies soon bore fruit as the Ismaili *daʿwa* and Fatimid cause were reinvigorated outside the Fatimid state. Most notably, Abū Yaʿqūb al-Sijistānī (d. after 361/971), the *dāʿī* of Sīstān, Makrān and Khurāsān, who had earlier belonged to the dissident faction, transferred his allegiance to the Fatimids; and, consequently, many of his followers in Persia and Central Asia acknowledged the Fatimid imam-caliph.

Ismailism also acquired a permanent stronghold in Multān, Sind, where an Ismaili principality was established for a few decades.

In the course of the 4th/10th century, the *dāʿīs* Muḥammad b. Aḥmad al-Nasafī (d. 332/943), Abū Ḥātim al-Rāzī (d. 322/934) and Abū Yaʿqūb al-Sijistānī set about harmonizing their theology with Neoplatonic philosophy which led to the development of a unique intellectual tradition of philosophical theology in Ismailism. These *dāʿīs* wrote for the educated classes of society and aimed to attract them intellectually. This is why they expressed their theology, always revolving around the central Shiʿi doctrine of the imamate, in terms of the then most intellectually fashionable terminologies and themes. After the initial efforts of al-Nasafī and al-Rāzī, the Iranian *dāʿīs* elaborated complex metaphysical systems of thought with a distinct Neoplatonized emanational cosmology. In this cosmology, fully elaborated in al-Sijistānī's *Kitāb al-yanābīʿ* and other works, God is described as absolutely transcendent, beyond being and non-being, and thus unknowable. These *dāʿīs* also expounded a doctrine of salvation as part of their cosmology. In their soteriology, the ultimate goal of salvation is the human soul's progression towards its Creator in quest of a spiritual reward in an eternal afterlife. This, of course, would depend on guidance provided by the authorized sources of wisdom in every era of sacred history. Later, Ḥamīd al-Dīn al-Kirmānī (d. after 411/1020) acted as an arbiter in the prolonged debate that had taken place earlier among these Iranian *dāʿīs*. He reviewed this debate from the perspective of the Fatimid *daʿwa* in his *Kitāb al-riyāḍ* (*Book of the Meadows*), and in particular upheld certain views of Abū Ḥātim al-Rāzī against those of al-Nasafī in affirming the indispensability of both the *ẓāhir* and the *bāṭin*, the letter of the law as well as its inner meaning.

Neoplatonic philosophy also influenced the cosmology elaborated by the Ismaili-connected Ikhwān al-Safā', a group of anonymous authors in Baṣra who produced an encyclopedic work of fifty-two epistles, *Rasā'il Ikhwān al-Ṣafā'*, on a variety of sciences during the 4th/10th century, or just before the foundation of the Fatimid state. At any rate, the Ikhwān al-Ṣafā', usually translated as the 'Sincere Brethren' or 'Brothers of Purity,' drew on a wide variety of Greek and other pre-Islamic sources and traditions which they combined with Islamic teachings, especially as upheld by the Shiʿis. Like the contemporary Iranian *dāʿīs*, they aimed to harmonize religion and philosophy. Indeed, the Ikhwān offered a new synthesis of reason and revelation – representing a new world order under the hegemony of the Ismaili imam reminiscent of Plato's philosopher-king. However, the Ikhwān do not seem to have had any discernible influence on the Ismaili thought of the Fatimid period. It was only in the 6th/12th century that the *Rasā'il* were introduced into the literature of the Ṭayyibī Mustaʿlian *daʿwa* in Yaman. Henceforth, these epistles were widely studied by the Ṭayyibī *dāʿīs* of Yaman and, later, by their successors in the Dā'ūdī Bohra community of the Indian subcontinent.

It was also in al-Muʿizz's time that Ismaili law was finally codified. The process had started already in ʿAbd Allāh al-Mahdī's reign as caliph (297–322/909–934), when the precepts of Shiʿi law were put into practice. The promulgation of an

Ismaili *madhhab* resulted mainly from the efforts of al-Qāḍī Abū Ḥanīfa al-Nuʿmān b. Muḥammad (d. 363/974), who was officially commissioned by al-Muʿizz to prepare legal compendia. Al-Nuʿmān had started serving the Fatimids in different capacities from the time of al-Mahdī. In 337/948, he was appointed by the Fatimid Imam-Caliph al-Manṣūr (334–341/946–953) as chief judge (*qāḍī al-quḍāt*) of the Fatimid state. It is to be noted that from the time of Aflaḥ b. Hārūn al-Malūsī, the Fatimid chief judge was also placed in charge of the affairs of the Ismaili *daʿwa*. Thus, responsibilities for explaining and enforcing the *ẓāhir*, or the commandments and prohibitions of the law, and interpreting its *bāṭin* or inner meaning, were united in the same person under the overall guidance of the Ismaili imam of the time.

Al-Nuʿmān codified Ismaili law by systematically collecting the firmly established *ḥadīth*s transmitted from the *ahl al-bayt*, drawing on existing collections of earlier Imāmī as well as Zaydī authorities. His initial efforts resulted in a massive compendium entitled *Kitāb al-īḍāḥ*, which has not survived except for one fragment. Subsequently, he produced several abridgements of the *Īḍāḥ*, which was treated as semi-official by the Fatimids. Al-Nuʿmān's efforts culminated in the *Daʿāʾim al-Islām* (*The Pillars of Islam*), which was scrutinized closely by al-Muʿizz and endorsed as the official code of the Fatimid state. Similarly to the Sunnis and other Shiʿi communities, the Ismailis, too, now possessed a system of law and jurisprudence, also defining an Ismaili paradigm of governance. Ismaili law accorded special importance to the Shiʿi doctrine of the imamate. The authority of the infallible ʿAlid imam and his teachings became the third principal source of Ismaili law, after the Qurʾan and the *sunna* of the Prophet which are accepted as the first two sources by all Muslims. In the *Daʿāʾim*, al-Nuʿmān also provided Islamic legitimation for an ʿAlid state ruled by the *ahl al-bayt*, elaborating the *ẓāhirī* doctrinal basis of the Fatimids' legitimacy as ruling imams and lending support to their universal claims. The *Daʿāʾim al-Islām* has continued through the centuries to be used by Ṭayyibī Ismailis as their principal authority in legal matters.

Absent from Ismaili literature in general are two branches of Islamic sciences, viz., *ḥadīth* and *tafsīr* or Qurʾan commentaries. This is because the Ismailis had a living and present imam, who represented the Prophetic tradition as well as the traditions of the earlier imams. As a result, the Ismailis felt no need to compile *ḥadīth* collections or produce philological commentaries on the Qurʾan. And the true, inner meaning of the Qurʾan could be made available to the faithful only through *taʾwīl*, which was again the prerogative of the imam and the hierarchy of teachers authorized by him. Amongst numerous such Ismaili works on *taʾwīl* related to particular chapters of the Qurʾan, mention may be made of al-Qāḍī al-Nuʿmān's *Asās al-taʾwīl*, and Jaʿfar b. Manṣūr al-Yaman's *Sarāʾir al-nuṭaqā* and *Kitāb taʾwīl al-zakāt*.

The Ismailis had high esteem for learning and elaborated distinctive traditions and institutions of learning under the Fatimids. Foremost among these was al-Azhar, initially founded as a mosque under al-Muʿizz, which subsequently became a leading college and centre of learning in the Muslim world. The Fatimid *daʿwa* was particularly concerned with educating the Ismaili converts in esoteric doctrine, known as *ḥikma* or 'wisdom.' As a result, a variety of lectures or 'teaching sessions,' generally designated as *majālis* (singular, *majlis*), were organized. The private lectures on Ismaili esoteric doctrine, known as the *majālis al-ḥikma* or 'sessions of wisdom,' were reserved exclusively for Ismaili initiates who had already taken the oath of allegiance and secrecy. The lectures, delivered by the *dāʿī al-duʿāt* at the Fatimid palace, were approved beforehand by the imam. Only the imam was the source of the *ḥikma*; and the *dāʿī al-duʿāt* or chief *dāʿī*, commonly called *bāb* (the gate) in Ismaili sources, was the imam's mouthpiece through whom the Ismailis received their knowledge of esoteric doctrines. Many of these *majālis* were in due course collected and committed to writing, such as al-Nuʿmān's *Taʾwīl al-daʿāʾim* and the *Majālis al-Mustanṣiriyya* delivered by Abu'l-Qāsim b. Wahb al-Malījī. This Fatimid tradition of learning culminated in the *Majālis al-Muʾayyadiyya* of the *dāʿī* al-Muʾayyad fi'l-Dīn al-Shīrāzī (d. 470/1078). Another of the main institutions of learning founded by the Fatimids was the Dār al-ʿIlm, the House of Knowledge, some times also called the Dār al-Ḥikma. Established in 395/1005 by the Imam-Caliph al-Ḥākim (386–411/996–1021), a variety of religious and non-religious subjects were taught at this academy which was also equipped with a major library. Many Fatimid *dāʿī*s received at least part of their training at the Dār al-ʿIlm.

Information on the structure and functioning of the Ismaili *daʿwa* organization was among the most guarded secrets of the Ismailis. The religio-political messages of the *daʿwa* were disseminated by networks of *dāʿī*s within the Fatimid dominions as well as in other regions referred to as the *jazāʾir* (singular, *jazīra*, 'island'). Each *jazīra* was placed under the charge of a high-ranking *dāʿī* referred to as *ḥujja*; and every *ḥujja* had a number of *dāʿī*s of different ranks working under him. Organized in a strictly hierarchical manner, the Fatimid *daʿwa* was under the overall supervision of the imam and the *dāʿī al-duʿāt*, or *bāb*, who acted as its administrative head. The *daʿwa* organization developed over time and reached its full elaboration under the Imam-Caliph al-Mustanṣir. It was, however, in non-Fatimid regions, the *jazīra*s, especially Yaman, Persia and Central Asia, that the Fatimid *daʿwa* achieved lasting success. The *daʿwa* was intensified in Iraq and Persia under al-Ḥākim. Foremost among the *dāʿī*s of this period was Ḥamīd al-Dīn al-Kirmānī. A learned philosopher, he harmonized Ismaili theology with a variety of philosophical traditions in developing his own metaphysical system, presented in his *Rāḥat al-ʿaql* (*Repose of the Intellect*), completed in 411/1020. In fact, al-Kirmānī's thought represents a unique tradition within the Iranian school of philosophical Ismailism. In particular, he expounded a modified cosmology, replacing the Neoplatonic dyad of intellect and soul in the spiritual world by a system of ten separate intellects in partial adaptation of al-Farābī's Aristotelian cosmic system. Al-Kirmānī's cosmology, however, was not adopted by the Fatimid *daʿwa;* it later provided the basis for the Ismaili cosmology of the Ṭayyibī *dāʿī*s of Yaman.

The Fatimid Imam-Caliph al-Ḥākim's reign also coincided with the opening phase of what was to become known as the Druze religion, founded by a number of *dāʿī*s who had come to Cairo from Persia and Central Asia, notably al-Akhram and al-Darazī. These *dāʿīs* proclaimed the end of the historical era of Islam and advocated the divinity of al-Ḥākim. Al-Kirmānī was officially invited to Cairo around 405/1014 to refute the new extremist doctrines from a theological perspective. He wrote several treatises in defence of the doctrine of imamate in general and al-Ḥākim's imamate in particular, including *al-Maṣābīḥ fī ithbāt al-imāma*, the *Risālat mabāsim al-bishārāt* and *al-Risāla al-wāʿiẓa*. In fact, the doctrine of the imamate provided essential subject matter for a number of theological treatises written by Ismaili authors of different periods.

The Ismaili *daʿwa* activities outside the Fatimid dominions reached their peak in the long reign of al-Mustanṣir (427–487/1036–1094), even after the Sunni Saljūqs replaced the Shiʿi Būyids as overlords of the Abbasids in 447/1055. The Fatimid *dāʿīs* won many converts in Iraq and different parts of Persia and Central Asia. One of the most prominent *dāʿīs* of this period was al-Muʾayyad fiʾl-Dīn al-Shīrāzī who after his initial career in Fārs, in southern Persia, settled in Cairo and played an active role in the affairs of the Fatimid *dawla* and Ismaili *daʿwa*. In 450/1058, al-Mustanṣir appointed him as *dāʿī al-duʿāt*, a post he held for twenty years, with the exception of a brief period, until his death in 470/1078. He left an invaluable account of his life and early career in his *Sīra*, which reveals his central role as an intermediary between the Fatimids and the Turkish military commander al-Basāsīrī who briefly led the Fatimid cause in Iraq against the Saljūqs. Al-Basāsīrī seized Baghdad in 450/1058 and had the *khuṭba* read there for one whole year for al-Mustanṣir before he was eventually defeated by the Saljūqs. Al-Muʾayyad established closer relations between Cairo and several *jazīras*, especially Yaman, where Ismailism had persisted in a dormant form throughout the 4th/10th century. By the time of al-Mustanṣir, the leadership of the *daʿwa* in Yaman had fallen into the hands of the *dāʿī* ʿAlī b. Muḥammad al-Ṣulayḥī, an important chieftain of the Banū Hamdān in the mountainous region of Ḥarāz. The *dāʿī* ʿAlī al-Ṣulayḥī rose in Ḥarāz in 439/1047, marking the effective foundation of the Ṣulayḥid dynasty ruling over different parts of Yaman as vassals of the Fatimids until 532/1138.

Meanwhile, the Ismaili *daʿwa* had continued to spread in many parts of the Iranian world, now incorporated into the Saljūq sultanate. By the early 460s/1070s, the Persian Ismailis in the Saljūq dominions were under the leadership of ʿAbd al-Malik b. ʿAṭṭāsh who had his secret headquarters in Iṣfahān, the main Saljūq capital. He was also responsible for launching the career of Ḥasan-i Ṣabbāḥ who in due course led the Ismaili *daʿwa* in Persia. In Badakhshān and other eastern parts of the Iranian world, too, the *daʿwa* had continued to spread after the downfall of the Sāmānids in 395/1005. One of the most eminent *dāʿīs* of al-Mustanṣir's time, Nāṣir-i Khusraw (d. after 462/1070) played an important part in propagating Ismailism in Central Asia, becoming known as the *ḥujja* of Khurāsān. He also spread the *daʿwa* to Ṭabaristān and other Caspian provinces of Iran.

The genuine and spurious works attributed to Nāṣir-i Khusraw (d. after 462/1070) have been preserved throughout the centuries by the Ismailis of Badakhshān (now divided between Tajikistan and Afghanistan) and their offshoot communities in the Hindu Kush region, now situated in Hunza and other northern areas of Pakistan. After a memorable journey to Fatimid Cairo, recorded in his *Safar-nāma*, Nāṣir-i Khusraw played a key role in propagating Ismailism in the remote eastern regions of the Iranian world. Fleeing persecution, he took refuge in the valley of Yumgān in Badakhshān, where he spent the final decades of his life. It was during his period of exile in Yumgān that Nāṣir produced most of his poetry and prose, including several theological works such as the *Zād al-musāfirīn* and the *Jāmiʿ al-ḥikmatayn*, his last known composition completed in 462/1070 at the request of his Ismaili patron in Badakhshān, the *amīr* Abu'l-Maʿālī ʿAlī b. Asad. Amongst his other Ismaili works preserved in Central Asia, mention may be made of the *Gushāyish wa rahāyish*, the *Shish faṣl* and the *Wajh-i dīn*, Nāṣir's major treatise on *ta'wīl* containing esoteric interpretations of a range of religious commandments such as prayer, fasting and pilgrimage. The *Wajh-i dīn* is esteemed very highly by the Ismaili communities of Badakhshān that in due course became a stronghold of the Nizārī branch of Ismailism. Nāṣir's writings contributed significantly to shaping the later distinctive literary tradition of the Central Asian Nizārī Ismailis. Nāṣir-i Khusraw may also have been the person who translated al-Sijistānī's *Kashf al-maḥjūb* (*Unveiling the Hidden*) from Arabic into Persian, the only version of the work that has actually survived.

During the long reign of al-Mustanṣir, the Fatimid caliphate had already embarked on its decline resulting from factional fighting in the Fatimid armies and other political and economic difficulties. The ravaging activities of the Turkish regiments which led to a complete breakdown of law and order finally obliged al-Mustanṣir to appeal for help to Badr al-Jamālī, an Armenian general in the service of the Fatimids. Badr arrived in Cairo in 466/1074 and soon assumed leadership of civil, judicial and religious administrations in addition to being 'commander of the armies' (*amīr al-juyūsh*), his main title and source of power. He managed to restore peace and relative prosperity to Egypt in the course of his long vizierate of some twenty years when he was the effective ruler of the Fatimid state. Badr died in 487/1094 after having arranged for his son al-Afḍal to succeed him to the vizierate. Henceforth, real power in the Fatimid state remained in the hands of viziers who were normally commanders of the armies, whence their title of 'vizier of the sword' (*wazīr al-sayf*), and they were normally also in charge of the *daʿwa* organization and activities.

Al-Mustanṣir, the eighth Fatimid caliph and eighteenth Ismaili imam, died in Dhu'l-Ḥijja 487/December 1094, a few months after Badr al-Jamālī. Thereupon, the unified Ismaili *daʿwa* split into two rival factions, as al-Mustanṣir's son and original heir-designate Nizār was deprived of his succession rights by al-Afḍal who quickly installed Nizār's younger half-brother to the Fatimid throne with the title of al-Mustaʿlī bi'llāh (487–495/1094–1101). The two factions were later designated as the Nizāriyya and Mustaʿliyya after al-Mustanṣir's sons who had claimed his heritage. Al-Afḍal immediately obtained for al-Mustaʿlī the allegiance of the notables of the Fatimid court and most leaders of the Ismaili *daʿwa* in Cairo who also recognized al-Mustaʿlī's imamate. Nizār refused to pay homage to al-Mustaʿlī and fled to Alexandria where he rose in revolt, but was defeated and killed in 488/1095. The imamate of al-Mustaʿlī was recognized by the Ismaili communities of Egypt, Yaman and western India. These Ismailis who depended on the Fatimid regime later traced the imamate in the progeny of al-Mustaʿlī. The bulk of the Ismailis of Syria, too, joined the Mustaʿlīan camp. On the other hand, the Ismailis of Persia who were then already under the leadership of Ḥasan-i Ṣabbāḥ supported the succession rights of Nizār. The Central Asian Ismailis seem to have remained uninvolved in the Nizārī-Mustaʿlī schism for quite some time.

The Fatimid state survived for another 77 years after the Nizārī-Mustaʿlī schism of 487/1094. These decades witnessed the rapid decline of the Fatimid caliphate which was beset by continuing crises. Al-Mustaʿlī and his successors on the Fatimid throne, who were mostly minors and remained powerless in the hands of their viziers, continued to be recognized as imams by the Mustaʿlian Ismailis who themselves soon split into Ḥāfiẓī and Ṭayyibī branches.

The Ayyūbid Ṣalāḥ al-Dīn, who had acted as the last Fatimid vizier, ended Fatimid rule on 7 Muḥarram 567/10 September 1171, when he had the *khuṭba* read in Cairo in the name of the reigning Abbasid caliph al-Mustaḍīʾ. A few days later, al-ʿĀḍid (555–567/1160–1171), the fourteenth and final Fatimid caliph, died after a brief illness. The Fatimid *dawla* had, thus, ended after 262 years. On the collapse of the Fatimid caliphate, Egypt's new Sunni Ayyūbid masters began to persecute the Ismailis, also suppressing the Ḥāfiẓī Ismaili *daʿwa* organization there, and all the Fatimid institutions. The immense treasures of the Fatimids and their vast libraries were also pillaged or sold.

NIZĀRĪ ISMAILI TRADITIONS OF THE ALAMŪT PERIOD

By the time of the Nizārī-Mustaʿlī succession dispute of 487/1094, Ḥasan-i Ṣabbāḥ, who preached the Ismaili *daʿwa* within the Saljūq dominions in Persia, had emerged as the leader of the Persian Ismailis. He was then clearly following an independent policy, and his seizure of the fortress of Alamūt in 483/1090 had, in fact, signalled the initiation of the Persian Ismailis' open revolt against the Saljūqs as well as the foundation of what would become the Nizārī Ismaili state. The Nizārī state, centred at Alamūt, with its territories scattered in different parts of Persia and Syria, lasted some 166 years until it was destroyed by the Mongols in 654/1256.

The circumstances of the Nizārīs of the Alamūt period were radically different from those faced by the Ismailis of the Fatimid state and the Ṭayyibīs of Yaman. From early on, the Nizārīs were preoccupied with a revolutionary campaign and their survival in an extremely hostile environment. As a result, they produced military commanders rather than theologians. Furthermore, Ḥasan-i Ṣabbāḥ and his seven successors at Alamūt used Persian as the religious language of their community. This made it very difficult for the Nizārīs of Persia and adjacent Persian-speaking, eastern lands to have ready access to the Ismaili literature produced in Arabic during the Fatimid period, although the Syrian Nizārīs who used Arabic did preserve some of the earlier texts. At any rate, the Persian Nizārīs did not produce a substantial literature; the bulk of their literature, including the collections of the famous library at Alamūt, was either destroyed in the Mongol invasions or lost soon afterwards during the Mongol Īlkhānid rule over Persia (654–754/1256–1353). The Syrian Nizārīs were spared the Mongol catastrophe and were permitted by the Mamlūks to remain in their traditional strongholds. Subsequently, many of the literary sources, produced or preserved by the Syrian Nizārīs, perished in the course of prolonged hostilities with their Nuṣayrī (ʿAlawī) neighbours.

The Nizārī Ismailis of the Alamūt period did, nevertheless, maintain a sophisticated intellectual outlook and a literary tradition, elaborating their teachings in response to changing circumstances. Ḥasan-i Ṣabbāḥ himself was a learned theologian and was credited with founding an impressive library at Alamūt. Later, other major Nizārī fortresses in Persia and Syria were equipped with significant collections of books, documents and scientific instruments. In the doctrinal field, only a handful of Nizārī works have survived directly from that period. These include the *Haft bāb-i Bābā Sayyidnā*, or the *Seven Chapters* of Bābā Sayyidnā, two honorific titles reserved for Ḥasan-i Ṣabbāḥ. This is an anonymous work written around 596/1200, several decades after Ḥasan-i Ṣabbāḥ's death in 518/1124. There are also those Ismaili works written during the final decades of the Alamūt period and attributed to Naṣīr al-Dīn al-Ṭūsī (d. 672/1274), who spent some three decades in the Nizārī fortress communities of Persia. Among these works, mention should be made of the *Rawḍa-yi taslīm* (*Paradise of Submission*), which is the single most important source on the Nizārī teachings of the Alamūt period, and al-Ṭūsī's spiritual autobiography *Sayr wa sulūk*, in which he explains his conversion to Ismailism. A few Nizārī texts, which are not extant otherwise, have been fragmentarily preserved in the *Kitāb al-milal wa'l-niḥal* of Ḥasan-i Ṣabbaḥ's contemporary, Muḥammad b. ʿAbd al-Karīm al-Shahrastānī (d. 548/1153), the famous heresiographer and theologian who was influenced by Ismaili ideas if not an Ismaili himself, as well as in some post-Alamūt Nizārī writings. Al-Shahrastānī himself wrote several works, including a partial Qur'an commentary called *Mafātiḥ al-asrār wa maṣābīḥ al-abrār*, and a philosophical treatise in refutation of Ibn Sīnā's metaphysics, *Kitāb al-muṣāraʿa*, using Ismaili ideas and the methodology of *ta'wīl* or esoteric interpretation.

The Nizārī Ismailis of the Alamūt period also maintained a historiographical tradition in Persia. They compiled chronicles in the Persian language recording the events of their state according to the reigns of the successive lords of Alamūt. This historiographical tradition commenced with the *Sargudhasht-i Sayyidnā*, covering the biography of Ḥasan-i Ṣabbāḥ, designated as *Bābā* and *Sayyidnā* ('our master') by the contemporary Nizārīs, and the events of his rule as the first lord of Alamūt. All the Nizārī chronicles kept at Alamūt and other strongholds in Persia perished in the period of Mongol rule. However, some of these chronicles and other Nizārī documents, such as the *fuṣūl* or epistles of the lords of Alamūt, were seen and used extensively by three Persian historians of the Īlkhānid period, namely, ʿAṭā-Malik Juwaynī (d. 681/1283), Rashīd al-Dīn Faḍl Allāh (d. 718/1318), and Abu'l-Qāsim ʿAbd Allāh Kāshānī (d. ca. 738/1337). The Ismaili histories of these authorities remain our main sources on the Nizārī *daʿwa* and state in Persia during the Alamūt period. Having joined the entourage of Hülegü, Juwaynī accompanied the Mongol conqueror on his military campaigns against the Nizārīs in 654/1256; he also participated in the peace negotiations between Hülegü and the Nizārī Imam Rukn al-Dīn Khurshāh. Juwaynī received permission to visit the Alamūt library before the destruction of that fortress by the Mongols. As a result, he succeeded in saving a number of what he called 'choice books,' including the *Sargudhasht-i Sayyidnā*, and used these Ismaili sources in writing his history of Ḥasan-i Ṣabbāḥ and his successors at Alamūt, which he labelled the *daʿwa* of the 'heretics' (*malāḥida*) and the 'new preaching' (*daʿwat-i jadīd*). He composed this account soon after the fall of Alamūt and added it to the end of his *Ta'rīkh-i jahān-gushā* on Mongol victories, completed in its present form in 658/1260. Juwaynī's history of the Persian Nizārīs, permeated with invective and curses against them, is preceded by sections relating to the earlier history of the Ismailis, a pattern adopted by later Persian historians. Rashīd al-Dīn's history of the Ismailis is contained in the second volume of his vast *Jāmiʿ al-tawārīkh* (*Collection of Histories*) completed in 710/1310. Few details are known about the life of Kāshānī, a Persian Twelver Shiʿi historian belonging to the Abū Ṭāhir family of leading potters from Kāshān. It is known, however, that he was associated with Rashīd al-Dīn and was probably involved in producing parts of the *Jāmiʿ al-tawārīkh*. He included a section on the Ismailis in his *Zubdat al-tawārīkh*, a general history of the Muslim world until the demise of the Abbasids. Kāshānī's account, which came to light in 1964, is the fullest of the three sources. Later Persian historians who produced summary accounts of Ḥasan-i Ṣabbāḥ and his successors, based themselves mainly on Juwaynī and Rashīd al-Dīn, occasionally drawing also on sources of legendary nature.

The Nizārīs of Syria produced their own religious literature, including numerous poetical works in Arabic, during the Alamūt period. This literature has not been sufficiently studied in modern times, as the relevant manuscript sources are not readily accessible. The Syrian Nizārīs have also preserved many of the Ismaili texts of the Fatimid period, works of al-Qāḍī al-Nuʿmān, Jaʿfar b. Manṣūr al-Yaman and others. The Persian Nizārī works of the Alamūt period were evidently not translated into Arabic in Syria, and similarly, the religious literature of the Syrian Nizārīs was not rendered into Persian. Nor did the Syrian Nizārīs compile official chronicles like those produced by their Persian co-religionists. Amongst the few surviving Syrian Nizārī works, a special place is occupied by the *Faṣl min al-lafẓ al-sharīf*, which includes a biographical account of Rāshid al-Dīn Sinān (d. 589/1193), the most famous *dāʿī* of the community, in addition to sayings attributed to him. This hagiographic work containing anecdotes based on the oral tradition of the Syrian Nizārīs, may have been compiled much later by the *dāʿī* Abū Firās Shihāb al-Dīn al-Maynaqī (d. 937/1530 or 947/1540), or possibly by another Syrian Abū

Firās who lived two centuries earlier. The main literary sources on the history of the Syrian Nizārīs, from the arrival of the first *dāʿīs* dispatched from Alamūt in the earliest years of the 6th/12th century until the complete subjugation of the Nizārī castles by Mamlūks in 671/1273, are the local histories of Syria as well as general Arab chronicles. Amongst the relevant authorities, the most important are Ibn al-Qalānisī (d. 555/1160), the Damascene chronicler, Ibn al-ʿAdīm (d. 660/1262), the historian of Aleppo, and Ibn al-Jawzī's grandson known as Ṣibt (d. 654/1256). Of particular interest here are also works of several lesser known historians, notably al-ʿAẓīmī (d. after 556/1161). For the later decades, the histories of Abū Shāma (d. 665/1267) and Ibn Wāṣil (d. 697/1298), amongst others, are of significance.

The non-literary sources on the Persian Nizārīs of the Alamūt period are rather insignificant. The Mongols demolished the major Nizārī fortresses of Persia, which may have provided valuable archaeological evidence. At any rate, these fortresses have not been scientifically studied and the few excavations undertaken in modern times probably caused more damage to the sites than they yielded results. All in all, no epigraphic evidence has been recovered from the Nizārī castles of Persia, which were equipped with impressive defence and water supply systems, while relatively limited hoards of Nizārī coins minted at Alamūt have also been recovered. On the other hand, the Nizārī castles of Syria, which have been much better preserved, have yielded valuable archaeological, including epigraphic, information.

By 487/1094 Ḥasan-i Ṣabbāḥ, as noted, had emerged as the leader of the Persian Ismailis. As an Ismaili Shiʿi, he could not tolerate the anti-Shiʿi policies of the Saljūqs who, as the new champions of Sunni Islam, aimed to uproot the Fatimids. Ḥasan's revolt was also an expression of Persian 'national' sentiments, as the alien rule of Saljūq Turks was detested by Persians of different social classes. This may explain why he substituted Persian for Arabic as the religious language of the Persian Ismailis, accounting also for the popular success of his movement. It was under such circumstances that in al-Mustanṣir's succession dispute, Ḥasan supported Nizār's cause and severed his relations with the Fatimid regime and the *daʿwa* headquarters in Cairo which had lent their support to al-Mustaʿlī. By this decision, Ḥasan founded the independent Nizārī Ismaili *daʿwa* on behalf of the Nizārī imam who then remained inaccessible; and, as a result, the Nizārī *daʿwa* survived the downfall of the Fatimid dynasty, similarly to the subsequent fate of the Ṭayyibī *daʿwa* in Yaman.

Ḥasan-i Ṣabbāḥ did not divulge the name of Nizār's successor to the imamate. In fact, numismatic evidence shows that Nizār's own name appeared on coins minted at Alamūt for about seventy years after his death in 488/1095, while his progeny were blessed anonymously. The early Nizārī Ismailis were, thus, left without an accessible imam in another *dawr al-satr*; and, as in the pre-Fatimid period of concealment, the absent imam was represented in the community by a *ḥujja*, his chief representative. Ḥasan and his next two successors as heads of the Nizārī *daʿwa* and state, were indeed recognized as such *ḥujja*s. It seems that already in Ḥasan-i Ṣabbāḥ's time many Nizārīs believed that a son or grandson of Nizār had been secretly brought from Egypt to Persia, and he became the progenitor of the line of the Nizārī imams who later emerged at Alamūt.

From early on in the Alamūt period, outsiders had the impression that the Persian Ismailis had initiated a 'new preaching' (*al-daʿwa al-jadīda*) in contrast to the 'old preaching' (*al-daʿwa al-qadīma*) of the Fatimid times. The 'new preaching' did not, however, represent any new doctrines; it was merely a reformulation of the old Shiʿi doctrine of *taʿlīm*, or authoritative teaching by the imam. It was mainly Ḥasan-i Ṣabbāḥ himself who restated this doctrine in a more rigorous form in a theological treatise entitled *al-Fuṣūl al-arbaʿa* or *Four Chapters*. This treatise, originally written in Persian, has been preserved only fragmentarily by al-Shahrastānī and Persian historians. This doctrine is also reiterated in Naṣīr al-Dīn al-Ṭūsī's spiritual autobiography. The doctrine of *taʿlīm*, emphasizing the autonomous teaching authority of each imam in his own time, became the central doctrine of the Nizārīs who, henceforth, were designated as the Taʿlīmiyya. The intellectual challenge posed to the Sunni establishment by the doctrine of *taʿlīm*, which also refuted the legitimacy of the Abbasid caliph as the spiritual spokesman of all Muslims, called forth the reaction of the Sunni establishment. Many Sunni scholars, led by Abū Ḥāmid al-Ghazālī (d. 505/1111), wrote refutations of the Ismaili doctrine of *taʿlīm*. It is to be noted that the Nizārīs do not seem to have responded to these polemics.

By 489/1096, when the fortress of Lamasar was seized, Ḥasan had acquired or built numerous mountain strongholds in Daylamān, the centre of Nizārī power in northern Persia. Meanwhile, the Ismailis had come to possess a network of fortresses and several towns in Quhistān, in south-eastern Khurāsān, which remained the second most important territory of the Nizārī state in Persia. Later, the Nizārīs acquired Gird Kūh and other fortresses in the regions of Qūmis, Arrajān and Zagros. In the opening years of the 6th/12th century, Ḥasan began to extend his activities to Syria by sending Persian *dāʿī*s from Alamūt, led by al-Ḥakīm al-Munajjim (d. 496/1103). In Syria, the *dāʿī*s confronted many difficulties in the initial phases of their operations in Aleppo and Damascus; and it took them several decades before they finally succeeded in acquiring a network of castles, collectively referred to in the sources as the *qilāʿ al-daʿwa*, in the Jabal Bahrāʾ (present-day Jabal Anṣāriyya), a mountainous region between Ḥamā and the Mediterranean coastline in central Syria. These castles included Qadmūs, Kahf and Maṣyāf, which often served as the headquarters of the chief *dāʿī* of the Syrian Nizārīs. There, the Nizārīs confronted the enmity of various local Sunni rulers as well as the Crusaders who were active in adjacent territories belonging to the Latin states of Antioch and Tripoli. By the final years of Ḥasan's life, however, the anti-Saljūq revolt of the Nizārīs had lost its momentum, much in the same way that the Saljūqs under Barkiyāruq (d. 498/1105) and Muḥammad Tapar (d. 511/1118) had failed in their prolonged military campaigns to uproot the Persian Ismailis from their mountain strongholds. Ismaili-Saljūq relations had now entered a new phase of stalemate.

On Ḥasan-i Ṣabbāḥ's death in 518/1124, Kiyā Buzurg-Ummīd succeeded him as the head of the Nizārī *daʿwa* and state. A capable administrator like his predecessor,

Buzurg-Ummīd (518–532/1124–1138) maintained the policies of Ḥasan and further strengthened and extended the Nizārī state. The Ismaili-Saljūq stalemate essentially continued during the long reign of Buzurg-Ummīd's son Muḥammad (532–557/1138–1162) as the third lord of Alamūt. By then, the Nizārī state had acquired its distinctive administrative structure. Each Nizārī territory was placed under the overall leadership of a chief *dāʿī* appointed from Alamūt; the leader of the Quhistānī Nizārīs was known as *muḥtasham*. These *dāʿī*s as well as the commanders of major fortresses enjoyed a large degree of independence and local initiative, contributing to the dynamism and resilience of the Nizārī movement. Highly united with a remarkable sense of mission, the Nizārīs acknowledged the supreme leadership of Alamūt and obeyed without any dissent the religious policies initiated at that fortress by the imam's *ḥujja*s and, subsequently, by the Nizārī imams themselves. Meanwhile, the Nizārīs had been eagerly expecting the appearance of their imam, who had remained inaccessible since Nizār's murder in 488/1095.

The fourth lord of Alamūt, Ḥasan II, to whom the Nizārīs refer with the expression *ʿalā dhikrihi'l-salām* (on his mention be peace), succeeded to the leadership in 557/1162 and soon after declared the *qiyāma* or resurrection, initiating a new phase in the religious history of the Nizārī community. On 17 Ramaḍān 559/8 August 1164, in the presence of the representatives of different Nizārī territories who had gathered at Alamūt, he delivered a sermon in which he proclaimed the *qiyāma*, the long awaited Last Day. About two months later, a similar ceremony was held at the fortress of Muʾminābād, near Bīrjand, and the earlier *khuṭba* and message were read out by Raʾīs Muẓaffar, the *muḥtasham* in Quhistān. There, Ḥasan II's position was more clearly equated with that of al-Mustanṣir as God's caliph (*khalīfa*) on earth, implicitly claiming the status of imam for the lord of Alamūt.

Ḥasan II relied heavily on Ismaili *taʾwīl* and earlier traditions, interpreting *qiyāma* symbolically and spiritually for the Nizārīs. Accordingly, *qiyāma* meant nothing more than the manifestation of unveiled truth (*ḥaqīqa*) in the person of the Nizārī imam; it was a spiritual resurrection only for those who acknowledged the rightful imam of the time and were now capable of understanding the truth, the esoteric and immutable essence of Islam. It was in this sense that Paradise was actualized for the Nizārīs in this world. They were now to rise to a spiritual level of existence, transcending from *ẓāhir* to *bāṭin*, from *sharīʿa* to *ḥaqīqa*, or from the literal interpretation of the law to an understanding of its spirituality and the eternal truths of religion. On the other hand, the 'outsiders,' the non-Nizārīs who were incapable of recognizing the truth, were rendered spiritually non-existent. The imam proclaiming the *qiyāma* would be the *qāʾim al-qiyāma*, 'lord of resurrection,' a rank which in Ismaili religious hierarchy was always higher than that of an ordinary imam.

Ḥasan II's son and successor Nūr al-Dīn Muḥammad devoted his long reign (561–607/1166–1210) to a systematic elaboration of the *qiyāma* in terms of a doctrine. The exaltation of the autonomous teaching authority of the present imam now became the central feature of Nizārī thought; and *qiyāma* came to imply a complete personal transformation of the Nizārīs who were expected to perceive the imam in his true spiritual reality. Nūr al-Dīn Muḥammad also made every Nizārī imam potentially a *qāʾim* capable of inaugurating an era of *qiyāma*. Nūr al-Dīn Muḥammad also explicitly affirmed the Nizārī Fatimid descent of his father and, therefore, of himself. He explained that Ḥasan II was in fact an imam and the son of a descendant of Nizār b. al-Mustanṣir who had earlier found refuge in Alamūt. Henceforth, the Nizārīs recognized the lords of Alamūt, beginning with Ḥasan II, as their imams.

Meanwhile, the Syrian Nizārīs had entered into an important phase of their own history under the leadership of Rāshid al-Dīn Sinān, their most famous leader, who had been appointed chief *dāʿī* in Syria by Ḥasan II soon after his own accession in 557/1162. Sinān reorganized and strengthened the Syrian Nizārī *daʿwa*, also consolidating their network of fortresses in the Jabal Bahrā'. Aiming to safeguard his community, Sinān entered into intricate and shifting alliances with the major neighbouring powers and rulers, notably the Crusaders, the Zangids and Ṣalāḥ al-Dīn. The Syrian Nizārīs had intermittent conflicts with the Templars and the Hospitallers, Frankish military orders which often acted independently in the Latin East. The only one of the Syrian *dāʿīs* to act somewhat independently of Alamūt, Sinān evidently taught his own version of the doctrine of *qiyāma*. He led the Syrian Nizārīs for almost three decades to the peak of their power and fame until his death in 589/1193.

Nūr al-Dīn Muḥammad's son and successor, Jalāl al-Dīn Ḥasan (r. 607–618/1210–1221), was concerned largely with redressing the isolation of the Nizārīs from the larger world of Sunni Islam. Consequently, he publicly repudiated the doctrine of *qiyāma* and ordered his followers to observe the *sharīʿa* in its Sunni form, inviting Sunni jurists to instruct his people. Indeed, Jalāl al-Dīn Ḥasan did his utmost to convince the outside world of his new policy. In 608/1211, the Abbasid caliph al-Nāṣir acknowledged the imam's rapprochement with Sunni Islam and issued a decree to that effect. Henceforth, the rights of Jalāl al-Dīn Ḥasan to Nizārī territories were officially recognized by the Abbasid caliph, as well as the Khwārazm Shāhs, who were then establishing their own empire in Persia as successors to the Saljūqs, and by other Sunni rulers. The Nizārīs viewed Jalāl al-Dīn Ḥasan's declarations as a restoration of *taqiyya*, which had been lifted in the *qiyāma* times; the observance of *taqiyya* could imply any type of accommodation to the outside world deemed necessary by the infallible imam. Be that as it may, the Nizārī imam had now successfully achieved peace and security for his community and state.

Under ʿAlāʾ al-Dīn Muḥammad (r. 618–653/1221–1255), Jalāl al-Dīn Ḥasan's son and successor as the penultimate lord of Alamūt, gradually the Sunni *sharīʿa* was relaxed within the community and the Nizārī traditions associated with *qiyāma* were once again revived. The Nizārī leadership now also made a sustained effort to explain the different doctrinal declarations and religious policies of the lords of Alamūt. As a result, all these teachings were interpreted comprehensively within a coherent theological framework, aiming to provide satisfactory explanations for the seemingly contradictory policies adopted at Alamūt. Intellectual life indeed flourished in the long reign of ʿAlāʾ al-Dīn Muḥammad, receiving a special impetus from the influx of outside scholars who fled the first waves of the Mongol invasions and took refuge in the Nizārī fortress communities. Foremost among such scholars who availed themselves of the Nizārī libraries and patronage of learning was Naṣīr al-Dīn al-Ṭūsī (d. 672/1274), who made major contributions to the Nizārī Ismaili thought of the late Alamūt period during his prolonged stay amongst them.

It is mainly through al-Ṭūsī's extant Ismaili writings, including notably the *Rawḍa-yi taslīm*, a collective work to which he probably contributed substantially, that we have an exposition of the Nizārī thought of the Alamūt period, especially as it developed after the declaration of the *qiyāma*. The author explained that *qiyāma* was not necessarily a final, eschatological event, but a transitory condition of life when the veil of *taqiyya* would be lifted so as to make the unveiled truth accessible. In the current cycle of history, however, the full *qiyāma*, or Great Resurrection (*qiyāmat-i qiyāmāt*) would still occur at the end of the era initiated by the Prophet Muḥammad. The identification of *sharīʿa* with *taqiyya*, implied by the teachings of Ḥasan II, was now made explicit by an identification of *qiyāma* with *ḥaqīqa*. Thus, the imposition of the Sunni *sharīʿa* by Jalāl al-Dīn Ḥasan was presented as a return to *taqiyya*, and to a new period of *satr* or concealment, when the truth (*ḥaqīqa*) would be once again concealed in the *bāṭin* of religion. The condition of *qiyāma* could, in principle, be granted by the current Nizārī imam at any time, because every imam was potentially also an *imām-qāʾim*. In this integrated theological presentation, human life could alternate between periods of *qiyāma*, when reality is manifest, and *satr*, when it would be concealed requiring the observance of *taqiyya*. In this sense, the term *satr* was redefined to imply the concealment of the religious truths and the true spiritual reality of the imam, and not just the physical inaccessibility of the imam, as had been the case in the pre-Fatimid and early Alamūt times. The teachings of the late Alamūt period brought the Nizārīs even closer to the esoteric traditions more commonly associated with Sufism.

Nizārī fortunes in Persia were rapidly reversed after the collapse of the Khwārazmian empire which brought them into direct confrontation with the invading Mongols. When the Great Khan Möngke decided to complete the Mongol conquests of western Asia, he assigned first priority to the destruction of the Nizārī Ismaili state, a task completed with some difficulty in 654/1256 by his brother Hülegü who led the main Mongol expedition into Persia. Shortly before, in 653/1255, ʿAlāʾ al-Dīn Muḥammad had been succeeded by his eldest son Rukn al-Dīn Khurshāh, who would rule for exactly one year as the last lord of Alamūt. The youthful imam engaged in a complex and ultimately futile series of negotiations with Hülegü. Finally, on 29 Shawwāl 654/19 November 1256, Khurshāh descended from the fortress of Maymūndiz in Rūdbār in the company of Naṣīr al-Dīn al-Ṭūsī and Nizārī dignitaries, and surrendered to the Mongols. With the fall of Alamūt a month later, the fate of the Nizārī state was sealed. Alamūt and many other fortresses were demolished, though Gird Kūh resisted its Mongol besiegers for another fourteen years. In the spring of 655/1257, Khurshāh himself was killed by his Mongol guards in Mongolia, where he had gone in order to meet the Great Khan. By then, the Mongols had massacred large numbers of Nizārīs who had been placed in their protective custody.

In the meantime, the Syrian Nizārīs had been led by other *dāʿīs* after Rāshid al-Dīn Sinān. From the time of the Imam Jalāl al-Dīn Ḥasan's rapprochement with Sunni Islam, relations between the Syrian Nizārīs and their Muslim neighbours had improved significantly, while periodic encounters of different kinds continued with the Franks. The last important encounter between the Nizārīs and the Crusaders, who still held the Syrian coastline, occurred in the early 650s/1250s in connection with embassies exchanged with Louis IX, the French king better known as St. Louis (d. 1270), who led the Seventh Crusade (1248–1255) to the Holy Land. John of Joinville (d. 1317), the king's biographer and secretary has left a valuable account of these dealings, including a curious disputation between an Arabic-speaking friar and the chief *dāʿī* of the Syrian Nizārīs. Subsequently, the Nizārīs collaborated with the Mamlūks and other Muslim rulers in defeating the Mongols in Syria. Baybars, the victorious Mamlūk sultan, now resorted to various measures for bringing about the submission of the Nizārī strongholds in Syria. Kahf was the last Nizārī outpost there to fall in 671/1273. However, the Syrian Nizārīs were permitted to remain in their traditional abodes as loyal subjects of the Mamlūks and their Ottoman successors. Having lost their political prominence, the Nizārīs henceforth lived secretly as religious minorities in numerous communities scattered in Syria, Persia, Afghanistan, Central Asia and the Indian subcontinent.

POST-ALAMŪT NIZĀRĪ ISMAILI TRADITIONS

The post-Alamūt period in Nizārī Ismailism covers more than seven centuries, from the fall of Alamūt in 654/1256 to the present time. The Nizārī communities, scattered from Syria to Persia, Central Asia and South Asia, now elaborated a diversity of religious and literary traditions in different languages. The first five centuries after the fall of Alamūt represent the longest obscure phase of Ismaili history. Many aspects of Ismaili activity in this period are not still sufficiently studied due to a scarcity of primary sources. A variety of factors, related to the very nature of Nizārī Ismailism of this period, have caused special research difficulties here. In the aftermath of the destruction of their state and fortress communities in Persia, the Nizārīs were deprived of the centralized leadership they had enjoyed during the Alamūt period. After Rukn al-Dīn Khurshāh's son and successor, Shams al-Dīn Muḥammad, there was a split in the line of the Nizārī imams and their followers, further dividing the community into rival Muḥammad-Shāhī and Qāsim-Shāhī branches. The Nizārī imamate was, thus, handed down through two parallel lines while the imams remained in hiding and were inaccessible to the bulk of their followers for about two centuries.

More complex research difficulties arise from the widespread practice of *taqiyya* by the Nizārīs of different regions. During much of the post-Alamūt period of their history, the Nizārīs were obliged to dissimulate rather strictly to safeguard themselves against rampant persecution. They concealed their true beliefs and literature in addition to resorting to Sunni, Sufi, Twelver Shiʿi and Hindu disguises in different parts of the Iranian world and the Indian subcontinent. It is important to note that in many regions, the Nizārīs observed *taqiyya* for very long periods with lasting consequences in terms of their religious identity. Although this phenomenon has only recently been studied by a few scholars, notably cultural anthropologists, it is certain that long-term dissimulation under any guise would eventually result in irrevocable changes in the traditions and the very religious identity of the dissimulating community. Such influences might have manifested themselves in a variety of manners, ranging from total acculturation or full assimilation of the Nizārīs of a particular locality into the community chosen originally as a protective cover, to various degrees of interfacing and admixture between Ismaili and 'other' traditions without necessarily entailing the loss of the Ismaili identity. Probabilities for complete assimilation or disintegration were particularly high during the early post-Alamūt times when the Nizārīs were effectively deprived of any form of central leadership, including the guidance of their imams. In the event, for several centuries, the Nizārī communities developed independently of one another under the local leadership of their *dāʿī*s, *pīr*s, *shaykh*s, *khalīfa*s, etc., who often established their own hereditary dynasties. The difficulties of studying post-Alamūt Nizārī Ismailism are further aggravated by the fact that the Nizārīs produced relatively few religious texts, while, following the demise of their state in 654/1256, they had lost their earlier interest in historiography as well.

In the light of these problems, further progress here would require the acquisition of a better understanding of the historical developments as well as the religious and literary traditions of major Nizārī communities of this period, especially those in South Asia and different parts of the Iranian world. The Nizārī Ismaili literature of the post-Alamūt period can be classified into four main categories, namely the Persian, the Badakhshānī or Central Asian, the Syrian, and the South Asian or the *ginān* corpus. The Nizārī sources produced in Persia, Afghanistan and the upper Oxus region are written entirely in the Persian language, while the Syrian texts are in Arabic. The Nizārīs of South Asia, some of whom were designated as Khojas, elaborated a distinctive Ismaili tradition known as Satpanth or 'true path,' and used various Indian languages in committing their doctrines to writing in the form of devotional hymns known as *ginān*s.

The Nizārīs of Persia and adjacent regions did not produce any doctrinal works during the earliest post-Alamūt centuries. Only the versified works of Ḥakīm Saʿd al-Dīn Nizārī Quhistānī (d. 720/1320), a poet and government functionary from Bīrjand in south-eastern Khurāsān, remain extant from that period. He was perhaps also the first post-Alamūt Nizārī author to have chosen verse and Sufi forms of expression to conceal his Ismaili ideas, a model adopted by later Nizārī authors in Persia. Nizārī's vast *Dīwān*, containing some 10,000 verses in *ghazal* form, was recently published in Tehran. The subsequent revival of *daʿwa* activities during the Anjudān period also encouraged the literary activities of the community, and a number of better-educated Persian Nizārīs began to produce the first doctrinal works of the period. The earliest amongst these authors were Abū Isḥāq Quhistānī (d. after 904/1498), and Khayrkhwāh-i Harātī (d. after 960/1553), a *dāʿī* and poet who visited the contemporary Nizārī imam in Anjudān. The writings of these authors contain important historical references as well. Amongst later authors, mention may be made of the poet Imām Qulī Khākī Khurāsānī (d. after 1056/1646) and his son ʿAlī Qulī, better known as Raqqāmī Khurāsānī; they too, resorted to poetry and Sufi expressions. More doctrinal works by Persian Nizārī authors appeared during the 13th/19th century and later times, marking a modern revival in Nizārī literary activities. This revival was encouraged by the Nizārī imams following the transference of their residence to India. Amongst such works written in Persian, mention may be made of the *Risāla dar ḥaqīqat-i dīn* and the *Khiṭābāt-i ʿāliya* of Shihāb al-Dīn Shāh al-Ḥusaynī (d. 1302/1884), the eldest son of the forty-seventh Nizārī Imam Āqā ʿAlī Shāh, Āghā Khān II, and the works of Muḥammad b. Zayn al-ʿĀbidīn, known as Fidāʾī Khurāsānī (d. 1342/1923), who was also the only Persian Nizārī author of modern times to have written a history of Ismailism, entitled *Hidāyat al-muʾminīn al-ṭālibīn*.

The Nizārī Ismailis of Badakhshān and the adjacent areas in the upper Oxus have retained their distinctive literary tradition, drawing on the Persian Ismaili literature of different periods with particular reference to the writings of Nāṣir-i Khusraw as well as the Sufi traditions of Central Asia. Consequently, the Badakhshānī Nizārīs have preserved and transmitted the anonymous *Umm al-kitāb*, which does not contain any specific Ismaili ideas, the genuine and spurious writings of Nāṣir-i Khusraw, all written in Persian, as well as the Nizārī literature of later times representing the coalescence of Nizārī Ismailism and Sufism. They have also preserved many anonymous works as well as the writings of the great mystic poets of Persia, who are regarded as their co-religionists. The Nizārīs of these remote regions in the Pamirs do not seem to have produced many noteworthy authors in the post-Alamūt period, with some exceptions such as Sayyid Suhrāb Valī Badakhshānī (d. after 856/1452); but they have preserved the bulk of the Ismaili literature of different periods written in Persian elsewhere. These manuscript sources have been held in numerous private collections, especially by the local religious leaders known as *khalīfa*s, in Shughnān, Rūshān, Ishkāshīm and other districts of the Gorno-Badakhshān province of Tajikistan. The Nizārīs of Afghan Badakhshān, too, have extensive collections of manuscripts about which information is not yet readily available. The Central Asian Ismailis concentrated in Badakhshān also have a rich tradition of oral poetry of different genres in Tājik Persian, including specifically religious poetry in praise of Imam ʿAlī b. Abī Ṭālib, other imams, and Nāṣir-i Khusraw, known as *maddāḥ* and delivered in special ceremonies by *maddāḥ*-reciters and singers. They have also preserved a number of local rituals such as the *Cherāgh-rawshan* rite for the dead (based on variants of a Persian text entitled *Cherāgh-nāma*).

The Nizārīs of Hunza, Chitrāl and the districts of Gilgit, now all situated in northern areas of Pakistan, have preserved a selection of Persian Nizārī works, although they themselves speak a host of local languages and dialects such as Burushaskī and Wakhī rather than Persian. This literature was originally made available to them by their Badakhshānī neighbours, who themselves speak a number of local dialects, like Shughnī, in addition to a Tājik version of Persian. The Ismailis of Badakhshān do not seem to have compiled histories of their community, but there are references to Ismailis in a few local histories of the region. Small Nizārī communities have existed in Yārkand and Kāshgar, in the Singkiang (Xinjiang) Uyghur province, in the Tashkorghan region of China, about whose literary traditions no specific details are available. Ethnically defined as Tājiks, the Nizārīs of China speak mainly Sarikoli and Wakhī dialects of the Pamiri languages. They seem to have had the same religious rituals and literature as those found in the neighbouring Badakhshān.

The Syrian Nizārīs, who adhered almost entirely to the Muḥammad-Shāhī branch of Nizārī Ismailism until the 13th/19th century, developed their own limited literature in Arabic. As they also preserved some of the Ismaili works of the Fatimid period, certain earlier Ismaili traditions continued to be represented in the Nizārī texts of the Syrian provenance. The most famous Syrian *dāʿī* author of this period was Abū Firās Shihāb al-Dīn al-Maynaqī, who died in 937/1530 or ten years later. The Nizārīs of Syria were evidently not persecuted by the Ottomans, who mention them and their castles in their land registers of the region. In fact, the Syrian Nizārīs did not attract much outside attention until the early decades of the nineteenth century, when they became entangled in recurrent conflicts with their Nuṣayrī neighbours. It was around the same time that European travellers and orientalists began to make references to them. In the 1840s, the Syrian Nizārīs successfully petitioned the Ottoman authorities for permission to restore Salamiyya, then in ruins, for the settlement of their community. Meanwhile, the Syrian Nizārīs belonging to the Muḥammad-Shāhī line had not heard, since 1210/1796, from their last known imam, Muḥammad al-Bāqir, who lived in India. As they failed to locate him, the majority of the Muḥammad-Shāhī Nizārīs of Syria transferred their allegiance in 1304/1887 to the Qāsim-Shāhī line, then represented by Aga Khan III. An Ismaili minority, centred in Maṣyāf and Qadmūs, remained loyal to the Muḥammad-Shāhī line, and are still awaiting the reappearance of their last known imam as the Mahdī.

The Nizārī Ismailis of the Indian subcontinent, as noted, elaborated their own literary tradition in the form of the *ginān*s, containing a diversity of mystical, mythological, didactic, cosmological and eschatological themes. Many *ginān*s contain ethical and moral instructions for the conduct of religious life and guiding the spiritual quest of the believer. As an oral tradition, some *ginān*s also relate anachronistic, hagiographic and legendary accounts of the activities of *pīr*s, as the chief *dāʿī*s in India were called, and their converts. The *ginān*s are composed in verse form and are meant to be sung and recited melodically. The earlier Ismaili literature, produced in

Arabic and Persian, was not until recently available to the South Asian Nizārīs. The authorships of the *ginān*s are attributed to Pīr Shams al-Dīn, Pīr Ṣadr al-Dīn and other early *pīr*s. Originally transmitted orally, the *ginān*s began to be collected and recorded from the 10th/16th century. The *ginān*s exist in a mixture of Indian languages, including Sindhī, Gujarātī, Hindi, Panjābī and Multānī. The bulk of the recorded corpus of the *ginān* literature, comprised of about one thousand separate compositions, has survived in the specific Khojkī script developed and used extensively by the Nizārī Khojas. Since the middle of the nineteenth century, an increasing number of *ginān*s have been published in India.

In the aftermath of the Mongol debacle, the Nizārī Ismailis of Persia survived the downfall of their state. Many migrated to Badakhshān and Sind, where Ismaili communities already existed. Other isolated Nizārī groups soon disintegrated or were assimilated into the religiously dominant communities of their locality. The centralized *daʿwa* organization also disappeared, to be replaced by a loose network of autonomous *dāʿī*s and *pīr*s in the various regions. Under these circumstances, scattered Nizārī communities developed independently while resorting to *taqiyya* and different external guises. Many Nizārī groups in the Iranian world, where Sunnism prevailed until the rise of the Safawids, disguised themselves as Sunni Muslims. Meanwhile, a group of Nizārī dignitaries had managed to hide Rukn al-Dīn Khurshāh's minor son, Shams al-Dīn Muḥammad, who succeeded to the imamate in 655/1257. Shams al-Dīn was taken to Ādharbāyjān, in north-western Persia, where he and the next few successors to the imamate lived clandestinely. Certain allusions in the unpublished versified *Safar-nāma* (*Travelogue*) of the contemporary poet Nizārī Quhistānī indicate that he may have seen the Nizārī imam in Tabrīz in 679/1280. Shams al-Dīn, who in certain legendary accounts has been confused with Mawlānā Jalāl al-Dīn Rūmī's spiritual guide Shams-i Tabrīz, died around 710/1310. An obscure dispute over his succession split the line of the Nizārī imams and their following into the Qāsim-Shāhī and Muḥammad-Shāhī (or Muʾmin-Shāhī) branches. The Muḥammad-Shāhī imams, who initially had more followers in Persia and Central Asia, transferred their seat to India in the 10th/16th century and by the end of the 12th/18th century this line had become discontinued. The sole surviving Muḥammad-Shāhī Nizārīs, currently numbering about 15,000, are to be found in Syria where they are locally known as the Jaʿfariyya. The Qāsim-Shāhī community has persisted to the present time, and their last four imams have enjoyed prominence under their hereditary title of Āghā Khān (Aga Khan). It was in the early post-Alamūt times that Persian Nizārīs, as part of their *taqiyya* practices, disguised themselves under the cover of Sufism, without establishing formal affiliations with any of the Sufi *ṭarīqa*s then spreading in Persia and Central Asia. The practice soon gained wide currency among the Nizārīs of Central Asia and Sind as well.

In early post-Alamūt times, the Nizārīs had some success in re-grouping in Daylam, where they remained active throughout the Īlkhānid and Tīmūrid periods. Only a few isolated Nizārī groups survived a while longer in Daylam during the Safawid period when Alamūt was used as a prison. In Badakhshān and other parts of

Central Asia, the Ismailis evidently acknowledged the Nizārī imamate only during the late Alamūt period as a result of the activities of *dāʿīs* dispatched from Quhistān. These *dāʿīs* founded dynasties of *pīrs* and *mīrs* who ruled over Shughnān and other districts of Badakhshān. In 913/1507, Shāh Raḍī al-Dīn b. Ṭāhir, a Muḥammad-Shāhī imam, established his rule briefly over a part of Badakhshān with the help of his followers there. Subsequently, the Badakhshānī Nizārīs were severely persecuted by the local Tīmūrid, and then, Özbeg rulers.

By the middle of the 9th/15th century, Ismaili-Sufi relations had become well established in the Iranian world. Indeed, a type of coalescence had emerged between Persian Sufism and Nizārī Ismailism, two independent esoteric traditions in Islam which shared close affinities and common doctrinal grounds. As an early instance of this coalescence, mention may be made of the celebrated Sufi *mathnawī* poem, *Gulshan-i rāz* (*The Rose-Garden of Mystery*), composed by the Sufi master Maḥmūd-i Shabistarī (d. after 740/1339), and its later commentary, *Baʿḍī az taʾwīlāt-i Gulshan-i rāz*, by an anonymous Persian Nizārī author. Among other examples, Central Asian Nizārīs consider ʿAzīz al-Dīn al-Nasafī (d. ca. 700/1300), a local Sufi master, as a co-religionist, and they have preserved his treatise *Zubdat al-ḥaqāʾiq* as an Ismaili work. Owing to their close relations with Sufism, the Persian-speaking Nizārīs have also regarded several of the great mystic poets of Persia, such as Sanāʾī, ʿAṭṭār and Jalāl al-Dīn Rūmī, as their co-religionists. The Nizārī Ismailis of Persia, Afghanistan and Central Asia have preserved their works and continue to use their poetry in their religious ceremonies. Soon, the dissimulating Persian Ismailis adopted the more visible aspects of the Sufi way of life. Thus, the imams appeared to outsiders as Sufi masters or *pīrs*, while their followers adopted the typically Sufi appellation of disciples or *murīds*. By then, the Nizārī imams of the Qāsim-Shāhī line had emerged in the village of Anjudān, in central Persia, and initiated the Anjudān revival in Nizārī Ismailism. With Mustanṣir bi'llāh (II) (d. 885/1480), who carried the Sufi name of Shāh Qalandar, the Qāsim-Shāhī imams became definitely established in the locality where a number of their tombs are still preserved. Taking advantage of the changing religio-political climate of Persia, including the spread of ʿAlid loyalism and Shiʿi tendencies through Sunni Sufi orders, the imams successfully began to reorganize and reinvigorate their *daʿwa* activities to win new converts and reassert their authority over various Nizārī communities, especially in Central Asia and India where the Ismailis had been led for long periods by independent dynasties of *pīrs*. The imams gradually replaced these powerful autonomous figures with their own loyal appointees who would also regularly deliver the necessary religious dues to the imam's central treasury

The Anjudān period witnessed a revival in the literary activities of the Nizārīs, especially in Persia, where the earliest doctrinal works of the post-Alamūt period were now produced. In the context of Nizārī-Sufi relations during the Anjudān period, valuable details are preserved in a book entitled *Pandiyāt-i jawānmardī*, containing the religious admonitions of Imam Mustanṣir bi'llāh (II). In this book, later translated into Gujarātī for the benefit of the Khojas, the Nizārīs are referred to with common Sufi expressions such as *ahl-i ḥaqīqat*, or the 'people of the truth,' while the imam is designated as *pīr* or *murshid*. The imam's admonitions start with the *sharīʿat-ṭarīqat-ḥaqīqat* categorization of the Sufis, describing *ḥaqīqat* as the *bāṭin* of *sharīʿat* which could be attained only by the believers (*mu'min*s). The *Pandiyāt* further explains, in line with the earlier Nizārī teachings of the *qiyāma* times, that *ḥaqīqat* consists of recognizing the spiritual reality of the imam of the time. The Nizārīs now essentially retained the teachings of the Alamūt period, especially as elaborated after the declaration of the *qiyāma*. The current imam retained his central importance in Nizārī doctrine, and the recognition of his true spiritual reality remained the prime concern of his followers.

The advent of the Safawids and the proclamation of Twelver Shiʿism as the state religion of their realm in 907/1501, promised more favourable opportunities for the activities of the Nizārīs and other Shiʿi communities in Persia. The Nizārīs were now able to reduce the intensity of their *taqiyya* practices. However, this new optimism was short-lived as the Safawids and their *sharīʿat*-minded *ʿulamā* soon suppressed all popular forms of Sufism and those Shiʿi movements which fell outside the confines of Twelver Shiʿism. The Nizārīs too, received their share of persecutions. Shāh Ṭāhir al-Ḥusaynī (d. ca. 956/1549), the most famous imam of the Muḥammad-Shāhī line whose popularity had proved unacceptable to the founder of the Safawid dynasty, was persecuted in Shāh Ismāʿīl's reign (907–930/1501–1524). However, Shāh Ṭāhir fled to India in 926/1520 and permanently settled in the Deccan where he rendered valuable services to the Niẓām-Shāhs of Aḥmadnagar. It is interesting to note that from early on in India, Shāh Ṭāhir advocated Twelver Shiʿism, which he had obviously adopted as a form of disguise. He achieved his greatest success in the Deccan when Burhān Niẓām-Shāh, after his own conversion, proclaimed Twelver Shiʿism as the official religion of his state in 944/1537. Shāh Ṭāhir's successors as Muḥammad-Shāhī imams continued to observe *taqiyya* in India under the cover of Twelver Shiʿism. In this connection, it is to be noted that in the *Lamaʿāt al-ṭāhirīn*, one of the few extant Muḥammad-Shāhī texts composed in India around 1110/1698, the author (a certain Ghulām ʿAlī b. Muḥammad) conceals his Ismaili ideas under the double cover of Twelver Shiʿi and Sufi expressions; he eulogizes the Ithnāʿasharī imams whilst also alluding to the Nizārī imams of the Muḥammad-Shāhī line.

Meanwhile, the second Safawid monarch Shāh Ṭahmāsp persecuted the Qāsim-Shāhī Nizārīs of Anjudān and had their thirty-sixth imam, Murād Mīrzā, executed in 981/1574. By the time of the greatest Safawid monarch Shāh ʿAbbās I (995–1038/1587–1629), the Qāsim-Shāhī Nizārīs of Persia, too, had successfully adopted Twelver Shiʿism as a second form of disguise. By the end of the 11th/17th century, the Qāsim-Shāhī *daʿwa* had gained the allegiance of the bulk of the Nizārīs at the expense of the Muḥammad-Shāhīs. The *daʿwa* had been particularly successful in Afghanistan, Central Asia and several regions of the Indian subcontinent.

In South Asia, the Hindu converts originally belonging to the Lohāṇā caste, became known as Khoja, derived from the Persian word *khwāja*, an honorary title meaning lord or master corresponding to the Hindi term *ṭhākur* by which the

Lohāṇās were addressed. As noted, the Nizārīs developed a religious tradition, known as Satpanth or the 'true path' (to salvation), as well as a devotional literature, the *ginān*s. The earliest Nizārī *pīr*s, missionaries or preacher-saints, operating in India concentrated their efforts in Sind. Pīr Shams al-Dīn is the earliest figure specifically associated in the *ginān* literature with the commencement of the Nizārī *daʿwa* there. By the time of Pīr Ṣadr al-Dīn, a great-grandson of Pīr Shams, the *pīr*s in India had established a hereditary dynasty. Pīr Ṣadr al-Dīn, who died around the turn of the 9th/15th century, consolidated and organized the *daʿwa* in India; he is also credited with building the first *jamāʿat-khāna* (literally, community house), in Kotri, Sind, for the religious and communal activities of the Khojas. In India, too, the Nizārīs developed close relations with Sufism. Multān and Uchch in Sind, in addition to serving as centres of Satpanth *daʿwa* activities, were the headquarters of the Suhrawardī and Qādirī Sufi orders. Ṣadr al-Dīn was succeeded as *pīr* by his son Ḥasan Kabīr al-Dīn, who reportedly visited the Nizārī Imam Mustanṣir bi'llāh (II) in Anjudān. Ḥasan Kabīr al-Dīn's brother Tāj al-Dīn was evidently the last person appointed as *pīr* by the Nizārī imams who were then making systematic efforts to end the hereditary authority of the *pīr*s in India.

South Asian Nizārīs periodically experienced internal dissensions, while many reverted back to Hinduism or converted to Sunnism, the dominant religions of contemporary Indo-Muslim society. It was under such circumstances that a group of Nizārīs of Gujarāt seceded and recognized the imamate of Nūr Muḥammad (d. 940/1533); they became known as Imām-Shāhīs, named after Nūr Muḥammad's father Imām Shāh (d. 919/1513), one of Ḥasan Kabīr al-Dīn's sons who had attempted in vain to become a *pīr* in Sind. The Imām-Shāhīs, who produced their own *ginān* literature and split into several groups following different *pīr*s, soon denied any connections with Ismailism. Meanwhile, in the absence of *pīr*s, the Nizārī imams maintained their contacts with the South Asian communities through lesser functionaries known as *wakīl*s.

The origins and early development of the South Asian form of Ismailism known as Satpanth remain obscure. In particular, it is not clear whether Satpanth resulted from the conversion policies developed locally by the early *pīr*s who operated in India at least from the 7th/13th century, or whether it represented a tradition that had evolved gradually over several centuries dating further back, possibly even to Fatimid times. Be that as it may, Satpanth Ismailism may be taken to represent an indigenous tradition reflecting certain historical, social, cultural and political circumstances prevailing in the medieval Indian subcontinent, especially in Sind. On the evidence of the *ginān*s, it seems plausible that the *pīr*s did attempt ingeniously to maximize the appeal of their message to a Hindu audience of mainly rural castes. Hence, they turned to Indian vernaculars, rather than the Arabic and Persian used by the educated classes. And for the same reasons, they used Hindu idioms and mythology, interfacing their Islamic and Ismaili tenets with myths, images and symbols already familiar to the Hindus. The teachings of Satpanth Ismailism are clearly reflected in the *ginān* literature.

In the meantime, with the fortieth Qāsim-Shāhī imam, Shāh Nizār (d. 1134/1722), the seat of this branch of the Nizārī *da'wa*, then representing the only branch in Persia, was transferred from Anjudān to the nearby village of Kahak, in the vicinity of Qumm and Maḥallāt, effectively ending the Anjudān period in post-Alamūt Nizārī Ismailism. By the middle of the 12th/18th century, in the unsettled conditions of Persia after the demise of the Safawids and the Afghan invasion, the Nizārī imams moved to Shahr-i Bābak in Kirmān, a location closer to the pilgrimage route of Khojas who then regularly travelled from India to see their imam and deliver the religious dues, the *dassondh* or tithes, to him. The Khojas were by then acquiring increasing influence in the Nizārī community, both in terms of their numbers and financial resources. Soon, the imams acquired political prominence in the affairs of Kirmān. The forty-fourth imam, Abu'l-Ḥasan 'Alī, also known as Sayyid Abu'l-Ḥasan Kahakī, was appointed to the governorship of the Kirmān province by Karīm Khān Zand (r.1164–1193/1751–1779), founder of the Zand dynasty in Persia; earlier this imam had been the *beglerbegi* or governor of the city of Kirmān. It was in his time that the Ni'mat Allāhī Sufi order was revived in Persia. Imam Abu'l-Ḥasan had close relations with Nūr 'Alī and Mushtāq 'Alī Shāh among other Ni'mat Allāhī Sufis then active in Kirmān. On Abu'l-Ḥasan's death in 1206/1792, his son Shāh Khalīl Allāh succeeded to the Nizārī imamate and eventually settled in Yazd. Shāh Khalīl Allāh was murdered in 1232/1817 and was succeeded by his eldest son Ḥasan 'Alī Shāh, who was later appointed to the governorship of Qumm by Fatḥ 'Alī Shāh (1212–1250/1797–1834) and also given properties in Maḥallāt. In addition, the Qājār monarch of Persia gave one of his daughters in marriage to the youthful imam and bestowed upon him the honorific title of Āghā Khān (Aga Khan), meaning 'lord' or 'master' – this title has remained hereditary among Ḥasan 'Alī Shāh's successors. This Nizārī imam, who maintained his own close relations with the Ni'mat Allāhī Sufi order, has left a valuable autobiographical account of his early life and career in Persia in a work entitled *'Ibrat-afzā*.

Ḥasan 'Alī Shāh was appointed to the governorship of Kirmān in 1251/1835 by the third Qājār monarch, Muḥammad Shāh. Subsequently, after some prolonged confrontations between the imam and the Qājār establishment, Āghā Khān I, also known as Āghā Khān Maḥallātī, left Persia permanently in 1257/1841. After spending some years in Afghanistan, Sind, Gujarāt and Calcutta, the imam finally settled in Bombay in 1265/1848, marking the commencement of the modern period of Nizārī Ismailism. Subsequently, the Nizārī imam launched a widespread campaign for defining and delineating the distinct religious identity of his Khoja following. The contemporary Nizārī Khojas were not always certain about their religious identity as they had dissimulated for long periods as Sunnis and Twelver Shi'is, while their Satpanth tradition had been influenced by Hindu elements. With the help of the British courts in India, however, the Āghā Khān's followers were, in due course, legally recognized as Shi'i Imāmī Ismailis. In the event, the bulk of Khojas reaffirmed their allegiance to Āghā Khān I and acknowledged their Ismaili identity while minority groups seceded and joined Twelver Khoja and other communities.

Āghā Khān I died in 1298/1881, and was succeeded by his son Āqā ʿAlī Shāh who led the Nizārīs for only four years (1298–1302/1881–1885). The latter's sole surviving son and successor, Sulṭān Muḥammad Shāh, Aga Khan III, led the Nizārīs for seventy-two years, and also became internationally known as a Muslim reformer and statesman. Aga Khan II also made systematic efforts to set his followers' identity apart from those of other religious communities, particularly the Twelvers who for long periods had provided dissimulating covers for Nizārīs of Persia and elsewhere. The Nizārī identity was spelled out in numerous constitutions that the imam promulgated for his followers in different regions, especially in India, Pakistan and East Africa. Furthermore, the Nizārī imam became increasingly engaged with reform policies that would benefit not only his followers but other Muslims as well. He worked vigorously to consolidate and reorganize the Nizārīs into a modern Muslim community with high standards of education, health and social well-being for both men and women, also developing a new network of councils for administering the affairs of his community. The participation of women in communal affairs was a high priority in the imam's reforms. Aga Khan III, who established his residence in Europe in the early part of the twentieth century, has left an interesting account of his life and public career in his *Memoirs*.

Aga Khan III died in 1376/1957 and was succeeded by his grandson, known to his followers as Mawlana Hazar Imam Shāh Karīm al-Ḥusaynī, Aga Khan IV. The present, Harvard-educated imam of the Nizārī Ismailis, the forty-ninth in the series, has continued and substantially expanded the modernization policies of his predecessor, also developing numerous new programmes and institutions of his own which are of wider interest to Muslims and Third World countries at large. He has created a complex institutional network generally referred to as the Aga Khan Development Network (AKDN), which implements projects in a variety of social, economic and cultural areas. In the field of higher education and academic institutions, his major initiatives include The Institute of Ismaili Studies, founded in London in 1977 for the promotion of general Islamic as well as Ismaili studies, and the Aga Khan University, set up in Karachi in 1985. More recently, he founded jointly in Kazakhstan, the Kyrgyz Republic and Tajikistan, the University of Central Asia, to address the specific educational needs of the region's mountain-based societies. The Institute of Ismaili Studies is already serving as a point of reference for Ismaili studies, while making significant contributions to the field through a variety of research and publication programmes, as well as making its large collection of Ismaili manuscripts accessible to scholars worldwide.

By 2007, when the Nizārīs celebrated the fiftieth anniversary of his accession to the imamate, Aga Khan IV had established an impressive record of achievement not only as an Ismaili imam but also as a Muslim leader deeply aware of the demands of modernity and dedicated to promoting a better understanding of Islamic civilizations with their diversity of traditions and expressions.

PART ONE

HISTORY AND MEMOIR

Introduction

SAMIRA SHEIKH

From the time of their origins, the history of the Ismailis was largely depicted in the words of their detractors. It is only recently that their own traditions of recording and remembering the past have become better known. As Ismailis were often persecuted and reviled, their records tended to be closely guarded within the community. Many records were also lost in the widespread destruction that followed the fall of the Fatimid dynasty in 567/1171 and the demise of the Nizārī state centred at Alamūt in 654/1256. Nevertheless, Ismaili historiography spans a variety of genres, from official chronicles to personal memoirs.

The first text included here is the *Kitāb al-munāẓarāt* (*Book of Discussions*), the memoir of Ibn al-Haytham, a north African *dāʿī* of the 4th/10th century, which concentrates on the opening phase of the Fatimid caliphate. Ibn al-Haytham's words bring out the fervour of the *daʿwa* of those early times when a pair of charismatic brothers – the *dāʿī*s Abū ʿAbd Allāh al-Shīʿī and Abu'l ʿAbbās – were the chief agents of Ismaili activities in North Africa. It was about this time that the Ismaili Imam al-Mahdī (d. 322/934) decided, in the face of danger and dissidence in Syria, Iraq and Yemen, to travel towards Egypt. The imam and his followers endured a long and perilous journey to North Africa, eventually entering the town of Raqqāda (now in Tunisia) in 297/910, where he was proclaimed caliph.

The Fatimid era of the subsequent two and a half centuries is perhaps the period of Ismaili history that is best recorded in surviving historical texts. Works that chronicle this period include official histories such as the *Iftitāḥ al-daʿwa* (*Commencement of the Mission*) written by the *dāʿī* and jurist al-Qāḍī al-Nuʿmān in 346/957 and *ʿUyūn al-akhbār* (*Choice Stories*) composed centuries later by the Ṭayyibī *dāʿī* Idrīs ʿImād al-Dīn (d. 872/1468). The Fatimid caliphate and its outposts in Persia are recalled in the vigorous memoirs of the *dāʿī* al-Muʾayyad fī'l-Dīn al-Shīrāzī (d. 470/1078) and in the journey to Egypt made by the poet Nāṣir-i Khusraw (d. after 462/1070).

The records of the Nizārī state in Persia were systematically destroyed by the Mongols who sacked the Ismaili fortresses in 654/1256. Although some court chronicles and archival sources were selectively used by later Persian historians, few histories or memoirs from this period have yet been found, with the major exception of Nizārī Quhistānī's *Safar-nāma* (*Book of Travels*), recollections of the poet's journey to northwestern Persia written in verse. After the fall of Alamūt, the Nizārī *daʿwa* spread towards South Asia. The *pīrs* or preacher-saints in India, seeking followers in an unfamiliar and often hostile environment, observed *taqiyya*, the Shiʿi practice of precautionary dissimulation, and kept a low profile, refraining from producing formal histories or records of their activities. While the history of the mission is recalled in some of the devotional poetry of South Asian Ismailis, much of this poetry is oblique and coded. The history of the post-Alamūt period in Iran, Central Asia and South Asia must, perforce, be pieced together from scattered sources, regional histories and devotional poetry.

While historical context can be discerned in many Ismaili texts, the extracts chosen here offer glimpses into ways in which Ismailis recorded their own experiences and traditions. In the following pages we see the past through the words of eyewitnesses to various events. From Ibn al-Haytham's emotional encounter with a charismatic *dāʿī*, we turn to the picaresque adventures of Jaʿfar, the chamberlain to the Imam-Caliph al-Mahdī, in the bazaar of Tūzar. Jaʿfar's vivid and intimate description of al-Mahdī's great reception complements al-Qāḍī al-Nuʿmān's account, in which the new imam-caliph's administrative measures play a greater role. A history of the Fatimids written in 15th-century Yemen preserves details of al-Qāḍī al-Nuʿmān's entire oeuvre and shows that the Imam al-Muʿizz personally supervised some of his writing.

Finally, extracts from journeys made almost nine hundred years apart demonstrate how the faith of individual Ismailis enabled them to undertake hazardous journeys into unknown lands. In the mid 11th century, the *dāʿī* al-Muʾayyad fi'l-Dīn al-Shīrāzī left Shīrāz in southern Iran after the local Būyid ruler had turned against him and travelled in disguise through hostile territory until he reached safety in Egypt. Around the same time, the Persian poet and philosopher, Nāṣir-i Khusraw, experienced a spiritual awakening and journeyed through distant territories to the Fatimid capital. His descriptions of Cairo reveal him to be an urbane and critical observer. Nine centuries later, in the 1920s, Pīr Sabzālī made a very different journey when he was dispatched by the then imam, Sulṭān Muḥammad Shāh Aga Khan III to visit the Ismaili communities deep in the mountains of Central Asia. Among the snowbound Pamirs, far from home in India, he and his entourage were buoyed by their faith in the imam.

1

Ibn al-Haytham

Abū ʿAbd Allāh Jaʿfar b. Aḥmad al-Aswad b. al-Haytham lived in the 4th/10th century and was a prominent *dāʿī* in North Africa. His *Kitāb al-munāẓarāt* (*Book of Discussions*) was preserved in a 16th-century compendium of Ismaili texts. When he met the *dāʿī*s Abū ʿAbd Allāh al-Shīʿī and his brother Abu'l-ʿAbbās in Qayrawān between 296/909 and 297/910, the author was a young and eager recruit to the Ismaili cause. He wrote the *Book of Discussions* much later, around 334/945, recalling his conversations with them during the early years of the movement in Ifrīqiya. In the first of the following extracts, Ibn al-Haytham visits the victorious *dāʿī* Abū ʿAbd Allāh, and tears well up as he recalls the sufferings of the Prophet's family. The *dāʿī* beckons him close and exhorts him to be steadfast to the Ismaili cause. On another occasion, the *dāʿī* tests his understanding of the imamate by presenting the arguments of the opponents of ʿAlī. In this dialogue, Ibn al-Haytham eloquently defends the virtues of Imam ʿAlī. Subsequently, Ibn al-Haytham takes an oath of allegiance to the faith. Finally, the author describes the *dāʿī*s of the Kutāma Berbers, who made their message accessible by teaching people with reference to their own lives.

Kitāb al-munāẓarāt
The Book of Discussions[1]

IBN AL-HAYTHAM MEETS THE *DĀʿĪ* ABŪ ʿABD ALLĀH

In the company of Abū Mūsā Hārūn b. Yūnis al-Azāyī al-Masāltī,[2] we called upon Abū ʿAbd Allāh two days after his arrival in Raqqāda, and that was Monday, the third of Rajab in the year 296 [27 March 909]. My aim in going to him and my predilection in his favour was due to their unanimous agreement regarding his discernment, understanding, culture, intelligence, and knowledge. I had been staying with Abū Mūsā for those two days. He conveyed news of me to Abū ʿAbd Allāh and informed him about my seeking to visit him and what there was between him and me. On the third night Abū Mūsā set out with me on foot.

1. Ibn al-Haytham, *Kitāb al-munāẓarāt*, ed. and tr. Wilferd Madelung and Paul E. Walker as *The Advent of the Fatimids: A Contemporary Shiʿi Witness* (London, 2000), pp. 65–67, 76–80, 95–97, 166–168.
2. Abū Mūsā was one of the earliest supporters of Abū ʿAbd Allāh, having joined him in 280/893.

We passed by the abode of Abū Zākī,[1] and Abū Mūsā sent in to him word that I was present. He came out and Abū Mūsā introduced me to him, and he greeted me. Thereupon, we entered into the courtyard of the palace in which Abū ʿAbd Allāh had settled. Then the door was opened for us and Abū Mūsā informed them of my name. The doorway to Abū ʿAbd Allāh was entrusted to fifty men of proper faith, understanding, and surety. They expressed their greetings and crowded about me, embracing me with the welcome of the people of faith who truly desire God's reward. Abū Mūsā then entered before me and informed Abū Abd Allāh of my presence. He came out to me again and I now entered with him into his presence. Abū Mūsā said to me, 'Do not hold back but rather debate with him like your first debates with me. He will surely humour your entertaining a different opinion.'

Abū ʿAbd Allāh rested on a fine couch on which he was sitting, its covering a single *Yansānī* (*sic*) saddle. I extended him my greetings standing and thanked God for what He had granted to us through his being close at hand and God's investing him and supporting him and giving him victory. There then sprang up in me such a flow of tears that I could not restrain them as I remembered our lord al-Ḥusayn b. ʿAlī, may the blessing of God be upon him, and what harm the criminals had done to him and what was inflicted on his followers. We were at that time still more tender of heart, damper of eye and more copious in tears. Grief had given notice to our hearts, and our souls were wont to remember the humiliation of the family of Muḥammad, blessings be upon them, enfolding hearts with regret, sadness, and pain, and a rising anger against the enemies of God, those criminals. Each day prior to his arrival we had anticipated his days, and we had expected his advent with great longing. Hopes created in us the expectation of attaining that, and of the coming of victory and the vanquishing of the iniquitous. Among our Shiʿi companions, our watchword had been none other than the words of the poet:

When will I see the world without a determinist?
    And no Ḥarūrī[2] or opponent of ʿAlī?
When will I behold the sword that signifies
    the love of ʿAlī, the son of Abū Ṭālib?

Then he sat and made me come closer to him until my right knee was on his couch. At that I said to him, 'We have come to you as students hoping for the knowledge that you possess. It has been proven about the Apostle of God, may God's blessings be on him and his family, that he said, "Whosoever listens to the summoners of my family and does not respond positively to them, God will throw him down on his face in hellfire".'

He responded: 'Why then did you fail to join up with us and come to where we were?'

---

1. This is Abū Zākī Tammām b. Muʿārik, another early supporter of Abū ʿAbd Allāh.
2. A Khārijī.

I answered: 'Fear, youth, and being too weak to undertake it, even though our hearts and prayers were with you.'

He said: 'That is weak support indeed! Whoever combines with the heart his tongue and hand, he has truly fulfilled his obligation and done what is required of him. God, exalted is His mention, has declared, "Whosoever leaves his home as an emigrant to God and His Apostle and then death overtakes him, his recompense falls due to God" [Qur'an 4:100], and He said also, "And for those who believe and do not emigrate, nothing obliges you to associate with them until they emigrate" [8:72].'

So I replied: 'And He, glorified is His name, also said, "Do not deliver yourselves by your own hands into destruction" [2:195], and God excused "those men who are weak and the women and children who do not have the means" [4:98].'

He responded: 'If you are resigned to being in the position of women, children, and the weak among men, I hope that God will make a path for you hereafter.'

THE PROOF OF THE EXCELLENCE AND PURITY OF IMAM ʿALĪ

He said: 'What proof do you have of the excellence of ʿAlī, peace be upon him, and his worthiness for the imamate you have mentioned?'

I said: 'Every word of ours previously stated is in fact a proof, but our real proof is the Book, the Sunna, the consensus, reason, reflection, the revelation, and historical report. All of these certify it to the person who considers carefully, thinks it over and listens attentively as a true witness and avoids personal bias.'

He said: 'With respect to historical reports and the revelation, they may be construed in the general sense, and the opponent can also invoke them in an argument with you.'

I answered: 'It is necessary for someone who discusses the imamate to be of sound faith and a piety that restrains him from putting forward claims for something that does not belong to him, and that he be thoroughly familiar with the reported accounts and neither repudiate them nor steal them from their owners. When the disputant is like this, that is, he does not repudiate or steal, and does not claim something that does not belong to him, we prove it by citing what no other can claim. Thus, it is firmly reported that ʿAlī was the brother of the Apostle of God, who established brotherhood between the two of themselves when he fraternized as brothers among his Companions on two occasions. He said to him, "You, ʿAlī, are my brother and you are to me in the position of Hārūn in respect to Moses," and he stated in reference to him, "Whosoever I am the master of, ʿAlī is his master." He prayed for him and for his party and he cursed those who would forsake him and make war against him. He removed all of his Companions from his neighbourhood and left behind only ʿAlī, when he evicted the polytheists of the Quraysh from the vicinity of the sacred sanctuary. Thus he removed all of them from himself and kept behind ʿAlī alone in his presence. In the *sūra*, "Does there not pass over man…,"[1] there is sufficient mention of him and of God's promising him paradise. And God

1. *Sūrat al-insān* (76), which begins with these words.

promised him paradise, and there is the statement of the Most High, "Your protectors are God, His Apostle, and those who believe, who observe prayer and give alms, while they kneel down in worship" [5:55], and the verse of confidential discourse in which is His statement, "O you who believe, if you have a private conference with the Apostle, pay something as alms for your conference" [58:12]. No one did this except ʿAlī alone. There is also the Exalted's statement, "Do you consider providing water [*siqāya*] for the pilgrims and repair of the sacred mosque to be like believing in God and the Last Day and fighting on behalf of God? They are not equal with God. God does not guide those who do wrong" [9:19]. The whole of this verse to its end was revealed about ʿAlī and al-ʿAbbās and Shayba.[1] God, the Mighty and Glorious, judged ʿAlī superior to both of them. Also there is the verse of mutual imprecation. All that and similar passages in the Qur'an are about ʿAlī and all those who oppose nevertheless confirm that this is about him and do not deny it, praise be to God, Lord of the two worlds.

'As for implied and obscure indications or examples and allusions, they are incalculably numerous, such as the statement of God's Apostle about him, "ʿAlī is among you like the ark of Noah; whoever sails upon it is saved and whoever stays away from it, sinks and is destroyed," and his saying, "I am leaving with you two weighty items such that if you cleave to them, you will not fall into error, the Book of God and my descendants, the members of my family." And there is the statement of the Most High, "And he made this a word to remain among his descendants" [43:28]. All of this is quite clear and well known and is in addition to the early merits, knowledge, *jihād*, and nearness to the Apostle of God in which ʿAlī stands alone. Thus he combined in himself every excellence by which one merits the imamate because of his closeness to God, the Mighty and the Glorious, and that he was owed the obedience linked to the Apostle in the statement of the Most High. 'Obey God and obey the Apostle and those with authority among you' [4:59]. There was thus combined in ʿAlī the excellence of every one who had any excellence, whereas God, the Mighty and Glorious, singled him out to have what none of them have. He had purity of birth, superiority of knowledge and kinship, and about ʿAlī, God revealed, "Is then the man who believes no better than the wicked; no they are not equal" [32:18]. None are the like of ʿAlī and he resembles no one else of those who are believers after him and were termed abominable prior to finding faith. And about him and his companions, God, the Exalted, revealed, "…men who have been true to their covenant with God. Of them some have already redeemed their pledge; others still wait but have not changed in the least" [33:23]. They have all agreed that this verse was revealed about ʿAlī, Ḥamza, ʿUbayda b. al-Ḥārith b. al-Muṭṭalib, and Jaʿfar b. Abī Ṭālib, peace be upon them all.'

1. Al-ʿAbbās, the Prophet's uncle, held the hereditary right of *siqāya*, the privilege of providing water for the pilgrims. This right was restored to him upon the conquest of Mecca by the Muslims. Shayba b. ʿUthmān b. Abī Ṭalḥa was a member of the Banū ʿAbd al-Dār who were collectively the guardians or keepers (*sadana*) of the Kaʿba, and this Shayba is reported to have been one of those confirmed in his role (along with his cousin ʿUthmān) by the Prophet at the conquest of Mecca.

He said to me: 'The Islam of 'Alī, according to your opponents, was like the Islam of a child who does not truly believe.'

I replied: "Alī's submission [*islām*] was in response to the summons of God's Apostle by the command of God, the Mighty and Glorious, and he was not a child devoid of belief but rather he was thirteen years old. Boys of eleven years have produced children just as women have attained puberty at ten. The Apostle of God commanded that youths be taught prayers from the age of six and five, and to discipline them for prayers from seven. 'Alī had then passed these limits. The Apostle of God was not one who would deceive himself about the religion of God and disclose it to someone who will not believe anything. It has been universally agreed that the Apostle of God entered the ravine with him, and with them was Khadīja. They remained in it three years and seven months, eating poor bread and date pits, and cracking bones and splitting them apart. If 'Alī had not been a believer, he would have abandoned this hardship in favour of ease and joined his uncles and kin. Moreover no one relates that the Apostle of God summoned any of the young boys of the Banū Hāshim or others. In this is a proof that 'Alī was the remnant of God on His earth after Muḥammad and that from him came the progeny of the Apostle of God. He was the summons of Abraham, peace be upon him, and however the ignorant belittle his case, that merely increases his excellence.'

He said: 'How could this be, given that the one who benefits from Islam is the adult who prefers what he enters to what he leaves, because of a proof whose evidence is plain to him or a sign that is firm in his perception and whose explanation is for him sound?'

I said: 'But the adult may enter it out of fright and fear and humiliation and of being overpowered, and his Islam might be for worldly gain or leadership over the people of this world, or in order to attain status with the one who rules over them. A child gains nothing of this kind by entering Islam, and especially not 'Alī b. Abī Ṭālib in particular since his father was the supporter of the Apostle of God and the one who stood up for him and defended him. Thus, 'Alī was loved by the Apostle of God and was his chosen, his intimate, and the one brought up by him. For that reason he selected him to be his associate and his legatee, and singled him out by adopting him as his brother, turning over to him the government of his community after him, designating him as successor and approving of him, and choosing him as deputy and friend. Furthermore the virtue of the Islam of the young boy is confirmed in the Book of God. An example of that is Abraham who was properly guided by inferences when he was only thirteen; "and he said, I will not hold dear those that fade away" [6:76]. The setting of the stars was for him a proof of their having come into being and that the exalted Creator, glory be to Him, does not set or cease or move about or belong to a place. Similarly Abraham desired the Islam of his sons and to acquaint them with faith prior to their reaching maturity and before they would know and worship the idols. That was confirmed in the mind of Abraham by the word of God and His making it clear in the statement of Him who has no partner, "And Abraham was tried by his Lord with certain edicts which he carried out;" He then said, "I will make you the leader [*imām*] of the people;" He asked, "And also from my offspring?" He said, "My assurance does not apply to the evildoers" [2:124]. At that Abraham desired more and he said, "Preserve me and my children from worshipping idols" [14:35], and he said, "My Lord give me a righteous son" [37:100]. God, the Mighty and Glorious, thus informed Abraham that the imamate will not be inherited by someone who embraces polytheism nor one who reaches maturity as a polytheist, even if he then accepts faith and Islam. None will inherit the imamate who is not pure from the beginning. Likewise was Moses, peace be upon him, of such purity in his birth that the milk of harlots was forbidden him in order that he be as pure in his nursing as he was in his birth. Likewise was Jesus, peace be upon him, in the purity of his beginnings, and similarly Muḥammad, may God bless him and his family, and ʿAlī, peace be upon him, after him. One aspect of the complete purity of ʿAlī is that his grandmother and the grandmother of Muḥammad was the same woman, the mother of ʿAbd Allāh, father of Muḥammad. The mother of Abū Ṭālib was the same woman and they were thus full brothers.'

IBN AL-HAYTHAM TAKES THE OATH OF ALLEGIANCE

Following that he [Abū ʿAbd Allāh] summoned me to the faith and he gave permission for our colleagues whom he had summoned before me to enter into his presence. Thus, they joined in the *daʿwa*. When it was time for the oath, he said, 'Know, may God have mercy on you, that this oath is a sunna from God in respect to His people and His servants. God took it from His prophets, and each prophet took it from his own community. The proof for this is from the Book of God, since He says, "When We took a covenant from the prophets, from you, from Noah and Abraham and Moses and Jesus, the son of Mary, and We took from them a solemn pledge" [33:7]; and His saying, "When We took the pledge of the tribe of Israel not to worship any except God" [2:83]; and His statement, "God took a pledge from the tribe of Israel and We sent among them twelve leaders" [5:12]; and His saying, "From those who said that they were Christians, We took their pledge" [5:14]; and His saying, "When We took your pledge not to shed each other's blood" [2:84]; and His statement to the Apostle of God, "Those who swear allegiance to you swear allegiance to God Himself, his hand above theirs; whoever violates it violates himself and whoever remains true to what he promised to God shall be due a great reward" [48:10].' Thereafter he reviewed everything in the Qur'an mentioning the covenant and fidelity to it. He said, 'There is no religion except on the basis of covenant. Of whomever God has not taken a covenant, has no one to guard him nor any religion to restrain him. Prior to this "you were a dissolute people" [48:12].' He said, 'Truly God has said, "God has purchased from the believers their souls and their wealth in exchange for paradise when they will fight on behalf of God, killing and being killed, a promise He made truly in the Torah, the Gospels and the Qur'an. And who is truer to his covenant than God? Rejoice therefore in your pledge of allegiance which you have pledged to Him. That is a wondrous triumph" [9:111].' And He said, '"God was pleased with the believers when they swore allegiance to you under the tree" (to the end of the verse) [48:18].'[1] Then he said, 'Today you have pledged allegiance to God and you are truly His servants and you have acknowledged Muḥammad and pledged allegiance to him.' He continued, 'God has explained that He was not satisfied with the worship of those who came first except upon their pledging allegiance to Muḥammad, His Prophet. How could He then approve your worship without a pledge?'

I said: 'By God, O by God, I had never heard this and yet I have read all that reached us concerning the teachings of the sects and the many doctrines of both heretics and believers, but I never heard of this. Surely, it is quite obviously true, and its proof and veracity are certainly evident. We used to think and maintain that God extracted the descendants of Adam from his back and took from them the covenant.'

He said: 'This is wrong and no proof will support it, nor would an intelligent person consider it to be valid, since God, the Most High, says, "Be mindful of the favour God showed you and of His pledge with which He bound you when you said: we hear and we obey" [5:7]. How could it be that He reminded them of something they could not remember, and then they gave Him this understandable reply. No, it is as we see it; it was those from before you.'

I said: 'There is no religion in the absence of a covenant.'

He said: 'That is correct. Have you not heard God's words, "None shall have the power of intercession except those who have taken a covenant with the Most Merciful" [19:87], and, "They said, the fire will touch us only for a limited number of days; say, have you taken a covenant with God – God will never go back on His covenant – or do you assert of God what you have no knowledge of?" [2:80]. Thus, the covenant is a pre-condition for worship and an intercession for him with God. Whoever violates it has a painful punishment. The covenant is the means. God, the most High, said, "O you who believe, fear God and seek the means to approach Him" [5:35].'

I said: 'Praise be to God, we have faith and believe. We would not have been led rightly if it were not that God guided us by the arrival of the apostles of our Lord with the truth.'

THE *DĀʿĪS* OF THE KUTĀMA

We were together with the *shaykh*s of the Kutāma, their *dāʿīs*, learned men, and the devotees of religion among their men, 'on raised mats' [56:34], 'with set drinking glasses, arrayed cushions, unfolded carpets' [88:14], 'under a thornless lote tree, stacked acacias, shade extended, water poured out' [56:28–31] that we drank from them 'in a cup from a running spring, white, a pleasure for those who drink'

1. The verse continues, 'He knew what was in their hearts; He sent down upon them tranquillity and He rewarded them with a speedy victory.'

[37:45–46], there being no headiness in it nor accusation of offence, 'reclining between strands of gold and brocade' [18:31]. We plucked from the fruits of their thoughts and inhaled from the fragrances of their flowers matters whose benefit was great with me and whose outcome was lofty. The mercy of God be upon all the believers who have gained certitude, are true to their covenant, and patient, and God is compassionate and merciful to us and to them all.

There was no duly authorized *dāʿī* among them but that I learned from him with the permission of the shaykh Abū Mūsā.[1] I harvested from their fruits both the exterior and the interior, and there was not one of them who did not stay with me and visit my home. And whatever I may forget, I shall[2] never forget the *dāʿī* of Malūsa, the shaykh of the community and their legal authority, Aflaḥ b. Hārūn al-ʿIbānī.[3] He combined his activity as a *dāʿī* with the sciences of the religious law, and he reached back to the time of Abū Maʿshar and al-Ḥulwānī, and transmitted on their authority from al-Ḥalabī.[4] I frequently met with him and visited him. He stayed with me many times and copied many books on law, traditions, and the virtues and speeches of our master and our lord, the Commander of the Faithful, ʿAlī b. Abī Ṭālib, may the blessings of God be upon him and on the imams among his offspring. I heard from him the summons for the women and what types of proofs he would address to them that their minds will accept and retain. He would say, 'God has the convincing proof' [6:149]. He said, 'This means the proof with which the scholar addresses the one he teaches or the ignorant person, using only what that person comprehends.' He would address women and employ as evidence in their case items of their jewellery, rings, earrings, headgear, necklaces, anklets, bracelets, dresses, head binding. Next he would cite examples pertaining to spinning, weaving, costume, and hair, and other items that suit the natural disposition

1. Abū Mūsa was known as the 'shaykh of shaykhs' (*shaykh al-mashāʾikh*) and obviously played an important part in the mission of Abū ʿAbd Allāh. The account of Ibn al-Haytham confirms this judgement. Nonetheless, there is remarkably little information about him in the other sources, perhaps because of his later treason and execution.

2. The passage that follows here was also quoted by Idrīs ʿImād al-Dīn. *Taʾrīkh al-khulafāʾ al-Fāṭimiyyīn biʾl-Maghrib: al-qism al-khāṣṣ min Kitāb ʿuyūn al-akhbār*, ed. Muḥammad al-Yaʿlāwī (Beirut, 1985), pp. 211–213, and published in Samuel Stern, *Studies in Early Ismāʿīlism* (Jerusalem, 1983), pp. 102–104.

3. The praising of Aflaḥ by the author is particularly noteworthy because he was a Kutāmī. As a *dāʿī* of the prominence accorded him by the author, he is evidence of a learned elite among the Kutāma. Al-Mahdī first appointed him *qāḍī* of Raqqāda in 297/910. He died apparently in 310/922 at the time holding the post of *qāḍī* of Raqqāda and possibly al-Mahdiyya.

4. In his investigation for 'The Sources of Ismāʿīlī Law' (*Journal of Near Eastern Studies*, 35 [1976]: 29–40), Madelung found that al-Qāḍī al-Nuʿmān cited two works by al-Ḥalabī, a *Kitāb al-masāʾil* and a *Jāmiʿ*. He gives a possible identification there for this al-Ḥalabī as ʿUbayd Allāh al-Ḥalabī, who transmitted directly from Jaʿfar al-Ṣādiq and who died in the latter's lifetime. See pp. 30, 34–35. Al-Ḥulwānī is reported to have been sent by the Imam Jaʿfar to the Maghrib, along with a certain Abū Sufyān, in 145/762 to spread Shiʿism there. See al-Qāḍī al-Nuʿmān, *Iftitāḥ*, pp. 26–29, 34, 41–42, 131–132, 182. Al-Ḥulwānī, who is specifically reported to have converted many of the Kutāma, is said also have lived such a long time that persons who related directly from him were still alive when Abū ʿAbd Allāh arrived in the Maghrib. But it is virtually impossible that Aflaḥ and the others extended back to the time of al-Ḥulwānī if he in fact came at the time of the Imam Jaʿfar since the time elapsed was a century and a half or more.

of women. He would speak to the craftsman using the terms of his craft and thus, for example, address the tailor by reference to his needle, his thread, his patch, and his scissors. He addressed the shepherd using references to his staff, his cloak, his horn, and his two-pouched travelling bag.[1] Today I know of no one who can do that or of anyone to take my place in it or who has preserved the memory of it as I have. All that was due to the success given by my Lord and Creator and my Benefactor and Sustainer. May God's mercy be upon him. Whenever he spoke, in his speech he was humble toward God, seeking what is with Him, and was tender of heart, amply tearful and moist of tongue, and he mentioned God submissively, humbly and affectionately. Of his maxims and his recommendations to me, I remember that he once said, 'Be wary of placing your trust in anyone until he is firmly established. When he is firmly established, what he was concealing, as well as what he was making public, will both become manifest in him.'

(Translated by Wilferd Madelung and Paul E. Walker)

1. Or possibly 'his sash,' depending on the reading of this word and the exact meaning of *kurziyyatihi*. The other items are things the shepherd carries on himself.

2

Jaʿfar b. ʿAlī

Jaʿfar b. ʿAlī was a chamberlain to the Fatimid Imam-Caliph al-Mahdī (d. 322/934) who accompanied him faithfully on his long journey from Salamiyya in Syria to North Africa (289–297/902–909). His account was compiled some years later by Muḥammad b. Muḥammad al-Yamānī, an Ismaili scribe. Jaʿfar's narrative is a personal and often amusing rendition of events which took place on the way to Raqqāda (in modern Tunisia), where al-Mahdī was installed as the first Fatimid caliph. In the first of the following extracts, we get a glimpse of the affectionate relationship between Jaʿfar and al-Mahdī. The second extract vividly relates the grand spectacle of al-Mahdī's inspection of his troops.

Sīrat al-ḥājib Jaʿfar
Account of the Chamberlain Jaʿfar[1]

AN INCIDENT FROM AL-MAHDĪ'S JOURNEY TO NORTH AFRICA

Jaʿfar said [continuing the narration]: Al-Mahdī chanced upon a caravan heading for Sijilmāsa[2] by way of Qasṭīliya[3] after I returned to him with the money for which he had dispatched me.[4] He thanked God for my safe return and his good fortune, and he departed from (Tripoli). We took the road to Nafūsa territory,[5] heading for Sumāṭa territory[6] in the district of Qasṭīliya. We stopped in a town of (Qasṭīliya)

1. Muḥammad b. Muḥammad al-Yamānī, *Sīrat al-ḥājib Jaʿfar b. ʿAlī wa-khurūj al-Mahdī min Salamiyya wa-wuṣūluh ilā Sijilmāsa wa-khurūjuh minhā ilā Raqqāda*, ed. W. Ivanow, in *Bulletin of the Faculty of Arts, University of Egypt*, vol. 4 (1936), pp. 107–133, 129–131, tr. Hamid Haji. The integral text was previously translated into English by Wladimir Ivanow in his *Ismaili Tradition Concerning the Rise of the Fatimids* (London, etc., 1942), pp. 184–223, (trans. pp. 198–201, 217–219).

2. The site of this ancient town lies in south-eastern Morocco in the oasis of the Tafilelt, immediately to the west of the modern town of Rissani. Sijilmāsa, famous for its wealth, was founded by the Miknāsa Berbers in 140/757. See M. Terrasse, 'Sidjilmāsa,' *EI2*, vol. 9, p. 545.

3. The name Qasṭīliya refers to the district, and sometimes to its administrative centre Tūzar or Tawzar, ancient Thusuros, now Tozeur, in the region of Djerid in south-western Tunisia.

4. After his departure from Salamiyya in 289/902, al-Mahdī stayed briefly in Damascus. Then he passed through Tiberias, without entering the town. He proceeded to al-Ramla where he stayed with its governor who was his follower, and from there proceeded to Egypt. Here al-Mahdī ordered Jaʿfar to go back to Salamiyya to recover his buried valuables and rejoin him. Jaʿfar rejoined al-Mahdī in Tripoli.

5. The Nafūsa Berbers were particularly spread in the north-western region of Tripolitania. One of their chief towns was Sabra (Roman Sabratha) on the coast, west of Tripoli.

6. The Sumāṭa are a branch of the Nafzāwa Berbers. The name also applies to their territory which

called Tūzar, where we stayed for a few days to celebrate the feast day. Then we left (Tūzar) for Sijilmāsa on the feast day.

I remember – narrates Jaʿfar – that while we were in (Tūzar) al-Mahdī told me one day, 'Go and find for me a small, fat lamb. If you do find one, buy it, roast it, and serve it to me.' So I left to look for it. A local man told me, 'I have what you are looking for. Come with me to my house.' I went with him and he ushered me in a room where there was a hairy dog with a thick chain around its neck. Its eyes had turned red. The man told me, 'It is now two months that I have been feeding it dates while it has been chained without being able to move. Its skin is bulging with fat.' It seems that the local people eat dogs, referring to them with names of lambs. The dog jumped towards me pulling its chain like a lion when it pounces. I had no doubt that it would break its chain and tear my stomach. I turned back and fled from it outside the house, not believing that I could escape from it, while the owner of the house followed me, calling me back; but I did not turn back. I had no desire to be saved until at last I reached al-Mahdī. My reason had gone and I put my hand on my heart. When (al-Mahdī) saw me terrified and pale, he asked me, 'Who was chasing you?' I replied, 'My lord, may God's curse be upon this town and its people.' He asked, 'What is the matter?' I replied, 'I went to look for what you commanded me to do and such and such happened to me,' and I related to him what had happened, while (al-Mahdī) and my lord al-Qāʾim[1] could not stop laughing. They consoled me until I became calm.

A day or two later, (al-Mahdī) commanded me to find for him a barber. He told me, 'Try and make sure that he is a stranger.' I went and found a barber who appeared to be a traveller. I asked him, 'Are you a stranger?' He replied, 'Yes.' I asked, 'When did you arrive in this town?' He replied, 'I just arrived today.' So I took him with me to (al-Mahdī) and informed him that he was a stranger. When (al-Mahdī) saw him, he asked him his name and from which town he was and whether he was a freeman or a slave. This was al-Mahdī's habit whenever he saw someone whom he did not know. He would never talk to anyone or treat anyone with familiarity without asking the person his name, his lineage and his country of origin. When he asked him all those questions, the man informed him that he originated from Ifrīqiya, from al-Qayrawān, and that he had been away from his country for a long time in Kutāma territory and it was from there that he had come to this town. (Al-Mahdī) asked him, 'How were you able to enter Kutāma territory and stay there considering what is said about it that there is trouble there and that norms (*sunan*) have changed there?' The man replied, 'By God, my Lord, every authentic norm of God and His messenger is found in Kutāma territory.' Al-Mahdī said, 'This contradicts reports coming from everywhere about the man from abroad who reigns there.[2] It is said that he has seduced the inhabitants, making lawful to them their

was located to the north-west of Qasṭīliya.

1. Abu'l-Qāsim Muḥammad al-Qāʾim bi-Amr Allāh (d. 334/946) was the son and successor of al-Mahdī.

2. A reference to the *dāʿī* Abū ʿAbd Allāh al-Shīʿī. On him and his mission among the Kutāma

daughters and sisters and dispensing them from fasting and prayers.' The barber replied, 'By God, other than whom there is no God, none of that is true. There is no religion of God except that which this man who reigns in Kutāma territory follows.' Al-Mahdī asked him, 'What act of his do you consider to be good, because I see that you praise him so much that no one will agree with you?' (The barber) replied, 'By God, O my lord, I had a companion with whom I resolved to go to the town of Saṭīf[1] and work there for a month, and to share with him whatever sustenance God the Mighty, the Glorious, provided us. We set out together. When we wanted to enter the town from its gate, we were not allowed to enter the town with our weapons. We told (the guards), 'What shall we do? We do not know anyone here to whom we could hand our weapons for safe keeping.' They told us, 'Leave (the weapons) behind the wall of the town.' We said, 'How can we do that? We shall lose our weapons.' We were told, 'Just leave them and have no fear for them.' So we left (our weapons) and entered the town and remained there, because it was difficult for us to turn back after having reached the town. We remained there for a month. When we left the town, we were surprised to see that our weapons were in the same condition as when we left them; nothing was missing from them. That, my lord, is how governs a man who has been accused of impiety and replacing the law (*sharīʿa*). Jaʿfar said [continuing the narration]: Thereupon I saw al-Mahdī's face becoming radiant. Then (the barber) finished his work, and (al-Mahdī) ordered him to be paid handsomely and he retired.

AL-MAHDĪ GREETS HIS TROOPS[2]

Jaʿfar said [continuing the narration]: We saw al-Mahdī sitting on his throne in the middle of the tent like the shining sun, emanating elegance and brilliance. We kissed the ground, weeping, while he was smiling and prostrating before God, praising Him, thanking Him and glorifying Him – blessed be His name. Then he told Ṣandal,[3] 'Bring the two robes of honour which I have set aside in such and such wardrobe. (Ṣandal) brought (the two robes). (Al-Mahdī) put one on himself and clad al-Qāʾim with the other. Then he ordered to bring him clothes and swords which had been set aside for them. He called me and, after having put with his own

---

Berbers, see al-Qāḍī al-Nuʿmān b. Muḥammad, *Iftitāḥ al-daʿwa*, ed. Wadād al-Qāḍī (Beirut, 1970); ed. F. Dachraoui (Tunis, 1975). English tr. Hamid Haji, *Founding the Fatimid State: The Rise of an Early Islamic Empire* (London, 2006).

1. The town of Saṭīf (Sétif), ancient Sitifis, in present-day Algeria. Abū ʿAbd Allāh conquered Saṭīf after a siege and a fierce battle. See al-Qāḍī al-Nuʿmān, *Iftitāḥ* (ed. al-Qāḍī) pp. 154–156 (trans. pp. 126–128).

2. After al-Mahdī and his entourage reached Sijilmāsa, they were arrested and held in captivity. They regained their freedom after the *dāʿī* Abū ʿAbd Allāh conquered Sijilmāsa. Here Jaʿfar relates the events shortly after the conquest of Sijilmāsa. On the conquest of Sijilmāsa see al-Qāḍī al-Nuʿmān, *Iftitāḥ* (ed. al-Qāḍī), pp. 237–241 (trans. pp. 195–199).

3. Ṣandal was a eunuch and a slave, originally from Aleppo, who at that time had come to Sijilmāsa. He was named Ṣandal by al-Mahdī. For details of this Kutāma uprising, see al-Qāḍī al-Nuʿmān, *Iftitāḥ* (ed. al-Qāḍī), p. 273 (trans. pp. 226–227).

hand the robe of honour on Abū ʿAbd Allāh and presenting him a turban and a sword, he presented me a cloth lined with *dabīqī*[1], a turban, trousers and boots, and he girded me with a sword. He presented to Ṭayyib[2] garments similar to mine and he girded him with a sword. He did likewise with Muslim,[3] Ṣandal and Abū Yaʿqūb,[4] and girded the latter with a sword and he girded Ṣandal with a sword. He had prepared all this before our departure from Salamiyya. Then he ordered Abū ʿAbd Allāh to pitch a large tent for him and for us. This he did, and he spread in it exquisite carpets for al-Mahdī.

(Al-Mahdī) ordered (Abū ʿAbd Allāh) to instruct the troops to come the following morning to greet him according to the order of their ranks and dignity, and to introduce them to him. Abū ʿAbd Allāh said, 'Our lord, among the troops there are those with rough manners. They are waiting impatiently to look at the face of our lord al-Mahdī. May our lord command those of his slaves that he wishes to stand outside the marquee (*samāʾ*). I myself shall stand in front of the troops and bring forward those who deserve to be presented first, ten at a time. I shall convey them to (this servant), and he will bring them forward. They will greet our lord and then retire. When the *dāʿīs* and the commanders have finished, I shall bring forward those that are lower than them, 50 at a time, then 100 at a time, and then 500 at a time. Then I shall parade the remaining troops in procession in front of our lord, until everyone is able to look at the face of our lord and present their greetings fully to him.'

'Here is the man to assist you,' said al-Mahdī, pointing at me. The following day, al-Mahdī sat on the throne which was set up under the marquee. It appeared as if the sun rose from his face. Al-Qāʾim stood to his right, girded with his sword and touching his throne like the full moon. Ṭayyib stood to the right of the throne near al-Qāʾim at a distance of two steps. Muslim was to the left of the throne, at a distance of two steps from the throne. Near him was Abū Yaʿqūb. Bushrā[5] and Ṣandal stood to the right and left of the throne, each of them holding a fly-whisk, waving them over al-Mahdī's head.[6] I was standing at the entrance of the marquee leaning on my sword. Abū ʿAbd Allāh was standing at a distance of 200 cubits from the marquee with 1,000 guards (*bawwāb*) who were standing in two rows. He was calling by name the *dāʿīs* and the commanders, bringing them forward ten by ten. As soon as ten of them had assembled, he told them, 'Walk gently to the chamberlain who is standing at the entrance of the marquee. Conform strictly to

1. An adjective relating to Dabīq, a locality in the outer suburbs of Damietta, noted for the manufacture of high quality woven fabrics. The term *dabīqī* was then applied to fabrics manufactured in Upper Egypt and elsewhere.
2. Ṭayyib was al-Mahdī's slave.
3. Muslim was a Greek slave bought by Jaʿfar for al-Qāʾim in Sijilmāsa on al-Mahdī's orders.
4. Abū Yaʿqūb was a Christian slave and head servant (*qahramān*) of al-Mahdī.
5. Bushrā was a slave of Slavic (Ṣaqlabī) origin purchased by Abū ʿAbd Allāh in Īkjān in Kutāma territory and presented to al-Mahdī in Sijilmāsa.
6. This is the earliest reference to the two fly-whisks (*al-midhabbatān*) which were part of Fatimid regalia.

what he instructs you in order to greet our lord and invoke prayers for him. Then when he signals you to retire, you will retire.'

Ja'far said [continuing the narration]: It is from that day that I was called 'chamberlain' (*ḥājib*). I brought them forward ten by ten, and I was the first to serve al-Mahdī when he acceded to the caliphate.[1] They continued to greet him, and invoke prayers for him, while he blessed them and thanked them for their devotion. He informed them that God had prepared for them immense reward in this world and the Hereafter. (This ceremony) lasted for the whole day. Then al-Mahdī continued to sit for three days for (the officers) and the soldiers [to go through the same ceremony].

(Translated by Hamid Haji)

1. After leaving Sijilmāsa together with the *dā'ī* Abū 'Abd Allāh, al-Mahdī passed by Īkjān in Kutāma territory and then proceeded to Raqqāda, the former capital of the Aghlabids, where he assumed supreme authority as caliph and imam.

3
al-Qāḍī al-Nuʿmān

The jurist and scholar al-Qāḍī al-Nuʿmān (d. 363/974) was the author of perhaps the most important historical text on the early history of the Fatimids. The *Iftitāḥ al-daʿwa* was completed in 346/957, twelve years before the Fatimid conquest of Egypt, during the reign of the Imam-Caliph al-Muʿizz li-dīn Allāh (r. 341–365/953–975). It relates the momentous events preceding the establishment of the caliphate in 297/910 by ʿAbd Allāh al-Mahdī and goes on to offer a vivid and detailed account of the early days of the Fatimid caliphate. In the first of the following extracts, we accompany al-Mahdī on the perilous journey from Sijilmāsa to his triumphant arrival in Ifrīqiya, covering present-day Tunisia and eastern Algeria. Next, we see how al-Mahdī was accepted by the populace and speedily established peace, justice and administration in his realms.

Iftitāḥ al-daʿwa
Commencement of the Mission[1]

AL-MAHDĪ'S COMING FROM SIJILMĀSA AND HIS ARRIVAL IN IFRĪQIYA

Then al-Mahdī arrived accompanied by al-Qāʾim. At that time al-Mahdī was in the prime of his youth without any grey hair, while al-Qāʾim was at an age when his moustaches sprouted. Abū ʿAbd Allāh returned from the expedition with him together with all his troops. He handed over the command to (al-Mahdī) and informed the *dāʿī*s that he was the imam in whose favour he had been carrying out the mission. He presented him to all the believers, saying, 'He is my lord and your lord, the guardian of your destiny, your guide in the straight path, your awaited Mahdī whose glad tidings I had announced. God, the Mighty, the Glorious, has caused him to triumph, just as He had promised. He granted assistance to his followers and his soldiers.'

The first of his proofs and portents which the followers saw with their own eyes was that they observed that God, the Mighty, the Glorious, had willed to accomplish (al-Mahdī's) cause; that God, the Blessed and Sublime, protected him from his enemy by putting fear of him in his heart, in spite of the fact that he was in his dominion and swords were sharpened against him. His followers and helpers were

1. al-Qāḍī al-Nuʿmān, *Iftitāḥ al-daʿwa*, tr. Hamid Haji as *Founding the Fatimid State: The Rise of an Early Islamic Empire* (London, 2006), pp. 202–213 (nos. 37–38).

being killed for him, but (the enemy) was unable to inflict any harm upon him. Nor could (al-Yasaʿ b. Midrār)[1] stretch his hand to do any misdeed, in spite of the fact that one of his courtiers had advised him to kill him saying, 'These people have only flocked to him, but when they are disappointed with him, they will disperse. So if you kill him, it will give a lie to what his companion is preaching about him among them, that he would reign and triumph. Kill him because that will certainly give a lie to what his companion is preaching about him among them. That will create discord among them and divide them.'

However, God, the Mighty, the Glorious, abandoned him so that he did not accept this advice from the one who gave it and the one who advised him to do so. God killed the one who gave this advice at the hands of His friend and enabled (al-Mahdī) to be protected from his enemy.

Al-Mahdī, peace be upon him, approached. When he was alongside Kutāma territory, he turned towards it and arrived in Īkjān. He ordered funds to be brought forth. These had been under the custody of the *dāʿī*s and the elders who had buried them there. They submitted (the funds) to him. He ordered that the custody of the funds be taken over from them. He packed them in loads and proceeded with them. This was the first matter which changed the corrupt hearts.[2] They had imagined that they would be as Abū ʿAbd Allāh had accustomed them: commanding, forbidding, collecting taxes and disbursing.

When al-Mahdī arrived in Īkjān,[3] he instructed Abū ʿAbd Allāh to write a letter to Abū Zākī[4] informing of his arrival. Abū ʿAbd Allāh wrote the letter and sent it with a courier. The letter was read out from the pulpit of the mosque. Here is its copy:

> In the name of God, the Compassionate, the Merciful. Now then! Praise be to God, protector of His religion and cherisher of His friend. He caused His religion to triumph over all religions, and His friend over oppressors and aggressors who were hostile to him. This letter of mine to you is from Īkjān, the abode of emigration, and the established home of the faith. The imam, our lord and master, al-Mahdī bi'llāh, may God's blessings be upon him, has arrived together with his son, may God fulfil through him his best hopes, at the head of all the supporters of religion (*awliyāʾ al-dīn*) and the believers who were accompanying him. The arrival was excellent, most auspicious, joyous and satisfying. He has illuminated with his arrival the abode of emigration of his followers and gladdened the believers, men as

1. Al-Yasaʿ b. Midrār was the ruler of Sijilmāsa who placed al-Mahdī and al-Qāʾim under captivity soon after their arrival there. After the conquest of Sijilmāsa by Abū ʿAbd Allāh, Ibn Midrār was captured and put to death.

2. A reference to those who plotted with Abu'l-ʿAbbās and Abū Zākī against al-Mahdī.

3. The exact position of Īkjān is difficult to establish. See Mohamed Talbi, *L'émirat Aghlabide 184–296/800–909, histoire politique* (Paris, 1966), pp. 600–601, note 4. Information in the *Iftitāḥ* allows us to locate Īkjān to the north of Saṭīf and Mīla.

4. Abū Zākī Tammām b. Muʿarik, from the Kutāma clan of Ijjāna, became Abū ʿAbd Allāh's most faithful companion to whom the latter entrusted the government of Ifrīqiya during his expedition to Sijilmāsa in 296/909. Abū Zākī was among those later accused of treason and executed on the orders of al-Mahdī.

well as women, who had remained behind, being excused from fighting (*jihād*), as well as those whom we had stationed there to secure the place. They approached from all sides to reach him and from every horizon hastened towards him, seeking to be blessed by looking at him and to be healed by his glance, praising God for having conveyed to them the accomplishment of His promise and the manifestation of His cause. They hastened to deliver to him the deposits of God which they had held in trust and delivered to him what God has enjoined upon them.[1] The war is over by the grace of God. God extinguished its fire, and destroyed those who provoked it and scattered and divided those who thereby intrigued against the religion of God. The Commander of the Faithful is coming straight to Ifrīqiya. With success, capacity, help and facilitation granted by God, he will be able to arrive on Thursday 20 Rabīʿ II 297/6 January 910, God willing. Let this be known. Be ready for him with those who are with you. Praise God for having entrusted you that favour and that He has your appointed time of death until you reached him. Solicit from him that this be completed for you by glancing at your lord and his satisfaction with you. Salutation!

When the letter bearing this statement arrived, it was read out. The news spread and the followers were overjoyed. It put an end to the slander and rumours which had spread. The people got ready and prepared themselves to meet him. Their eyes aspired towards him and their souls looked up to him and to his coming. (Al-Mahdī), may God's blessings be upon him, arrived on the appointed Thursday as stated in the letter. The people met him according to their rank. The inhabitants of al-Qayrawān received him in their multitude. Among them on that day were elders, notables and jurists who had perception, intelligence, forbearance and eloquence. Those who lived before that time were also like them, but all that vanished from them with the manifestation of the friends of God among them and from all those like them who opposed their authority. God eclipsed their light, abated their splendour and took away their joy, because this can only reside in the friends of God and those who follow them. Glory, brilliance, beauty, perfection and splendour appertain to them alone, just as the sun, when it rises, takes away the light of the stars and their shapes, overcomes the light of the lamps and eclipses their rays, so that doubt does not accompany the truth, nor should there be any obscurity which could cause doubt about those who are its rightful owners.

Al-Mahdī, peace be upon him, approached, leading the supporters of his realm and multitudes of troops of his followers, like the full moon of completeness and the lamp of darkness. Abū ʿAbd Allāh led the group of *dāʿīs*, while the elders and the followers marched in front of him. Al-Qāʾim followed behind him, while the cortege and the troops marched along the length and breadth of the plain of al-Qayrawān. The jurists (*shuyūkh*) of the people of al-Qayrawān greeted (al-

1. These deposits held in trust (*amānāt*) included monies due to the imam from the wealth of the believers, in accordance with Shiʿi practice. See al-Qāḍī al-Nuʿmān, *Kitāb al-himma fī ādāb atbāʿ al-aʾimma*, ed. Muḥammad Kāmil Ḥusayn (Cairo, [1948]), pp. 41–44.

Mahdī) as caliph and imam. They congratulated him on his victory and safety. He reciprocated towards them kindly and agreeably. He asked them to retire and they left. He told Abū ʿAbd Allāh and those accompanying him, 'It is as if we have seen a people who resemble the inhabitants of towns of the east. The inhabitants of the Maghrib that we have seen [so far] are only like the Bedouins.' He settled in his palace in Raqqāda. The followers settled in their quarters and dispersed to their regions. Every group of the people of Ifrīqiya went to their place, and went by his order and permission to their towns.

EARLY DECREES OF AL-MAHDĪ

On Friday morning, the day after his arrival, (al-Mahdī) issued a decree, ordering it to be invoked from the pulpits of mosques. He addressed it to the two preachers of Raqqāda and al-Qayrawān, prescribing invocation of blessings upon himself after the invocation of blessings of God upon the Prophet, ʿAlī, Fāṭima, al-Ḥasan, al-Ḥusayn and the imams from his posterity, which had been put into practice by Abū ʿAbd Allāh. The decree contained the following invocation:

> O Lord! Bless your servant and vicegerent who presides in Your lands upon the destiny of Your servants, the Servant of God, Abū Muḥammad al-Imām al-Mahdī bi'llāh, Commander of the Faithful, just as You blessed his ancestors, Your rightly-guided vicegerents led on the right path, who ruled and rendered justice, observing the truth. O Lord! Just as You have designated him for Your guardianship and chosen him for Your vicegerency, and have made him a protection and pillar for Your religion, as well as an asylum and refuge for Your subjects, may You also cause him to triumph over Your enemies in rebellion, heal through him the hearts of the believers, and cause him to conquer the earth, the east as well as the west, just as You promised him. Grant him Your support against the unjust rebels. God of all the beings, Lord of the worlds.

He ordered the transcription of another decree which was read from the pulpit in al-Qayrawān. Copies of the decree were sent to the towns and read from the pulpits. Here is its exemplar:

> In the name of God, the Compassionate, the Merciful. We seek His help. From the Servant of God, Abū Muḥammad al-Imām al-Mahdī bi'llāh, Commander of the Faithful, to his followers among the believers and all the Muslims. Peace be with you. The Commander of the Faithful praises God before you. There is no god except Him. He prays to Him that He may bless Muḥammad, His servant and Messenger. May God bless him and his progeny. Now then! All praise is due to God who raised the flag of truth and honoured its adherents. He overturned the banners of falsehood and humiliated its party. The Powerful who cannot be opposed in His power, the Exalted in might whose decree cannot be resisted. The Protector of His religion which He chose for Himself and which He honoured with the most noble of His prophets, the highest in rank among them before Him, the most noble among them in status, the nearest of them as intermediary before

Him, Muḥammad, may God bless him, bearer of His wisdom and depository of His mystery. After him there will be no deception of the deceivers, no treason of the traitors, no oppression of the oppressors for the members of his household, for He promised him help, assistance, glory and authority concerning them, just as He says in His clear Book and revelation that '*no falsehood can approach from before or behind*' [41:42], '*And We wished to show favour unto those who were oppressed in the earth, and to make them examples and to make them the inheritors, and to establish them in the earth, and to show Pharaoh and Hāmān and their hosts that which they feared from them*' [28:5–6]. And He says, '*And verily we have written in the Scripture, after the Reminder: My righteous servants will inherit the earth. Behold! This is a plain statement for folk who are devout*' [21:105–106]. (God), may His praise be exalted and His names sanctified, fulfilled His promise to His Messenger, may God bless him and his progeny, by restoring the inheritance of prophethood and the keys of the imamate to the family of His Prophet. He honoured religion and the believers, saving them from disaster in every situation with the advent of the Servant of God, Abū Muḥammad al-Imām al-Mahdī bi'llāh, Commander of the Faithful. (God) manifested the splendour and beauty of Islam with his advent. He secured the heritage of his ancestor the Prophet, and his forefather ('Alī), the legatee (*waṣī*). May the blessings of God be upon them both. (God) endowed His friends and the supporters of His right, Arab chiefs and valiant Kutāma, with perspicacity. The imamate cast its staff in its house with delight; its solitude became tamed, and its basis became firm.[1] The Commander of the Faithful became a high, lofty mountain, a firm mountain on earth and a sheltering shadow for its inhabitants. The foothold of guidance became firm and the fright of piety was calmed by him. He straightened its support which had become crooked, and strengthened its foundations which had become loose. He reinforced its rope (*ḥabl*) which had dissolved, restoring its unity which had been dispersed. What was scattered was repaired by the blessing of the Commander of the Faithful, the good fortune of his nature, the good omen of his star and the breeze of his zephyr. He treated Islam from incurable disease and repaired its fissures. He mended cracks in it which could not be mended, and reconciled splits in it which could not be reconciled. He is the key of mercy and the guide of the good, defending the truth, protecting religion, taking care of the affairs of Muslims, and watchful of that which thwarts the aspirations of the peddlers of falsehood. Praise be to God, Lord of the worlds. By the grace of God, whenever the Commander of the Faithful attempted a great and difficult feat, God facilitated it. When he met any hardship, (God) subdued it. When he came to any rough terrain, (God) made it smooth. Unity was established through him, harmony was continuous and calamity was averted. The farthest and closest regions of the earth are secure through him. His friend is powerful and protected, while his enemy is humble and restrained. Whoever strikes fire with his flint and gathers firewood in his rope (*ḥabl*) is assured help and ordained for him is victory. Whoever breaks his oath to him, betrays his trust, violates his

1. The wording is reminiscent of a poet's words in which the expression 'to cast one's staff' (*alqā 'aṣāhu*) is used of a traveller who settles down at the end of a long journey.

treaty and breaks his commitment will incur the wrath of God for opposing him and causing sedition. War will burn with its fire whoever kindles against him the fire of war (*nār al-ḥarb*) and will wound him with its claws, and whoever holds on to obedience to him grasps '*the firm hand-hold*' [2:256], and will be victorious in the Hereafter and in this world. Whoever solicits a confidant other than it, '*he loses both this world and the Hereafter. That is the sheer loss*' [22:11]. Therefore, praise God who has let you attain the time of the Commander of the Faithful, and distinguished you with the blessing of his reign and good fortune of his dominion. May your hopes be high and your optimism grow with confidence in his justice. May your expectation rise to recognize the excellence of his attention. May your adherence to the rope of obedience to him and the bonds of loyalty to him become strong, for indeed, no bond connects God and His servants except through their love for the family of Muḥammad, may God bless him and grant him salvation. God, exalted be His mention, has said, '*Say: "No reward do I ask of you for this except the love of those near of kin"*' [26:23]. The Messenger of God says, '*My family among you are like Noah's ark. He who sails in it will be safe, but he who holds back from it will drown.*' So renew thanks to God for having granted you the compassion and mercy of the Commander of the Faithful, and his constant care for your affairs, compensating for your shortcomings. Indeed, giving thanks is the surest preserver for the one benefiting from His bounties, and the surest custodian for His abundant kindness, and the most effective means derived for the beginning of His benefit and the provision of its abundance. The Commander of the Faithful prays to God, possessor of benevolence and bounties, and bestower of favours and graces, that He may bless Muḥammad, the key of His mercy and conveyor of His message, to whom He granted all His virtues and nobility. May He cause (the Commander of the Faithful) to be filled with His fear and regard. May he carry out with good fortune His precepts. May He grant him the best inspiration in fulfilling the leadership which He has granted him and carrying out the affairs of His servants that He has entrusted to him, just as He inspired His rightly-guided vicegerents. May He support him in his good intention and grant him the best trial. May He grant him success to act in obedience to Him and to uphold His right so that he can restrain infidelity and heresy, and subjugate the outlying regions of the land. May He make him the best leader who is kind to his subjects. May He make his subjects the best subjects who discharge the right of their leader. Indeed, success lies with Him and abundance proceeds from Him. Salutation!

(Al-Mahdī) was proclaimed caliph on Friday 21 Rabīʿ II 297/7 January 910 at Raqqāda, al-Qayrawān, and al-Qaṣr al-Qadīm. This letter was read out from the pulpit of al-Qayrawān and was dispatched to the provinces with the *dāʿīs*. He was proclaimed thereafter and it was read out from the pulpits when it reached there. The people were happy and pleased with this and invoked blessings upon him profusely. Delegations of the towns came from every region and place in proportion to the proximity of their settlements. (Al-Mahdī) continued to sit in assembly for the people. Abū Jaʿfar al-Khazarī[1] arrived with the womenfolk from the city of Tripoli in the best manner.

EULOGY OF AL-MAHDĪ

Whenever (al-Mahdī) sat for his assembly, he allowed his close followers to come in his presence. When he had satisfied their needs, he allowed those who were below them in rank, and often allowed the common people to come in his presence to greet him. Poets composed verses about him and eulogized him. The first poet of Ifrīqiya to eulogize him was Saʿdūn al-Warjīnī. He was a poet who had eulogized the Aghlabids and held their functions. He had been taken prisoner in Byzantium and had been ransomed. He was permitted to come before (al-Mahdī) and recite to him what he had composed about him. This happened immediately after the arrival of the womenfolk, while (al-Mahdī) was seated and the followers congratulated him on their safe arrival. (The poet) came in his presence and recited the poem in which he says:

Stop with the mounts on the pastures of regions.
Their features are wearing garments of dust,
Two winds play with them until their traces are erased,
An easterly and a westerly wind.

Then he reached these verses:

The agile she-camel ran turning away from the destination,
While the hand of destination ruled the rein of my journey.
She feared that mishap might befall me because I
Previously had been absent then returned after a long time.
Then after that we met, re-united.
O what a captive was united with a captive!

When he had recited these verses, al-Mahdī shed tears. His tears fell on his sleeve. Saʿdūn became silent. (Al-Mahdī) gestured to him to recite. (The poet) continued until he came to the verses:

Will you deter a man from the son of Fāṭima,
Daughter of the Prophet and the family of purification?
Abstain from distracting, I shall visit
The best one visited from the members of the household of the revelation.

Abū ʿAbd Allāh, who was standing before al-Mahdī, told (Saʿdūn), 'You have spoken the truth. Indeed, he is the best of creatures!' Thereupon, Saʿdūn kissed the

---

1. He was a senior *dāʿī* entrusted with the task of escorting the womenfolk on their journey.

ground in front of al-Mahdī and continued to recite the verses until he reached these verses:

> This is the Commander of the Faithful with whose coming
> The supports of every commander were demolished.
> This is the Fatimid imam through whom feel secure from threat
> The western lands of (the earth).
> And the east, in spite of its Syria and Iraq, is no
> Refuge from his victorious army,
> Until he attains what he desires of the caliphate
> And is obtained from him his extended justice.

The Commander of the Faithful said, 'Whatever God wills (*mā shā'a llāh*)!' He continued to recite the poem until he referred to Abū 'Abd Allāh saying:

> O chosen one from his finest *dā'īs*.
> The one most hoped for by them in difficulty and in ease,
> Until he won over every tribe for (al-Mahdī)
> And he threw to him the reins of every persistent stumbler,
> You (al-Mahdī) resemble Moses and he (Abū 'Abd Allāh) is your serpent
> Which is cast and snatches every falsehood of the magician.[1]

At this al-Mahdī looked at Abū 'Abd Allāh and smiled. Abū 'Abd Allāh kissed the ground in front of (al-Mahdī) and said to al-Warjīnī, 'I am beneath that (praise), as much as the distance between the sky and the earth!'

The Commander of the Faithful ordered (the poet) to be granted plentiful recompense and that it should be bestowed upon him every year. Abū 'Abd Allāh also offered (the poet) a gift. It would be too long to mention the poets who have eulogized al-Mahdī. The elegies they have composed are so many that they are outside the scope of this book.

THE ADMINISTRATIVE SYSTEM OF AL-MAHDĪ

(Al-Mahdī) organized the administrative departments and gave orders to levy taxes. The land register was burnt when Ziyādat Allāh fled.[2] He ordered it to be restored.[3] He set up an intelligence service, a department for real estate and a department for property which belonged to those who fled with Ziyādat Allāh. He confiscated their property, leaving alone what was due to their wives, whose safeguard and protection he guaranteed. He took in his service black slaves and white slaves of Christian

1. Cf. Qur'an 7:117; 26:45.
2. Ziyādat Allāh III (r. 290–296/903–909), the last ruler of the Aghlabid state in Ifrīqiya, who fled his capital of Raqqāda as the Fatimid forces led by Abū 'Abd Allāh approached the city in 296/909.
3. Al-Mahdī entrusted this task to Ibn al-Qadīm, who had held the same functions under the reign of Ziyādat Allāh.

origin (*al-rūm*), and established a department for pensions where he ordered the registration of freed slaves and sons of slaves and applicants who had hastened to be registered for maintenance. Many offices were thus established. He gave order to recover the pillage of Raqqāda, of which a great deal was recovered from the hands of people who were prosecuted and from whom large sums were gathered. He instituted a public treasury for which a department was set in place. It is said that the director of the public treasury presented to him an account of allowances for the month of Ramaḍān amounting to 100,000 dinars, and which the director of the treasury had considered enormous. However, al-Mahdī replied, 'If I would attain my dues by the grace of God and realize my hopes, I would not be satisfied with all this as the pay for a single one of my followers.'

He was very generous with money which is a characteristic of the Mahdī, peace be upon him, as reported of old in traditions. Nevertheless he would neither waste nor neglect the least sum, and he would not get involved in expenses which could not be justified. Such are the characteristics of the imams. It has been reported that a man came to al-Ḥasan b. 'Alī,[1] peace be upon him, to beg from him without recognizing who he was, for he had been led to him. He saw (al-Ḥasan) asking someone for something trivial which was due to him of his right. So he refrained from begging from him and thought of giving up. Then he dared to approach him and begged from him. (Al-Ḥasan) gave him many times more than he had expected. He told him, 'By God! I don't know at what to marvel. Should I marvel at your giving this or at your asking for what I saw you previously demanding?'

(The beggar) related to him what had caused him to lose hope. (Al-Ḥasan) said, 'O man! The one whom you saw us asking for the paltry thing you saw wanted to deceive our intelligence, so we declined, while you appealed to our generosity and we donated to you.'

Members of the Aghlabid family, their clients, troops and servants who had remained behind feared (al-Mahdī), even though Abū 'Abd Allāh had granted them a guarantee of safety. So al-Mahdī confirmed it to them. Their dignitaries and chiefs entered before him when he sat for audience together with others who did. (Al-Mahdī) granted them proximity and was friendly with them. He was kind to them and employed some of them. He sent on missions and military campaigns all those who were suitable for that, and granted them the status of followers. Hence they felt secure and became confident, and their fear calmed down. People observed his discipline, resolve, sound administration, kindness and generosity to the extent which they had not expected of him. He spread justice, established it and ordered it to be enforced in places distant and remote as well as near and close. He redressed injustices and would hear such cases himself. He accepted written petitions from complainants while riding or sitting. He would hear from them their complaints and would redress their grievances on the basis of justice and equity. Consequently he gained the sympathy of the elite as well as the commonalty who regarded him

1. Al-Ḥasan b. 'Alī b. Abī Ṭālib (d. 41/669), the elder son of Imam 'Alī and Fāṭima, and grandson of the Prophet Muḥammad.

highly. Abū ʿAbd Allāh was disregarded and his light was eclipsed by the light of al-Mahdī. People turned away from (Abū ʿAbd Allāh) and turned towards (al-Mahdī). In spite of this, (Abū ʿAbd Allāh) showed humility, self-abasement, reverence and submission, and acknowledged (al-Mahdī's) kindness, confirmed his authority and wished him well, much more than he used to do before. This showed sincere intention, purity of innermost thought and commitment to duty, until something happened to him which we shall relate in the next chapter, God, the Most High, willing.

(Translated by Hamid Haji)

4
Idrīs ʿImād al-Dīn

Idrīs ʿImād al-Dīn (d. 872/1468) was the chief *dāʿī* of the Ṭayyibī Ismaili *daʿwa* in Yemen. His *ʿUyūn al-akhbār wa-funūn al-āthār* is the only extant history of the Fatimid caliphate written by an Ismaili author. Drawing upon eyewitness accounts of the dynasty, it provides a unique, Ismaili perspective on the Fatimids. Below are two excerpts from the reign of the fourth Fatimid Imam-Caliph al-Muʿizz. The first, taken from the fourth volume of the *ʿUyūn*, preserves an eyewitness account of the first Fatimid imam-caliph explicating the concept of *imāma*, drawing parallels with prophets of earlier eras, and highlighting the uniqueness of the occasion when four future imam-caliphs were present at his court. The second excerpt provides a rare insight into the close relationship between al-Muʿizz and the Fatimid jurist al-Qāḍī al-Nuʿmān. More importantly, it demonstrates al-Muʿizz's role in mentoring the compilation of al-Nuʿmān's writings, in particular his *Daʿāʾim al-Islām*, which represents the foundations of Fatimid Ismaili law.

ʿUyūn al-akhbār
Choice Stories[1]

ON THE NURTURING OF THE IMAMS

Al-Qāḍī al-Nuʿmān[2] was among those who had precedence in serving the Imam al-Mahdī bi'llāh during the later part of his caliphate. He was also the beneficiary of the favours of al-Qāʾim bi-Amr Allāh[3] as were others. Then Imam al-Mahdī bi'llāh disclosed to him the distinction of his grandson Imam al-Manṣūr bi'llāh[4] who was the third of the imams of the [period of] manifestation. He (al-Nuʿmān) said: 'O Commander of the Faithful, three imams in one age?' The [number] astounded

1. Idrīs ʿImād al-Dīn, *Tāʾrīkh al-khulafāʾ al-Fāṭimiyyīn bi'l-Maghrib: al-qism al-khāṣṣ min Kitāb ʿuyūn al-akhbār wa-funūn al-āthār*, ed. Muḥammad al-Yaʿlāwī (Beirut, 1985), tr. Shainool Jiwa as *Springs of Knowledge: An Annotated Translation of Idrīs ʿImād al-Dīn's* ʿUyūn al-akhbār wa-funūn al-āthār. vol. 4, (forthcoming), on the reign of al-Muʿizz li-Dīn Allāh. The introduction to this extract is by the translator.

2. Celebrated Ismaili jurist and historian of the 4th/10th century.

3. The second Fatimid imam-caliph (r. 322/934–334/946).

4. Ismāʿīl al-Manṣūr bi'llāh (d. 341/953) was the third caliph of the Fatimid dynasty in Ifrīqiya. He succeeded to the imamate on the death of his father al-Qāʾim in 334/946 and in his short reign restored peace and secured the future of the Fatimid state in Ifrīqiya.

him. Then Imam al-Mahdī bi'llāh showed him al-Muʿizz li-Dīn Allāh[1] who was a babe in his cradle and said, 'And this is the fourth of us, O Nuʿmān!'

In the time of the Prophet Ibrāhīm al-Khalīl[2] there were four [prophets]: Ibrāhīm al-Khalīl, the prophet who was the messenger of his cycle, to whom God sent the revelation and said, 'I will make thee an imam to the nations.' He pleaded, 'And also (imams) from my offspring!' [Qur'an 2:124] With him were Ismāʿīl, Isḥāq and Yaʿqūb.[3]

Then at the time of Mūsā b. ʿImrān he had with him his brother Hārūn, Yūshaʿ b. Nūn and Finḥāṣ b. Hārūn.[4]

Subsequently, during the time of our Prophet Muḥammad, the best of the prophets and their seal, by whose prophethood and messengership God completed the messenger-prophets, He distinguished him among all His creation and made his law (*sharīʿ*) eternal until the Day of Judgement. During his era there was his brother and helper, his supporter in establishing the religion of God and his aide, the father of the imams of his progeny and his son-in-law, ʿAlī, his legatee (*waṣī*), the Commander of the Faithful and the seal of the legatees (*khātim al-waṣiyyīn*), and their two sons al-Ḥasan and al-Ḥusayn. With Jaʿfar al-Ṣādiq[5] were his sons Ismāʿīl b. Jaʿfar[6] and his grandson Muḥammad b. Ismāʿīl,[7] three imams in one era.

That was also the case with al-Mahdī bi'llāh, al-Qā'im bi-Amr Allāh, al-Manṣūr bi'llāh and al-Muʿizz li-Dīn Allāh.

Indeed, the *imāma*[8] can only reside with one [imam] after the other, with the one who is distinguished by its merits and is deserving of its exalted status. He

1. Abū Tamīm Maʿadd, fourth Fatimid imam-caliph who reigned 341/953 to 365/975, adopted the regnal title 'The Commander of the Faithful, al-Muʿizz li-Dīn Allāh' upon his ascension to the Fatimid caliphate.

2. Biblical Abraham, mentioned several times in the Qur'an.

3. Biblical Ishmael, Isaac and Jacob.

4. Biblical Moses, Aaron, Joshua and Phinehas.

5. The early Shiʿi imam Jaʿfar al-Ṣādiq (ca. 702–765), son of Muḥammad al-Bāqir, was a distinguished *ḥadīth* transmitter, cited as an authority in Shiʿi and Sunni *isnād*s alike. Numerous traditions defining Shiʿi doctrine and several prayers, homilies and books are ascribed to Jaʿfar. He is also a celebrated figure in Sufism.

6. The eldest son of Jaʿfar al-Ṣādiq by his first wife, Fāṭima, granddaughter of al-Ḥasan b. ʿAlī. According to several sources, Imam al-Ṣādiq designated Ismāʿīl as his successor but the mystery surrounding Ismāʿīl's disappearance caused disagreement in the Shiʿi community and saw the emergence of what subsequently came to be known as the Ismaili and Ithnāʿasharī branches of Shiʿa Islam. See Farhad Daftary, *The Ismāʿīlīs: Their History and Doctrines* (2nd ed. Cambridge, 2007), pp. 90–93.

7. The eldest son of Ismāʿīl b. Jaʿfar. Born around 120/738, he was eight years older than his uncle Mūsā, who also contended the imamate and was accepted by the majority of the Imāmiyya. He escaped Medina and headed to the east to avoid Abbasid persecution, initiating the *dawr al-satr* or period of concealment in early Ismaili history, which ended with the establishment of the Fatimid caliphate. Idrīs provides the most detailed biographical account on him in his *ʿUyūn al-akhbār*, vol. 4, pp. 351–356, and *Zahr al-maʿānī*, tr. W. Ivanow, *Ismaili Tradition Concerning the Rise of the Fatimids* (London, 1942), pp. 53–58, trans. pp. 240–248. See also Ivanow, 'Ismailis and Qarmatians,' *JBBRAS*, New Series, 16 (1940), pp. 60–63; Daftary, *The Ismāʿīlīs*, pp. 95–96.

8. The Shiʿi concept of the imamate is based on the premise that mankind is in permanent need of a divinely-inspired teacher or *imām* to lead believers to spiritual salvation. Endowed with authoritative knowledge of the Qur'an, the imam has the sole legitimate claim to the leadership of the Muslim community.

indicates his successor and designates him (*yanuṣṣu ʿalayhi*),[1] and makes his successor evident to the adherents of his *daʿwa* (mission), and surrenders the imamate to him. The virtues of al-Muʿizz li-Dīn Allāh were apparent and the worthiness of his succession to his pure ancestors was evident.

In one of al-Qāḍī al-Nuʿmān b. Muḥammad's reports on Imam al-Muʿizz li Dīn Allāh he said: 'I recollect what the Commander of the Faithful al-Mahdī bi'llāh said one day when I was carried to him – for I was a toddler then – and I could understand what was said and remember what took place. He held me, kissed me and placed me under his cloak. He uncovered my navel and placed it against his own. Then he moved me [from under his cloak], blessed me and asked me how I was. He sat me on his lap and ordered some food for me. I was offered a silver gilded plate. On it were bananas, autumn apples and grapes. It was put in front of me but I did not eat any of it. He lifted it and offered it to me. So I took it in my hands. He said: "Take it and eat what is on it and give the plate to so and so," and he mentioned a girl who was similar in age to me.

'I replied, "No, rather, I will take the plate and will give her what is on it." He laughed and was astonished by my alertness to that. He bade me well and said to the servant, "Carry him!" So I was carried while I was holding the plate in my hand. He added, "He will become prominent." I did not confirm these words with al-Muʿizz.[2]

'Then al-Muʿizz remarked: "Al-Mahdī was unique in his time. He was vested with the secrets of the progeny of Muḥammad, the most knowledgeable of them, and the one who shielded them from calamities."'

He [al-Nuʿmān] said: 'From a young age, al-Muʿizz li Dīn Allāh had a special status with his grandfather al-Qāʾim. He used to keep him in his company, be close to him and confide in him in preference to his father. He was his messenger and intermediary to the people conveying his orders and prohibitions and doing whatever he needed him to do. Whenever he (al-Qā'im) was alone, he (al-Muʿizz) was with him and whenever he was absent, he (al-Qāʾim) would send for him.

'Similarly, Imam al-Manṣūr had the same status with his grandfather al-Mahdī, who was inseparable from him. He (al-Manṣūr) used to confide secrets in him and no one knew what transpired between them. One of the people who used to enter the presence of al-Mahdī frequently, as it was imperative for him to do so, said to me that there was never a time when he (al-Mahdī) was alone without al-Manṣūr being present and al-Mahdī would be speaking in confidence to him. When he (al-Manṣūr) saw him (the visitor) he would step back until the man's need had been attended. When he left, he (al-Manṣūr) returned to him.

---

1. In Shiʿi tradition *naṣṣ* refers specifically to the imam's designation, based on divine knowledge, of his successor. See Arzina Lalani, 'Naṣṣ,' *The Qur'an: An Encyclopaedia*, ed. Oliver Leaman (London and New York, 2006), pp. 488–451.

2. al-Qāḍī al-Nuʿmān, *Kitāb al-majālis wa'l-musāyarāt*, ed. al-Ḥabīb al-Faqī, Ibrāhīm Shabbūḥ and Muḥammad al-Yaʿlāwī (Tunis, 1978), p. 541.

'He (the visitor) remarked: "I never heard what was said between them. I did not know of anyone who was closer to al-Mahdī and had the same status with him, as did al-Manṣūr. I knew of no one speaking with him (al-Mahdī) in seclusion, and upon my entry, I could not hear what was said between them, except in the case of al-Manṣūr."

'One day al-Muʿizz mentioned a similar instance to his situation, saying that al-Mahdī bi'llāh used to nurture him (al-Manṣūr) with wisdom and prepare him for the imamate, just as al-Qā'im did so with him.'[1]

UNDER THE GUIDANCE OF THE IMAM: AL-QĀḌĪ AL-NUʿMĀN'S COMPOSITIONS

Al-Qāḍī al-Nuʿmān was one of the knowledgeable and virtuous people. He authored many books and had famed knowledge. Even adversaries conceded his virtues and vast knowledge. In fact, all that he wrote, gathered and compiled was learned from the imams of his time, based on what they reported from their pure ancestors. He did not compose any writing nor compile a work without checking it with them, step by step. They corroborated the truth and straightened out the mistakes with the correct information. He drew from their sea of knowledge, and by them he knew, and by their benefactions he was able to compile and write his works.

The following are among his works on jurisprudence [list of books]. Then he composed the work, *Daʿā'im al-Islām fī'l-ḥalāl wa'l-ḥarām wa'l-qaḍāyā wa'l-aḥkām* (*Pillars of Islam regarding the Permitted and the Prohibited, the Decrees and Judgements*)[2] on the authority of the Commander of the Faithful, al-Muʿizz li-Dīn Allāh. That was because al-Nuʿmān and a group of *dāʿī*s came to the Commander of the Faithful, al-Muʿizz. They mentioned some invented sayings, doctrines (*madhāhib*) and opinions, which had caused disagreement among Muslim groups as well as mentioning what their scholars had agreed upon, deviated, claimed knowledge of and disseminated without clear proof. So the Commander of the Faithful, al-Muʿizz li-Dīn Allāh, recounted the sayings of his forefather, the Messenger of God, which had been confirmed by his pure ancestors: 'You will follow the path of the peoples who preceded you, step by step and feather by feather so that if they entered a lizard hole,[3] so will you.' In another saying he said: 'You will follow the path of those who preceded you hand-span by hand-span and arm's-length by arm's-length so that if they entered a wasp nest, so will you.' Then al-Muʿizz mentioned the words of the Messenger of God to them: 'If deviation occurs in my community (*umma*), the scholar should manifest his knowledge, or else God's curse be upon him.' He turned to al-Qāḍī al-Nuʿmān and said, 'You are meant by that, O Nuʿmān.' Then he instructed him to compose the *Kitāb al-daʿā'im*; he confirmed its foundations and divided its sections. He apprised him of the sound traditions from his pure

1. al-Qāḍī al-Nuʿmān, *Majālis*, pp. 501–502.
2. al-Qāḍī al-Nuʿmān, *Daʿā'im al-Islām*, ed. Asaf A. A. Fyzee (Cairo, 1951–61); English trans. Asaf A. A. Fyzee, revised by I. K. Poonawala, as *The Pillars of Islam* (New Delhi, 2002–2004).
3. al-Suyūṭī, *al-Jāmi' al-saghīr*, 122/2, as cited by al-Yaʿlāwī, *'Uyūn*, p. 560.

ancestors and from the Messenger of God, avoiding those that the narrators had disagreed upon and were fabricated, according to their types and categories. He added: 'Indeed, we have related from Imam Jaʿfar al-Ṣādiq b. Muḥammad who said: "Islam was founded on seven pillars: obedience and devotion (*al-walāya*)[1] – this is the best, by it and by the master (*walī*), gnosis (*maʿrifa*) can be achieved – purity, prayer, almsgiving, fasting during the month of Ramaḍān, pilgrimage to the sacred House of God, and *jihād*."'[2]

He (al-Muʿizz) instructed him, so he began by mentioning *walāya* to the Commander of the Faithful, ʿAlī b. Abī Ṭālib, demonstrating how the Messenger distinguished his merits and that he was the foremost person to succeed him over the community (*umma*). This was after he had referred to faith (*īmān*), without which God does not accept any work and only the one who belongs to its people is righteous. He mentioned obedience and devotion (*walāya*) to the imams from the Messenger's progeny and the obligation to pray for them, and explained the appointment of the imams and that the imams can only be appointed by divine designation (*naṣṣ*) and notification; and the status of the imams with God, their dissociation from those who hold extreme views about them,[3] some of their admonishments to their followers (*awliyāʾihim*) and their supporters (*shīʿatihim*). He recounted that God has enjoined love for them (the imams), urging [believers] to take knowledge from those whom God has appointed for that.

Then he (al-Muʿizz) explained the obligations in Islam concerning purity, prayer, almsgiving, fasting, pilgrimage and *jihād* and what ensues from these concerning what is permitted and prohibited, cases and rulings, selling and buying, food and drink, divorce and marriage, inheritance and bloodwit, testimony and the rest of the established, obligatory categories of jurisprudence.

Al-Qāḍī al-Nuʿmān completed this work called *Daʿāʾim al-Islām* according to the precepts established by the Commander of the Faithful, al-Muʿizz li-Dīn Allāh. He used to present it to him section by section and chapter by chapter. He (al-Muʿizz) confirmed parts of it, corrected the errors in it and filled the gaps until it was complete. Thus the work emerged as a comprehensive synopsis with utmost precision. That was a miracle of the Commander of the Faithful, al-Muʿizz li-Dīn Allāh which he manifested through his *dāʿī* and supporter (*walī*) al-Nuʿmān b. Muḥammad, explicating the law (*sharīʿa*) of his forefather Muḥammad, the

1. *Walāya/wilāya*, derived from the root *w-l-y*, to be near, is a crucial concept in Islamic social and spiritual life which revolves around notions of authority and succour. In Shiʿi tradition the concept of *walāya* appears to have developed very early and centres on devotion and obedience to the *ahl al-bayt*. In the *Daʿāʾim*, al-Qāḍī al-Nuʿmān, following Jaʿfar al-Ṣādiq, names *walāya* as one of the seven pillars of Islam. In Sunni tradition, the concept of *walāya/wilāya* focuses more on the principle of kinship. See H. Landolt, 'Walāyah,' *The Encyclopedia of Religion*, ed. Lindsay Jones (Detroit, 2005), vol. 14, pp. 9656–9662.

2. The notion of a just war has been interpreted over the course of time both in the military sense and as an inner struggle for purification; from the root *j-h-d*, meaning exertion, struggle, application.

3. 'Those who hold extreme views about them' refers to the *ghulāt* (sg. *ghālī*) or extremists, the notion being 'those who go too far in religion.' See M. G. S. Hodgson, 'Ghulāt,' *EI2*, vol. 2, pp. 1093–1094, and 'How Did the Early Shiʿa become Sectarian?' *JAOS*, 75 (1955), pp. 1–13.

Messenger of God, elevating it as a landmark of Islam, to rule by his example (*sunna*), and to abandon heresy, about which the Prophet said, 'Every deviation is an error and every error leads to Hellfire.'

Then the Commander of the Faithful instructed al-Qāḍī al-Nuʿmān to abridge the *Daʿāʾim al-Islām* in another work titled *Iqtiṣār al-āthār fī mā ruwiya ʿan al-aʾimma al-aṭhār* (*Summary of the Traditions related from the Pure Imams*). He made it accessible and elucidated it for those who sought it.

Al-Qāḍī al-Nuʿmān said: 'Some *qāḍīs*, governors and seekers of knowledge asked me for a work which would provide an abridged exposition of the sayings of the *ahl al-bayt* which explicates their meaning, facilitates memorization and is light on the pocket. So I began to write it and I reckoned that when the book is complete it would cost no more than a dinar for those who wished to transcribe it. Hence, I named it *Kitāb al-dīnār* and I mentioned that in the introduction. I presented what I had begun to write to al-Muʿizz. I requested him to peruse the work and to confirm that the traditions were transmitted from him. I sent that with a note in which I made the request.

'He (al-Muʿizz) wrote back in his own hand on the reverse of the note: "In the name of God the Merciful, the Gracious. May God safeguard you, O Nuʿmān. I have leafed through and examined the book and am pleased with the sound traditions and the excellent summation. However, it contains words which many of our followers (*awliyāʾ*) would find abstruse, so elucidate them such that they can comprehend, so as to ensure that everyone can grasp the knowledge through the words, whether they are exalted or common. That way it will become valuable and digestible and name it *Kitāb al-iqtiṣār li ṣaḥīḥ al-āthār ʿan al-aʾimma al-aṭhār* (*Summary of the Sound Traditions from the Pure Imams*). This is better than calling it *Kitāb al-dīnār* because it contains the knowledge of the Friends of God which all people should seek for their souls let alone by their money. This name will devalue the work among the rich who will think that they can easily procure it. Moreover, they can aim for something more expensive than that with the vanities of their world. They consider that the money that they have collected and hoarded is a gain; however, this will vanish if they deviate and stinginess takes over their mind. This is so except for those who are protected by God, and they are but a few."

'Then he corrected, modified and deleted some sections of what I had submitted to him and confirmed the others by mentioning or marking them. Thereafter, I read it to him, incorporating all his corrections and suggestions, and deleting all that he had recommended to remove, copying his words into the text. He permitted that the one who reports from me should mention that I relate from him (al-Muʿizz), from those of his pure ancestors whom he mentioned, after he authenticated the reports from them. I benefited tremendously from that and I was exalted by his benefactions. I only presented this work to him so that he could confirm to me what I had collected and read and heard on the authority of the preceding narrators from his (al-Muʿizz's) ancestors was correct. Through the work, he opened and made accessible his sea of knowledge, which enabled me to include in this book all that is prohibited and permitted, the cases and rulings. In that work, he confirmed for me duties and responsibilities I should fulfil towards those who seek my opinion and when I pronounce judgements, by the praise and grace of God and the benefaction of His Friend (*walī*). I hope that if God extends my life, I shall present everything else in my religion for his review, record it and take the sound [traditions] from him. May God let me attain that by His power and strength.'

Al-Qāḍī al-Nuʿmān said: 'The Commander of the Faithful instructed me to collect the reports of the reign and the virtues of the Banū Hāshim[1] in a book and the flaws of the Banū ʿAbd Shams[2] in a work, so I did. I collected enough material on these two themes to compile a comprehensive work in many parts, in accordance with his classification and guidance. I presented them to him. He liked them, was satisfied with them, praised their content and said: "Concerning the reports of the reign, those who ruled it and those *dāʿīs* and believers who established it, I would like information on them to be perpetuated in this manner with those who follow, so that the positive mention of those from bygone times is perpetuated and the prayers of those who succeed them and hear their name is upon them and so that those who succeed them know the honour that God has prepared for them in the hereafter. That is our duty towards them for they are not present with us for us to offer this to them.

"'It is imperative that the successors, the progeny and the friends know about the ancestors' merits and virtues and the enemies' flaws and failings. The adversaries and the enemies should be censured and should be publicized among the people and for posterity, even though the virtues of the people of merit and the vices of the base are well known and unconcealed, apparent and unveiled. They harbour many suspicions and are steeped in deceit in different ways. In this they are as God has said: 'Their intention is to extinguish God's light [by blowing] with their mouths. But God will complete [the revelation of] His light, even though the unbelievers may detest it.'" [61:8]

Amongst what has been related from al-Qāḍī al-Nuʿmān b. Muḥammad is that he said: 'I received a letter from al-Manṣūr in which he said: "O Nuʿmān, excerpt from the Book of God what the commoners have rejected and dismissed." I said to myself: "What can there be in the Book of God that any believer in the religion of Islam would reject and dismiss?" This weighed heavily on me and I thought at the time that I would not find a single letter of this; yet I did not consider referring back to him appropriate. Then I sought succour from God, for I knew that the Friend (*walī*) of God would not have said so without its existence. So I opened the Qur'an

1. The Hāshimiyya, descended from Muḥammad's great-grandfather Hāshim b. ʿAbd Manāf, were a Qurayshī tribe charged with guardianship of the Kaʿba at Mecca. The Fatimid imam-caliphs traced their descent from the Prophet and hence from the Banū Hāshim.

2. The Banū ʿAbd Shams, named after Hāshim's brother ʿAbd Shams b. ʿAbd Manāf, was a clan within the Meccan Quraysh who opposed Muḥammad for most of his prophethood under the leadership of Abū Sufyān b. Ḥarb. The Umayyads were descendants of the Banū Shams through ʿUthmān b. ʿAffān.

to read it and the first sentence that caught my eye was: "In the name of God the Merciful, the Gracious." I recalled that some people said that this was not in the Qur'an, but I established that it is. The material began to become disclosed to me until I had collected a twenty-folio section on it. I presented it to al-Manṣūr. He approved of it and was pleased with it. Then he said: "Continue!" So I reached *Sūrat al-Mā'ida*, having begun from *Sūrat al-Fātiḥa* followed by *Sūrat al-Baqara* and I collected examples that amounted to over 600 pages. Whenever I met al-Manṣūr, I presented the work to him. He was pleased with it and said: "No one has done such work before." Then he passed away; however, I had not yet completed it.'

The virtues of al-Qāḍī al-Nuʿmān b. Muḥammad are well known and his merits are famous and oft-related. He is the one concerning whom the Commander of the Faithful al-Muʿizz li-Dīn Allāh said: 'Whoever presents a tenth of what al-Nuʿmān has accomplished, I guarantee him heaven on behalf of God! As for Jaʿfar, we have other things to say about him.' He meant Jaʿfar b. al-Ḥasan Manṣūr al-Yaman,[1] whose father was among the greatest and best *dāʿī*s.

(Translated by Shainool Jiwa)

1. Jaʿfar b. Manṣūr al-Yaman, son of the first Ismaili *dāʿī* in the Yemen. He came to the Maghrib during the reign of al-Qā'im and opposed the Khārijī rebel Abū Yazīd under al-Manṣūr (946–953). He wrote many works, which deal for the most part in Qur'anic exegesis and ritual duties. For extracts from his *Kitāb al-ʿālim wa'l-ghulām* (*Book of the Master and the Disciple*), see Part Two, III, 1.

5

al-Mu'ayyad fi'l-Dīn al-Shīrāzī

The *dā'ī* al-Mu'ayyad al-Shīrāzī (d. 470/1078) was active on behalf of the Fatimids in the mid 11th century in southern Iran, the region of his birth. He was a formidable scholar, poet and diplomat, apart from being an effective *dā'ī*. In the course of his activities in Shīrāz, al-Mu'ayyad won the Būyid ruler, Abū Kālījār Marzubān (r. 415–440/1024–1048) to the Ismaili cause and also came to be revered by the sultan's soldiers, many of whom were from the northern region of Daylam. Not surprisingly, al-Mu'ayyad's rising influence provoked strong opposition from the Abbasids as well as the court-affiliated clergy, who used their influence to turn the sultan against him. Al-Mu'ayyad was eventually forced to flee Shīrāz in disguise. This vivid description of his escape and his subsequent travels brings out the enormous risks faced by the intrepid *dā'ī*s of the early Fatimid *da'wa* and shows also that al-Mu'ayyad had a turn of phrase as gripping as that of any modern thriller writer.

Sīrat al-Mu'ayyad
Autobiography of al-Mu'ayyad[1]

FLEEING FROM SHĪRĀZ TO AHWĀZ

The king [Sultan Abū Kālījār] was on the point of travelling to Ahwāz with his troops. I concluded that if I remained in Shīrāz, I would not be safe from whatever trickery or subterfuge might be used to fulfil the desires of [my enemies]. Accordingly, I told myself that it would be most prudent to remain with the group and not to separate from the collective.[2] Thus, I sought permission to travel with them but was refused. This refusal only increased my forebodings. I continued to send written requests for permission, but I met with no approval, and in spite of

1. al-Mu'ayyad fi'l-Dīn al-Shīrāzī, *Sīrat al-Mu'ayyad fi'l-Dīn*, ed. M. Kāmil Ḥusayn (Cairo, 1949) tr. Joseph E. Lowry, in Dwight F. Reynolds, ed., *Interpreting the Self: Autobiography in the Arabic Literary Tradition* (Los Angeles, London, 2001), pp. 140–143. For a detailed study of the *sīra*, see Verena Klemm, *Memoirs of a Mission: The Ismaili Scholar, Statesman and Poet al-Mu'ayyad fi'l-Dīn al-Shīrāzī* (London, 2003).

2. Al-Mu'ayyad adds a touch of humour and irony here by using a phrase at the end of this sentence that is a slogan of Sunni Islam. The Prophet Muḥammad is reported to have said, 'Do not separate from the collective,' commonly understood by Sunni Muslims as a condemnation of all non-Sunni sectarianism. But al-Mu'ayyad, who is fleeing Sunni enemies and seeking safety by hiding among a group of Sunnis, wryly quips that he is doing so according to the Sunni teaching not to separate from the collective!

more urgent requests, I met with nothing but more obstinate refusal. I therefore undertook the difficult course of clandestine flight. It had not occurred to me, and certainly not to anyone else, that I was capable of such a thing. I gave my followers and companions in Shīrāz to understand that I had received approval for my request to join the troops but would be travelling in the entourage incognito, while I gave those travelling in the entourage to understand that I would be remaining in Shīrāz, in hiding, but that I would be sending along with them some of my baggage, riding beasts, and servants. I then donned a disguise and assumed an unfamiliar demeanour, wearing old and ragged clothes. I acquired two new servants, unknown to anyone, and set off on back roads, hiring at each way station an ass to ride, or a camel, or a steer, as circumstances dictated.

The travails of journeying that I endured during that time – descending into ravines and mires, bearing the freezing cold, alighting in filthy places – was something for which, had it been a disease, death would have seemed a cure! The most difficult thing I had to bear was that every time I hired an ass to ride, I wanted to go down the road alone so no one would see me. Its owner, however, would want to accompany us to keep an eye on his animals, squarely defeating the entire purpose. He would ask what caused me to prefer travelling alone when the custom among travellers was to prefer the opposite, namely, that they would ask to be accompanied. I was tongue-tied, unable to give a reasonable excuse for this. Along the way I would alight with people from the countryside and backcountry. I listened as they mentioned me in very unflattering terms and I realized that if they recognized me, they would have performed ritual ablutions in my blood and gone to prayer! May you never have to go down such roads and hear with your own ears such horrible things about yourself!

Among the places in which I wished neither to be, nor to be apprehended, and in which my safety was preserved only through the subtle graces of Almighty God, was a place called Jannāba. [...] I felt this way because I arrived there on a rainy day, and my search for some shelter from the rain led me to the congregational mosque. The town market was next to it, and someone came in to pray who knew my name, ancestry and everything else about me. When his gaze fell upon me, he came closer, approaching as you would approach someone who enjoys an elevated station in life. Then he saw my demeanour, my state, my clothes and what I was doing, and he realized right away that I was fleeing. He offered himself and his money to me, saying, 'If there is anything you need, I can help you, or, if you need a little extra money to take with you, I have some and cannot think of a better use for it than you.' 'God bless you and your money,' I replied. 'I have no need more pressing than that you have not seen me, nor I you.'

Then a second person came over to me, an ʿAlid [i.e., a Shiʿi], and asked one of my servants about me. My servant replied that I was a *sharīf* [i.e., a descendant of the Prophet Muḥammad through ʿAlī and the Prophet's daughter, Fāṭima] travelling from Kirmān to Baghdad. He said that this was not what people were saying about me. He approached and greeted me, and I greeted him politely and welcomed him.

He said, 'It seems as if I know you, sir – may God protect you.' 'Perhaps that is the case,' I said. He said, 'I met you in Ahwāz.' I replied, 'I have indeed been there.' 'In the place known as the Palace of al-Ma'mūn, I remember that you were building a building there,' and in saying this alluded to the shrine that was the cause of the current misery afflicting me.[1] 'I do not know that place; I have only gone to Ahwāz when passing through. Anyway, where would I get the means to build something? I am too busy looking out for myself to pay attention to such a thing.' 'Well, what have I been doing trying to cover for you then? They said you were so-and-so and spoke of you with terms of great honour and respect.' 'I have on occasion heard of that man,' I said. 'He is a man of important affairs, the leader of the Daylamīs, a powerful position. Still I have never seen him, but some people resemble others and perhaps someone would liken me to him.' He continued, 'Some people said to the local governor, "You should take him into custody, perhaps he is fleeing the sultan. If you capture him you may gain favour with the court." He was about to detain you until I pointed out to him that he should really ignore that sort of talk completely.' I said to him, "You are neither commanded nor required to do so. He may be the man they mean and he may not. If he is the one they mean, exposing yourself to his enmity together with the enmity of all of the Daylamīs would outweigh whatever reward you might earn by seizing him. And if he is someone else, then you have frightened a stranger, detained him on his way to some place or another, and earned yourself the embarrassment of it." "You are right," replied the governor, and he accepted my counsel regarding you. But now I would like for you to take as much money from me as you want and let it help you along your way. You would both honour me and favour me by doing so.' I thanked him profusely.

Then a third person approached me carrying himself differently than had the other two. He greeted me, came up to me, and said, 'There has been much talk of you in this town. Some say that you are Ẓahīr al-Dīn, lord of Baṣra, escaped from prison and making your way back to Baṣra. Another says you are so-and-so,' and he called me by a name which only a passionate and ardent devotee would use, showing himself to be a fervent adherent of Shiʿism and its doctrines. I said, 'Sir, I am neither the one nor the other of these two men, but rather merely an ʿAlid passing through.' The man replied, 'Then I would ask something of you.' 'What is it?' I asked. 'That you write for me, in your own hand, a prayer from which I might receive some blessing.' 'As for writing the prayer,' I replied, 'there is nothing which could keep me from doing that, but as for your taking it as a blessing because it is written in the hand of the man to whom you referred, I am not he, and there is no blessing in my hand or in his, in my opinion and according to my creed.' 'That would be fine,' he said, 'please write it.' I said to him, 'Then I have a favour to ask of you, too, so please do it, one favour for another.' 'What is that?' he inquired. 'I would like you to rent a riding ass for me, so that I can leave this place.' 'I hear and obey,' he replied.

1. Al-Mu'ayyad had restored a mosque, an act that caused him difficulties with the sultan Abū Kālījār.

So the man left in search of a riding ass to rent, and I busied myself with writing what he had asked for. He returned after a while with the muleteer, having agreed with him on a price, and so he was paid. I said, 'Where is the ass for me to ride so that we can travel?' 'I will bring it to you shortly,' he said, 'It is in an outlying village.' He then left me while it was still morning. The time came for the first afternoon prayer and he had not yet returned. Dusk approached and he had still not returned. I had no doubt that I had been delayed by the local governor and that he would arrest me, having forbidden the muleteer from returning and sent spies to follow me if I left the place. I was in no position to run and escape my pursuers had I wished to flee. This gave me a fright of apocalyptic proportions, so I sent for the man who had brought the muleteer and said to him, 'That man has left me high and dry, for he has not returned, despite the fact that it was settled that he would do so within a short time. So, if you please, could you track him down and bring him back with the riding ass? If you would, it would be most kind and I would not be able to thank you enough.' 'I hear and obey,' he said. He set off at once, and suddenly there he was approaching with the muleteer and the ass, shortly before sunset. So we set off, I not believing that I had escaped from that predicament, and looking back to see if anyone was following us. We travelled and stopped overnight in a ruined palace on the riverside. It was in fact haunted by demons, but when I entered it, I felt as though I had been plucked out of Hellfire and dropped into Heaven.

When we awoke, we travelled wherever God in His munificence led us. Such was my wont for an entire month, experiencing all of life's hardships, wrapped in the garments of terror, undergoing every genus and type of torment and travail, until I entered my home in Ahwāz one evening, prior to the sultan's return. For he had remained en route between Shīrāz and Ahwāz for some time, engaged in diversions and pastimes, until he encamped for a month in a town called Sābūr, three days' march from Shīrāz. During his stay there, a letter from the intelligence network reached him informing him that I had disappeared, and that, since the time his entourage had departed, no trace of me had been seen, but that there was a rumour that I was travelling in his company in disguise. He was shaken by these rumours and I heard that he placed spies and agents in the tents of the Daylamīs and in their camps to ascertain my whereabouts. He stepped up his efforts to narrow the search, examining the cavalry and the infantry man by man, and in a number of cases laid bare the faces of some who had disguised themselves. But all that was lost effort, for I was tucked away in my hiding place and not among them, kept safe by God in His mercy.

(Translated by Joseph E. Lowry)

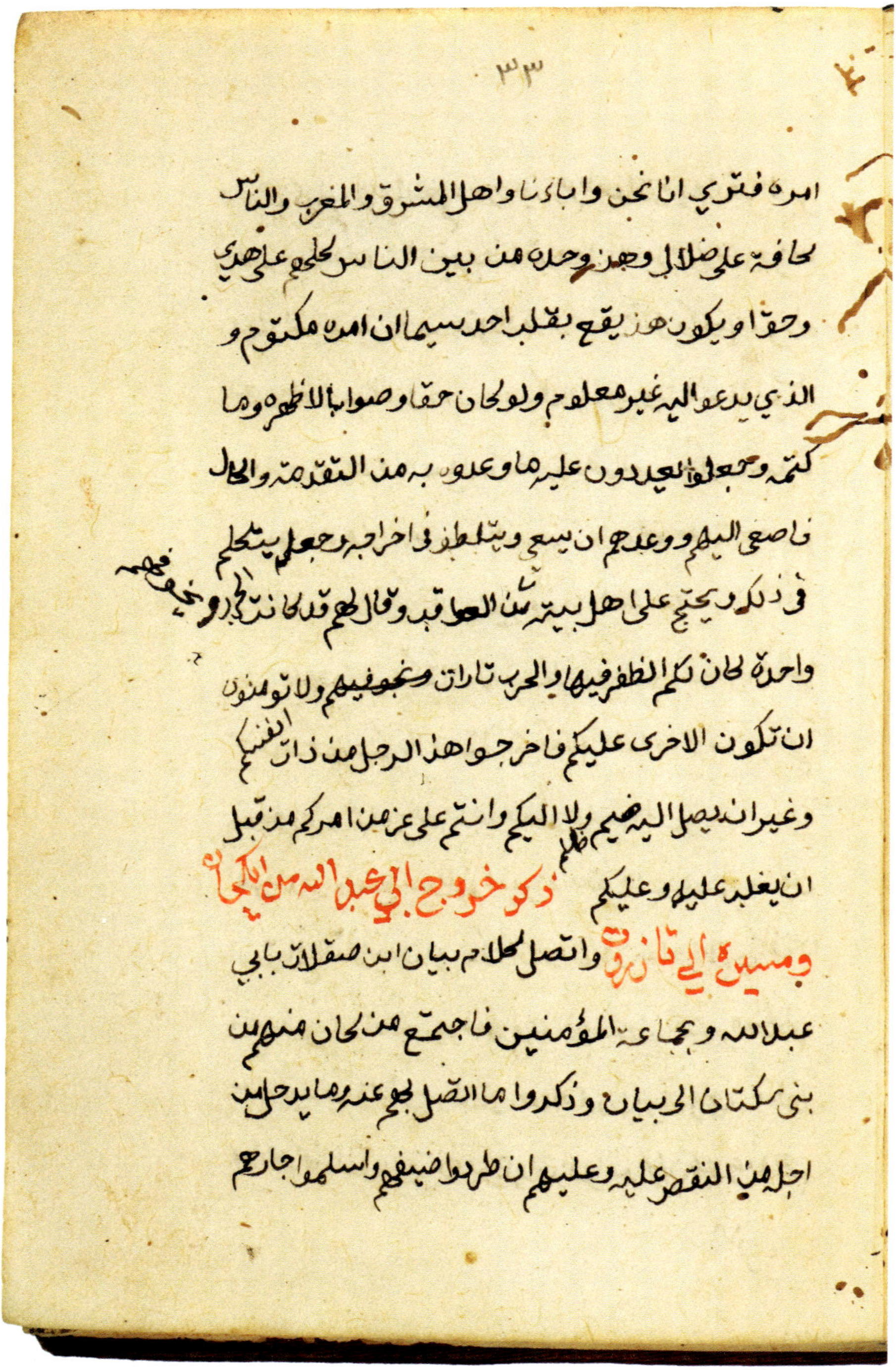
٣٣

امره فترى انا نحن واباؤنا واهل المشرق والمغرب والناس
كافة على ضلال وهذا وحده من بين الناس كلهم على هدى
وحق او يكون هذا يقع بقلب احد سيما ان امره مكتوم و
الذي يدعو اليه غير معلوم ولو كان حقا وصوابا لاظهره وما
كتمه وجعلوا يعددون عليه ما علموا به من المتقدمة والحال
فاصغى اليهم وعدهم ان يسعى ويتلطف في اخراجه وجعل يتكلم
في ذلك ويحتج على اهل بيته ثم العاقد وقال لهم قد كانت لكم دور وحروب فيهم
واحدة لكان لكم الظفر فيها او الحرب تارات وتخوفهم ولا تؤمنون
ان تكون الاخرى عليكم فاخرجوا هذا الرجل من ذات انفسكم
وغير انه يصل اليه ضيم ولا اليكم وانتم على عز من امركم من قبل
ان يغلب عليه وعليكم ذكر خروج ابي عبد الله من ايكجان
ومسيره الى تازروت واتصل الكلام بيان ابن صقلان بابي
عبد الله وبجماعة المؤمنين فاجتمع من كان منهم من
بني سكتان الجيان وذكروا ما اتصل بهم عنه وما يدخل من
اجله من النقص عليه وعليهم ان طردوا ضيفهم واسلموا جارهم

PLATE 1

This page from a 19th-century manuscript of the *Iftitāḥ al-daʿwa* of al-Qāḍī al-Nuʿmān describes incidents during the *dāʿī* ʿAbū ʿAbd Allāh's journeys in North Africa around 289/902.

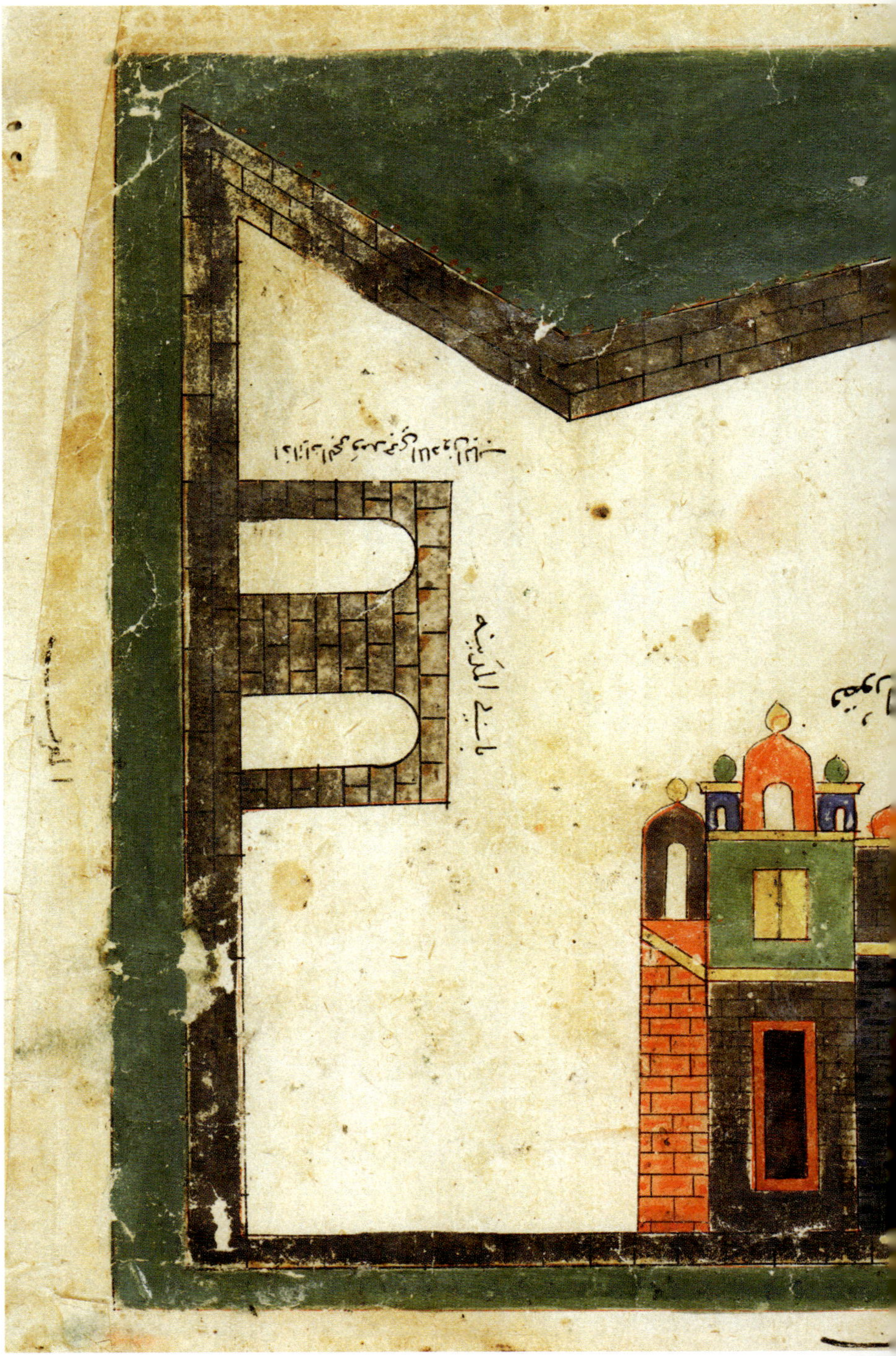

PLATE 2

This painting of the Fatimid palace at Mahdiyya in Ifrīqiya is from a 3rd/11th-century manuscript, the *Kitāb gharā'ib al-funūn wa-mulaḥ al-ʿuyūn* (*Book of Curiosities*). The colourful buildings represent the palaces of the imams,

surrounded by a wall with arched gates leading to the city. The writing in the upper left indicates distances from port to port on the way from Mahdiyya to Sicily.

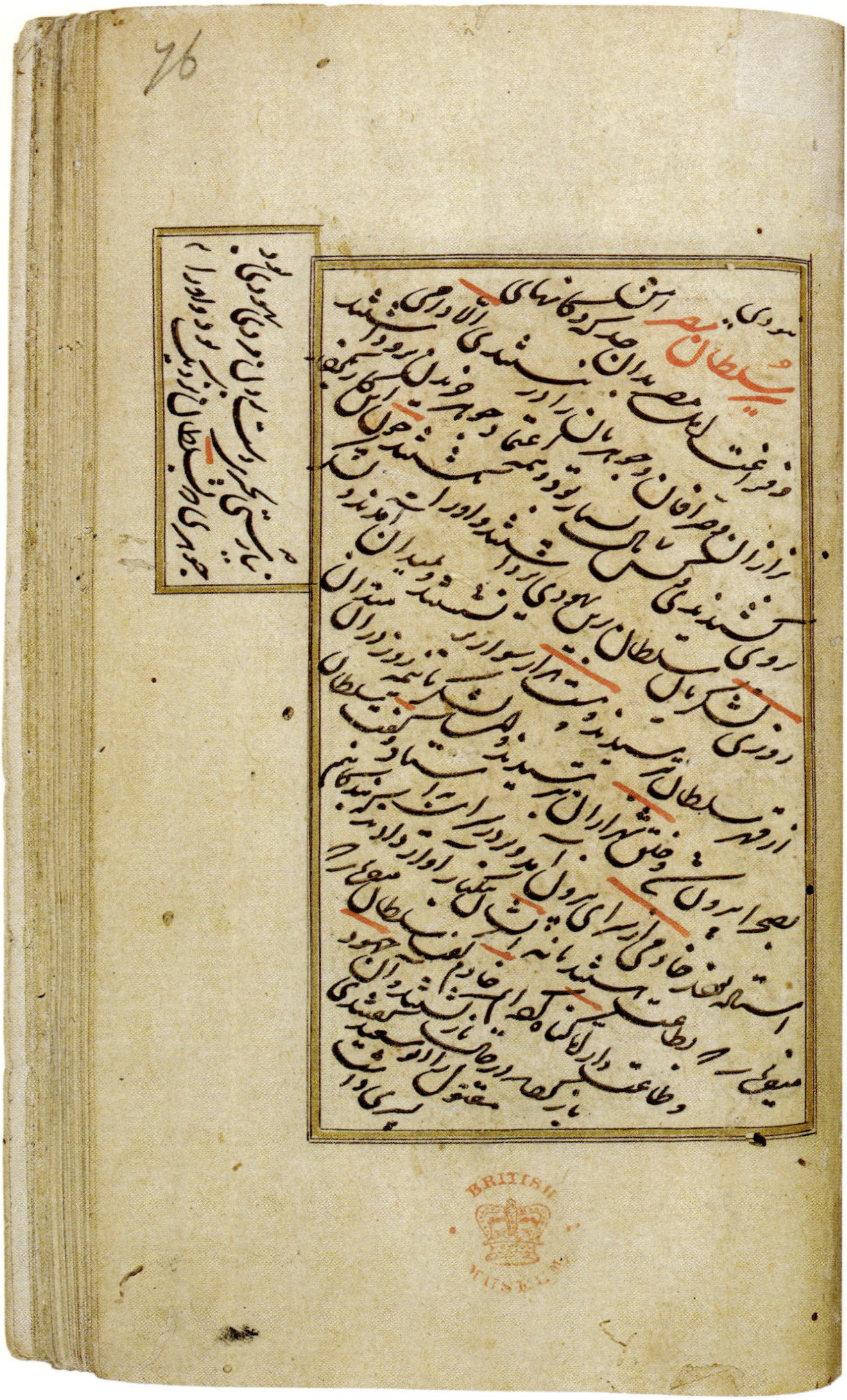

PLATE 3

Nāṣir-i Khusraw visited the Fatimid capital of Cairo in the mid 11th century. In this page from a 17th-century manuscript of his *Safar-nāma* (*Book of Travels*), he describes the just reign of the Imam-Caliph al-Mustanṣir bi'llāh.

6
Nāṣir-i Khusraw

Nāṣir-i Khusraw (d. after 462/1070), the great Persian poet and prose writer, was a middle-aged official in the Saljūq administration in Marw, in eastern Khurāsān, when he had a dream in which he was urged to give up a life of pleasure and search for 'that which increases reason and wisdom.' This exhortation woke Nāṣir from what he called a 'forty-year sleep' and impelled him to set out on pilgrimage. He travelled for seven years (437–444/1045–1052) through Central Asia, Persia, the Near East (including several visits to Mecca) and to Fatimid Egypt which was then ruled by the Imam-Caliph al-Mustanṣir bi'llāh (d. 487/1094). Nāṣir probably received doctrinal training from al-Mu'ayyad fi'l-Dīn al-Shīrāzī during his sojourn of more than two years in Cairo. His *Safar-nāma* (*Book of Travels*) includes an observant and detailed account of the Fatimid capital as seen by a visitor from the east. The following extract is an account of the extent and abundance of the great royal capital in the reign of Imam al-Mustanṣir, where citizens – Muslims, Christians and Jews – were protected by the grace of their ruler. Nāṣir refers to the imam as *sulṭān-i Miṣr* (ruler of Egypt) and as *amīr al-mu'minīn* (Commander of the Faithful), recognizing both his temporal and spiritual sovereignty.

Safar-nāma
Book of Travels[1]

A DESCRIPTION OF THE CITY OF OLD CAIRO

The city of Old Cairo is situated on a promontory. To the east of the city is a hill, not too high, of rock and stone. On one side of the city is the Ibn Ṭūlūn Mosque, built on a rise with two reinforced walls. With the exception of the walls of Āmid and Mayyāfāriqīn, I never saw the likes of this mosque. It was built by one of the Abbasid *amīrs* who was governor of Egypt. During the reign of al-Ḥākim bi-Amr Allāh, the grandfather of the present sultan, the descendants of Ibn Ṭūlūn sold the mosque to al-Ḥākim for thirty thousand dinars. Later, they were about to have the minaret torn down when al-Ḥākim sent word to them to inquire what they were

1. Nāṣir-i Khusraw, *Safar-nāma*, ed. Muḥammad Dabīr Siyāqī (5th ed. Tehran, 1977); tr. Wheeler M. Thackston, Jr. as *Nasir-i Khusraw's Book of Travels (Safarnama)*, (Costa Mesa, CA, 2001), pp. 66–75. For a comprehensive study of Nāṣir-i Khusraw's life and writings, see Alice C. Hunsberger, *Nasir Khusraw, The Ruby of Badakhshan: A Portrait of the Persian Poet, Traveller and Philosopher* (London, 2000).

doing, since they had sold him the mosque. They replied that they had not sold the minaret, so he gave them another five thousand dinars for it. During the month of Ramaḍān the sultan prays there, and also on Fridays.

The city of Old Cairo was built on a hill for fear of the Nile waters. Once the site was just large boulders, but they have all been broken up and the ground levelled. Now they call such a place an *ʿaqaba*.

Looking at Old Cairo from a distance, because of the way it is situated, you would think it was a mountain. There are places where the houses are fourteen stories tall and others seven. I heard from a reliable source that one person has on top of a seven-story house a garden where he raised a calf. He also has a waterwheel up there turned by this ox to lift water from a well down below. He has orange trees and also bananas and other fruit-bearing trees, flowers, and herbs planted on the roof.

I was told by a credible merchant that there are many houses in Old Cairo where chambers can be hired. These chambers are thirty cubits square and can hold 350 people. There are also markets and lanes there where lamps always must be kept lit because no light ever falls upon the ground where people pass to and fro.

In Old Cairo alone, not counting New Cairo, there are seven Friday mosques built one next to the other. In the two cities there are fifteen Friday mosques, so that on Fridays there is a sermon and congregation everywhere. In the midst of the market is the Bāb al-Jawāmiʿ Mosque, built by ʿAmr b. al-ʿĀṣ when he was appointed governor of Egypt by Muʿāwiya. The mosque is held aloft by four hundred marble columns, and the wall that contains the *miḥrāb* is all slabs of white marble on which the entire Qur'an is written in beautiful script. Outside, on all four sides, are markets into which the mosque gates open. Inside there are always teachers and Qur'an readers, and this mosque is the promenade of the city, as there are never less than five thousand people – students, the indigent, scribes who write checks and money drafts, and others.

Al-Ḥākim bought this mosque from the descendants of ʿAmr b. al-ʿĀṣ. As they were in financial distress, they had asked the sultan to give permission for them to tear down the mosque their ancestor had built in order to sell the stones and bricks. Al-Ḥākim gave them one hundred thousand dinars for the mosque with all the people of Old Cairo as witnesses. Then he built many amazing things there, one of which is a silver lamp holder with sixteen branches, each of which is one and a half cubits long. Its circumference is twenty-four cubits, and it holds seven hundred-odd lamps on holiday evenings. The weight is said to be twenty-five *qinṭār*s of silver, a *qinṭār* being a hundred *raṭl*s, a *raṭl* being 144 silver dirhams. After it had been made, it was too large to get in through any of the existing doors, so they removed one of the doors and got it inside, after which the door was replaced. There are always ten layers of coloured rugs spread one on top of the other in this mosque, and every night more than a hundred lamps are kept burning. The court of the chief justice is located in this mosque.

On the north side of the mosque is a market called the Lamp Market, and no one ever saw such a market anywhere else. Every sort of rare goods from all over the world can be had there. I saw tortoise-shell implements such as small boxes, combs, knife handles, and so on. I also saw extremely fine crystal, which the master craftsmen etch most beautifully. [This crystal] had been imported from the Maghrib, although they say that near the Red Sea, crystal even finer and more translucent than the Maghribī variety had been found. I saw elephant tusks from Zanzibar, many of which weighed more than two hundred maunds. There was a type of skin from Abyssinia that resembled leopard, from which they make sandals. Also from Abyssinia was a domesticated bird, large with white spots and a crown like a peacock's. Throughout Egypt is much honey and sugarcane.

On the third of the month of Day of the Persian year 416 [December 1048] I saw the following fruits and herbs, all in one day: red roses, lilies, narcissus, oranges, limes and other citrous fruits, apples, jasmine, basil, quince, pomegranates, pears, melons of various sorts, bananas, olives, myrobalan, fresh dates, grapes, sugarcane, eggplants, fresh squash, turnips, radishes, cabbage, fresh beans, cucumbers, green onions, fresh garlic, carrots, and beets. No one would think that all these fruits and vegetables could be had at one time, some usually growing in autumn, some in spring, some in summer, and some in fall. I myself have no ulterior motive in reporting all this, and I have recorded what I saw with my own eyes, although I am not responsible for some of the things I only heard, since Egypt is quite expansive and has all kinds of climate, from the tropical to the cold; and produce is brought to the city from everywhere and sold in the markets.

In Old Cairo they make all types of porcelain, so fine and translucent that you can see your hand behind it when held up to the light. From this porcelain they make cups, bowls, plates and so forth and paint them to resemble *būqalamūn* so that different colours show depending on how the article is held. They also produce a glass so pure and flawless that it resembles chrysolite, and it is sold by weight.

I heard from a reputable draper that they buy a stone-dirham's weight of thread for 3 Maghribī dinars, which is equal to three and a half Nīshāpūrī dinars. In Nīshāpūr I priced the very best thread available and was told that one dirham-weight of the finest was sold for five dirhams.

The city of Old Cairo is situated laterally along the Nile and has many kiosks and belvederes so that the people can draw water in buckets directly from the river if they want to; however, all water for the city is handled by water carriers, some by camel and some on their backs. I saw brass ewers, each of which held three maunds of water, and one would think they were made of gold. I was told that there is a woman who leases out no less than five thousand of these ewers for one dirham a month each. When returned, the ewers must be in perfect condition.

Opposite the city of Old Cairo is an island in the Nile that at one time was turned into a city. It is to the west of Old Cairo and has a Friday mosque and gardens. The island is a rock in the middle of the river, and I estimated each branch of the river to be the size of the Oxus, but the water flows gently and slowly. Between the city and the island is a bridge made of thirty-six pontoons. Part of the city is on the other side of the river and is called Giza. There is also a Friday mosque there but no bridge, so you have to cross by ferry or skiff. There are more ships and boats in Old Cairo than in Baghdad and Baṣra.

The merchants of Old Cairo are honest in their dealings, and if one of them is caught cheating a customer, he is mounted on a camel with a bell in his hand and paraded about the city, ringing the bell and crying out, 'I have committed a misdemeanour and am suffering reproach. Whosoever tells a lie is rewarded with public disgrace.' The grocers, druggists, and peddlers furnish sacks for everything they sell, whether glass, pottery, or paper; therefore, there is no need for shoppers to take their own bags with them. Lamp oil is derived from turnip seed and radish seed and is called *zayt ḥārr*. Sesame is scarce, and the oil derived from it is expensive, while olive oil is cheap. Pistachios are more expensive than almonds, and marzipan is not more than one dinar for ten maunds. Merchants and shopkeepers ride on saddled donkeys, both coming and going to and from the bazaar. Everywhere, at the heads of lanes, donkeys are kept saddled and ready, and anyone may ride them for a small fee. It is said that every day fifty thousand beasts are saddled for hire. No one other than soldiers and militiamen rides a horse, while shopkeepers, peasants, and craftsmen ride donkeys. I saw many dappled donkeys, much like horses, but more delicate. The people of the city were extremely wealthy when I was there.

In the year 439 [AD 1047] the sultan ordered general rejoicing for the birth of a son. The city and markets were so arrayed that, were they to be described, some would not believe that drapers' and moneychangers' shops could be so decorated with gold, jewels, coins, goldspun cloth, and linen that there was no room to sit down!

The people are so secure under the sultan's reign that no one fears his agents or informants, and they rely on him neither to inflict injustice nor to have designs on anyone's property. I saw such personal wealth there that were I to describe it, the people of Persia would never believe it. I could discover no end or limit to their wealth, and I never saw such ease and security anywhere.

I saw one man, a Christian and one of the most propertied men in all Egypt, who was said to possess untold ships, wealth, and property. In short, one year the Nile failed and the price of grain rose so high that the sultan's grand vizier summoned this Christian and said, 'It has not been a good year. The sultan is burdened with the care of his subjects. How much grain can you give, either for sale or as a loan?' The Christian replied, 'For the happiness of the sultan and the vizier, I have enough grain in readiness to guarantee Egypt's bread for six years.' At that time there were easily five times the population of Nīshāpūr in Cairo, so that anyone who knows how to estimate can figure out just how much grain he must have had. What a happy citizenry and a just ruler to have such conditions in their days! What wealth must there be for the ruler not to inflict injustice and for the subjects not to hide anything!

I saw a caravanserai there called Dār al-Wazīr where nothing but flax was sold, and on the lower floor there were tailors while above were specialists in clothing repair. I asked the keeper how much the fee for this caravanserai was. He told me that it was twenty thousand dinars per year but that just then one corner had been demolished for reconstruction so that only one thousand a month, or twelve thousand per annum, was being collected. They said that there were two hundred caravanserais in the city the size of this one and even larger.

A DESCRIPTION OF THE SULTAN'S BANQUET

It is customary for the sultan to give a banquet twice a year, on the two great holidays, and to hold court for both the elite and the common people, the elite in his presence and the commoners in other halls and places. Having heard a great deal about these banquets, I was very anxious to see one with my own eyes, so I told one of the sultan's clerks I had met and with whom I had struck up a friendship that I had seen the courts of the Persian sultans, such as Sultan Maḥmūd of Ghazna and his son Masʿūd, who were great potentates enjoying much prosperity and luxury, and now I wanted to see the court of the Commander of the Faithful. He therefore spoke a word to the chamberlain who was called the *ṣāḥib al-sitr*.

The last of Ramaḍān 440 [8 March 1049] the hall was decorated for the next day, which was the festival, when the sultan was to come after prayer and preside over the feast. Taken by my friend, as I entered the door to the hall, I saw constructions, galleries, and porticos that would take too long to describe adequately. There were twelve square structures, built one next to the other, each more dazzling than the last. Each measured one hundred cubits square, and one was a thing sixty cubits square with a dais placed the entire length of the building at a height of four ells, on three sides all of gold, with hunting and sporting scenes depicted thereon and also an inscription in marvellous calligraphy. All the carpets and pillows were of Byzantine brocade and *būqalamūn* [fabric], each woven exactly to the measurements of its place. There was an indescribable latticework balustrade of gold along the sides. Behind the dais and next to the wall were silver steps. The dais itself was such that if this book were nothing from beginning to end but a description of it, words would still not suffice.

They said that fifty thousand maunds of sugar were appropriated for this day for the sultan's feast. For decoration on the banquet table I saw a confection like an orange tree, every branch and leaf executed in sugar, and thousands of images and statuettes in sugar. The sultan's kitchen is outside the palace, and there are always fifty slaves attached to it. There is a subterranean passageway between the building and the kitchen. Every day fourteen camel-loads of snow have to be provisioned for use in the royal sherbet-kitchen. Most of the *amīr*s and the sultan's entourage received emoluments there, and, if the people of the city make requests on behalf of the suffering, they are given something. Whatever medication is needed in the city is given out from the harem, and there is also no problem in the distribution of other ointments, such as balsam.

THE CONDUCT OF THE SULTAN

The security and welfare of the people of Egypt have reached a point that drapers, moneychangers, and jewellers do not even lock their shops – they just lower a net across the front, and no one tampers with anything.

There was once a Jewish jeweller who was close to the sultan and who was very rich, having been entrusted with buying all the sultan's jewels. One day soldiers attacked this Jew and killed him. After this act was committed, and fearing the sultan's wrath, twenty thousand mounted horsemen appeared in the public square. When the army appeared thus in the field, the populace was in great fear. Until the middle of the day the horsemen remained in the square, when finally a servant of the sultan came out of the palace, stood by the gate, and addressed them as follows: 'The sultan asks whether you are in obedience or not.' They all cried out at once, saying, 'We are his slaves and obedient, but we have committed a crime.' 'The sultan commands you to disperse immediately,' said the servant, and they departed. The murdered Jew was named Abū Saʿīd, and he had a son and a brother. They say that God only knows how much money he had. They also say that he had on the roof of his house three hundred silver pots with fruit trees planted in them so as to form a garden. The brother then wrote a note to the sultan to the effect that he was prepared to offer the treasury two hundred thousand dinars immediately for protection. The sultan sent the note outside to be torn up in public and said, 'You rest secure and return to your home. No one will harm you, and we have no need of anyone's money.' And they were compensated for their loss.

(Translated by Wheeler M. Thackston, Jr.)

7

Pīr Sabzālī

Pīr Sabzālī (Sabz ʿAlī) Ramzānalī (d. 1938) grew up in Mumbai. His widowed mother, worried about her teenage son's waywardness, sent him to Gwādar, on the coast of Balochistan, to apprentice with the learned Vāras Muḥammad Remu. Under the latter's tutelage, his character began to change and he soon became known as one of the most dynamic volunteers and gifted orators in the Ismaili community. In 1923, the Imam Sulṭān Muḥammad Shāh Aga Khan III sent Pīr Sabzālī on a difficult mission to Central Asia to contact the isolated Ismaili communities in that mountainous region. Sabzālī kept a diary in Gujarātī of this harrowing journey, first serialized in *The Ismaili* from 1924 to 1926. Below are Episodes 10 and 23 from his fascinating travelogue in which he describes his travels through Chitrāl, now in Pakistan. In Episode 10, written in a literary style, Pīr Sabzālī relates his thoughts about the mission ahead and his complete trust in and reliance on the imam. In Episode 23, Sabzālī encounters large numbers of Mawlāīs, Central Asian Ismailis, in the mountains of Badakhshān. He marvels at their dedication in the harshest of circumstances, revels in their all-night spiritual assembly and fervent recitation of the poetry of Nāṣir-i Khusraw, comments on their eagerness to hear the *farmāns*, i.e. the commands, blessings and instructions of their imam, and expresses his admiration at the devotion of even their youngest children.

Madhya Eshiyā nī rasik vigato
Journey to Central Asia[1]

EPISODE 10

It was midnight and silence enveloped everything. All the members of my convoy slumbered soundly. Only the quiet roar of the waterfall crashing down disturbed the eerie silence. I tried to appease sleep's enchantress with my tossing and turning, but she was displeased and my efforts to placate her were in vain. Thoughts flooded my mind; thoughts that would return so many times during the journey over the snow-capped mountains. Tomorrow's expedition was to be through those very

1. Pīr Sabzālī Ramzānalī, '*Ālījāh Mishanarī Sabajā-alī-bhāī nī musāfarī: Madhya Eshiyā nī rasik Vigato*,' *The Ismaili*, Mumbai (27 April 1924), p. 4 and (19 October 1924), p. 2; tr. Nizarali J. Virani and Shafique N. Virani in *Journey to the Roof of the World: The Travels of Pir Sabzali in Central Asia* (forthcoming). The introduction to this chapter is by the translators.

mountains. That evening, I had heard the strangest tales about these mountains, and such images flashed before my eyes.

The ensuing journey would be neither on horseback, nor by mule, but on foot. The owners of the mules had already taken our leave in the evening and departed, as the animals were no longer of use to transport the baggage. We had asked our local brethren to arrange for coolies, who would carry our gear from here on – so that was one matter taken care of. But now another worry had reared its head. That very evening, a few Pathāns had arrived and informed us that a massive amount of snow had accumulated on Mount Lohārī [Lawārī], blanketing the road. They advised that the onward trek would not be possible until it melted. We were shocked to learn that two or three travellers had already been buried in the snow. A predicament now confronted us – should we delay our journey or continue onward? It was a difficult decision, but finally I resolved to carry on and leave everything to Mawlā. All night long, such thoughts swam through my mind.

The coolies were ready bright and early in the morning. We weighed the baggage and entrusted it to them. Labour charges were by weight in that region. For carrying one 'butty,' which is around ten of our pounds, from where we were to the camp of Daroz [Drosh], it would cost about seven to eight *kābulī*s, or roughly five of our rupees. It turned out that we could still take a horse or mule to the next way-station, so we let the coolies set out first, and we readied ourselves to follow them. Our local brethren entreated us to delay the trip until we received favourable news, but I was set on our plan. An experienced elder suggested, 'carry dried onions and apricots in your pockets, because when you arrive at the peak of Mount Lohārī, there will be an awful stench from the snow. It overpowers some people and they pass out. At that time, the onions and apricots will come in handy [for overcoming the smell], not to mention how useful they will be to eat while travelling.'

After breakfast, we were on our way. Though we had taken a horse with us, we often had to lead it on foot because of the heavy snowfall. The entire road was covered in snow and walking was tortuous. The snow-capped mountains towered even higher with the accumulation of snow, just as they seemed smaller when the snow melted. So mountains that had appeared small from a distance now loomed much larger as we approached them. The encounter was quite unnerving, as we had never experienced anything quite like it before.

It was impossible to see far, as the dazzling silvery-white mountains were blinding. These terrifying scenes erased from our hearts the whole muddle of thoughts that had occupied them. All we could think about now was what lay ahead. At such a place, a person, no matter how unflinching, could not help but think of death's minions hovering over his head. The mountains appeared more and more fearsome as we progressed, but even in this frightful place, we could make out the roofs of houses, now engulfed in snow. Such was the power of nature! Some of the houses lay completely buried. I just couldn't imagine how people managed to subsist in such treacherous environs, so I asked the attending orderly about it. He explained that nobody lived there in the snowy season, but that once the snow melted, the houses would once again become visible and the residents would even come back to inhabit them. This explanation amazed me, but on our return journey, we did, in fact, see hundreds of houses with people in them, as the snow had melted by then.

After some time, we arrived at Gurjar [Gujur], an encampment in the midst of the colossal snow-covered mountains. The darkness of evening now enveloped the area. Even the local mountain people dared not be out at this time, but fate had dictated that we now break in the midst of the terrifying mountains, so we entered the camp. The guard was a Panjābī who respectfully cleared the bungalow and also prepared the guest house for the staff. The coolies had not yet arrived with the baggage. As time passed, the blizzard became more fierce. We were famished, so the guard brought us refreshments. After about two hours, the baggage train, for which we had been waiting, arrived. We were to pass the night in this snow-covered place.

The coolies asked permission to spend the night in the neighbouring mountains. Touched by the courtesy and politeness of their request, I was inclined to accede. However, the learned guard, who was wise to the ways of the coolies, told me not to consent as they would not show up on time the following morning, and it would be impossible to recruit other labourers there. Moreover, if word of our presence spread, new problems could arise. The advice was sound, so we just permitted four or five of them to go out to obtain foodstuff and return immediately. Two of the labourers were exhausted and they made arrangements for replacements, so we allowed them to go as well. Now, everything was in order for our sojourn at this place. It was impossible to sleep though. The day's frightening scenes flashed before my eyes. An icy wind began to howl furiously and with it, the blizzard intensified. We lay in our beds remembering Mawlā.

EPISODE 23

We left Kogaj [Koghuzi] at about 7:30 in the morning, arriving in Morai [Muroi] at around 10:00 am. After some tea and refreshments, we set out on our journey once again. At about 12:30 pm, we arrived in Barenish [Barenis]. It was here that Chitrāl's current ruler, the honourable Mihtar-saheb, had grown up. At this point, I should tell you about a local practice. In these parts, any child born of aristocratic lineage is entrusted, in its early days, to be brought up by a family in a suitable town. In accordance with custom, the present leader, the honourable Mihtar-saheb, was raised here. The man who accompanied us at the Mihtar-saheb's bidding was a resident of this area and it was in his very home that the Mihtar-saheb had grown up. He made all the arrangements for us to be accommodated at his house, and insisted that we rest there.

After a short respite, we continued onwards until we reached a place where we were forced to stop in our tracks. From atop the mountain, large rocks were constantly raining down. As there was a gushing stream next to the road, we had no choice but to continue on our current course. Dismounting from our horses, we waited. Whenever there was a gap of a few seconds between falling rocks, one by one we dashed across to safety. Despite our precautions, one of our companions was severely injured on the face by a rock. Our colleague, Ramzān Alībhāi, immediately set about tending the wound. This mountain of tumbling rocks is known as Dārā Galāsh [Draghalosh].

At around 7:00 in the evening, we arrived at a place called Reshun. Mawlāīs had gathered here in large numbers. After a full day of travel, we were completely exhausted, but our fatigue dissipated as soon as we saw the joyous faces of the Mawlāīs. Elaborate arrangements for our accommodation had been made at the residence of Bahādur Fidāī Jamādār Shermuhammad. At each station, the affection and hospitality displayed by the Mawlāīs was ever more praiseworthy. Their hearts were overflowing with the purest love. We spent the entire night in a *majlis*, a spiritual assembly. Enraptured, those devotees sweetly sang odes to the illustrious missionary, Nāṣir-i Khusraw, and recited his poetry. They were ever-ready to sacrifice their lives and possessions for Mawlana Hazar Imam's *farmān*. In those regions, they are severely persecuted for their devotion to Mawlana Hazar Imam, and for honouring the missionary, Nāṣir-i Khusraw. If they praise him openly, they have to endure all manner of oppression. However, they care not a whit for this and live their lives openly as true devotees. Words fail me in praising how the night was imbued with splendour by the *majlis*.

At the break of dawn, hundreds of women and children had gathered and were sitting with great anticipation so that they could hear the *farmān* of Mawlana Hazar Imam. As soon as the reading commenced, all listened attentively with immense respect and decorum. Hearing the *farmān*, their eyes brimmed over with tears of joy. How fortunate they were today! Among them were those who were saying, 'Our ancestors yearned longingly their entire lives to hear these very words of blessing, but never had that chance. Today, our Mawlā has sent those blessings right to our threshold. Can there be any day more joyous than this?'

We would marvel to realize that the minds of even their tender-aged children are imbued with such lofty principles. Here, a single example will suffice. At the time of Mawlana Hazar Imam's blessed visit to Mumbai in 1923, I had gone to Apollo Port, accompanied by a nine-year-old Badakhshānī boy. Never before had he received the *dīdār*, the beatific vision of Mawlana Hazar Imam. Noticing how euphoric he was, I asked, 'What was it that you saw today that has made you so happy?' His reply was beautiful. He said 'Today, I have witnessed the *dīdār*, the beatific vision, of that king for whose name I would give up my life.' On uttering these words, his eyes filled with tears of joy. Such love for the imam of the time from a nine-year-old child. What devotion!

Almost all the residents of Reshun are Mawlāīs. In the evening, exiting the compound, a mighty river flowed before us. Off in the distance were snow-clad peaks. A company of men and women could be seen on the mountain. After a spell, five Mawlāī horsemen came from that direction. They entreated us to go to the opposite mountain. No matter how tired we were, we couldn't refuse their heartfelt request.

It was a gruelling way ahead. As our Badakhshānī companions were familiar with the road, even they began commenting that the path was difficult, and suggested that perhaps the Jamat should be asked to meet us midway at a place called Kosht. However, we didn't feel right about this, because it would cause immense discomfort for them to go there, a journey of two days, with young children. So instead, all of us set forth to meet them. We had traversed some pretty rough terrain in the past, so even hearing about this road, we couldn't really imagine that it would be any more difficult. However, the more we progressed, the more rocky and broken the road became. Though we had horses with us, they were useless for riding on these paths. In addition, a lot of snow had fallen and it was bitterly cold.

Finally, we completed the route and reached the rest stop. After a brief respite, food was prepared. Some green vetches that grew in the area were cooked as a curry. We were thrilled to see vegetable curry after many days. However, as soon as we had eaten a bit of it, we started to vomit violently. We realized that some poisonous leaves had been cooked in the curry. With God's grace there were no further ill effects. We spent the night here with the Mawlāīs and departed for Gupis at 10:00 the next morning.

(Translated by Nizarali J. Virani and Shafique N. Virani)

PART TWO

FAITH AND THOUGHT

Introduction

HERMANN LANDOLT

In keeping with the Qur'anic promise, 'We shall show them Our signs in the horizons and in themselves, till it is clear to them that it is the truth' (41:53), Ismaili thought as a whole may perhaps be characterized as a major endeavour to read the 'signs of God' in nature and history rather than to make the divine essence itself the subject of theological discourse. The classical Ismaili thinkers represented in Section I of this part, such as Abū Yaʿqūb al-Sijistānī, Ḥamīd al-Dīn al-Kirmānī, or Nāṣir-i Khusraw, distinguished themselves from both the 'attributist' and the 'anti-attributist' schools of mainstream Muslim theology by refusing to project any notions that could be seen as explicitly or implicitly anthropomorphic, including those hidden in the simple profession of monotheism or *tawḥīd*, on the absolutely transcendent Originator of all. By the same token, they also set themselves apart from the mainstream philosophical tradition, arguing that 'existence' itself belongs to the domain of the originated and thus cannot be applied to the Originator, whose pure identity is beyond intellectual reach. 'Absolute existence,' therefore, refers not to the Originator, but to the absolutely primordial act of origination (*ibdāʿ*) – a crucial point made particularly explicit by Nāṣir-i Khusraw, and which was similarly taken up later by Sufi and Shiʿi critics of the popular version of the mystical doctrine of the 'unity of existence.' The 'necessary being,' then, is the 'First-Originated,' that is, the Cosmic or Universal Intellect, which, paired with its immediate 'Follower,' the Universal Soul, sets the stage for everything else in creation. Adopting earlier Neoplatonic models of thought with variations, Fatimid as well as related thinkers, such as the anonymous author(s) of the *Epistles of the Brethren of Purity*, rediscovered harmony in spiritual hierarchies that mark and govern both the visible and the invisible worlds, and beauty in nature and art.

From the point of view of the philosophy and sociology of religion (Section II), the most important contribution of the *dāʿīs* was doubtless their embedding of the 'world of religion' (*ʿālam al-dīn*) into such universal patterns. As can be seen from the place occupied by prophecy in the very structure of al-Sijistānī's *Kashf al-maḥjūb*, a universal process of prophetic revelation (which tends towards total unveiling [*kashf*] with the coming of the *mahdī* or *qāʾim*), esoterically patterns the history of mankind as a whole. For Nāṣir-i Khusraw, human reason, being a 'trace' of the Universal Intellect, is far from contradicting Revelation. In his *Jāmiʿ al-ḥikmatayn*, a book which suggests that the 'two wisdoms' are ultimately one and the same, he strongly argues – as the celebrated Sunni philosopher Ibn Rushd

(Averroës) would do later – that scientific enquiry into nature is itself a religious duty. In the words of Nāṣir's teacher, the grand *dāʿī* al-Muʾayyad fiʾl-Dīn al-Shīrāzī, 'The conviction of the people of truth is that all the sciences, including the rational ones which the philosophers claim [as their own], are collectively present in the sciences of the prophets – may [God's] peace be upon them – and have diverged and branched out from there.' As a result, a general hierarchy of Being and Knowledge is being suggested, which of course entails the affirmation of the continued existence of the imamate in one form or another, and its function as a guiding principle. This is the main theme of Section II, which also includes samples taken from famous Nizārī texts.

With Section III, we turn from the universal to the individual, and more specifically to the individual believer's way of acquiring spiritual growth and higher levels of knowledge through initiation. The section begins with two lively descriptions of a beginner's approach to Ismailism, taken from quite different milieus: the classical initiatory tale known as the *Book of the Master and the Disciple*, and Naṣīr al-Dīn al-Ṭūsī's personal account of his own initiation. The need for higher knowledge through interpretation of scripture is, then, demonstrated in a series of rational arguments propounded by al-Kirmānī, while al-Sijistānī points to the very source of prophetic inspiration in a more mystical way. Finally, a number of concrete examples of Ismaili *taʾwīl*, suggesting a common spiritual origin of religious symbols in various scriptural traditions, conclude this section.

Section IV begins with a discussion of the notions of 'faith' (*īmān*) and *islām* as conducted by the widely recognized 'founder' of Fatimid Law, al-Qāḍī al-Nuʿmān, who is known for his faithful recording of the imam's instructions. Next, the less well-known but important 'rules of conduct' for a *dāʿī* by Aḥmad al-Naysābūrī, paves the way for ethics proper, in which field a significant part is naturally given to the great philosopher Naṣīr al-Dīn al-Ṭūsī. The chapter on 'The refinement of character' from the standard philosophical account of Nizārī Ismailism, the *Paradise of Submission*, which bears the mark of al-Ṭūsī's influence though not necessarily of his pen, shows how ethics is governed by the recognition of, and love for, the 'truthful master of the time,' the imam. The following sample, al-Ṭūsī's short but masterful treatise on the deeper sense of the profoundly Shiʿi notions of 'solidarity' and 'dissociation' (known in Persian as *tawallā* and *tabarrā* respectively) ends up on a distinctly mystical note. As is known, certain mystical trends also characterize later Nizārī developments, which are represented here by an as yet little-known epistle on spiritual edification by the 10th/16th-century *dāʿī* and poet Khayrkhwāh-i Harātī.

I

GOD AND CREATION

1
Ḥamīd al-Dīn al-Kirmānī

The leading Ismaili intellectual of the late 4th/10th century, Ḥamīd al-Dīn al-Kirmānī (d. after 411/1020) lived in the reign of the Fatimid Imam-Caliph al-Ḥākim bi-Amr Allāh. He became a prominent *dāʿī* in Iraq and Persia and was granted the title *ḥujjat al-ʿIrāqayn* (Proof of the Two Iraqs, i.e. including the parts of Persia known as al-ʿIrāq al-ʿAjamī). A prolific author, al-Kirmānī wrote widely on many of the doctrinal and social debates of his day. In this short work, reproduced here in full, he explains the nature of God's oneness (*tawḥīd*) and offers a discussion of the connotations of this fundamental concept of Islam.

al-Risāla al-durriyya
The Brilliant Epistle[1]

ON THE MEANING OF *TAWḤĪD* (UNIFICATION), *MUWAḤḤID* (THE UNIFIER) AND *MUWAḤḤAD* (THE UNIFIED)

In the name of Allah, the Beneficent, the Merciful.

Praise be to Allah, Who is too mighty to have an equal and too sublime to be described by speech in any way. The intellects are perplexed about Him, therefore they barely begin to search for a path to attain something to name Him therewith, but the incapability of reaching Him surrounds them. And the insights (*albāb*) are baffled (about Him), therefore they barely think of something, intending to make it an attribute of Him, but the ignorance of how to judge Him with it seizes them.

I praise Him with the praise of the one who affirms only that which is comprehended of itself by His essence. And there is none among His originated things that is a deity, and there is none among His originated creatures but a supplicant to Him through glorification. And I truly bear witness according to my creation, and thereby I hope to attain salvation and success when there will be no longer time to escape, that divinity is not among the things that can be comprehended by an intellect or a soul, nor is it among those that can be judged by an imagination or a sense, except that while affirming Him they are compelled to say that He is

1. Ḥamīd al-Dīn al-Kirmānī, *al-Risāla al-durriyya fī maʿnā al-tawḥīd wa'l-muwaḥḥid wa'l-muwaḥḥad*, ed. M. Kāmil Ḥusayn (Cairo, 1952) tr. Faquir M. Hunzai. An earlier version appeared as '*al-Risālat al-durriyah*' in *APP*, pp. 192–200.

Allah, other than Whom there is no deity. Nor is there anyone worthy of worship (*maʿbūd*) other than Him.

And I bear witness that Muḥammad, the one crowned with the lights of *ta'yīd* (divine help) and holiness and honoured with the leadership of (all of) mankind, the former and the latter, His servant and messenger, invited to the principles of faith (*aḥkām al-īmān*) and to the attainment of mercy in the neighbourhood of God, through a law (*sharīʿa*) that he spread and introduced, and practices (*sunan*) that he established and laid down, and obedience that he urged as beneficial and disobedience that he abstained from and prohibited, and pillars of truth that he raised high, and motives of falsehood that he eradicated as something repelled, and a trust that he conveyed yet prevented its assumption. May God bless him with ever-increasing and pure (*zākiya*) blessing so long as a night becomes dark and a morning shines. And may the peace (of God) continue eternally and multiply sempiternally upon the one who is (divinely) helped (*mu'ayyad*) with the comprehensive lights and is rich with the blessed and reverent imams from his progeny, his legatee, inheritor of his knowledge, his successor and protector of his authority, ʿAlī b. Abī Ṭālib, the guardian of the religion and its crown and the custodian of the straight path and its course. And may the best of blessings and salutations of God be upon the pure imams, the forefathers of Imam al-Ḥākim bi-Amr Allāh, the Commander of the Faithful, and upon him and those who are waiting to come till the Day of Resurrection.

Now then, when the trial pervaded the people of the guiding mission (*al-daʿwa al-hādiya*), may God spread its lights, due to the withholding by the sky of the rain, and perplexity seized them due to the stopping by the earth of the nurturing of the seeds, and distress surrounded them due to the domination of the famine, and the causes of insanity alternated among them, and the teeth of test bit them, and the vicissitudes of time snubbed them, the wisest of them was flabbergasted and the most clement of them was dismayed. Their hope and expectation diminished. They gave up all hopes and thought that they were doomed to perdition. Then by the favour of the friend (*bi-naẓar walī*) of God [i.e., the imam] and the son of His Prophet... His succour came to them as a mercy. He illuminated for them what was dark and elucidated what was obscure. And that was his chosen, ... the one who was the most truthful in speaking, the most trustworthy in executing the duty, the most steadfast in the religion, the most firm in obedience and the most long-standing in migrating among them, namely Khattigīn al-Ḍayf,[1] may God guard him in the best obedience. He appointed him as the gate (*bāb*) of his mercy and the chief *dāʿī* (*dāʿī al-duʿāt*) with the title of *al-ṣādiq al-ma'mūn* (the truthful and trustworthy), so that he may reunite them and preserve the order.

On this renewal of the gift for them, they rejoiced. For (his) favour for them became greater by his gift (*minḥa*). And (for this) they thanked God, may He be exalted, and His friend on the earth, may peace be upon him. They used to attend

1 Chief *dāʿī* under the Imam-Caliph al-Ḥākim (d. 411/1021).

his circle (*majlis*) and converse with one another. Some of the people of *daʿwa* (mission), may God protect its lights, put some questions to make them a means of testing and a way of spreading discord. I thought it appropriate to answer each of the questions according to what has been extended from the blessings of the friends of God on the earth … and devote a separate epistle to what I am going to write, so that thereby the pillars of intimacy, by confidential conversation between me and my brethren, may become strong and the soul may be prepared with training to encounter the antagonists and the hypocrites. Thus I decided and wrote this epistle answering the first of the questions and named it *al-Risāla al-durriyya* (The Brilliant Epistle). For it is a light in its meanings and a pearl in its contents. The rest of them will follow it. I ask God for help to complete them, by His strength and power.

The actual question: A questioner asked and said, 'What is *tawḥīd*?' It is known in our saying that it means 'making *muwaḥḥad* (unified, one) (*fiʿl al-muwaḥḥad*)' and the *muwaḥḥad* is the object of the *muwaḥḥids*. But it is not permissible for us to say that God is the object of the *muwaḥḥids*. Further, he said that *tawḥīd* is not possible without the imagination of a multiplicity; it is applicable only to what is made *wāḥid* (one) of the entire multiplicity. But in the divinity there is no multiplicity to make *wāḥid* out of it. Explain this for us.

First we say that the *Mubdiʿ* (Originator) … having no similitude, does not depend on the unification of the unifiers (*tawḥīd al-muwaḥḥidīn*), nor on the purification of the purifiers (*tajrīd al-mujarridīn*), so that He would leave His having no similitude if the unifiers do not unify Him, or that He would leave His transcendence (*min ʿuluwwihi*) from the characteristics of His originated things if the purifiers do not purify Him. But He … has no similitude whether the unifiers unify Him or not, whether the purifiers purify Him or not.

And it is the element (*ʿunṣur*) and nature of speech that, when someone intends to inform about the traces and essences that transcend the comprehension of the senses, its meanings become too narrow and too subtle (to convey them), let alone that which (even) the propositions of the intelligence and the soul cannot comprehend. Thus, speech is unable to denote that which is not like it. Thus, there is nothing in that which is composed of letters, such as a word or speech, which can denote the reality sought in *tawḥīd*. For what is intended to be comprehended about the *Mubdiʿ* … through a description, is far beyond the noblest meanings that the composed letters can convey.

Since this is the case and it is inevitable to speak and affirm what the rudiments of the intellect necessitate, namely, an agent from whom the existing actions came forth, nor is it possible to dispense with the expression of the subtleties of the imaginary thoughts that flash in the mind, and (since) the simple letters to which recourse is taken in expression and whence the speech and demonstration come forth, due to their limitation in bearing the subtle meanings, are unable to convey what is not from their element and incapable of informing about what is not from their substance, the speaker is compelled to speak with the most noble, most sublime and most subtle meanings that the letters can convey from their cognation (*sunkh*) and origin. When there is compulsion (to speak), then there is no more noble and more subtle meaning in the speech than *wāḥidiyya* (being one) and no more exalted than the meaning of our saying '*fard*' (single), owing to the fact that, to that which has no similitude, *fard* may be applied more appropriately, from among that which is composed of letters, to Him than *Mubdiʿ* even if it does not befit Him. Since the name referring to His being *Mubdiʿ* is due to Him (only) by virtue of His *ibdāʿ* (origination) and He was there while there was no *ibdāʿ*, and He is not He without being *fard*. But He is *fard* forever. And He, as such, is *fard* due to the impossibility of the existence of His similitude.

Again, when the field of thinking is extended in attaining the most appropriate of the meanings which the composite letters convey to be said about the *Mubdiʿ* in bewilderment and compulsion, it is the *fard* which can be applied to Him – even though the meaning (of *fard*) is applicable to some of His originated things (*mukhtaraʿāt*), the field of thinking remaining confined to what the intellect comprehends through its light and to that which its propositions may comprehend of what is beyond it [i.e., the field of the intellect], namely, the meaning conveyed by our saying '*fard*.' For the meaning of *fardiyya* (being single) in *wāḥidiyya* (being one) exceeds the meaning of *wāḥid* (one), *aḥad* (unique) and *waḥīd* (alone) in *wāḥidiyya* by virtue of its being *ṣamad* [one to whom people resort in their needs, that which has no emptiness, i.e., is self-sufficient]. And the meaning of *fard* in *wāḥidiyya* is not, upon careful examination, to be distinguished from the meaning of *wāḥid* by virtue of its having an additional meaning in *wāḥidiyya*, except by virtue of its being the cause of *wāḥid*. And that which is the cause always precedes the effect, about which we have spoken in our book known as *Rāḥat al-ʿaql* (*Repose of the Intellect*), with which the darkness of ignorance disappears and through which the light of justice speaks. We have written it as a preface and have extended the field of definition so that it may be helpful for what we want to speak about.

Tawḥīd does not mean – as we have said about the meaning of *fard*, the careful examination of the meaning in communicating about God – that He is *fard*, so that the one who carefully examines (the meaning) may be a *muwaḥḥid*. Nor is it the case that God is restricted to one particular meaning so that by virtue of that meaning, it may be established that He is *fard*. For the glory of His grandeur is in a veil making it impossible for the letters to render it by any means. And how can it be possible for the letters to render it while they barely erect in their composition a lighthouse to guide, whereas the water of His power overflows and they barely announce any information to speak with a meaning, small or great, but the incapability (of that) establishes itself and spreads? God, the Existentiator, the Worthy of worship, thus, transcends the rational propositions and the physical qualifications.

Tawḥīd, indeed, is an infinitive on the (grammatical) measure of *tafʿīl*. The philologists do not use this kind of quadrilateral verb-forms except for the one whose action is abundant. For instance, if someone massacres, it is said: '*qattala fulānun yuqattilu taqtīlan fa-huwa muqattil*.' The one who kills only once is called *qātil*, but the one who massacres many times, *qattāl*. *Tawḥīd*, with respect to its meaning, has two aspects: One is related to the *ibdāʿ* of the *Mubdiʿ*... and the other to the act of the *mu'min* (believer) who is a *muwaḥḥid* (unifier). With respect to the aspect related to the *ibdāʿ* of the *Mubdiʿ*, *tawḥīd* necessitates a *muwaḥḥid* who is the agent of *wāḥid* (*al-fāʿil li'l-wāḥid*) and a *muwaḥḥad* (unified), which is the object (of the *muwaḥḥid*) in the sense of *wāḥid* (one). And *wāḥid* is used in many ways, such as:

(i) A *wāḥid* is *wāḥid* by virtue of the finiteness of its essence (*dhāt*) toward the sides by which it separates itself from others, such as the bodies of sensible things. In this respect, it deserves to be called *wāḥid*. And its limitation toward the sides and the comprehension of its limits, all this shows that this *wāḥid* is contingent.
(ii) A *wāḥid* is *wāḥid* in the sense that it is given a specific meaning that is not found in others, such as the property of the magnet in attracting iron. In this respect, it deserves to be called *wāḥid*. And its specification with this meaning, with the exclusion of the others, necessitates it to be contingent.
(iii) A *wāḥid* is *wāḥid* in the sense of essence (*ʿayn*), such as the essence of whiteness, the essence of blackness, the essence of a substance and the essence of a thing. In this respect, all of them deserve to be called *wāḥid*. And the fact that this *wāḥid*, in its existence, depends on the existence of someone other than who precedes it, and that its existence does not detach itself from its essence, being always with it, as long as it has an essence within existence, necessitates its being contingent.
(iv) And the *wāḥid* is *wāḥid* in an absolute sense. The absolute *wāḥid* betrays its essential 'pairedness (*izdiwāj*),' which consists of the *waḥdah* (oneness, unity) and its receptacle.

All these aspects (of *wāḥid*) necessitate that *wāḥid* be absolutely contingent. When it is established that *wāḥid* is absolutely necessarily contingent, then it necessitates that *tawḥīd*, which means 'making one (*fiʿl al-wāḥid*),' which latter pronounces the contingency of its (own) essence, does not befit the glory of the *Mubdiʿ* ... Thus the *Mubdiʿ*, may He be sanctified, is *muwaḥḥid* in the sense that He is the *Mubdiʿ* of *wāḥid* and *aḥad*.

As to (the aspect of) *tawḥīd* related to the *mu'min* who is a *muwaḥḥid*, it does not mean that he 'makes one (*yafʿalu al-wāḥid*);' rather, it changes from its previous meaning that is 'making one (*fiʿl al-wāḥid*)' to another one. As when the particle '*ʿan*' is used with the verb '*raghiba*,' its meaning changes (from the previous one). For instance, when it is said, '*raghiba fulānun ʿan al-shay'*,' it means 'so-and-so disliked the thing,' but the '*raghiba*' alone means contrary to it [i.e., to like]. Thus, the meaning of *tawḥīd* of the *muwaḥḥid* (in the case of the *mu'min*) is to divest the *muwaḥḥad* from a certain meaning. As in the sense of isolating (*tajrīd*) or separating (*ifrād*) a thing from another thing, it is said, '*waḥḥadtu al-shay'a 'an al-shay'* (I isolated a thing from another thing).'

When *tawḥīd* (in this case) means divesting the *muwaḥḥad* from a certain meaning, as we mentioned, and divinity is a necessity whose existence cannot be repudiated, and the fact of the agency (*fā'iliyya*) is a power that cannot be negated; and from among the things falling under existentiation, from the Originated Intellect (*al-'aql al-ibdā'ī*) to the Emanated Intellect (*al-'aql al-inbi'āthī*), there is that which possesses the highest degree of knowledge, beauty, power, light, might, grandeur, nobility and sublimity, such as the Intellect, the Precursor (*sābiq*) in existence; and there is that which is below it in rank, such as the Successor (*tālī*) in existence, and so on till what is below them from the world of nature, and what it contains till the human intellect at the end – it is not impossible for an ignorant to think that the divinity lies in some of them. Each of these things (under existentiation) because of the subsistence of the traces (of creaturehood) in it, bears witness against itself that it is not God; then from that proposition it follows that the *tawḥīd*, which means to divest the *muwaḥḥad* (unified) – which because of the subsistence of the traces in it bears witness against itself that it is not God – from divinity, and to negate it from it and to isolate it from it and sustainership (*rubūbiyya*) and what is related to it, is the act of the *mu'min* who is a *muwaḥḥid*, so that by that *tawḥīd* it may be established that the divinity belongs to someone else. As it is known from the things that fall under existence, there are things that have no intermediaries opposite to those that have intermediaries, such as blackness and whiteness that have intermediaries, such as redness, yellowness and so on. The things that have no intermediaries, they as such, have two sides, two states and two aspects. That is to say, when one of the two sides is negated by that negation, the other side is established, such as eternal and contingent. They do not have intermediaries between them; when eternity is negated from a thing, contingency becomes inseparable from it. And like substance and accident that have no intermediaries between them; when the characteristic of substance (*jawhariyya*) is negated from a thing, the characteristic of accident (*simat al-'araḍ*) becomes inseparable from it. Then it is not imaginable that there is an intermediary between the Lord (*rabb*) and the vassal (*marbūb*), or between the *Mubdi'* (Originator) and the *mubda'* (originated), as we have explained the meaning of our sayings, 'the *mubda'* is the essence of the *ibdā'*,' in the book *Rāḥat al-'aql*.[1] Then the *mu'min* is a *muwaḥḥid* (unifier) in the sense that he divests the *muwaḥḥad* (unified), who is the *mubda'*, from divinity, as he finds the trace of *ibdā'* and the subjects and predicates in itself. Thus, the Prophet ... said: '*Al-mu'min muwaḥḥid wa-Allāh muwaḥḥid* (The believer is a *muwaḥḥid* and God also is a *muwaḥḥid*).'

Again, the meaning of the multiplicity that is necessitated by our saying that '*tawḥīd* stands in two aspects' is: either with respect to the *fard* (Single), may He be exalted ... that is the *ibdā'* of multiplicity, that is multiple singles (*afrād*) and

1 Hamīd al-Dīn al-Kirmānī, *Rāḥat al-'aql*, ed. M. Kāmil Ḥusayn and M. Muṣṭafā Ḥilmī (Leiden, 1953), pp. 73–75.

units (*āḥād*), or with respect to the *mu'min*, who is divesting all these numbers and singles from the divinity, one by one.

And then, first we will tersely show the truth contained in our saying that 'the *fard* is the cause of *wāḥid*,' according to the capacity of the epistle, even though we have explained it in our books. We say that the existence of all those things that are the essence of the first effect (*al-ma'lūl al-awwal*) is from the essence of the cause, which is the effect, and the effect is the cause (*hiya huwa wa-huwa hiya*) by virtue of the effect in its existence being from the element of the cause. And it is the nature of the effect that nothing is granted to and nothing exists in it except what its cause itself has poured forth over it, for what exists in the effect exists in the cause out of which the effect came into existence. For if the existence of what exists in the effect were not in the cause, it would have been impossible to grant the effect that did not exist in its cause. For instance, fire that is the cause of heating in what adjoins it: had the heat not been existing and subsisting in the essence of the fire, it would not have been found in what adjoins it. And how can a thing grant a thing from itself while the field of its element is empty of it? Or how can it bestow a thing while the bones of its existence are worn out?

When this is the case, we thought to investigate whether the *fard*, which is the cause of numbers, can from its essence indicate the ranks of countable things or not. We found it by virtue of what is hidden in it, such as the letters, their conjunction, their disjunction, their signs, their kinds, their multiplication, their calculation, that it comprises and indicates the entire ranks which God has originated. And the ranks in arithmetic are twelve, even though in form they are nine, vis-à-vis existents. This is the form of twelve ranks hidden in the *fard*....

And corresponding to those kinds are the letters of '*lā ilāha illa'Llāh* (There is no deity but God),' which show the *ḥudūd* (ranks), over whom the light of Oneness pours forth, and upon whom are based the heavens and the earth and what they contain....

The brilliant proof of what we have said in this regard is the existence of the seven letters vis-à-vis the lords of the cycles, through whom and through what is poured forth over the souls from them, the purpose of the spiritual form that is created in their cycles becomes complete. If you calculate the numerical values (of the letters) according to the calculation of the *jummal*, they stand vis-à-vis the days of the sun in one revolution, which are three hundred sixty-five days; the result of the multiplication of the rank four into rank seven stands vis-à-vis the mansions of the moon in one revolution, which are twenty-eight mansions; the result of the values of the letters of the fourth rank according to the calculation of the *jummal* stands vis-à-vis the numbers of the lords of *ta'yīd* (divine help) from the *ḥudūd* (ranks) of every cycle, except the supreme of them which is one, stands vis-à-vis the Names of God ... which he who counts them enters paradise, and which are ninety-nine names.[1]

1. See T. Fahd, 'Ḥurūf, 'Ilm al-', *EI2*, vol. 3, p. 595.

Had we not chosen brevity and decided that prolixity does not befit the epistles, we would have similarly expounded these ranks and numbers with which the abundance of the oceans of the friends of God, may peace be upon them, in sciences and the subtlety of the deduction of their followers from them, specifically and generally, would have been conceived. But this we have left so that the one who thinks about it may have happiness in every moment, and the one who reflects on it may renew for him a good deed in every instant from what shines to him from the wonders of wisdom.

Thus, it is evident that in the *fard*, by virtue of its being the cause of the *wāḥid*, are contained the ranks of all the countable [lit., that which fall under the number] existents, and that *tawḥīd* with respect to God is the *ibdāʿ* of the *wāḥid* and units (*āḥād*), and with respect to the *muʾmin* is to divest the divinity from the units.

We say that the community, due to its deviation from the lords of guidance [i.e., the imams] and due to relinquishing the injunctions of obedience, does not reach (even) the remotest end of the ways of *tawḥīd*, except a few who follow the friends of God, the Exalted, on His earth, may peace be upon them. Therefore, the One Whom they worship with their descriptions of and belief in Him, is not searched for except (in) the one who exists and falls under origination (*ikhtirāʿ*), and His Essence is comprehended by the power of *ibdāʿ*. When the One Whom they worship is originated and over-powered, then their *tawḥīd* is short of that by which they would deserve the garden of paradise and its felicity, and falls short of that by which they can enter the garden of eternity and dwell in it.

And how can they reach the eternal blessings while the prerequisite of attaining them is to reach their source? It is unimaginable that a traveller may reach peace, pleasures, bounty and blessings in a desired abode while he is miles away from it. Nay, 'Verily, the wicked will be in hell' [Qur'an, 82:14]. And indeed the negligent are in excruciating punishment. 'Say, shall We inform you who will be the greatest losers by their works? Those whose effort goes astray in the life of the world, and yet they reckon that they do good work. Those are they who disbelieve in the signs of their Lord and in the meeting with Him. Therefore their works are vain, and on the Day of Resurrection We assign no weight to them' [18:103–105]. God has refused to pour forth His light except over one who surrenders to His friends, and enters the house of His worship through its gate; one who made his *tawḥīd* to divest His originated things from (divinity) and his worship is surrendering to His friends; Whose obedience is his purpose and Whose disobedience his object of fear. And he knows that this world is the abode of tribulation whose star never falls and it is a dwelling of humiliation whose screw never turns. Its delights have to come to an end and what is loved from it is going to perish; its children are bound to extinction and mankind among them to resurrection [lit., gathering and dispersing]. We ask God … for help to attain peace from its ruses and to take a share from its benefits. May God make us and the community of the believers among the righteous and sincere servants and unite us with our pure lords in paradise (*ḥaẓīrat al-quds*) and in the vicinity of the Lord of the worlds.

I completed this epistle with the praise of God, the High, and with the blessing and peace upon the pure Prophet Muḥammad, the revered and righteous, and with the peace upon the one who is true to his word, ʿAlī, the legatee, and the imams from their progeny, the intercessors of their followers and the genera of their species. May the peace of God be upon all of them and the best of peace and greetings upon the *qāʾim* (Resurrector) among us, al-Manṣūr Abū ʿAlī Imām al-Ḥākim bi-Amr Allāh, the Commander of the Faithful. With the praise of God and His help, the *Brilliant Epistle* is completed.

(Translated by Faquir M. Hunzai)

2

Abū Yaʿqūb al-Sijistānī

Very little is known about the Iranian *dāʿī* Abū Yaʿqūb al-Sijistānī who appears to have been active in various parts of Iran and Iraq for some four decades of the 4th/10th century (from 322/934 to at least 360/971). His writings are of great importance in the history of early Ismailism, especially to its engagement with philosophical themes. The *Book of Wellsprings* was probably written around 350/961. Each of al-Sijistānī's 'wellsprings' explicate themes ranging from proofs of the intellect and the soul to the nature of creation itself. The following extracts draw out the transcendent nature of the Originator, the metaphysical worlds of the intellect and the soul and the nature of origination itself.

Kitāb al-yanābīʿ
The Book of Wellsprings[1]

ON THE PURE IDENTITY OF THE ORIGINATOR

That pure identity that is attributable to the Originator, exalted is He above both 'Himself' and 'not-Himself,' is nothing other than the existentiality of the Preceder that derives from the existentiality of the Originating as bestowed on the Preceder. This is to say that the Originator is that which the Preceder knows through its own existentiality. Thus its becoming aware in its own existentiality of what originated it is, in fact, the identity of the Originator. Not that an identity is there that actually exists or does not exist. It is merely something that appears to the Preceder within its own existentiality. For the Originator is not 'Himself' as would be the case with the identity of existential beings, nor is He 'not-Himself' as would be the case with the nonidentity of nonexistential beings, but rather His identity is simply the manifestation of the negating of the Originator, exalted is He, of both identities and nonidentities.

If it were the case that the Originator, exalted is He, has an acknowledged identity within originated being other than this negating of both identities and nonidentities, then in what thing would originated being affirm this identity to be? Would it be in its existentiality, which is the intellect, or in its nonexistentiality,

1. Abū Yaʿqūb al-Sijistānī, *Kitāb al-yanābīʿ*, ed. and French trans. Henry Corbin in his *Trilogie Ismaélienne* (Tehran and Paris, 1961); ed. Muṣṭafā Ghālib (Beirut, 1965); English trans. Paul E. Walker as *The Wellsprings of Wisdom* (Salt Lake City, 1994), Wellsprings 2, 4, pp. 49–50, 52–54.

which is the originating? If it were to affirm an identity for the Originator within its own existentiality, its own existentiality being the intellect, the Originator would then be intellect; but the intellect is the originated. A conclusion must follow that the originated is the Originator (or vice versa) and that is an obvious absurdity. If it wanted to affirm that the identity lies in the nonexistentiality of the [divine] Command, how could an identity be established in nonexistentiality? This is a greater impossibility than the first.

Beware thus of seeking behind the Preceder any identity following the appearance of the Preceder. The Word [of God] is the cause [of the latter], and since the appearance of the Preceder has as its cause the very first cause, when the Preceder appeared, that cause united with it and came to exist henceforth as if it is the identity of the Preceder itself. This is something the Preceder possesses solely – something that it does not emanate to its effect, i.e., the Follower – although whatever [in it] is lower than this pure identity that is united with its own identity, that it does emanate to its effect. Exalted is God above all effects, whether they be identities or nonidentities. He is hallowed above these high indeed.

We deny identities for the true Originator because every identity requires a cause. We found that the most noble of those things possessing identity is the intellect, and the identity of the intellect necessitates a cause, which is the Command of God, may His glory be exalted. It is thus He who is the true Originator without a cause – exalted is He above that – and accordingly He does not require an identity. Since He does not require an identity, denial of it, given that He is not a 'he,' is also not required, as there cannot be behind nonidentities an affirmation of a thing that is 'Himself.' We have thus extolled Him above this, exalted and sanctified is He beyond that which the heretics attribute to Him.

THE EXPLANATION OF THE WORLD OF INTELLECT AND THE WORLD OF SOUL AND THEIR RESPECTIVE QUALITIES

In that we find that the physical world resembles those [individual] physical things that it contains and that the physical things in it resemble the physical world in general, it will follow necessarily that the world of intellect and of soul resembles each one of them and that they – that is, intellect and soul – resemble their own worlds. Thereupon we find also that it cannot be said of partial intellect or partial soul either that they are within the physical world in the sense of being a thing located in it or outside of it in the sense of a substance enveloping it bodily. In a similar way, we say that universal intellect and soul cannot be said to be either within or without the world, meaning thereby that they are either in an encompassed position or an enveloping locus. Rather, they are inside it in the sense of being outside and outside it with the meaning of being inside. We will clarify this for you on the basis of the most accessible bit of knowledge you have.

Knowledge of this occurs only in respect to the soul. You are aware of such knowledge as being within the things you know at the moment of perception and outside at the time of the cessation [of this perception]. Likewise, as the physical world is being informed, given shape and subject to predication, the intellect and the soul are seen by you as if they are both inside it. But, having completed their execution [of this role], they are understood as being outside of it. And you cannot imagine something possessing physical dimension beyond the [furthest] sphere, because all physical dimensions are within that sphere. Thus, were you to formulate an image of a spiritual or an intellectual dimension that is beyond the sphere, your formulated image in such a case would be pernicious, false, and fraudulent. Notwithstanding this [limitation of the physical dimension], it sometimes happens that the spiritual dimension between a pure, partial soul and the universal soul experiences corruption and yet as a result that soul is then no longer impatient with its progress [in this world] because there exists within it everlasting joy, delight, power, and felicity. This happens when it forgets the corporeal world and embarks on a path toward its own spiritual world.

Among the noble distinctions of that world is that nothing of its substantiality ceases. Ordinary things, in contrast, cease being what they are and become something else. Unlike ordinary things, spiritual things are not rooted in a place that makes possible their ceasing to be [what they are]. It is possible, because of this, for the physical world, in its entirety and in the sum of its parts, to exist within the world of intellect and soul without causing them to give up spatial location and without inducing in them change or transformation. When the True Originator originated the first [being], He originated it perfect and without defect. He did not leave anything out of it. If He had left anything at all out of intellect, intellect would be defective to the extent of the forms of those things secluded from it.

Since origination left nothing out of the first originated being, the physical world is therefore within it. Yet, because this physical world has no standing in the spiritual world, it exists without cessation or change or contact with fatigue, illness, or harm due to this world being in it. Although the connecting link between the partial soul and the universal soul during its progress [through the physical world] is but the smallest fragment of that radiant world, yet because of that fragment it forgets this world. If this world had some worth vis-à-vis that fragment, the partial soul would not forget. But when it does forget, it knows that this world has no affinity with the spiritual world on account of which it might be held in regard, being worthless against but a fragment of the other. Understand this!

Among the specific properties of the world of intellect and soul is the possibility of imagining that it is greater than any measurement whether rational or imaginary. It may also be conceived of as a single rational or imaginary point – a point representing a circle with infinite circumference or a circle with infinite circumference signifying a single point. Among that world's specific characteristics also is that it differs from the physical world with respect to potentiality and actuality. That is, the physical world perpetuates the forms of the kingdoms as potentialities, and if and when they become actualities, it causes them to corrupt so that they return again to the stage of potentiality. But the intellectual world preserves the psychic forms that have passed on to actuality and it retains them in their form and in their [degree of] substantiality. Understand this!

(Translated by Paul E. Walker)

3

Nāṣir-i Khusraw

The Persian poet and philosopher Abū Muʿīn Nāṣir b. Khusraw b. Ḥārith al-Qubādiyānī al-Marwazī has already been introduced as an observant traveller (see Part One, 6). Widely known as the 'Proof of Khurāsān' (*ḥujjat-i Khurāsān*), he was evidently commissioned by the Imam-Caliph al-Mustanṣir bi'llāh (427–487/1036–1094) to spread the Ismaili *daʿwa* in the eastern Muslim lands. In about 450/1058, he moved to the valley of Yumgān in Badakhshān, where he was able to spend the rest of his life at a safe distance from Saljūq persecution, spreading his message through numerous prose works as well as his poetry. The present work, translated as *Knowledge and Liberation*, is a set of responses to theological and philosophical queries and is divided into five parts. The part on ontology, which discusses the nature of 'existents,' the human soul and its relation to the body and the world of nature, is reproduced here in full.

Gushāyish wa rahāyish
Knowledge and Liberation[1]

ONTOLOGY

On different kinds of existents

O brother! You asked: 'What [is meant by] the term 'existent' (*hast*), how many kinds of existents are there, what is each one called, and how can it be recognized? In the *tawḥīd* [profession of One God], should God be called existent or not, for if we do not call Him existent, then He becomes non-existent (*nīst*) which is *taʿṭīl* [negation of God's existence]? Explain this so that we may know.'

Know, O brother, that the existent is of two kinds: one is called necessary (*wājib*) and the other contingent (*mumkin*).[2] The necessary existent is higher than the contingent existent [because] without the necessary existent the contingent cannot exist. For instance, the necessary existent is like a bird and the contingent existent

1. Nāṣir-i Khusraw, *Gushāyish wa rahāyish*, ed. and tr. Faquir M. Hunzai as *Knowledge and Liberation: A Treatise on Philosophical Theology* (London, 1998), Part II, 'Ontology,' pp. 41–53. This selection has been slightly revised.

2. 'Contingent' has been retained here for conventional reasons. An alternative translation of *mumkin* would be 'possible' or 'potential' – that which has the potentiality to be or not to be. As the subsequent examples make clear, Nāṣir uses it also for the 'potential' existence of the palm-tree in the date-stone, fire in water, the bird in the egg.

like its egg; it is not possible for the egg to reach the state of a bird without the help of the bird from which it has come into existence and whose position is like that of the necessary existent.

We say that the world in its entirety is the contingent existent, not the necessary existent, because all its parts are contingent existents. The contingent existent is that which is intermediate between the existent and the non-existent. For instance fire, which is one of the constituent parts of the world, is a contingent existent because its heat may be transformed into cold and its dryness into moisture, thus turning fire into water. The cooling of heat and the drying of moisture in this world testify to the correctness of this state. Therefore, fire is water in contingency, and similarly all components of the world are in [a state of] contingency. Likewise, plants and animals are contingent and not necessary, because the plants and animals which exist today may or may not exist tomorrow. All such things are called contingent existents, including the two entities of plant and animal, each of which is a part of the world.

According to this explanation, the entire world is a contingent existent which cannot come into existence without the necessary existent. Inevitably, the maker of the world has to be a necessary existent, because if we say that it is a contingent existent, then it should also have a necessary existent. Then let us stop at this point [and say] that the creator of the world is a necessary existent whereas the world itself is a contingent existent, just as a date-stone is like a contingent existent because from it the palm-tree may or may not come into existence. Since, as we mentioned, the existent is of two kinds and both of them are species, and whatsoever is a species must have a genus, it is inevitable for the genus to be superior to both species, the necessary and the contingent, in rank and not in time or anything else. That is the Command of God – may His name be mighty – which is the Absolute Existent (*hast-i muṭlaq*), the existent which has come into existence not from an existent. Under it there are the necessary existent, which is the (Universal) Intellect, and the contingent existent, that is, the (Universal) Soul which is under the Intellect. The Soul has the potential, through effort, to become one day like its source (*aṣl*), just as it is possible for a date-stone to grow one day into a palm-tree. However, it is not befitting for God to be a genus, because the status of genus is given only to that which has species under it. The genus then is like the cause and the species like its effect. It is not befitting for God to be either the cause or the effect, and it is therefore not appropriate to say that God is an existent. It should be known that the Absolute Existent [the Command of God] is originated by Him, and His ipseity transcends an existence whose opposite is non-existence.

It should be known further that whatever has one rank is superior and prior to that which consists of many ranks. The necessary existent has one rank. The contingent existent, which is intermediate between existence and non-existence, has three ranks: the spatial existent, the temporal existent, and the relative existent. The spatial existent [is exemplified in the statement] 'there are dates in Kirmān' or 'there are stars in the sky;' the temporal existent [in] 'there is light in the day,' and the relative existent in 'man has speech' or 'a cow has hooves.' All these ranks are included in the contingent existence. [Since] the contingent existent has ranks whereas the necessary existent does not, we come to know that the contingent existent is lower in rank than the necessary existent and is dependent on it for existence. The necessary existent is one, just as the genus of animal, which is like the necessary existent, is one, whereas bird and rational animal [mankind], which are species under it, are contingent existents. The existence of bird, reptile and man depends on the existence of the [genus] animal; if you remove the animal, all these species would [also] be removed. Thus, if in imagination you remove the necessary existent, the contingent existents would also be removed. Attain so that you may know! Recognize so that you may be liberated!

On the meanings of 'no-thing' and 'is not'

O brother! You asked: 'How should we understand [the word] "no-thing" (*na-chīz*) and how should we recognize "is not" (*nīst*)? Is there any difference between "no-thing" and "is not," or do they have the same meaning as "thing" (*chīz*) and "is" (*hast*)? Explain so that we may know.'

Know, O brother, that a group of people claim that 'no-thing' and 'is not' are only two names, otherwise they are one [in meaning]; similarly they say that 'thing' and 'is' both have the same meaning. If you have understood [this, know] that the word (*nām*) 'thing' is not applicable except to the meaning (*dhāt*) which is attainable (*yāftanī*), and the word 'is' is applicable only to a thing with respect to the present time in which it is found, not with respect to the past nor with respect to the future. [This is] because time is of three modes: the past which has elapsed, the future which is going to come such as tomorrow or the next year, and the present such as today or this year. The word 'is' is applicable to a thing only with respect to the present time, not with respect to the past or the future. Thus, we should not say 'yesterday is hot' or 'tomorrow is cold;' rather we should say 'today is hot' or 'this year is cold.' It would be absurd to say that 'is' and 'thing' are both one and have the same meaning, or to say that 'no-thing' and 'is not' have the same meaning. If it were possible to say so, then [in the case of 'no-thing' and 'is not'] we would have said 'so and so *no-thing* a thing,' in the sense of 'so and so *does not* have a thing,' or we would say '*is not* belongs to so and so' in the sense of '*no-thing* belongs to so and so;' [likewise], if 'is' and 'thing' were both one and the same thing, it would have been permissible for us to say 'so and so does not have an *is*' [in the sense of] 'so and so does not have a *thing*.'

As for the word 'no-thing,' it should be known that it means to nullify a thing by applying the prefix 'no' (*na*) to a thing which has an attainable meaning; otherwise if 'no-thing' necessarily had a meaning which could be applied to it or which it was possible to indicate, then it would itself have been a thing. Logically, when the word 'no' is prefixed to anything, that thing should have a meaning; but this is impossible because when you prefix the word 'no' or 'non' to one of the things or names, [you are negating] that particular thing or name to which you have applied the prefix and not any other thing apart from it. For instance, if someone says 'no-wall,' this utterance is not applicable to anything; or if he says 'no-cow' or 'no-man,' here a meaning does not become necessary. However, when the word 'no' or 'non' is prefixed to a name or a thing that comes alternately after another thing and between which there is no intermediary [state] – such as day and night, blind and seeing, odd and even – then the name of that [second] which follows [the first] becomes established. Thus, if you say 'no-night,' this amounts to saying 'day,' or if you say 'non-hearing,' this amounts to saying 'deaf,' or if you say 'non-blind,' this amounts to saying 'seeing.' But if the word 'no' or 'non' is prefixed to the word 'is,' then inevitably it is applied either to the past or to the future, and you would have said that something has been or will be. [The expression] 'has been' signifies the past and 'will be' the future; the former is a sign of the past and the latter of the future. [For instance], when you say 'it is not night,' it refers to something which has been in the past or will be in the future, but does not exist at the [present] time which is intermediate between these two times; it is a sign of a thing which has been in the past or will be [in the future].

Thus, we have established that [the meaning of] *nīst* ('is not') is not free from being either time which has passed or time which has not come, but it is not time in the present. For instance, in summer you may say, 'it is not spring, it is Tīr-māh,' in which one [the spring] is past and the other [the first month of summer] is present; but you cannot say [at the same time] 'it is not summer,' because it is the present time and 'is not' does not apply to the present. Thus, it has been explained that the meaning of 'no-thing' is not equal to that of 'is not' because the word 'no-thing' is not applicable to all the three [tenses] – that is, you cannot say that 'no-thing is not,' or 'no-thing has not been' or 'no-thing will not be,' [whereas 'is not' is applicable to both the past and the future]. Attain so that you may know! Recognize so that you may be liberated!

On the nature of the human soul

O brother! You asked about the doctrine of a group who say that the human soul is nothing but the equilibrium of elements (*iʿtidāl-i ṭabāyiʿ*), and that when the elements come together appropriately, they reach a point where movement and knowledge are generated. [The group] supports this doctrine by the argument that when the body loses its equilibrium, the soul ceases to exist. Thus, the soul is nothing but the equilibrium of elements, and when they return to their origins, the soul ceases to exist. If this is so, then you have neither reward nor punishment [for the soul in the hereafter]. You wanted a categorical answer to be given in this connection, so that you may refute this doctrine and have a firm belief in the survival of the soul, and so that observance of the Holy Prophet's law (*sharīʿat*) becomes pleasant. You will learn that the soul is not the equilibrium of elements such that when they return to their origins it ceases to survive; rather the soul is something other than the equilibrium of the elements. Peace!

Know, O brother, that had there not been 'how' and 'why,' then all people would have been wise, and had there not been someone to answer the questioner, then truth would not have been distinguishable from falsehood. Thus, by divine help, we say in response to that group who say that the soul is nothing but the equilibrium [of elements], that this equilibrium which they claim to be the soul is not free from being either substance or accident (*'araḍ*). If the soul is a substance [in] equilibrium, then it is [different from] the origins from which it comes into existence, [in which case] it would be the fifth element, not [a mixture of] the four elements. Then let them show us that fifth one which comes forth from these four elements but is not from them, the one which is harmonious whereas these four are [discordant], so that we may see it as we see these four. But they are not able to find that harmonious one which they claim to have come forth from the four elements which are different and not in equilibrium. They are unable to do so because it is absurd for someone to say that a body can produce another body like itself. Thus, it is evident that what they claim [to be the soul] is not a substance. Had it been a substance [composed of the elements], it would have been visible and accessible like they are visible and accessible [to our senses].

Then, inevitably, the equilibrium which they claim to be the soul will be called an accident. If they say that it is an accident, then they cannot say that it has action, because an accident is that which cannot subsist on its own, and action does not come into being from that which is not self-subsistent. Moreover, since the accident itself is an action [of an agent], it is not possible for that action to produce another action [on its own], just as it is not possible for a body to produce another body or to be originated by itself. And since that which is called equilibrium has no action, then those actions which we find from the soul – such as comprehension of things, discrimination of one thing from another, and so on – these do not belong to the equilibrium which they claim to be the soul. It is evident, therefore, that since equilibrium does not have action, their claim that it is the soul is false.

Another answer we give to the one who says that the soul is the equilibrium of elements is that whereas the elements are hot, cold, wet and dry, equilibrium is neither hot nor cold, neither wet nor dry. If it were possible that from hot, cold, wet and dry, something would originate which is neither hot nor cold, nor wet nor dry, then it would also be possible for fire to produce cold and for snow [to generate] heat. But this is absurd and impossible, [just as] it is equally absurd and impossible to say that something harmonious originates from different elements and which contains within itself nothing of them. If it were possible for the harmonious to originate from opposite elements then it would also be possible for something opposite to emerge from the harmonious. Then there would not be any difference between the one who says that these four opposites originate a harmonious thing [which they call the soul], and the one who says that it [the soul] consists of equilibrium and harmony, whose essence is the same without differentiation, and which originates death as well as life, blindness as well as sight, health as well as illness. This argument is absurd and no intelligent person would accept it. And if, according to their claim, one says that the soul is the equilibrium of elements, then opposite actions should not come forth from it because, as we have already explained, the opposite does not come from the harmonious. [But] the soul is that from which comes both generosity and parsimony, bravery and cowardice, piety and impiety, which makes it clear that it is not the equilibrium of the elements. Similarly, when two white bodies come together, it is not possible to originate something other than white, just as when two black bodies come together, there comes forth nothing but a black thing. [Hence], it is impossible and absurd to originate something harmonious from opposite things when they come together; and since the elements are opposite to one another, it is not possible that from their gathering there should originate something harmonious without any differentiation in it.

Thus, we have established that the soul is not the equilibrium [of elements]. It is a substance which brings opposite elements into harmony and puts them together by the power with which God has endowed it. And great is the wisdom which appears to the soul in its resurrection after [leaving] the body. As God says in the following verse after a detailed description of creation one after the other: 'And certainly We created man from a quintessence of clay, then We placed him as [a drop of] sperm in a resting place, then We made the sperm a clot, then We made the clot a lump of flesh, then We made the lump of flesh bones, then We clothed the bones with flesh, then We made him another creation. So blessed is God, the best of Creators' [23:12–14]. Then He has said: 'After that you will most surely die. Then surely on the Day of Resurrection you shall be raised' [23:15–16]. If this were not the purpose of creation, then no wisdom would have appeared in this world. But the soul, which brings together these opposite [elements] in the body, leaves them again. If it separates from them with the recognition of the Creator and in obedience and worship, then it will remain in the eternal world in delight, but if it does not acquire knowledge and departs in ignorance and disobedience, then it will remain in hell. Attain so that you may know! Recognize so that you may be liberated!

On the soul's existence and self-subsistence

O brother! You asked about the soul: 'Does it exist or not, and is it self-subsistent or does its subsistence depend on the body? Is it from among substances or from accidents? What is the proof that the soul is a substance and self-subsistent when we do not find it without a body, and without body, no action comes forth from it? Demonstrate [the proof] that we may know.'

Know, O brother, that our bodies are alive because of the soul, and the proof of the soundness of this statement is that our bodies are movable and that whatever is movable, its movement is [caused] either from outside or from inside. An entity whose movement is [caused] from outside is moved [either] by another entity, as wind moves a tree or water moves a water-wheel and a boat, or another entity pulls it towards itself, as an ox pulls a windlass and a magnet pulls iron. [However], our bodies move [voluntarily] without being pulled or repulsed by something else. Since the movement of our bodies is not [caused] from outside, it must of necessity be from inside. The movement of an entity which comes from inside is either natural [physical] or spiritual. [The entity with] natural movement is that which never rests and does not alter from one state into another. As for our bodies, as long as the soul is with them, they sometimes move and sometimes rest but they become [inactive] when the soul parts from them. Thus, it is evident that the movement of our bodies is not due to a physical [cause]; had it been physical, they would not become [motionless] by the separation of the soul from them. The movement of our bodies is caused by the soul.

From this explanation it becomes clear that it is the soul which keeps our bodies alive and that the souls of our bodies subsist by themselves. The soul is a substance and self-subsistent, the mover and keeper-alive of the body. The body is not a substance, nor self-subsistent, nor is it the mover of a substance, since that which moves a substance must itself be a substance. The soul which moves the body is a substance [because] the definition of a substance is that it admits opposite things, and yet [its essence always] remains the same; its state does not change from one to another by admitting them. Thus, the human soul admits opposite things, such as speaking and hearing, movement and rest, bravery and cowardice, and so on.

As for the statement that no action comes forth from the soul without a body, the answer is that the action of the soul by itself is to know, and in order to know it does not need a body. But when the soul wants to portray [the form of] that knowledge on a [material] body, it seeks the help of the [human] body which is linked to it, and it is able to do this because of compatibility [between the two bodies]. Ask so that you may know! Comprehend so that you may be liberated!

On the definition of substance

O brother! You asked: 'What is substance (*jawhar*), how many kinds of it are there, and what is each one called? Are we permitted to call God substance or not?'

Know, O brother, that substance is called genus of genera or *summum genus* [that is, the supreme genus], under which comes everything because all existents are under and within it. Substance has two species: one is called simple (*basīṭ*), that is dispersed, and the other compound (*murakkab*), which is mixed. [So] when you are asked what substance is, say that it is that whose essence is one, which brings together opposite things without changing its own state. When you are asked how many kinds of substance there are, say that there are two kinds, one is simple and the other compound. If you are asked which one is simple, say that it is the soul; and if you are asked which one is the compound, say it is this entire world and all things within it. If you are asked what opposite things the soul has brought together without changing its own state, say knowledge and ignorance, goodness and badness, well-being and mischief. And if you are asked what opposite things has the world brought together, say that it has brought together the six directions of which each one is opposite to another – that is, above and below, left and right, front and back – all three [pairs] being opposite to one another, like earth, water, air and fire, or like light and darkness, which are [also] opposite to each other.

This is the definition of a simple substance and a compound substance, so that you may know that, according to our explanation of the definition, it is not permissible to call and know God as a substance. When substance has this definition, then it is defined, and that which is defined is incapable of coming out of its definition. A definition necessitates a definer who has enclosed a substance within the domain [of that definition]. So that the wise may know, [we say]: that which is [confined] in a definition or a boundary does not deserve to be [called] God. He who keeps it in its defined boundary is God who is free from substance and accident, and all things are contained within the enclosure of His creation. As God says: 'He created everything and measured it as ought to be measured' [25:2]. This is the measure of substance. Study so that you may know! Recognize so that you may be liberated!

On the soul's relation with the body

O brother! You asked: 'How and where in the body is the human soul? Previously you have established that the movement of the human body is [caused by the soul] from within. Explain how [the soul] is inside [the body]? Is it like someone who is in a house, and if that is the case how is it that when its ways are closed, the soul can leave the body all at once?' Peace!

Know, O brother, that one entity can be within another entity in twelve different ways: first, it is as a part in the whole, such as a hand or a foot in the human body; the second is as the whole in the part, as is the human body in its organs, which is the totality of the organs; the third is as water in a pitcher; the fourth is as an accident in a substance, such as the whiteness of hair in old age; the fifth is as one thing mixed with another, such as vinegar and honey which is called oxymel; the sixth is as a captain in a ship; the seventh is like a king in a country; the eighth is like a genus in a species such as animal in man, that is to say, man is a species of animal and animal is included in man; the ninth is like a species in a genus, as man is in animal; the tenth is as form in matter, as is the form of a signet ring [set] in silver; the eleventh is as matter in form, as is silver in the form of a signet ring; and the twelfth is as an entity in time.

It is inevitable, therefore, that the soul in the body must be like one of these [twelve] ways which have been mentioned. We say that the soul in the body is not like a part in the whole, as is a hand in the human body, because the hand is of the body but the soul is not of the body. Also, the soul in the body is not like the whole in its parts, because the whole of the organs is the body, that is, the body is nothing but the organs, but the soul itself is not the body, rather it is a different substance. Also, the soul in the body is not like water in a pitcher or jar, [because] the jar or pitcher is a place for water, but the soul does not need a place [in which to locate itself]. Also, the soul in the body is not like a captain in a ship, in that the captain is in one place and the rest [of the ship] is devoid of him, but in the human body there is no place devoid of the soul; if a place were to be devoid of it, that place would not be alive and moveable. Also, the soul in the body is not like an accident in a substance, because the soul itself is a substance and not an accident; and when an accident leaves a substance, the substance remains in its state, but the body does not remain in its state when the soul leaves it. Also, the soul in the body is not like vinegar and honey in oxymel, because vinegar and honey have both changed from their states; wherever such a thing is mixed its state changes, as when you mix vinegar and water neither remains in its previous state, but the soul and the body remain in their state despite being mingled. Also the soul in the body is not like a species in a genus as man is in animal, in that both are alike in eating and reproduction, but the soul leaves the body and is [therefore] not its species. Also, the soul in the body is not like a genus in a species as animal is in man, since genus and species are linked together in many aspects except in their form which is different, but the soul has no connection with the body as a genus because the soul is subtle and the body is dense. Also, the soul in the body is not like an entity in time, because time is prior to an entity which is in time and comes into being in time, but the body has not been and is not prior to the soul.

We say, therefore, that the soul in the body is like a subtle form in dense matter, as is the form of a signet ring in silver, because the soul is subtle like the form and matter is dense like the body, and the soul is not the body. Ask so that you may know! Learn so that you may be liberated!

(Translated by Faquir M. Hunzai)

4

Abū Yaʿqūb al-Sijistānī

Another important work of the 10th-century Iranian *dāʿī* Abū Yaʿqūb al-Sijistānī (see Chapter 2 of this section), was *Kashf al-maḥjūb* or *Unveiling the Hidden*. This composition was written originally in Arabic, but has survived only in a Persian translation made perhaps a century after his death. Divided into seven chapters or 'Discourses,' each of which is further subdivided into seven 'Streams' (*jastār),* the book seeks to 'unveil' the hidden sources of divine knowledge. Beginning with a summary discussion on the absolute incommensurability of the unique Creator in Discourse One, the next six Discourses present an original theory of six 'creations,' or phases of a universal process, in the following order: intellect, soul, nature, the species, prophethood, resurrection. This extract, taken from the Discourse on the 'third creation,' or nature, is a lucid exposition of the spiritual quality of natural beauty.

Kashf al-maḥjūb
Unveiling the Hidden[1]

THAT THE BEAUTY OR ADORNMENT OF NATURE IS SPIRITUAL

Having noticed a certain resemblance between the natural forms and the forms produced by art with regard to figure and shape, and seen that the beauty found in the forms produced by art must be spiritual, because they are traces of the soul [of the artisan] and are acquired from something other [than their original matter], you should realize that natural beauty and its forms must be spiritual, too, rather than natural. Indeed, if the beauty of nature were itself from nature, it would have to be attributed to one among the natural elements. But the beauty of nature does not come from such an element which provides the matter of nature, and from which its potentiality may be known. Rather, it consists of spiritual 'colours' (*ranghā-yi rūḥānī*). Just as colours imbue the stuff prepared or made ready to receive the colours of the craftsmen, so the beauty of nature consists of spiritual colours which imbued the beings to be generated naturally with the traces of [the Universal] Soul, which encompasses nature. Thus it has been verified that the adornment of nature is spiritual. Understand this!

1. Abū Yaʿqūb al-Sijistānī, *Kashf al-maḥjūb*, ed. and tr. Hermann Landolt as *Creation and Resurrection: Divine Unity and the Universal Process* (forthcoming), Discourse IV, 'On the Third Creation, Which is Nature', Stream 6. An earlier version tr. Hermann Landolt appears in *APP*, pp. 102–104.

Further, if corporeal things come to exist in corporeal things, they constitute for the latter an increase and an addition, and if they are separated from them, there is a decrease and their quantity diminishes. But if a spiritual thing enters or leaves a material thing, its quantity remains as it is. Now, having thought about the adornment of nature and the adornment of art, we realize that it joins another thing and leaves it again without there being any increase or decrease in the thing joined. Take, for example, the brocade weaver: the beauty appearing in the brocade is [grounded] in the being (*nihād*) of the brocade weaver, for, if the brocade is torn apart or if its threads are pulled out one by one, the quantity of the brocade is neither diminished nor increased. The same applies to the silk used for the weaving of the brocade: [even] if the brocade weaver lets many ideas (*andīshahā*) appear in the silk, the quantity of the silk does not increase. This will make you understand that whatever beauty was joined to the brocade came from the brocade weaver; and the beauty that left the brocade when it was torn apart was spiritual, not corporeal. Or take the narcissus flower. We can see that people turn it from hand to hand, smell at it and tear up its beauty, yet the quantity of the flower does not thereby become less. So we learn from the narcissus flower that its beauty was spiritual, not natural. Understand this!

If a soul becomes an expert in the art of painting, it can imitate (*ḥikāyat kardan*) the beauty and the colours of those things, so that it can bring into appearance, if it so desires, the form of whatever it wishes: the form of the animals, or the form of the seat and the house, or the form of the human being. That it can thus imitate [the colours and forms] is due to their being spiritual and concordant (*mushākil*) with the spiritual substance. Do you not see that nobody can create a thing of nature, whether animal, vegetable or mineral? But one can bring into appearance whatever one wishes from the beauty of nature; and one can do so because that [beauty] is spiritual. Understand this!

Further, we can see that humans enhance the beauty of nature: they beautify their own face, they make animals beautiful by detaching hair and combing, they embellish trees and herbs by pruning [or trimming], they render gems beautiful by cutting them. Both kinds of beauty, of nature and of art, may thus add up in one place, producing utmost pleasure. But if the first beauty were not spiritual, the second beauty would not be in harmony (*mushākil*) with it. Thus it has been verified that the beauty of nature is spiritual. Understand this!

(Translated by Hermann Landolt)

5
Ikhwān al-Ṣafā'

The authors collectively known as the Ikhwān al-Ṣafā', the 'Pure' or 'Sincere' Brethren, are shrouded in mystery and there is considerable debate about when they lived. It is generally acknowledged that these scholars probably resided in Baṣra in the middle of the 4th/10th century and were of Ismaili affiliation. The *Rasā'il*, an encyclopedic collection of 52 epistles or essays, cover a range of the scientific and religious subjects then current and draw upon a variety of intellectual traditions to construct a synthesis of religion and philosophy. The collection is divided into four sections: on the mathematical sciences, the physical or natural sciences, the psychological and intellectual sciences, and the sciences of theology. The present extract, from Epistle 22, is written in the form of a fable and shows how the authors employed natural history to make philosophical arguments, contrasting the lives and activities of animals with the world of humans.

Rasā'il Ikhwān al-Ṣafā'
Epistles of the Brethren of Purity[1]

THE CASE OF THE ANIMALS VERSUS MAN BEFORE THE KING OF THE JINN

'Were it not for the ignoble nature of humans, their base characters, unjust lives, vicious mores, vile doings, foul acts, ugly, misguided, and depraved customs, and rank ingratitude, God would not have commanded them: '*Show gratitude to Me and toward your parents, for unto Me shall ye come in the end*' [Qur'an, 31:14]. He gave no such command to us and our offspring. For we show no such disrespect or thanklessness. Command and prohibition, promise and threat are addressed solely to you, the human race, not to us. For you are creatures of mischief. Conflict, deceit and disobedience are ingrained in you. You are more fit for slavery than we! We are more worthy of freedom. So how can you claim that you are our masters and we your slaves, if not by sheer effrontery, outrageous lies and calumnies?'

When the parrot had finished speaking, the *jinnī* sages and philosophers said, 'This speaker speaks truly in all that he states and relates.'

Again the assembled humans were chagrined and hung their heads in shame, crushed by the indictment directed at them.

1. *Rasā'il Ikhwān al-Ṣafā'*, Epistle 22, tr. Lenn E. Goodman and Richard J. McGregor in *Epistles of the Brethren of Purity* (new critical edition and translation, forthcoming).

But at this point in the parrot's discourse, the King said to the chief of the *jinnī* philosophers, 'Who are these kings that this speaker has mentioned and lauded so highly, describing their deep compassion and concern for their subjects, their kindness and affection, toward their forces and vassals, and how well they treat them? Tell me what these hints and suggestions really intend.'

'I shall, felicitous Majesty, as your obedient servant. The name king, you know, *malik*, derives from angel, *malak*. And kings' names are taken from those of angels. For there is no kind of these animals, no species or individual among them, great or small, over which God has not charged a band of angels to oversee its growth, preservation and welfare, at every stage. Every class of angels has its chief to look after it. And these chiefs are kinder, gentler and more compassionate than mothers toward their tiny sons or infant daughters.'

Said the King to the sage, 'Where do the angels get this kindness, mercy, tenderness, grace, and compassion of theirs?'

'From God's mercy and compassion on His creation, His kindness and love. All the mercy and tenderness of parents – fathers and mothers – and the angels themselves, all the grace and goodness of creatures toward one another, is but the millionth part of God's mercy and kindness toward His creation, His grace and beneficence upon His creatures.[1]

'One mark of the soundness of what I say and the truth of my account is that when He first created and gave them their start, fashioned, finished and reared them up, their Lord entrusted their care to angels, the purest of His creatures, and made them in turn compassionate, noble and pure. He formed them with all sorts of useful appurtenances and advantages, marvellous anatomical pathways, elegant forms, keen and subtle senses, inspiring them to avoid the harmful and seek the beneficial.[2] He made night and day subservient to them: sun, moon, and stars serving at His command.[3] He ordered their lives in winter and summer, on land and sea, mountain and plain. He made foodstuffs for them from trees and plants, a delight to them for the nonce.[4] '*He lavished blessings on you, seen and unseen*' [31:20], so manifold that if you tried to count them, you'd find them numberless. All this manifests and proves God's great mercy, compassion and grace on His creation.'

1. The Ikhwān use their play on the words king and angel to lay out their view of providence. Mortal kings should emulate God's governance. But even animal paragons fall short of the ideal. The real kings are the angelic forms/intellects that govern each species.

2. Stoics hold that providence inspires all creatures naturally to pursue what is good for them, see Diogenes Laertius, *Lives of the Eminent Philosophers* (London, 1925), 7.85–7.86; Galen, *De Usu Partium*, tr. Margaret T. May as *Galen on the Usefulness of Parts of the Body* (Ithaca, NY, 1968), 1.5, pp. 70–71; and the passage from Galen's lost work *Peri Ethon* (*On Dispositions*) preserved in Arabic by al-Marwazī (12th century) from the translation of Ḥunayn b. Isḥāq, in S. M. Stern, 'Some Fragments of Galen's *On Dispositions* in Arabic,' *The Classical Quarterly*, 6 (1956), pp. 91–101.

3. Cf. Qur'an 14:33 and 31:20. The Ikhwān relate the subordination of celestial beings to God's command to another Qur'anic theme dear to their hearts, God's adaptation of nature to creaturely needs. For the prostration of the stars (55:5–6), see al-Kindī, 'Essay on the Prostration of the Outermost Sphere and its Obedience to God,' ed., Abū Rīḍa, in *Rasā'il al-Kindī* (Cairo, 1950–1953), 1.245–1.246.

4. Cf. Qur'an 2:36 and 7:24.

Said the King, 'Who is the chief angel charged with the care and welfare of the children of Adam?'

'That,' said the sage, 'is the universal human rational soul, vicegerent of God on His earth.[1] She it was who was linked to Adam's body when he was formed from earth, *and the angels all bowed down to him together* [15:30]. They are the animal soul directed by the rational. The universal rational soul still remains in Adam's seed, just as the corporeal form of Adam's body survives in his seed. In the pattern laid down by this soul they grow, develop and thrive; through it they are rewarded or punished, to it they return, and with it they will be raised on Judgment Day, when by it they enter Paradise and with it – the rational soul, vicegerent of God on His earth – they rise to the realm of the spheres.'[2]

Then the King inquired, 'Why are angels and souls invisible?'

'Because they are luminous, diaphanous spiritual substances without colour or mass. They are not captured by the bodily senses like scent, taste and touch, but seen by a subtle sight like that of prophets and messengers, and heard by such as well. For these men of chaste soul have roused themselves from the slumber of apathy and the sleep of folly. Freed from the tyranny of sin, they have cleansed their souls and been reborn and sanctified. Becoming like the souls of angels, they see them and hear their discourse, take up their message and inspiration and pass it to their fellow mortals in their diverse tongues, being embodied and corporeal like them.'[3]

Said the parrot, 'As to your statement, O human, that you have artisans and masters of various crafts, that does not set you apart from the rest of us. Several kinds of birds, crawling and swarming creatures share with you in this. Bees are insects, but they make their cells and build dwellings more skilfully and adeptly than your artisans, better and more masterfully than your builders and architects. They build their homes as round, multi-storeyed hives that look like stacked shields, just by setting one chamber atop another. They form each apartment as a perfect equilateral and equi-angular hexagon, using their consummate wisdom, craft and builder's art. They need no compass to guide them, no straight edge to rule, or plumb line to drop, nor any angle to gauge their corners, as human builders do.

'Bees go out to forage and gather wax from the leaves of trees and plants on their legs, and nectar from the blossoms of plants and trees with their probosces. For this they need no basket, pouch or peck to collect it in, nor any tool or implement to ladle it, as your builders need their tools and implements, their hoe, shovel, spade, bucket and the like.

---

1. In Arabic, 'She is God's Caliph.'

2. Immortality here is spiritual, not bodily, ultimately won, as in Plato, when intelligence is disencumbered of the body.

3. Plato too uses Empedocles' notion that knowledge is of like by like as a tag on which to hang his concept that only through an eternal (formlike, hence universal) soul can we know Forms (here angels). Fārābī elaborates the Platonic and Aristotelian counsel that prophecy must accommodate its audience. Purity here is the epithet the Ikhwān adopt as their own. As the context shows, they mean not just formal sincerity (truth to one's principles) but candid insight, inquiry, and commitment, nobility of spirit and aspiration.

'The same is true of the spider. She is of the crawling creatures, yet in weaving her web and setting out her net she is more sage and dextrous than any of your weavers. For she spins as she weaves her web, first a single thread from one wall to another or from one branch to the next, from tree to tree or bank to bank of a stream, not walking on water but sailing across through the air. Then she treads on the thread she has stretched out and makes the warp of her web, straight lines like the taut guy-ropes of a tent. Next she weaves upon those in a circling pattern, leaving in the centre a small open ring where she sits, waiting to snare flies. All this she does without distaff, spindle, wheel, comb, loom, or any other tool or implement used by your weavers or spinners, who depend on the usual tools traditional in their craft.[1]

'The silkworms too, who are of the crawling creatures, are most skilled in their craft, more adroit than your artisans. When sated with feeding they find a place in the trees, shrubs and thorns, and from their saliva spin fine, glossy, strong threads that they entwine about themselves in a tough pouch-like nest to protect them from heat and cold, wind and rain. Then they sleep for a certain time – all this not needing instruction by a master or training by fathers or mothers. They are inspired, rather, by God, taught directly by Him. And all without need of a distaff, spindle, needle or scissors, such as your tailors, menders and weavers require.

'Likewise the swallow, a bird, builds a home for himself and his young out of mud, a cradle hung high in the air under the eaves, needing no ladder to reach it, or hod to carry his clay, no post to support it, nor any tool or implement at all.[2]

'So too the termites, who are of the crawling creatures. They build houses over themselves, of pure clay, like vaulted galleries, without digging up the ground or moistening their clay, or even drawing water. Tell us, then, O philosophers and sages, where do they get that clay? Where do they gather it, and how do they carry it, if you know?

'In the same way all sorts of birds and beasts build their houses, nests or bowers and rear their young. You will find them more skilful, wiser and more learned than humans. Thus the ostrich, a cross between a bird and a beast, treats her chicks: Having collected twenty or thirty or forty of her eggs, she divides them into three groups. One third she covers with earth, one third she leaves in the sun, and one third she broods. When her chicks emerge, she breaks the eggs that have been in the sun and lets the chicks drink the fluid the sun has thinned and melted within. When the chicks are stronger and sturdier, she unearths the buried eggs and pokes holes in them. Ants, flies, and worms, crawling and swarming creatures gather, and she feeds her chicks on these until they can forage and look after themselves.[3]

---

1. Spiders 'spin a long thread from their small body and tend their webs continually; never ceasing work on them, ever suspended in their handiwork,' Isidore of Seville, *Etymologies*, ed. Stephen A. Barney (Cambridge, 2006), 12.5.2.

2. A glossator adds the following: 'And when her young are blind she brings a certain grass called *māmīzān* from the mud, and rubs their eyes with it to treat their vision. All this is learned from God, not man. You need teachers and instructors to master the simplest arts and humblest crafts and can do nothing on your own without extensive training.'

3. See Lamentations 4:8; cf. Isidore. *Etymologies* 12.7.20. Ostriches incubate eggs that are not their

'Tell us, then, O human, which of your women takes such care in raising her children? Without a midwife to help with the delivery when they go into labour, draw out the newborn and cut the umbilical cord, or a nurse to show them how to suckle, swaddle and anoint the babe, put kohl on its eyes, and put it to sleep, your women would have not the faintest idea of how to do this.

'The same is true of your children. So ignorant and backward are they at birth that they have no idea what's good for them, or how to take care of themselves or stay out of trouble, until they're over four years old, or seven, or ten or twenty! Every day they need new knowledge, fresh training, to the end of their lives. But our young, as soon as they issue from the womb, egg or hive, are ready taught, inspired, aware of their interests and what their welfare requires. They need no instruction by fathers or mothers: With the chicks of hens, quail, partridges, mountain quail and the like, for example, you'll find that as soon as they hatch they immediately start racing around, pecking for grain, and running from anyone who chases them, so fast they rarely get caught, all without direction by fathers or mothers but by God's inspiration and guidance. This is a mark of God's mercy toward His creation, His kindness, bounty and grace. For in birds of this sort, unlike other birds – doves, and sparrows, and such – the male does not help the female brood and rear the young. So God gives them many chicks and makes them self-reliant, not needing nurture by fathers or mothers – milk to drink, or the cracking of seeds, or provision of food, as the young of other sorts of birds and beasts require. All this is by God's providence, glorified and sanctified be He, His concern in caring for these animals, as already mentioned.

'So tell us now, O human, who stands higher in God's eyes: those He cares for more amply and over whom His providence is fuller, or someone else?[1] Praised, then, be God, the compassionate Creator, who shows His creatures grace, caring and love. We praise and exalt Him when we rise with the dawn and go to our rest, chanting hallels and paeans by day and by night. For His are the praise, thanks and lauds, the meed and thanksgiving. He is All-gracious and All-wise, the best of creators.

'You said you have poets, orators, theologians and such. But if you could follow the discourse of the birds[2] – the anthems of the swarming creatures, hymns

---

own and may roll extras out of the nest – perhaps prompting the ancient story that they feed their young on them. The Book of Job (39:13–18) remarks that an ostrich treats her young as though they were not her own, perhaps by expecting the hatchlings to forage for themselves. Like the Bible, the Ikhwān are not judgmental about such behaviours; these too are facets of God's providence in nature.

1. Humans are highly dependent, especially at birth. But culture steps between need and nature. The Ikhwān score a point for animals here: humans rely on personal and collaborative efforts. But animal instincts, a gift of providence, typify the pietist ideal of *tawakkul*, reliance on God. The argument rests on the sophists' dichotomy of art and nature, although culture too is part of nature and itself, as the Ikhwān hold, a gift of grace.

2. The discourse of the birds, *manṭiq al-ṭayr*, is a Qur'anic phrase (27:16). The Biblical Solomon could discourse *of* the birds (1 Kings 5:13 = RV 4:33), but midrashic fancy has him talking with the birds. Taking flight from that fancy is 'Aṭṭār's allegory, translated by A. Darbandi and D. Davis, as *The Conference of the Birds* (New York, 1984). The birds speak again in many a medieval and renaissance narrative.

of the crawling creatures, hosannas of the beasts – the meditative murmur of the cricket, entreaty of the frog, admonitions of the bulbul, homilies of the larks, the sandgrouse's lauds and the cranes' celebration, the cock's call to worship, the poetry doves utter in their cooing and the soothsaying ravens in their croaking,[1] what the swallows describe and the hoopoe reports, what the ant tells and what the bee relates, what the flies portend and the owl cautions, and all the other animals with voice or buzz or roar, you would know, O human race, you would realize that among these throngs are orators and eloquent speakers, theologians, preachers, admonishers and diviners, just as there are among the sons of Adam. So why do you brag of your orators, poets and the like at our expense?

'There's ample argument and proof of what I say in God's words in the Qur'an: '*There is not a thing that does not praise and exalt Him, but ye understand not their praises*' [17:44]. God calls you benighted and dim when he says '*you understand not.*' He cites our insight, good sense and awareness when He says, '*Each knows His worship and praise*' [24:41]. And again: '*Are they alike who know and who know not?*' [39:9] – a rhetorical question expressing dismay. For anyone with any sense knows that ignorance is no equal of insight to God in the eyes of man.

'So what have you to vaunt over us, O humans, that makes you our masters and us your slaves – even with all your distinctions – beyond sheer slander and lies?'

(Translated by Lenn E. Goodman and Richard J. McGregor)

1. For the raven as a bird of omen, see Isidore, *Etymologies*, 12.7.44 and 12.7.76.

II

PROPHETHOOD AND IMAMATE

1
Abū Yaʿqūb al-Sijistānī

Al-Sijistānī's *Kashf al-maḥjūb* (see also Section I, 4) is arranged after a seven-fold pattern with an opening chapter on divinity followed by a *hexameron* of six phases or aspects of creation. In this framework, prophethood is understood as that which leads from the natural existence of the living species (the 'fourth creation') to 'resurrection' or spiritual renewal (the 'sixth creation'). It therefore occupies the place of the 'fifth creation.' Prophets are superior to ordinary humans by virtue of divine inspiration and assistance (*taʾyīd*). Each prophet belongs to the same essence but they succeed one another in a universal process of seven major cycles of revelation, expected to lead to an ultimate 'unveiling' and liberation with the full manifestation of their essence in the person of a mysterious seventh figure, the *qāʾim* or *mahdī*.

Kashf al-maḥjūb
Unveiling the Hidden[1]

ON THE FIFTH CREATION (PROPHETHOOD)

On how the prophethood of prophets is facilitated

Everything in creation has a quintessence [or 'marrow,' 'kernel,' (*maghz*)], which is bound to become visible [eventually] and to manifest its benefits – those benefits which are vested in it. We have already said that the quintessence of 'animal' is man, the living being capable of rational speech (*mardum-i nāṭiq-i zinda*) and the benefits of man are manifest. They are the amazing crafts that man invented with his intellect, his subtle intelligence and his pure skill. The whole purpose of creation ended up with man, and after the humans, no form appeared in creation that [would have] surpassed them in nobility. Necessarily, the quintessence of man lies in his capacity to express thought (*sukhan*). However, the totality of thoughts expressed by humans during one cycle is like milk which, once milked, is churned in a skin so that butter is gathered as a result.[2] Moreover, being of the subtle nature [of the quintessence], the human thoughts thus gathered during one cycle will be

1. Abū Yaʿqūb al-Sijistānī, *Kashf al-maḥjūb*, ed. and tr. Hermann Landolt as *Creation and Resurrection: Divine Unity and the Universal Process* (forthcoming), Discourse VI, 'On the Fifth Creation (Prophethood)'. An earlier version tr. Hermann Landolt appeared in *APP*, pp. 108–116.

2. The 'skin' presumably stands for the Universal Soul (*nafs-i kullī*). See Abū Yaʿqūb al-Sijistānī, *Kitāb al-yanābīʿ*, no. 164, paraphrased by Nāṣir-i Khusraw, *Khwān al-ikhwān*, chapter 90.

re-shaped[1] for the comprehension of one man, for whose tongue it will, then, be easy to enunciate them, so that he is capable of accepting the task of a prophet; and because this is so, that enunciation will settle in the hearts of his people. For this enunciation is the quintessence of those thoughts uttered by them in their own gatherings. As a result, to hear it is agreeable for their ear, because those are tones that had once been familiar to them. This is how prophethood of prophets is facilitated. Understand this!

There is still another meaning to this. The Creator knows what is to the advantage of His servants, and what they need with a view to an auspicious regime for this world. For this purpose, He made manifest firmly-tied knots in the celestial bodies, each knot facing a specific individual, so that, whenever it was the right time for a noble [human] to be born, He would open one of those knots. As a result, noble powers coupled with auspiciousness and virtues would join the person so fortunate. [This] possessor of charisma (*khudāwand-i karāmat*) would, then, at all times contemplate in himself something of the luminosity of the spiritual world (*ʿālam-i malakūt*) and of the overwhelming power of the divine (*jabarūt*), becoming thereby capable of receiving the Word of God and of being acquainted with that divine Law (*sharīʿat*) which contains both the colours of the spiritual [world] and the dispositions pertaining to religious governance, so that those accepting it will be of blessed destiny just as those rejecting it will be ill-fated. Understand this!

There is still another way to see how prophethood is facilitated for prophets, namely, by way of the manifestation of the activity of Intellect. For everything, from the beginning of creation to its end, has its [proper] activities: Thus, the elements and the celestial bodies manifest their activities in the beings pertaining to the realm of natural generation; Soul's intention is active in the plants and animals, and Soul's proper activity is manifest in Man as can be seen from his discourse (*sukhan*). In sum, then, nothing in creation had an unfulfilled desire to deploy its activity, except for Intellect's desire [to exercise] lordship and glory. Among all possible activities, nothing indeed would befit Intellect except manifestation of domination and deployment of glory; and this lordship, glory and domination must be such as to dominate the most eminent of all things, which is Man. Thus, lights were pouring forth from Intellect, and then, an individual body (*shakhṣ*) having the most complete harmony, the most subtle natural constitution and the most perfect disposition was fashioned from Nature and Soul in such a way that [this individual] was capable of receiving the spiritual support of Intellect (*taʾyīd-i ʿaql*). As a result, these blessings reached Soul and Nature, their good and sacred qualities were ready, and many things appeared from there. This is how prophethood of prophets is facilitated. Understand this!

1. Reading *mushakkal* instead of *mushkil*, a suggestion kindly made to me by Dr Faquir M. Hunzai.

That prophethood prevails against [mere] discourse and its professionals

Prophethood prevails because it is unique and without equal in its time, whereas discourse (*sukhan*) occurs among men who are equals. Therefore, the person endowed with prophethood is confident of the message that reaches him, and he knows that it does not reach anyone other than himself so that there could be dispute and contradiction between himself and that other person. The professionals of discourse, on the other hand, are many in the world, and there is much contradiction and dispute because of their multitude. One group wishes to approach prophets, seeking to contradict them on the grounds that their discourse makes them equals, while another group is incapacitated before the prophet due to the inimitable quality of the prophetic message. But those [presuming] to be his equals in discourse cannot prevail against him because the prophetic message he has is more than speech (*nuṭq*); rather, it is he who prevails against them. Understand this!

Further, prophethood is a mystery (*pinhān*), because it is from God, so no one can grasp it by mere discourse. If it were open to all, then it would indeed be accessible to all, as discourse is a public (exoteric, *ẓāhir*) matter, having been deposed in every human. But not everybody can grasp it, nor understand it. Esoteric and divine matters are always prevailing and more powerful than natural and exoteric matters. This is why prophethood prevails against [mere] discourse.

If the holder of prophethood did not have the power to govern their affairs, they would not obey him. The prevailing power of his office therefore makes it necessary for their souls to be attached to him in obedience, to take his example as a model, and to follow and respect his rulings and legal decisions. The strongest [argument for] prophethood's prevailing over discourse and its professionals is this: As you can see, many who claim to be professionals of discourse and to have legal expertise (*faqīhī*) are prevailing over the mere professionals of discourse, being aided by [their references to] the holder of the prophetic message, even though there is no share of the knowledge of prophethood and the divine Law among them. Now if prophethood were not prevailing by virtue of its own root (*aṣl-i khwud*), things would not have worked out for these pretenders the way they did, and their trade would have brought nothing. Thus it has been verified that prophethood prevails against discourse and its professionals. Understand this!

Further prophethood is associated with the sword, the scourge, and prison, but also with divinely granted success, assistance (*ta'yīd*) and help. As for that which is associated with the sword, it means to fight for the faith (*jihād wa ghazw*), to apply the talion,[1] to cut off the hands of the thieves and the feet of the highway robbers. The scourge is administered to fornicators and drunkards; and those who spread corruption on earth are hanged or exiled. As for divine assistance, success and help, it implies that the prophet has command of the pre-established order of things as

1. Punishment equivalent to the offence.

they happened and will happen. None of these capabilities lie within the scope of [mere] discourse. For this reason, [too], prophethood prevails against discourse and its professionals. Understand this!

Why the later prophet confirms the truthfulness of the earlier prophet[1]

Should a later prophet disown an earlier prophet, claiming that prophethood belongs to him [alone], that no prophet will come after him and that there was no prophet before him, people will disown him even more. His work will turn out to be more difficult, and people will have stronger arguments against him. But if he confirms the truthfulness of the earlier prophet, he will have placed his prophetic task on firm ground, because he could say: 'Before me, there was one who proclaimed the same call that I am proclaiming.' He will have a proof against those who disown him, saying [to them]: 'Why do you disown my prophethood when I am proclaiming the same call that was proclaimed by him who was before me and when I am following the same path he was following?' For this reason, it is necessary that the later prophet confirm the truthfulness of the earlier prophet. Understand this!

Furthermore, prophets are like the members of [one body, i.e.] prophethood; for prophethood will not stand good unless its members and limbs are a perfect whole. Whenever a deficiency appears in one member, this deficiency will affect most of the members, for prophethood has no firm standing unless that member is [also] perfect. And if a later prophet does not confirm the truthfulness of an earlier prophet, he will have made inoperative a member of his own and introduced a weakness. Understand this!

Further, there is a continuity and affinity (*mushākilat*) between two prophets that succeed one another. Both have truth by virtue of [their] spiritual essence being one and the same (*bi-yikī-i ḥaqīqat*), for the rank of the preceding prophetic messenger is like the stage of potentiality, and the rank of the succeeding prophetic messenger is like the stage of actuality; and nothing ever comes to the stage of actuality unless it has been at the stage of potentiality. Therefore it is necessary for that prophetic messenger who comes next, since he is at the stage of actuality, to confirm the truthfulness of the one who is at the stage of potentiality. For if he disowns him, he disowns his own potentiality from which he evolved to the stage of actuality; and if he disowns his own potential, his effectiveness will be weakened; and if his effectiveness is weakened, his words will not settle in the hearts of the people of his community. But if the later prophetic messenger confirms the truthfulness of the one before him, it will be necessary for the prophet who comes next to confirm his truthfulness as well. Thus, it is necessary for that prophet who comes last to confirm the truthfulness of all the prophets prior to him. Understand this!

1. For this theme, see Abū Yaʿqūb al-Sijistānī, *Kitāb ithbāt al-nubūʾāt*, ed. ʿĀrif Tāmir (Beirut, 1966), pp. 162–166.

Further, there is a great advantage for the later prophetic messenger in confirming the truthfulness of the earlier one, namely this: If the [later] prophet is seen by his people to confirm the truthfulness of their own [earlier] prophets and to praise their virtues, their hostility towards him will be waning, and they will be inclined [to listen] to him, just as [in the opposite case], if he disowns the earlier prophets, people's hostility towards him will consolidate itself, and they will hold him in abomination. Now those who remained hostile towards him were all those who did not understand anything from their own prophets except following them in blind imitation (*taqlīd-i maḥḍ*) devoid of inner Truth (*dūr az ḥaqīqat*). As a result, they became obstinate in following the path of error, proudly refusing to submit to his command and to accept his [new] community, and ended up as rogues – as can be seen from the lies they were telling. Understand this!

There is yet another major and subtle reason for the later prophet to confirm the truthfulness of the earlier prophet, which is the following: Many later prophets lived under the Law of earlier prophets and acted for some time under that Law, and [then] reached prophethood [themselves]. If [such a prophet] would give the lie to the one under whose Law he had himself been acting, he would be weakening his own person and would debase himself, since he had accepted the truthfulness of that [earlier] person as long as prophethood had not [yet] belonged to him. He would become suspect regarding his own prophethood, and bad thoughts would come up regarding himself, since he [would have to admit that he] had accepted the truthfulness of someone without having sure knowledge of that person's truthfulness, and that he may [in fact] have been deluded by someone who cheated him. Indeed [the later prophet] must not allow any doubt to come up in himself with regard to the noble quality he saw in himself when living in obedience of [the earlier prophet], having then accepted his truthfulness by acting under his Law and worshipped God under that religion. This way, he will be safe from suspicions and will avoid being slandered by the adversaries (*sukhanān-i ḍiddān*). Therefore, it is necessary for the later prophetic messenger to confirm the truthfulness of the earlier prophetic messenger. Understand this!

Why the preceding prophet announces the following prophet

By announcing the prophetic messenger following him, the preceding prophetic messenger [in effect] announces himself. This is so because the preceding spiritual rank (*ḥadd*) is in comparison to the subsequent one like something that exists *in potentia*, while the subsequent prophetic messenger is like something that exists *in actu*, as we have already said; and something that exists potentially desires to attain the rank of actuality. Thus it is because of the desire of the possessor of potentiality to evolve in actuality that he announces the prophet after him. Understand this!

Moreover, if the preceding prophetic messenger were to deny [the coming of] the prophetic messenger after him, although the coming[1] prophetic messenger is

1. Reading *pasīn* instead of *pīshīn*.

always more excellent and more eminent, and the Law and the Book he will bring are more perfect and more luminous – if he did not announce the one coming after him, the willingness of the people to embrace his religion would be weak. Therefore, if he does announce the coming of that spiritual rank (*ḥadd*)[1] after himself, they will embrace his religion most warmly, and they will expect [that person's] advent; for that spiritual rank coming after him is to have far more lights of the spiritual domain (*anwār-i malakūt*) than he has. Consider for example someone inviting people to a feast, preparing food and drink of many kinds, and saying to them: 'If you are eager to come to my feast and willingly consume my food, I shall give you another feast, better than this!,' they will be eager to come for the sake of the other feast. Understand this!

Further, if the preceding prophet does not announce the subsequent prophet, while the coming forth of that spiritual rank is bound to happen eventually, he necessarily denies him either out of ignorance or out of envy. Now if the predecessor turns out to have been ignorant of the coming of the successor, he was not among those informed by God about His mysteries; and a person not thus informed does not qualify for the office of prophethood of God. If, on the other hand, it was out of envy [that he denied the successor, then he did not qualify either, for] envy is contemptible while prophets are consecrated persons assisted by divine support and far beyond envy. Thus, if the previous prophetic messenger does announce the subsequent prophetic messenger – that is, the one whose coming forth is bound to happen eventually – this predecessor will have given evidence of his own knowledge and noble rank, having been informed of that mystery which God conferred and revealed [only] to His prophets; moreover, he will have been freed of envy, which is the opposite of this [prophetic] status. For this reason, [too], it is necessary that the preceding prophet announce the following prophet. Understand this!

Further, to announce the following prophet means for the preceding one to eliminate pride and glory from himself. He thus eliminates from himself that urge which has driven the deniers into denying the divinity of their Lord and claiming divinity for themselves. The dominion of prophethood is a great dominion indeed, and it holds great sway. The possessor of prophethood contemplates in himself things of such magnitude and power as cannot be described. [He might succumb to this urge] if God does not guard him from pride, so that he will not look at the eminence of his own rank in reality. When God makes him aware of the coming of that person who is to succeed him – and, moreover, of those glories (*āfarīnhā*) that exist for him in God's treasure-house, those shining lights of the spiritual domain (*rawshanāʾīhā-yi malakūt*) and things beyond description which He allows His servants to become aware of – his modesty and submission will then become manifest. He will announce his submission to that spiritual rank who is to come after himself; and it is precisely in this way that he manifests his

1. Probably an allusion to the coming of the *qāʾim*, or the 'Lord of the Final Rising.'

own noble rank and glory, eliminating [any claim to] lordship or divinity from himself. Thus, it is necessary that the preceding prophet announce the following prophet. Understand this!

That the proof of God is not established with one prophet alone

God Most Exalted made it necessary [for Himself] to take care of [His] proof (*ḥujjat*) and to send prophets; but you must know that he did not privilege any one prophet in particular. The reason for this is that time does not remain unchanged, rather, it rotates and causes the [human] creatures to change accordingly, due to the motion of the stars in the skies and the fact that in their rotation they travel through the signs of the zodiac and the degrees [of the Sphere]. In sending prophets, God has no purpose other than the benefit [of the humans]: He does it not in order to remove any disadvantage from Himself but for the sake of that regime (*siyāsat*) which will be best for the humans, so that they will have a permanent standing in this world and the other. Now, since what we have established is true and time does not remain unchanged, it follows that the regimes must vary just like time; and given that the world is in rotation and the moral norms of the people in this changing world turn in various ways, it follows that there must be a ruler for each regime specifically, since each regime is different. And it is not possible that different regimes have one and the same ruler; for if one and the same person were to manage all the regimes, he would be unable to lead the affairs of everybody to their fulfilment and could not take care of all. In effect this would amount to approving of lawlessness and giving up the choice of the best option. It is for this reason that the proof of God is not established with one prophet alone. Understand this!

Another point: Had God sent no more than one prophet, it would be inconceivable that [this] one prophet alone would have come up with all the religious Laws, nor would he have realized all the spiritual Realities (*ḥaqīqathā*) that are deposited on top of them, nor would he have grasped the meanings made accessible through the Books that came over the tongues of the subsequent prophets. For that which was allotted to the prior prophets is only a little of the lights from the spiritual domain of God, and of those regimes, Books and religious Laws of the later prophets, who were privileged to find the way to the spiritual domain of God. And the word of God is the proof of God for the servants of God. If this were not so, this would amount to invalidation of the proof of God – but God does not invalidate his own proof. Rather he keeps his own proof valid and manifests it so as to eliminate the invalid. Thus it has been verified that the proof of God is not established with one prophet alone. Understand this!

On the other hand: Had God not brought forth prophets, and had He postponed [revelation] until the Seal of the Prophets came forth, whom He would [at that time] have graced with the clearly-spoken Qur'an and the Law of the true religion (*sharīʿat-i ḥanīfī*), the people of the earlier periods would have been in want of the proof of God, and God would have rendered invalid his own proof for a long time. Therefore, since it is inconceivable that God would render his own proof invalid forever or for a long time, sending out prophets was a necessity [for Him] in the past times, and is so, likewise in the remaining times. Thus it has been verified that the proof of God is not established with one prophet alone. Understand this!

Why it is Jesus, among all the prophets, whose descent is traced to coming down [from Heaven]

The meaning of Jesus' descent being traced to coming down from Heaven to Earth is this: In Christ (*masīḥ*), the model (*mithāl*) set by Adam became visible reality (*dīdār*); for he tasted (*bi-chashīd*) from that tree from which [Adam] had been debarred. Indeed while spreading the True Knowledge and Wisdom, at the time he walked among his friends, Jesus did not alter the Law of Moses except that he changed the Sabbath to Sunday. His constant concern was to give his disciples [the capacity to see] 'colour,' that is, the colours of the spiritual [world], up to the moment when he left this world. But the pre-established 'measuring' (*taqdīr*) of God was such that the previous Law should be abrogated and a new Law should appear. Thus, after Jesus, one heptad among the [successive] heptads passed by and the pre-established 'measuring' came true from among the people living during the cycle inaugurated by him, that is, the Law which is now in the hands of the Christians was then codified and attributed to Jesus. Yet God has [also] given an account of Christ as the sign of the Final Rising of Liberation (*nishān-i rastakhīz*), which means that the True Knowledge and Wisdom Christ revealed to his disciples belongs [properly] to the Lord of the Final Rising of Liberation (*khudāwand-i rastakhīz*). [Therefore,] the descent of Jesus from Heaven signifies that the Knowledge and Wisdom revealed by Jesus will be manifest to the Lord of the Final Rising (*khudāwand-i qiyāmat*). Indeed in some traditions it is said that the Mahdī will be Jesus the son of Mary, which means that that which Jesus imagined about himself was predetermined to come true with the Mahdī. That is why it is Jesus, among all the prophets, whose descent is traced to coming down [from Heaven].[1]

Another possible meaning of this is the following: Each one among the prophets was granted triumph over his enemies so that his rule could stand firm, except Jesus, who experienced hardship from his enemies and left this world without having received any help against his enemies. So God promised to grant him triumph at the Final Rising (*qiyāmat*), and He will call him to arise (*bar angīzad ūrā*) with victory and in triumph. Understand this!

Furthermore, Christ is kindred to the Spirit of God and the Word of God, for it was blown into Mary so it would arise (*bar-rustan*) and he would be born.[2] You should know that all the religious Laws are like bodies for the Word of God, and the

1. See *Kitāb al-yanābī'*, nos. 143–146.
2 For the Qur'anic background, see notably, 3:45; 4:171; 19:16ff; 21:91.

Word of God is like the Spirit animating all the religious Laws. Now God promised that the Final Rising will be close to the [second] Coming down of Jesus, that is to say, the Descent of the Word of God, so that the religious Laws shall be alive and their benefits will appear, and that the inner realities and secrets hidden in them come out into the open. This, [too], is what is meant by the Coming down of Jesus from Heaven. Understand this!

Why the lord of the final rising is kindred to the Mahdī

The Mahdī is the one who shows humans the path. All the prophets before him guided humans to the path of God; but their words were veiled, and their sciences were concealed, because the times required this. But once the process had reached its end and the lifting of the veils has come near and the cycle of unveiling (*dawr-i kashf*) has arrived, clear proofs will come out into the open, and signs of that will be set. The person who will appear then will guide the humans without [having recourse to] veils and symbols, and he will unveil to them all of the True Knowledge that had been [veiled] in the religious Laws and the [prophetic] Books, and every wisdom and mystery that had been hidden. The name of that person [i.e. *mahdī*] is derived from [the root] H-D-Y [to guide], which implies that there is no way for anyone to avoid him and his call (*daʿwat*), or to escape from his arguments and proofs, because he guides the humans to that which is in their own inner reality (*ḥaqīqat-i īshān*) and shows the way to those sciences to which 'the Horizons and the Souls' [41:53] bear witness and opens the way for the souls to know the spiritual domain of God, so that the souls become one with the True Realities (*ḥaqāʾiq*) and the spiritual support [of the 'chosen ones,' *taʾyīd*). Then all will be peace and joy, and all the stubborn will join the religion of God out of their own choice, eagerly and truly, and offer their obedience. This is why the Lord of the Final Rising is kindred to the Mahdī. Understand this!

It is said that when the Mahdī comes, wolf and sheep will drink water in one and the same place. 'Wolf' means the adversary (*ḍidd*), those who harm the friends of God (*awliyā-yi khudāy*) and confront them with hostility, while 'sheep' means a person with whom they feel confident and in whose goodness they place their hope. In this sense, then, there will be agreement between the adversary and the friend [of God] due to the power of the Lord of the Final Rising. That they 'drink water' [in the same place] means that there will be agreement between them in knowledge, wisdom, and unveiling of the True Realities.[1]

Further, it is said that the Mahdī will kill Gog and Magog.[2] This means that during the time and cycle of the Lord of the Final Rising those who strayed from the path and stuck to corrupt creeds will be put to death. The 'spilling of their blood'

1. See *Kitāb ithbāt al-nubūʾāt*, pp. 168f.

2 For an overview of traditions related to Gog and Magog, two mysterious peoples mentioned in the Qurʾan (18:94 and 21:96) see, E. van Donzel and Claudia Ott, 'Yādjūdj wa-Mādjūdj,' *EI2*, vol. 11, p. 231.

[means that] the doubt will be removed from their hearts and souls. After that, 'justice will be spread and tyranny will be abolished,' that is, the justice which is knowledge will be spread and the tyranny which is ignorance will be abolished.[1]

Further: The souls during the cycle of concealment (*dawr-i satr*) may be likened to a serious illness affecting the body, and the cycle of unveiling (*dawr-i kashf*) may be likened to the state of health that one hopes for when leaving the illness behind. The Lords of the cycles of concealment may be likened to the physicians who cure the sick. Now by God's pre-established 'measuring,' the period of time appointed for these sick ones was a total of seven cycles, and with the completion of these seven cycles the illness was to leave these afflicted ones. The Lord of the first cycle (*khudāwand-i dawr-i pīshīn*) [i.e. Adam] may be likened to the kind of physician who prevents the sick from eating anything, as do the physicians of India.[2] The Lord of the second cycle is rather like the physician who prescribes drugs, and the third and the fourth, up to the seventh, may be compared to those physicians who prescribe, each in his turn, an appropriate medical treatment. When it comes to the Lord of the Final Rising, he liberates them from the fetters of illness altogether, sustains them with his comfort (*bi-i 'ādat-i khwīsh barad*), his own food and drink, and makes them reach the state of health. That is the sign of the Mahdī, while those [medical treatments administered by the prophets] are the benefits of the sciences and wisdoms of the one who guides mankind towards the Mahdī and Lord of the cycle of unveiling. It is in this sense that the Lord of the Final Rising is kindred to the Mahdī. Understand this!

(Translated by Hermann Landolt)

1 For the 'spreading of justice' see the forthcoming text, Discourse IV.4.2.

2. The 'preventive medicine' of Adam perhaps reflects al-Sijistānī's (and al-Nasafī's) doctrine that Adam did not bring a *sharī'a*.

2

al-Mu'ayyad fi'l-Dīn al-Shīrāzī

Al-Majālis al-Mu'ayyadiyya is an eight-volume collection of lectures delivered by the Ismaili chief *dāʿī* and poet al-Mu'ayyad fi'l-Dīn al-Shīrāzī (d. 470/1078) at the Dār al-ʿIlm in Cairo during his tenure as the Ismaili *dāʿī al-duʿāt* (see Part One, 5). The *Majālis* are a prime example of the emphasis in the Fatimid tradition on reason as a pervasive element in revelation and religion. The 800 lectures of the *Majālis* demonstrate this pervasiveness by discussing Qur'anic verses and *ḥadīth* to analyse such complex issues as the unity and attributes of God, His revelation and its significance, the pivotal role of prophets and imams, the process and nature of creation, the place of man in the universe, and the ultimate purpose of God in all of them, the hereafter and its nature and significance. The selection for this chapter is the full text of the first of these lectures, which sets the tone for the rest by establishing the crucial role of intellect in religion.

al-Majālis al-Mu'ayyadiyya
The Discourses of al-Mu'ayyad[1]

REASON AND REVELATION

All praise be to God who arranged between human beings and animals such that He created both from clay, then brought forth their progeny from dense water. Divine providence then willed such that amidst the humours of the human form there was thrown in the elixir of intellect (*al-ʿaql*) – in the language of the chemists – by which he was raised to the highest pinnacles of honour and loftiness; he thus came to be among those of whom God – may He be exalted – says, and is there anyone more truthful than Him in word? – 'Verily, We have honoured the progeny of Adam, have carried them on land and on sea, have provided for them of the bounties, and have exalted them upon most of those We have created.' [17:70] He (the human being) thus brought down, by his design, the bird from the sky; and extracted the fish from the depths of the sea; and subjugated various species of animals, birds, livestock and carnivores. Of some of them he benefited from their meat; of others he enjoyed

1. al-Mu'ayyad fi'l-Dīn al-Shīrāzī, *al-Majālis al-Mu'ayyadiyya*, vols. 1 and 3, ed., Muṣṭafā Ghālib (Beirut, 1974–1984); vols. 1–3, ed., Ḥātim Ḥamīd al-Dīn (Mumbai, 1975–2005). This selection is from Ḥamīd al-Dīn's edition (repr., Mumbai, 2002), vol. 1, *Majlis 1*, pp. 1–5, tr. Abdeali Qutbuddin. The introduction to this chapter is by the translator.

the use of their skin, wool and fur. He encompassed the all-encompassing celestial sphere (*al-falak al-muḥīṭ*) in all of its cosmic vastness, in the pavilion of his thought, in contrast to his body which is enclosed in the pavilion of its [the celestial sphere's] dominion and captivity, being subjected to generation and corruption. This is the advantage God has granted him in the first world. He then made this (his intellect) a staircase by which he would climb to eternal existence in the world of the hereafter. For if it were not for the light of his intellectual perception, no message from any message-sender would be accepted, nor would the instruction of any messenger be followed or applied, nor would any soul be inscribed or enlightened with the knowledge of professing the unity of God – may He be exalted – nor would any tongue turn around the uvula (*al-lahawāt*) voicing the sciences of the hereafter.

May Allah bless Muḥammad, the best of the messengers who enlightened himself with the light of its [God's] clear lamp[1] and marched on its clear path; and his *waṣī* (successor) who was elevated from the horizon of nobility and distinction to the pinnacle of [nobility's] ascendancy; and his progeny who call towards the fresh and sweet drink (*'adhb furāt*), and prohibit from the bitter and the salty (*milḥ ujāj*).[2]

O community of believers! May God place you among those whose hearts have been enlightened by the radiance of the intellect, and whose sides have shunned the couches of ignorance.

A group [of people] from among those who have taken their religion from custom and proceed in it in the footsteps of the fathers and the mothers, surmised that the *sharī'as* of the prophets – may peace be upon them – which are the means for salvation and the road to eternal life, are not based on intellect and reason and that they fall in a category different to reason.

Now, if they had looked closely, and had cleared their minds from the adulteration of zealous partisanship and arbitrary opinion, they would know that if it was put to one of them regarding something about his own specialization, and the words and actions which ensue from him, that this action of yours is not based on reason, nor does it rise from reason's horizon, he would fly into a rage and would immediately falsify the accusation and would find the exchange offensive. How then do they accept for the prophets – peace be upon them – who are the masters of their religion and the intermediaries between them and their Lord, such a thing that they would dislike for themselves?

Do they not consider that the address in the Book of God – may He be exalted – is all toward 'those possessing reason' by his saying, 'Then be fearful of God, O those possessing reason' [5:100 and other verses], and His saying, 'In that, indeed,

1. Reference to the Qur'anic verse on Light, 24:35–36. In Fatimid thought, the lamp and its light symbolize the intellect as a divine hypostasis manifested in prophets and imams.

2. This is an allusion to a Fatimid interpretation of the Qur'anic verse 25:53: 'And He it is who hath given independence to the two seas (though they meet), one palatable, sweet (*'adhb furāt*), and the other saltish, bitter (*milḥ ujāj*), and hath set a bar and a forbidding ban between them.' (tr. Pickthall). Verse 35:12 has a similar theme. The fresh, sweet and palatable sea represents the pure knowledge possessed by the Fatimid imams; the salty bitter sea represents the corrupted knowledge of their opponents.

is a remembrance for those possessing reason' [39:21], and similar verses which are numerous and oft-repeated.

It can either be the case that the Prophet had no reasonable proof (*burhān*) explanation for the matters of *sharīʿa* which he himself had instituted, or that he did have them but did not inform of them. If he did not have such explanation, it would be abominably unacceptable, so that if someone inquired as to the reason which required him to institute five obligatory prayers and not six, and he said 'I do not know,' this alone would be enough discredit to him that he would institute something which he did not know the reason for when asked about it. And if he himself did have an intellectual argument for it – and it is an intellectual argument which gives beauty to words and actions – and he did not reveal it, he would then not have fulfilled the duty of delivering [the message]. This, however, is ruled out outright about the Prophet – may God bless him and his progeny – because he did deliver and said in the assembly, 'O God, bear witness that I have delivered.'

Apart from this, it is well known that the Messenger – may God bless him and his progeny – did not charge with the obligation of the *sharīʿa* save the person with sound mind. Why would he then charge the one of sound mind with something whose basis was not on reason? The thing whose basis is not on reason is more fitting for those without intellect than those with intellect. What would be the reason for appointing reason in the first instance and then deposing it in the last. Why not uphold its appointment in the last as it was in the first, or depose it in the first as it was in the last? This is something which is clear to the fair-minded.

Another argument: It is well-known that the philosophers claim the intellectual sciences and the true affairs [for themselves]; and the Muslims declare them apostates at the same time for cutting themselves off from the means of the Message, and for their declaration that they have gained independence from the prophets – may [God's] peace be upon them – in attaining knowledge of the signs of their salvation, and that they (the prophets) are needed only for the political ordering of worldly society, for protecting lives and wealth and the weak from the strong. The conviction of the people of truth is that all the sciences, including the rational ones which the philosophers claim [as their own], are collectively present in the sciences of the prophets – may [God's] peace be upon them – and have diverged and branched out from there. The confirmation of their belief is to be found in God's saying – may He be exalted – 'there is neither wet [substance] nor dry but it is in the clear Book,' [6:59], and His saying – may His glory be exalted – 'We have not left out anything in the Book' [6:38]. Now if one of the philosophers were to come to the Prophet and question him about the angels, the throne, the chair, heaven, hellfire and the principles of his *sharīʿa*, its prayers, its *zakat* (alms-tax), its fasting, its *ḥajj*, and its *jihād*, to demonstrate their compatibility with reason, would the Prophet say, 'I am not able to demonstrate that intellectually?' God – may He be exalted – forbid.

Another argument: It is reported from the Prophet – may God bless him and his progeny – that he said, 'The first thing that God created was the Intellect; then He said to it, 'Come forward' and it did, then He said to it, 'Go backward' and it did, then He said to it, 'By My honour and My glory, I have not created a creature more glorious than you; by you shall I reward, and by you shall I punish.' Thus if the *sharī'as* were not based on intellect and reason, there would be no reward or punishment in them according to the report, 'By you shall I reward, and by you shall I punish.'

O community of believers! Leave aside the people of division and opposition, for they are the followers of error and transgression. God – may He be exalted – says to His Prophet – may God bless him and his progeny – 'Indeed, those who divide their religion and are broken up into factions, you are not of them in anything' [6:159]. And hold fast in your religion to the guides and recognize the appointed times by the crescent moons; mend and rectify your condition and purify your garments. And praise God – the Exalted – who opened your eyes for you towards the truth, and the people are blind to it, and removed the veils from it for you, so that you bask in the comforts of its gardens. And run swiftly in the arena of the repenters and the worshippers. And clothe yourself in the rough garments of those who perform *rukū'* and *sujūd,* and draw people towards your imams with the goodness of your actions, even without speaking, and stay up the night in worship of God.

May God place you among those who 'when His verses are recited upon them, they (the verses) increase them in faith' [8:2], and may He urge you to provide thanks for his bounties, for 'He brought your heart together in harmony so that by His grace you became brothers' [3:103]. All praise be to God Whose might is overpowering, Whose proof is dazzling, Whose place is great, Whose bounty is vast. May God pray blessings upon Muḥammad on whom the *Furqān* (Qur'an) was sent down, by whom the edifice of polytheism is quivering; and on his *waṣī* (legatee) who is the trustee for his knowledge and its interpreter, 'Alī b. Abī Ṭālib, by whom the hands of the Truth are spread out, and by whose tongue its tongue speaks; and on the imams in his progeny by whom the boundaries of religion and its foundations are safe; and may He shower them with peace. God suffices us and He is the best entrustee.

(Translated by Abdeali Qutbuddin)

3

Aḥmad b. Ibrāhīm al-Naysābūrī

A distinguished scholar of the Fatimid period, Aḥmad b. Ibrāhīm al-Naysābūrī (fl. 4th/10th – early 5th/11th century) came from Nishāpūr, the centre of the Ismaili *da'wa* in Khurāsān noted for its use of rationalistic philosophy. He has several works to his credit but the *Kitāb ithbāt al-imāma* is of decisive importance to the philosophical curriculum of medieval Muslim thought. It is here that al-Naysābūrī applies rational tools to expound his theology, allowing us to capture not only the significance of his own thought, but also the beliefs of his age. Beginning with the premise that supreme leadership, the imamate, is the pole and foundation of religion, he establishes his thesis by using several approaches, the most important being the theory of 'degrees of excellence.' God created each genera and species with a unique capacity and distinct advantage not existing in another. Citing examples from the ten Aristotelian categories and other natural metaphors from mineral, plant, tree and animal kingdoms, he acknowledges the disparities within each genus and species, while at the same time providing paradigms of perfect examples in each variety, demonstrating in a parallel manner that the imam is at the apex of humanity. The *Ithbāt al-imāma* provides an unparalleled insight into the intricacy of the Imam-Caliph al-Ḥākim's rule (386–411/996–1021), adding considerably to our understanding of that period.

Kitāb ithbāt al-imāma
Affirming the Imamate[1]

We say that the existence of differences and degrees of excellence in all things that comprise the elements, realms of nature and their derivations are the firmest evidence and proof in affirming the imamate and the imams.[2] This is because God the Exalted created all things different and disparate in excellence, with respect to all genera and species, and thereafter set for each and every genus and species

1. Aḥmad b. Ibrahīm al-Naysābūrī, *Kitāb ithbāt al-imāma*, ed. and tr. Arzina R. Lalani as *Degrees of Excellence: A Fatimid Treatise on Leadership in Islam* (forthcoming), nos. 3, 6, 11, 14, 29–30; see also her article, 'Aḥmad b. Ibrāhīm al-Naysābūrī,' in Oliver Leaman, ed. *Biographical Dictionary of Islamic Philosophy* (London and New York, 2006), vol. 2, pp. 158–160. The introduction to this chapter is by the translator.

2. See Abū'l-Fawāris, *al-Risāla fi'l imāma*, in *The Political Doctrine of the Ismā'īlīs (The Imamate)*, ed. and tr. Sami N. Makarem (Delmar, NY, 1997), where he says that the judgement of reason assumes and testifies that the disparity of mankind is conceived wisdom on God's part (trans. p. 34, Arabic text p. 18).

an upper limit (*ghāya*), a summit (*dhurwa*), an end (*nihāya*) and a virtue (*faḍīla*), which none other in that category can attain. He made those genera and species principles in creation, without which the world of humans cannot do, and without which their bodily existence and function would not be complete. Alternatively, He made them [a source of] nourishment, a remedy, an elegance, an adornment and an indispensable tool. He placed in all things an advantage (*manfaʿa*) that does not exist in anything else. He powerfully endowed in them a capacity that the creation would necessarily need, which they can neither avoid nor be able to maintain their physical affairs without it. He also put them to a test and made them seek to acquire that which would remove their deficiency. Thus, if one cannot find the cure of that neediness in its place, one seeks it [elsewhere] or hastens to [another] place where it may be found. As long as one remains in the world of one's body, one cannot for a moment dispense with breathing (*tanāsum*) and seeking to benefit from the elements of one's world, its derivations, realms of nature, vegetation and nourishment, [all of] which are a wisdom from God the Exalted and a mark of justice from Him. [This is] so these aspects would be witnesses and ephemeral, obligatory symbols (*al-mithālāt al-jabriyyāt*) for the symbolized realities that are religious, eternal and chosen. The benefit of all symbolized realities comprising principles, realms of nature, nourishment and religious remedies are more deserving, more worthy and more powerful than the obligatory symbols. Their need is more than the need of what is compulsory by nature because their benefit[s] go back to the body, while those of the symbolized realities go back to the spirit and the soul. Therefore, the extent of increase in merit of the intellectual symbolized realities over the natural symbols is according to the extent of the spirit's merit over the body. Furthermore, the merit of the symbolized over the symbol is according to the extent of the merit of the everlasting ones over the perishable ones. The merit in each of them reflects the deficiency in the other. For whoever is deprived of the physical aspects he is in need of, will not experience destruction from that. Even if there be [such a] destruction, it would [only] be that of his body which undoubtedly will perish and die. In the absence of the symbolized, religious reality, however, there would be destruction of the soul [which] plunges into perpetual punishment. Therefore, if people's struggle in seeking for what the soul needs were similar to their struggle and desire for seeking what the body needs, then no two people would doubt, stray or ascribe human qualities to God, that is, anthropomorphism (*tashbīh*)… .

Furthermore, just as the testimony of the outer horizons and the inner selves is compulsory and not chosen, thus becoming impossible for anyone to either alter or substitute it, likewise the Messenger, may God bless him, made the testimony compulsory, without entailing a choice for the witnesses to change, alter or conceal it. He has threatened whomsoever would change or conceal it with a painful punishment. God the Exalted ordered [man] to judge on the basis of the testimony of two witnesses, mentioning in His words: 'If one of them falls into error, the other will remind. And the witnesses must not refuse when they are summoned' [2:282].

By this, He meant that true judgement in religion and in affirming the imamate and the hierarchies is at the hands of two witnesses, one posited by law and the other compelled by nature. If people deny the legally established testimony, then the one bound by nature, namely the horizons and our [own] inner selves reminds, enforces and verifies the conventional witnesses, just as God the Exalted says: 'We shall show them Our signs on the horizons and within themselves until it becomes manifest to them that it is the Truth,' [41:53] and just as the Prophet, when asked, 'Who is the witness of your Prophethood?' answered: 'My witness is every stone and every [piece of] clay.'[1] He then pointed to the testimony of the horizons and the souls. Thus, when legal and natural witnesses testify and intellect becomes the criterion in assessing the witnesses without preference or partiality, then truth swiftly becomes manifest.

Now, we shall mention the differences and degrees of excellence in each principle and realm of nature. We shall also show that the ultimate limit and highest summit in each genus and species points to the imam in every age and time. If these genera and species show proof of the imamate and the imams in a different order from the theme of heptads, such as the seven planets being the testimony for the seven imams and other heptads, then that does not prevent there being [another] proof given through the peak and perfection in every genus and species for the imam as we have just mentioned.

The sages among the philosophers mention the ten categories and say that one cannot mention or discuss anything except in reference to these ten: substance (*jawhar*), quantity (*kammiyya*), quality (*kayfiyya*), relation (*iḍāfa*), place (*makān*), time (*zamān*), possession (*jida*), posture (*nuṣba*), action (*fāʿil*) and affection (*mafʿūl*).[2] The ultimate extent of the ten is the substance upon which all others rest and which excels over all others because the [remaining] nine are established from it. Therefore, the substance that they describe is a proof for the permanent, intellectual, luminous and authentic substance through which all souls are illumined and on which depend all the nine religious accidents (*al-aʿrāḍ al-dīniyya*). Yet, it is one that has no need of any created thing; it draws benefit from nothing or no one in the world, but rather, everything benefits from it and is in need of it. That is the Imam, peace be upon him, and all other ranks are below him in the same manner as the nine accidents are in respect to the substance.

We also say that among the four basic constituents (*al-anāṣir*) from which the first composites (*tarākib*) were composed, two are active and two passive. The two active ones are heat and cold while the two passive ones are dryness and humidity. The ultimate and the noblest among them is heat from which arises luminosity, light, motion, movement and elevation, while the other three are established through it. Heat has precedence in origin and in existence. No foundation or realm of nature would be complete without it. Likewise, the imam

1. Muḥammad Bāqir al-Majlisī, *Biḥār al-anwār* (Tehran, 1956), vol. 3, p. 333.

2 See J. N. Mattock, '*Maḳūlāt*,' *EI2*, vol. 6, pp. 203–205. In rephrasing the Aristotelian categories, al-Naysābūrī uses the same Arabic terms as al-Sijistānī; see *Wellsprings*, pp. 122–123.

illumines the souls[1] and from him comes intellectual light (*al-nūr al-ʿaqlī*), motion (*al-ḥaraka*) and elevation (*al-ʿulū*). No principle or religious realm is complete without him.

Additionally, among the celestial spheres, the most lofty and supreme is the outermost sphere (*falak al-aflāk*) in which all orbit. Likewise, the imam in his religion is the supreme religious sphere for all other spheres. All heavenly bodies and religious signs of the zodiac function under his command. If someone were to claim that this is rather a symbol for the *qāʾim* (Resurrector), given that the highest principle in the world points to the intellect in respect to the four principles, then we would answer that the imam is the *qāʾim* in his time, he is the proclaimer (*nāṭiq*) in his age and time, and he is the one who assumes the position of the *qāʾim*. The imam's position in his realm is that of the Universal Intellect (*al-ʿaql al-kullī*).

We also say that among the four elements (*al-arkān*), the highest and the noblest is fire which is the summit and peak, [at a level] to which no other element or nature can attain.[2] Likewise, the imam, in his age and time is the highest religious pillar through whom souls are illumined. If what has been said about Abraham is true, then it is on this basis that he ordered glorification of the fire, and prevented them from extinguishing and putting it out. However, the indication was towards glorifying the imamate, which no one must put out through the injustice of those who falsely claim its position. The fire worshippers fell into confusion not knowing its symbolized reality. God the Exalted related about the adversaries and the usurpers of the position of the imamate in His words: 'They would like to extinguish God's light with their mouths, but God will not allow that until He perfects His light even if the unbelievers may detest it' [9:32].

We also maintain that there are many planets (*kawākib*), and among them there are differences and disparities in degrees of excellence. Their peak and summit in nobility and merit is the sun through which physical eyesight draws its light, and through which all plants, animals and newly born grow and become perfect. No plant or newly born will grow without the effect of the sun. Likewise, the imam is the sun of the religion through which insight is enlightened and souls are illumined from the light of guidance and wisdom, radiating the hearts of God's friends. It is because of this that some people propose to glorify the sun. However, worshippers of the sun fell into confusion as they only understood the symbol, not recognizing the symbolized reality. It is for this reason the Prophet, may God bless him, indicated the rising of the sun from the west which signals the 'rising' of the imam, peace be upon him, in the Maghrib.

1. Literally, 'the imam is the light of the souls.'

2. According to the early Ismaili author, Muḥammad al-Nasafī (d. 332/943), the four elements became mixed to form the four composites, where ether is the fourth element with earth, water and air. In contrast, Abū Ḥātim al-Rāzī (d. 322/934) in his *Kitāb al-iṣlāḥ* identifies ether with fire. See al-Rāzī, *Kitāb al-iṣlāḥ*, ed. Ḥasan Mīnūchihr and Mehdī Mohaghegh (Tehran, 1998). But, in his *Aʿlām al-nubuwwa*, ed. Salāḥ al-Ṣāwī and G. R. Aʿwānī. (Tehran, 1977), p. 138, he enumerates ether as the fifth element. See Shin Nomoto, 'Early Ismaili Thought on Prophecy according to *Kitāb al-iṣlāḥ* by Abū Ḥātim al-Rāzī (d. ca. 322/934–5),' (PhD dissertation, McGill University, Montreal, 1999), pp. 165ff.

If the physical sun were to depart from its usual orbit and its ascent and descent from its centre, for even a blink of an eye, the entire world would be destroyed; which is impossible, both rationally and naturally. Therefore, the Prophet's statement holds true only on the basis of esoteric interpretation. In fact, his interpretation has proved to be true as we have witnessed it with our [own] eyes by the grace and favour of God.[1]

We also say that among the twelve signs of the zodiac, four are most glorious and excellent. One of the four is the peak and the summit in nobility. Likewise, among the twelve *ḥujaj* (proofs), the one who is connected to the imamate is the most excellent, the noblest and the most exalted of them all… .

In the same way, we maintain that humankind is the ultimate among animals and in the realms of nature. The advantage of all that preceded the creation of mankind, from the principles, derivatives and realms of nature, goes back to humankind. The merits of the world and that of animals, plants and other things are contained in humankind; their benefit, glory, value, goodness are all apparent in mankind. If it were not for mankind, the merit of all things would not become apparent and neither would the order of the world. Nothing would be complete, nor would any benefit accrue from it, nor would anything be preserved from it or from the plants and animals. For it is the human being who utilizes water and irrigates the land bringing it under his rational control, tapping it from valleys, rivers and wells. It is also man who tills the land, cultivates it, makes from it habitations, and irrigates the plants and fields with water bringing the land under rational control.

In addition, it is the human being who utilized the wind and air, and it is man who discovered fire by means of flint and also the crossbreeding of animals that was non-existent. Man grafted the different trees such that he produced fruits from them that were not available [before] in the world. He extracted jewels from minerals and brought beneficial trees, seeds and fruits under his rule and control. He protected the welfare of animals and plants, as well as their produce, and took animals under his command and control. So, just as man is the peak of animals, plants, minerals and realms of nature and through him the welfare of animals and whatever was before became perfected and ordered, likewise, the imam is the peak, summit, quintessence and perfection of all human beings. It is through the imam that the affairs of mankind are ordered. As the benefit of all that preceded human beings goes back to mankind, similarly the benefit of all humanity and their quintessence goes back to the imams, peace be upon them. Human beings learn virtues and knowledge from them, and acquire minds and comprehension from them. It is through them that their welfare is guarded in their worldly and religious matters as well as in their life hereafter. They are guided by the Imams towards the recognition of the Creator (*maʿrifa al-Ṣāniʿ*), learning the necessity of gratitude to the benefactor and the manner in which gratitude should be

1. This refers to the rise of the Fatimid Imam-Caliph al-Mahdī who established the Ismaili state in the Maghrib in 297/909. See al-Qāḍī al-Nuʿmān, *Iftitāḥ al-daʿwa*, tr. Hamid Haji as *Founding the Fatimid State: The Rise of an Early Islamic Empire* (London, 2006), pp. 19ff.

expressed. It is through the imams that mankind recognizes the Messengers and how they ought to be obeyed.

Just as the benefit of all animals and everything that preceded them goes back to mankind and man therefore became their leader, similarly the benefit of all human beings goes back to the imams, who became their leaders, their commanders and prohibiters. If it were not for the imams and the direction and guidance they give to humanity and the protection of their well-being in this life and in the life hereafter, as well as their encouragement to acquire virtues and avoid vices and animal habits, then there would be no difference between beasts and humans; rather animals would be better. If man did not accept training to acquire virtues for his soul and did not learn to stimulate his intellect from the imams, then he would be in a worse position than animals since animals are not as prone to evil as humans are and animals have numerous benefits. If man did not have intellect and religion he would be totally evil and corrupt. It is on this account that, God the Exalted and Glorious, said: '*For the worst of beasts in the sight of God are the deaf and dumb – those who understand not*' [8:22]. The Exalted also said: '*They are like cattle nay, more misguided, for they are heedless of warning*' [7:179].

If there were no humanity, there would be no wisdom in the creation of animals and plants as there would be no benefit in them. Similarly, if it were not for the Imams, peace be upon them, there would be no wisdom in creating humanity and their superiority would not become manifest. For indeed, human beings have been created for religion and for the acquisition of virtues and knowledge. So learn knowledge and religion from the imams, peace be upon them, for through them, religion is established and perfected. If the excellence of man were not made manifest through religion, then the value of plants and animals would not become known either, and there would be no wisdom in the creation of humanity, plants and animals. Further, if there were no wisdom in their creation, then there would be no wisdom in the creation of all the worlds....

Further, we say that there are disparities (*tafāwut*) and differences in degrees of excellence (*tafāḍul*) in the organs of the body; the foremost and the best among them is the head. It is in the head that the face [is situated] by which each human being is recognized and distinguished from others. Among the internal organs, the best one is the brain, which is their chief, being the source of the intellect. So likewise the imam has a position in the world similar to the head and in relation to the organs, similar to the brain. Around him revolve all affairs of the creation just as all actions pertaining to the body revolve around the brain. Amongst the faculties in man and the spirits, the best is the intellect, and the imam is the Universal Intellect (*al-ʿaql al-kullī*) in the world from and in whom all people of the world become united.

As we mentioned earlier, leadership in nature is present in everything. It is present in animals and in birds, such as the stallion protecting and disciplining the females. Thus the rooster protects its fowl, disciplining it. Every genus protects its young and children according to its capacity and defends its female, the weak among the genus as well as the female and the young ones according to their need for benefit and learning from those above. The crane obeys its leader and the bee obeys its chief.

Indeed, God the Exalted created the world and made the creatures as we mentioned earlier to a certain extent, according to this classification [of] disparity and difference in degrees of excellence, having more or less strength, nobility or inferiority, so that they would know that in each species and genus there is a peak, summit and chief in nobility and merit. Likewise, it is necessary that the whole of mankind also have a peak and summit in nobility and merit who would be their leader and guide in the world. It has thus been shown that headship and leadership is necessary in nature and creation as well as within natural disposition and intuition, and that those who deny the revelation and religion are not able to deny the leadership, headship and directorship of the world, either rationally or in witnessing it with [their own eyes] as it is obligatory and necessary. It is therefore mandatory that that leader be the best among them all, the most noble, the most perfect, the most knowledgeable and the most pure according to the arguments that we mentioned [earlier] from creation and nature, and that the foremost is the imam in everything as well as the chief and the head. The name 'supreme leader' (*al-imām)* cannot be placed on the one who is led (*ma'mūm)* nor the name 'the excellent' (*al-fāḍil)* on the 'one preferred' (*al-mafḍūl*), nor the name 'one who supersedes' (*al-sābiq)* on 'one who is preceded' (*al-masbūq)*. Moreover, people from all communities and religions, as well as philosophers, atheists and those who deny God all attributes, affirm that the leader of the world ought to be the best among them, the most perfect in merit, and the most knowledgeable of all the people. There is no leader in the world of this description except for the imams, peace be upon them.

(Translated by Arzina R. Lalani)

4
Ḥamīd al-Dīn al-Kirmānī

Ḥamīd al-Dīn Kirmānī (d. after 411/1020, see Section I, 1) wrote his *al-Maṣābīḥ fī ithbāt al-imāma* around 404/1013 as a defence of the imamate of al-Ḥākim, hoping to convince the Būyid *wazīr* in Baghdad to support the Fatimids. In the extract chosen for this chapter, al-Kirmānī explains, through a series of lucid and logical demonstrations, why the imamate is necessary to take forward the message of God and the example of His Messenger.

al-Maṣābīḥ fī ithbāt al-imāma
Lights to Illuminate the Proof of the Imamate[1]

IN PROOF OF THE IMAMATE AND OF ITS NECESSITY

The first demonstration: The Messenger set forth on behalf of God wisdom that is far-reaching and it was incumbent upon him to convey it to those of the human species to whom he was sent, both those in existence in his time and those humans who would come into existence through procreation after him up to the Day of Judgement. The humans who lived in his time were not able to accept that wisdom in one fell swoop, nor was it feasible for the humans who were to come into existence up to the Day of Judgement to exist all together. Yet it was impossible that the Messenger himself remain in this world until the protection of God would cover all the nations to whom it was to be conveyed. As a result it was necessary to appoint someone to occupy his place in conveying that protection and to set up the perpetual designation of another when the time of his passing approached. The person appointed for that purpose is the imam. Hence, the imamate is essential.

The second demonstration: What the Prophet brought in the way of the Holy Book, the authoritative law, obligatory practice, religious regulations and well respected precepts can be added to or subtracted from, and it is possible to alter his regulations and pronouncements and to introduce deviation in them. But, given the possibility of adding to or subtracting from them and the feasibility of altering his regulations and pronouncements, and if addition, subtraction or alteration should occur, that would lead to tyranny, injustice, oppression, the hands of the

1. Ḥamīd al-Dīn Aḥmad b. ʿAbd Allāh al-Kirmānī, *al-Maṣābīḥ fī ithbāt al-imāma*, ed. and tr. Paul E. Walker as *Master of the Age: An Islamic Treatise on the Necessity of the Imamate* (London, 2007), Part II, 'The First Light', pp. 71–79.

unjust reaching for forbidden things and its becoming the cause for the appearance of errors, the spread of fear and the absence of security, the course of wisdom [therefore] requires that there be a person put in charge of them who guards over them in this respect and prevents additions, subtractions or alterations in them. The community will thus follow his practice and the commandments of God will be ever fresh, His word exalted and evil eradicated. The person so charged is the imam chosen on behalf of God. Therefore, the imamate is necessary.

The third demonstration: The revelation and law brought by the Prophet came in the Arabic language and that language sustains a variety of meanings since a single phrase in the speech of the Arabs conveys a wide range of interpretation because of metaphors that allow for variations of meaning and symbolic expressions that point to a variety of objects. It is thus possible to interpret each verse and each report in accord with what the interpreter wants. In various situations we observe among the community that often happens in each sect's setting itself apart in regard to a verse of the Qur'an or one of the reports and using it to verify their own particular doctrine based on a meaning, which is not the meaning another sect adduces for the same verse, to validate its doctrine. An example is the statement of God: 'What prevents you from bowing down to what I created with my own hand (*bi-yadī*)?' [38:75]. The Mu'tazila hold a view, in regard to this verse, which confirms their doctrine by claiming that the intended meaning in God's saying 'by my own hand' is strength and power. The view of another group is that it indicates benefit and benevolence. Yet another group – and they are the Predestinarians (al-Mujbira) of various types – maintain, in confirmation of their doctrine, that it means simply the hand that is a part of the body and is one of its limbs. Each of their doctrinal statements is undeniably correct because our saying 'hand' denotes a meaning which is that adduced by each sect within the community and advocated by them. In its being open to whatever interpretation accords with the intention of the interpreter, it is parallel to a piece of cloth that can be cut for whatever purpose a person who cuts it desires. A person wants to cut from it a shirt because he needs one and that is quite possible. Another wants to cut from it pants because that is what he needs. Yet another hopes to cut from it a vest and stockings and a collar, because that is what he requires and that is also possible. This is also like fire. One person has a lamp and wick to ignite in it, another a candle to light, yet another firewood to set ablaze. This situation has three stipulations: either all the meanings that are adduced from the outward sense of what the Prophet brought are reasonable and must be apprehended in the right manner; or what is intended in the large number of meanings that can be adduced for one phrase is one or two meanings only and the rest are erroneous, and that one must be grasped in order to avoid the others; or all of the meanings that the outward sense of the phrase entails are entirely erroneous and the intention in the phrase is something other than what its outward sense indicates. Thus the phrase performs in that case the function of a simile and a metaphor, and it is necessary to come to understand what that metaphor refers to or the implications of that simile. If all the meanings contained in the one phrase are reasonable, wisdom requires that there be in the community someone who teaches them what, in the whole lot, is the direction of wisdom and not to leave anyone to single out one meaning rather than another, so that the word is one in worship and that differing ceases. If the intended meanings adduced from the one phrase is a single meaning or two, wisdom requires that there exist in the community a person who teaches them the intended aim and the meaning in which there is right guidance and to prevent them from believing any other, since none has the knowledge of what meaning is more worthy of believing than any of the rest due to the human need for a teacher to keep out mutual hatred and contention and to keep uniform the word in worship. If the meanings that are adduced from the outward sense are all erroneous and what is intended by the phrase is not its meaning, but rather it has the function of metaphor and symbol, wisdom requires there to be in the community someone who explains to them what those metaphors and similes refer to, lest they fall into error and believe what they should not. Thus, if there are these three possibilities in this case and all three require that there be someone in the community to guide and to teach, the guide and the teacher is the imam. Therefore, the imamate is obligatory.

The fourth demonstration: Dispositions differ, desires are disparate, events are not predictable or determined, and arrogance, transgression, love of conquest and domination are natural. The course of wisdom thus requires that among people there be a ruler who decides for them about what happens and from whom or from his rule they have no escape nor can they flee his decree. This was the case with the Prophet in his time. God said about him in His statement: 'Indeed, by your Lord, they will not believe until they make you judge their disputes and find no reservation in their souls about what you have determined but accept them fully' [4:65]. The ruler is the imam. Therefore, the imamate is necessary.

The fifth demonstration: God is just and does not act tyrannically nor unjustly. God singled out the community that existed at the time of the Prophet by the incredible virtue of His having brought into existence among them the Messenger as a safeguard for them against punishment. God noted as much in His saying: 'And God will not punish them while you are with them' [8:33]. He is also a means for them to seek forgiveness for themselves when they slip up. God confirmed that in His revelation when He said: 'If they, having sinned against themselves, should come to you and they ask forgiveness of God and the Messenger also asks forgiveness for them, they would find God most forgiving and merciful' [4:64]. As well in His commenting on the account of the hypocrites, when they had appealed to the Messenger to seek forgiveness for them: 'If it is said to them, "Come, let us ask the Messenger of God for forgiveness," they avert their heads and you observe them turning away in arrogance' [63:5]. That community had the virtue of having among them the Messenger to decide their judgements, instruct them on the waymarkers of their religion and its obligations, prompt them to seek the afterlife, to exert themselves in the way of God, and to ask God to forgive them their sins. None in existence was the like of him among them, but still they are not more favoured than any others, since the Messenger is the Messenger to all people and is the means for the [saving of the] whole. Accordingly, given that God is not unjust to His servants, it is necessary that after the Prophet there come to the community someone who takes up his role and replaces him in being its safeguard and the means whereby it [the community] asks forgiveness of God, who preserves for them the order of things, and who prompts them to do what is best for themselves. God imposed the seeking of a means to Him as a duty when He said: 'O, you who believe, fear God and seek the means to Him' [5:35]. It is impossible to imagine God not having provided the community such means when He also imposed on them the obligation to seek it. The person who assumes the role of the Messenger is the imam. Therefore, the imamate is necessary.

The sixth demonstration: We maintain that God made Muḥammad the Messenger to all the people, both those of them who existed in his time and those who come into being after his era up to the Day of Resurrection. He ordered him to summon them all to Him in His saying: 'Summon them to the way of your Lord with wisdom and fine words' [16:125]. The Prophet did what his Lord commanded him to do with his efforts and abilities in speech and in deed all the days of his life. But there remained more people than had already come to and followed him, who had not entered the law of his religion, who were, nevertheless, among those he was obliged to summon with words and efforts. It was well known that the Prophet would not remain in the world forever. Therefore, he set up an appeal to God on behalf of himself to carry on until his religion would appear above all religions, just as God had promised. Thus, given the consequences of the impossibility of the Messenger remaining among creation as a whole until the Day of Resurrection in order to sustain the appeal to them as God commanded, it is necessary that, since it is not possible for him to remain physically, someone assume the place of the Messenger who summons to the abode of Islam by inducement and a warning and in words and efforts so that the command of God will be fulfilled. The person who assumes the place of the Messenger is the imam. Therefore, the imamate is essential.

The seventh demonstration: We hold that, because God said to the Prophet Muḥammad, 'Take of their wealth alms to cleanse them and make them pure' [9:103], and because Muḥammad was a Messenger to those in his own time and as well as whoever was to be born after his death, and yet, even so, he was commanded to take alms payments from the wealth of all Muslims and thereby to make them all pure. Given the impossibility for the Messenger to be present with the entirety of Muslims until the Day of Resurrection in order to take those alms from them and thus to ensure their purity throughout, it is necessary that someone assume the role of the Messenger in taking what he was ordered to take and in purifying the people so that the command of God is upheld. The person who assumes the role of the Messenger is the imam. Hence, the imamate is necessary.

The eighth demonstration: The law closes the gates of sedition through the upholding of its regulations and the ending of the desire for injustice by carrying out its penalties. The law includes actions that are disagreeable, such as killing, crucifying, flogging, stoning, banishment and others. Even though, by nature, humans do not intend to injure and cause pain to themselves, nor be killed if that becomes necessary, or be crucified or any of the rest, they are not stopped from committing the acts of disobedience that merit the application to them of such actions. It is within the possible that, were the methods used in these acts like the methods used in others of those the provisions of which are assigned for the safeguarding of the people, such as prayer, almsgiving and others, if they are not done or are violated, the course of wisdom requires that, as with these actions, there be reliance on someone to uphold them and, in upholding them, maintain them for those deserving them, lest the regulations and penalties be neglected, public security be nonexistent, and the gates of evil opened. The person entrusted with that charge is the imam. Hence, the imamate is necessary.

The ninth demonstration: God made it obligatory to refer what one does not know about, or that in which there is a difference of opinion, to the Messenger. He decreed referring to him in His saying: 'If you quarrel concerning a matter refer it to God and the Messenger' [4:59]. In regard to what one wanted to know concerning matters that were the subject of contention and difference in respect to issues of religion during the time of the Prophet, the authority was him, but it was not possible nor feasible for him to remain in the world to be among his community to the end so that they could refer to him that in which there occurred a difference or an issue of religion regarding which they did not have sure knowledge. Accordingly, it was necessary to put in the place of the Messenger someone to whom to refer those issues of religion about which there were differences, so that the decision would be his in that matter and the command of God would be upheld. The person who assumes the place of the Messenger is the imam. Thus, the imamate is essential.

The tenth demonstration: Drawing an analogy is to appoint the self as the authority in regard to what one wants to know in respect to that in which there is a difference of opinion and doubt, and to refer to it concerning that matter and to extrapolate from what is there in seeking the latter. God barred the use of analogical reasoning in His statement: 'In whatever matter about which you differ, the ultimate authority belongs to God' [42:10]. He did not say, 'In whatever matter about which you differ, the authority belongs to you.' Thus, the use of analogy is precluded. And He confirmed it by His indicating to them to whom it should be referred when He said: 'If you disagree about a matter refer it to God and the Messenger' [4:59]. Thus, since they were barred from using analogy, it is necessary for there to exist among them, after the Prophet, someone to issue rulings in matters about which they differ when it is referred to him. That someone to whom it is referred is the imam. Hence, the imamate is necessary.

The eleventh demonstration: God has spoken of 'The day We shall summon all peoples with their imams' [17:71]. But, if in every era and time, there were not an imam and the earth were to be without one, even though people successively come into existence, the statement of God would be a lie. It is impossible to imagine that the words of God are a lie. Thus, it is essential that there be an imam for every age in whose name God summons his people. Hence, the imamate is necessary.

The twelfth demonstration: When He said, 'O, you who believe, obey God and obey the Messenger and those in authority among you' [4:59], God imposed on the believers three acts of obedience in one verse, each linked to the others. Obedience to those in authority is not obedience to the Messenger and obeying the Messenger is not obeying God, but no one can accept the first without the second or the second without the third. Those addressed in the verse are the mass of the believers, both those in the era of the Messenger and those after him; it is not specific. On the part of God, it is impossible to impose on His servant obedience to someone and connect it with obedience to His Messenger and yet not to make that same person exist – that would be to impose an obligation that could not be fulfilled – or not to make him infallible, like the Messenger, and crowned with sacred and sublime traits. With regard to the addressee in the verse being the masses among whom no group is singled out to the exclusion of another, added to the impossibility of God depriving any community of someone they are obligated to obey, it is necessary that there exist for the community someone who is rightly the subject of their obedience, and their following his command in regard to God and the religion of God. The person from whom one takes orders is the imam. Hence, the imamate is necessary.

The thirteenth demonstration: God, the Exalted, high is His glory, created souls and made them alive and able to do good and evil, and He made for them the reward. He was not content, in terms of His own, until He had let them know what He had allocated for them as a reward. This information came on the tongues of His messengers as a warning and admonition. If there were not to be, after the messenger, one imam after another to preserve the messages of God and His command and prohibition, and to report to those communities who come into existence about how God's justice takes the form of both advice and admonition, that would single out the community of the messenger and the people of his time over those who are born into the communities after them. If He singled out for advice and admonition one group over another, the justice of God would prove false, even with a common reward. With respect to the perfection of the justice of God and its certainty, it is necessary for there always to be, after the messenger, an imam who is charged with warning the people of his time and admonishing them, announcing to them glad tidings and cautioning them lest they claim 'there came to us neither announcer of glad tidings nor warner' [5:19]. When one imam passes on, another takes his place by his command and with his designation. Therefore, the imamate is necessary.

The fourteenth demonstration: The wisdom of the Creator is such that each thing He creates that does not know and lacks ability is under the charge of a thing that does know and has that ability which preserves it and looks after its welfare. Otherwise, creation of it would prove futile. He connects the two, as is the case with the macrocosm, which is this world with its celestial spheres, stars and elements, which He created devoid of knowledge and without power. Then He entrusted them to the closest angels to preserve their proper order and serve as a link between them. These angels have both knowledge and power; otherwise if it were not for them, their creation would prove futile. Another example is the microcosm, which is the individual human, consisting of his hands, legs, head, bowels, which God created ignorant and without power. He gave command of that microcosm to the soul to govern it and preserve its proper order until the end of the time determined for it, and He linked the two, and the soul knows and has power. If it were not for it, the individual would cease to function, just as it does when the soul leaves it. What the lord of the prophets and their seal, Muḥammad, brought on behalf of God as the law, is knowledge by its very existence. This world is the world of legal imposition, a combination of prayer, almsgiving, the pilgrimage and the rest, all taking the form of acts. Acts are deeds and deeds are in their essences without knowledge. Accordingly, wisdom requires, in respect to the obligation of preserving them lest they cease to exist, that it is necessary to give command over them to someone who will preserve and take of them, as with the other worlds. For that reason, the appointment of the imam is the ultimate obligation. In him the world of law is completed. God declared this principle when He imposed it; He said: 'Today I have perfected for you your religion and I have completed for you My favour' [5:3]. And he connected the silent prophet with the speaking prophet who said: 'I have left among you the two anchors, the Book of God and my family.' The family functions, with respect to the Book and the law, as does the soul with respect to the world of the individual, and as do the angels with respect to this world. Thus, the imamate is obligatory.

(Translated by Paul E. Walker)

5
Ḥasan-i Ṣabbāḥ

The *dāʿī* Ḥasan-i Ṣabbāḥ was born in the mid 440s/1050s to a Twelver Shiʿi family in Qumm. He converted to Ismailism at the age of 17 and after receiving training in Egypt returned to his native Persia. There he travelled widely, gaining local strength and support at a time when the Fatimid caliphate in Egypt was coming under considerable strain. In 483/1090, Ḥasan and his followers captured the castle of Alamūt, then in Saljūq hands and made it the headquarters of the Nizārī Ismaili state in Persia. It was during his rule that Persian emerged as the religious language of the Ismailis of Persia. As the leader of the Nizārīs, Ḥasan-i Ṣabbāḥ was eventually recognized as the *ḥujja*, or proof of the imam. His major theological work, *al-Fuṣūl al-arbaʿa* was originally written in Persian but has survived only in fragments quoted in the Arabic heresiographical work of al-Shahrastānī written around 521/1127 and in paraphrased versions by later Persian historians. In this text, Ḥasan establishes the need for the Ismaili imam as the unique authoritative teacher who would guide mankind towards its spiritual goals.

al-Fuṣūl al-arbaʿa
The Four Chapters[1]

THE DOCTRINE OF *TAʿLĪM*[2]

Then the partisans of the new *daʿwa* deviated from this way, when al-Ḥasan ibn al-Ṣabbāḥ proclaimed his *daʿwa*. His words failed to be compelling, but he got the help of men and fortified himself in strongholds. He first went up into the fortress of Alamūt in Shaʿbān of the year 483. That was after he had gone away to the land of his imam, and had come to know from him how the *daʿwa* should be preached to his contemporaries. He then returned, and summoned the people first of all to single out a trustworthy imam arising in every age, and to distinguish the saving

1. Marshall G. S. Hodgson, *The Order of Assassins: The Struggle of the Early Nizārī Ismāʿīlīs against the Islamic World* (The Hague 1955; repr., Philadelphia, 2005), Appendix II, pp. 325–328.

2 Abu'l-Fatḥ Muḥammad b. ʿAbd al-Karīm al-Shahrastānī, *Kitāb al-Milal wa'l-niḥal*, ed., A. Fahmī Muḥammad (Cairo, 1948), vol. I, p. 339, section on Nizārīs. I have compared my translation with two former ones, those of E. E. Salisbury, 'Translation of Two Unpublished Arabic Documents Relating to the Doctrines of the Ismāʿīlīs and Other Bāṭinian Sects.' *JAOS*, 2 (1851) pp. 257–324, and al-Shahrastānī, *al-Milal wa'l-niḥal*, translated into German by Th. Haarbrücker, as *Religionspartheien und Philosophenschulen* (Halle, 1850–51; reprint, Wiesbaden 1969), 2 vols.

sect from the other sects by this point: which was that they had an imam, and others did not have an imam. After the repetitions in what he says about it, the substance of his discourse reduces, ending up where he started from, in Arabic or in Persian, to just this. We will report in Arabic what he wrote in Persian, and no blame attaches to a reporter. He is well aided who follows the truth and avoids error; and God is the giver of aid and assistance.

We shall begin with the four chapters [*fuṣūl*] with which he began his *daʿwa*. He wrote them in Persian, and I have turned them into Arabic. He said, He who delivers opinions on the subject of the Creator Most High must say one of two things: either he must say, I know the Creator Most High through reason and speculation alone without need of the teaching (*taʿlīm*) of a teacher; or he must say, there is no way to knowledge (*maʿrifa*) even with reason and speculation except with the teaching of a trustworthy teacher (*muʿallimin ṣādiq*). [Ḥasan] said, If one asserts the first he cannot deny the reason and speculation of anyone else; for when he denies, he thereby teaches; so denying is teaching, and an indication that the one denied needs someone else. [Ḥasan] said, The twofold [dilemma] is necessary, for when a man delivers an opinion or makes a statement, either he is speaking on his own, or from someone else. Likewise, when he accepts a doctrine either he accepts it on his own or from someone else. This is the first chapter, which refutes the partisans of reflection and reason.

He notes in the second chapter: if the need for a teacher is established, is absolutely every teacher acceptable, or is a trustworthy teacher required? [Ḥasan] said, If one says that every teacher is acceptable, he has no right to deny the teacher opposing him; if he denies, he thereby admits that a dependable, trustworthy teacher is required. This is said to refute the partisans of *ḥadīth* [Sunnis].

He notes in the third chapter: if the need for a trustworthy teacher is established, is knowledge of the teacher required or not? – assuring oneself of him and then learning from him? Or is learning permissible from every teacher without singling out his person and demonstrating his trustworthiness? The second [alternative] is a reduction to the first [proposition]. He for whom it is not possible to follow the way without a leader and a companion, let him '[choose] first the companion, then the way.' This refutes the Shiʿa.

He notes in the fourth chapter: Mankind forms two parties. A party which says, For the knowledge of the Creator Most High, a trustworthy teacher is needed; who must be singled out and distinguished first, then learned from; and a party which accepts in every field of knowledge some who are and some who are not teachers. It has been made clear in the portions that have preceded that truth is with the first party. Hence their head must be the head of the truthful. And since it has been made clear that the second party is in error, their heads must be the heads of the erring. [Ḥasan] said, This is the way which causes us to know the Truthful through the truth, in a summary knowledge; then after that we know the truth through the Truthful, in detailed knowledge; so that a circular argument is not necessary.[1] Here

1. Following Cureton's *dawrān* rather than A. Fahmī's *dūn*. al-Shahrastānī, *al-Milal wa'l-niḥal*, ed. W. Cureton (Cairo, 1842–1846), 2 vols.

he means by 'the truth' only the *need*, and by 'the Truthful' the *one who is needed.* He said, By our need we know the imam, and by the imam we know the measures of our need. Just as by *possibility* we know *necessity*, that is, the necessarily existent [God], and by it we know the measures of possibility in possible things. [Ḥasan] said, The way to *tawḥīd* [declaration of God's unity] is that way, feather [of an arrow] balanced against feather.

Then he went on to chapters establishing his doctrine, either supporting or refuting [other] doctrines. Most of them were refutation and disproof; demonstrating error by variety of opinion, and truth by agreement. Among them was the chapter of truth and error, and the small and the great. He notes that there is truth and error in the world. Then he notes that the sign of truth is unity, and the sign of error is multiplicity; and that unity comes with *taʿlīm*, and multiplicity with reflection. *Taʿlīm* is with the community, and the community with the imam. But reflection is with the various sects, and they are with their heads.

He put truth and error and the similarity between them on the one hand, and the distinction between them on the other hand – opposition on both sides, and order on one of the two sides [?] – as a balance to weigh all that he uttered on the matter. He said, This balance is simply derived from the formula of *shahāda* [no god but God], which is compounded of negation and affirmation, or of negation and exception thereto. He said, It does not claim the negation is erroneous, nor does it claim the affirmation is true. He weighed therewith good and evil, truth and falsehood, and the other opposites. But his point was that he came back, in every doctrine and every discourse, to affirming the teacher. And *tawḥīd* was *tawḥīd* and prophethood, together, if it was *tawḥīd* at all; and prophethood was prophethood and imamate together, if it was prophethood at all. This was the end of his discourse.

Moreover he prevented ordinary persons from delving into knowledge; and likewise the elite from investigating former books, except those who knew the circumstances of each book and the rank of the authors in every field. With his partisans, in theology he did not go beyond saying, Our God is the God of Muḥammad. He said, Here we stand [?]; but you say, Our God is the God of our reasons, whatever the reason of every rational man leads to. If one of them was asked, What do you say of the Creator Most High, does He exist? Is He one or many? Knowing and powerful, or not? He answered only to this extent: My God is the God of Muḥammad; He is the one who sent His messenger with guidance; and the messenger is the one who guides to Him.

However much I argued with the people over the premises just related, they did not go further than to say, Are we in need of you, or should we hear this from you, or learn from you? And however much I acquiesced in the need, and asked, Where is the one needed, and what does he determine for me in theology, and what does he prescribe in rational questions? – for a teacher does not have meaning in himself, but only in his teaching; you have shut up the door of knowledge and opened the door of submission and *taqlīd* [blind acceptance of authority], but a rational man cannot willingly accept a doctrine without understanding or follow a way without proof – the beginning of the discussion was arbitrariness (*taḥkīm*), and what it led to was submission. 'And by your Lord, they are not at all faithful till they make you [Muḥammad] arbiter of what divides them, and then find no fault, in their hearts, with what you decide, but submit fully.' [Qur'an, 4:65]

(Translated by Marshall G. S. Hodgson)

6
Naṣīr al-Dīn al-Ṭūsī

The famous scientist-thinker Naṣīr al-Dīn al-Ṭūsī wrote some of the most important works of Shiʿi philosophy and ethics in the Muslim world. The *Paradise of Submission*, a Persian work traditionally attributed to him, was probably compiled with his concurring assistance in 640/1243, during the long productive period of his intimate association with the Ismailis in Quhistān and Alamūt (from 624/1227 to 654/1256). This work is one of the most important expositions of Nizārī thought and doctrine from the Alamūt period. The text is divided into 27 (originally perhaps 28) sections called *taṣawwurāt* or representations and discusses a range of topics pertaining to the inner meaning of religion. The first extract below explains the necessity for the seeker to submit to 'the wise and perfect man' to achieve knowledge. The second details the nature and necessity of prophecy and imamate.

Rawḍa-yi taslīm
Paradise of Submission[1]

CONCERNING VARIOUS KINDS OF SUBMISSION

The ontological need (*iḥtiyāj*) of possible beings for the Necessary Being – may its majesty be exalted – far transcends the scope of man's finite imagination. From the very centre of the earth (*markaz-i taḥt al-tharā*) unto the outermost extreme of the farthest firmament (*falak al-aʿlā*), even unto the Universal Soul (*nafs-i kullī*) and the First Intellect (*ʿaql-i awwal*), all beings according to their essences and ontological requirements, have been stirred into motion, turning their faces towards their [divine] whole and original principle (*kull wa mabdaʾ-i khwud*). Each being, according to the aptitude it possesses, progresses from inferior to superior degrees, eventually realizing its own perfection through submission (*taslīm*) to that which transcends it.

For example, when the earth submits itself to the domination of plants so that they can spread their roots therein, extracting their sustenance from, and making use of, the earth's best and most precious substances to nurture themselves, thereby growing tall and manifesting their properties, it effects the transition from the earthly to the vegetative state. [Similarly], when plants submit themselves over to

1. Naṣīr al-Dīn al-Ṭūsī, *Rawḍa-yi taslīm*, ed. and tr. S. J. Badakhchani as *Paradise of Submission: A Medieval Treatise on Ismaili Thought* (London, 2005), *taṣawwurāt* 23–24, pp. 104–117.

the dominion of animals, so that animals convert them into food and thereby perfect their bodily organism, shape and senses, there ensues a progress from the vegetative to the animal condition. When animals give themselves over to the control of man that he may make use of some of them to nurture himself, gaining physical sustenance and stimulating his animal spirit which provides [or guarantees] sense perception and motion – and [he] may accrue from some [animals] various other benefits and accomplishments – the transformation from the animal to the human condition is thereby effected.

[The same is the case] when an ignorant and imperfect human being submits himself to the control of a wise and perfect man (*insān-i ʿāqil wa kāmil*) and surrenders to him both his senses and intellect, that is, puts his own will (*ikhtiyār*) completely in the hands of the other, so that he might, in the manner [his master] considers to be most beneficial, transform him from one condition to another and take him from one place to another, until he reaches the point where he will not wish to die as long as the other wishes to live, nor wish to live as long as the other wishes for death; or if he tells him that bright daylight is the dark of night or that the dark of night is bright daylight, he will not object to this in his heart, nor ask the reason why and wherefore. Once this point has been reached, so that the free will and personal desire of the imperfect and ignorant person have become merged with, and annihilated in, the will and desire of the wise and perfect person, he, [the disciple] will have emerged from the pit of ignorance and reached the degree of knowledge.

That man of perfect intelligence (*ʿāqil-i kāmil*) to whom the ignorant imperfect person should submit himself exemplifies the teaching given by the teacher of the rightly-guided mission (*daʿwat-i hādiya*) – may God ensure its stability – whose understanding and judgement are linked to the truth and the truthful master (*ḥaqq wa muḥiqq*). He [the man of perfect intelligence] is not just any wise or learned savant who does not acknowledge the truthful master of the time (*muḥiqq-i waqt*) and is incapable of transcending the boundaries of his own reason and knowledge which he assumes to be [inspired] wisdom and knowledge. Such an attitude would be total unbelief (*kufr-i maḥḍ*) from which we seek refuge in God. This is because his reason bears but a semblance of reason, being itself unreason and his knowledge [merely of the type of which] it is said, 'Verily, some kinds of knowledge are mere ignorance.[1]

According to the same ontological order, the elements (*arkān*) mix and mingle with one another by virtue of their submission to the rotation of the spheres and the irradiation of the stars. The celestial spheres remain in their natural orbit by virtue of their submission to the Universal Soul. The Universal Soul, in turn, attains perfection by virtue of submission to the First Intellect. The pre-eminence of the

1. A Prophetic tradition cited in Badīʿ al-Zamān Furūzānfar, *Aḥādīth-i mathnawī* (Tehran, 1969), p. 99. Furūzānfar refers to a number of variants of this *ḥadīth*, including *'Inna min al-bayāni la-siḥran.'* See also Arent Jan Wensinck, ed. *al-Muʿjam al-mufahras li-alfāẓ al-ḥadīth al-nabawī* (Leiden, 1943), vol. 1, p. 393.

First Intellect over all other living beings lies in the fact that its submission to the sublime Word (*kalima-yi aʿlā*) is of superior purity and sincerity [than theirs]; its will, knowledge and power is better than that of other creatures due to its avoidance of associating others with the supreme Divine Word.

Since the purpose of the emanative effusion (*ifāḍat*) of the supreme Word upon the First Intellect was to grant it eternal repose (*sukūn*), absolute perfection and true wisdom, the emanative effusion of the Intellect upon the Soul consisted in the fact that the perfection which was in the Soul's power to receive was granted to it. Similarly, the activity of the Soul in Nature consisted in the fact that the forms of things which the Soul had received from the Intellect would be bestowed on Nature. [Likewise], the action of Nature upon matter lay in bringing into the reality of concrete existence the forms bestowed upon it by the Soul. The final purpose of all such emanations was that [the natural kingdoms], beginning with minerals, would combine with the vegetative [realm], and [the vegetative realm combine] with the animal realm, and [the animal realm] be terminated by humankind. Thus, the chain of being completes its circle in man. Therefore, it is in this fashion that submission (*taslīm*), which is the supreme perfection belonging to the [First] Intellect, came to be the singular property of man.

As men are different and varied in their aptitudes, their ways [of self-surrender] may be different. Thus, some have said that when a man submits to the lord of the Divine Command (*ṣāḥib-i amr*), he should be asked: 'Have you done this with full conscious understanding of your submission or blindly?' One may measure his perfection according to the character of his submission (*taslīm*).

Some have said that insight (*baṣīrat*) should precede submission, because any submission without insight is merely imitation (*taqlīd*) and not submission. Others have said that the foundation of the creation of the physical world is set on [the principles of] opposition and gradation (*taḍādd wa tarattub*).[1] [When man lives in the realm of] opposition, there is neither insight nor submission. Therein no benefit can be derived either from knowledge or action, and no result is produced by either personal endeavour (*jahd*) or trust on God (*tawakkul*); everyone who strives to gain religious knowledge (*hama-yi mujtahidān*) falls into error. The reason for this is that [in the realm of opposition], submission is not based on insight, action is not based on knowledge, and religious endeavour is not based on trust in God. In that realm the soul is as if turned upside down (*intikās*) and is 'in layer upon layer of darkness' [24:40]. Its every activity, whether in thought, word, or deed becomes a descent into the pit of Hell until it reaches the most infernal degree. Therefore, whatever the insight or submission one exercises while in the realm of opposition

---

1. The word *taḍādd* (from the Arabic root D-D-D), means to contradict, in the sense of two opposing things where the existence of one implies the non-existence of the other. Elsewhere (e.g. *taṣawwur* 13, no. 118), the word has been translated as 'opposition' or 'discord' where two contrary entities may continue to co-exist in a state of conflict. In early Nizārī Ismaili literature generally, *taḍādd* represents the lowest level of being, subordinate to *tarattub* (gradation) and *waḥdat* (unity), each of which corresponds to a specific state of being and group of people.

is, in reality, neither insight nor submission, but rather the semblance of insight and submission.

In [the realm of] gradation, both insight and submission truly exist. Therein, benefit can be derived from both knowledge and action; results are produced by both righteous endeavour and trust in God, and all those who strive to gain religious knowledge find the truth. The reason is that in this realm submission is based on actual insight, action is based on knowledge, and religious endeavour is based on trust in God. In this realm, the soul stands upright amid the lights of good things and meritorious acts (*anwār-i khayrāt wa ḥasanāt*) in such a way that it faces increase without decrease. Its every activity, whether in thought, word and action, elevates it to an ever more superior degree on up to the supreme and highest degree.

Now, what is signified by insight (*baṣīrat*) is simply that a man becomes conscious of, and awakens to, the need (*iḥtiyāj*) which lies within his imperfect self, and hence [his need for] a master (*mutammim wa mukammil*) who can bring him to perfection. Once he becomes conscious of this, his insight is perfected and he realizes to whom he should submit himself.[1] So when he is given certain prescriptions or prohibitions by such a perfect being who grants perfection, he becomes inwardly enlightened (*mustabṣir*) as far as his aptitude permits him, and he will submit to that which he is unable [to understand].[2]

If one delves into and begins [to study] some scientific problem as a novice and pupil, one's intention and belief should be that, through the intellectual pleasures one derives from this study, one's faith in submitting to a truthful teacher (*muʿallim-i ṣādiq*) will become stronger and purer – not that he should reach a position in knowledge where he knows all that which the true teacher knows. Such [an attitude] would be transgressing the limits of discipleship. We seek refuge from this in God.

To each of these realms of relative existence corresponds a different type of submission. [For instance], in the realm of physical senses (*kawn-i maḥsūs-i jismānī*), which is the first [or lowest] rung or degree of existence, the subject sees all the clearly distinguished realities (*mutabāyināt*) in the shape of obscure illusions or similitudes (*mutashābihāt*), and he is obedient to the lusts of the body, subservient to the dictates of nature, and blindly follows the passions of the soul. Then, on the second rung or degree of existence, which is that of spiritual imagination (*kawn-i mawhūm-i rūḥānī*), the subject has one face turned towards the clearly distinguished realities and another face towards illusions. Here he sometimes inclines towards worldliness and sometimes attends to the affairs of the Hereafter. [Lastly], in the realm of [purely] intelligible existence (*kawn-i mawjūd-i ʿaqlānī*), which is

1. Cf. Naṣīr al-Dīn al-Ṭūsī, *Sayr wa sulūk*, ed. and tr. S. Jalal Badakhchani as *Contemplation and Action: The Spiritual Autobiography of a Muslim Scholar* (London, 1988), p. 45, nos. 42–45.

2. In Shiʿi literature, the word '*mustabṣir*' is often used as a synonym for *mu'min*, 'true believer,' in contrast to those who profess Islam only verbally (*muslim*), in keeping with Qur'an 49:14: 'The desert Arabs say, "We are the faithful (*mu'min*)." Say [to them]: You have no faith, but rather say "we submit".' Thus, in the present context, 'he will submit' (*musallim*) could be read as *muslim*.

the third degree of existence where degrees extend into infinity, the subject beholds all indistinct semblances as clearly distinguished realities. Here, he sees both the master of truth (*muḥiqq*) and the truth (*ḥaqq*) itself resplendent in the aura of divine wisdom, free from vain speculation and satanic fantasies.

The submission of people of the realm of the physical senses is an artificial submission (*taslīm-i taṣannuʿī*) under legal constraints, the submission of the denizens of the realm of the spiritual imagination is voluntary (*ikhtiyārī*), and the submission of people of the realm of intelligible existence is an entirely natural one (*ṭabīʿī*).

Artificial submission made under legal constraints is when someone says something out of financial need, or [out of fear for his] life, or for some other reason, specifically for his own benefit to satisfy his own desire and purpose, but in his heart nothing in fact corresponds to his exterior utterances [i.e., he is not sincere in his submission].

Voluntary submission is, for example, someone who is busy in this world with something, in perfect happiness and serenity, and with no ulterior motive. Suddenly, the command of the truthful teacher (*amr-i muʿallim-i ṣādiq*) reaches him, saying that he should abandon all this and throw himself into the most unbearable hardship and difficulty. At first he resents this and is offended. Eventually however, he overcomes the effects of that resentment and offence, turns back to his faith and the divine mission (*daʿwat-i ḥaqq*), realizing that if he does not do what he says wholeheartedly and with no reluctance or compulsion, he will be existentially lower than the base mineral, that both his religious and worldly life will dissolve away '*like scattered motes*' [25:53], and he will miss the purpose of both this life and the next. Therefore he will at once wholeheartedly, with the purest of intentions and the utmost sincerity, renounce all that was the source of his [worldly] comfort, choosing to abide by his teacher's will rather than follow his own preference.

Natural submission is not within the reach of every pupil. It is reserved specifically for the *ḥujjat*s and the truthful imams (*imāmān-i ḥaqq*) – may salutations ensue upon mention of them – because their visions are enlightened by the light of primordial conscience (*fiṭrat*) which shines especially upon them from the horizon of divine assistance (*ta'yīd*). Things are to be seen there that few hearts can withstand.

As our lord Zayn al-ʿĀbidīn – may salutations ensue upon mention of him – said:

O God, You created us from frailty, built us up from feebleness, and began us from '*mean water*' [77:20]. We have no strength except through Your power and no power except through Your help. Help us to succeed, guide us the right way, blind the eye of our hearts towards everything opposed to Your love, and set not in any of our limbs passage to disobeying you.[1]

1. From ʿAlī b. al-Ḥusayn Zayn al-ʿĀbidīn, *al-Ṣaḥīfa al-kāmila al-Sajjādiyya*, ed. Fayḍ al-Islām (Tehran, 1955), prayer 9, verses 5–7, p. 87; tr. W. Chittick as *The Psalms of Islam* (London, 1988), p. 41.

ON PROPHETHOOD AND IMAMATE, WHERE WITH RESPECT TO PROPHETHOOD ARE DISCUSSED MIRACLES, PSEUDO-PROPHETS AND THE POSSESSED, AND WITH RESPECT TO THE IMAMATE ARE DISCUSSED PUPILS, TEACHERS AND THE *ḤUJJATS*.

Since the creation of this world is based on opposition and gradation (*taḍādd wa tarattub*), and human beings are also [acting on the basis] of opposition and gradation; and since there exists [in the realm of] opposition a privation of spiritual aptitude; and in the realm of gradation the perfection of aptitude: human souls are therefore varied and differ with respect to their receptivity to the resplendent lights of the Divine Command (*anwār-i ishrāq-i amr-i ilāhī*), just as material objects are variously and differently receptive to the physical light of the sun. [Consider] stones, for example: one [kind] is pitch black, while others are progressively less dark, and their essences are more receptive to illumination, up to translucent glass which receives light from one side and emits it from the other.

In so far as human beings are unable to be receptive to His Almighty Command without mediation, it was necessary that there should be intermediaries vis-à-vis the Divine Command. Those people whose consciousness (*khāṭir*) behaved as does a [translucent] glass held up to the sun were the prophets.

The prophets were necessary (*bāyistand*), in the first instance, because men initially acquire [knowledge through] names (*asmā'*) before they can attain to their meanings; they first need to set foot on the road in order to reach the destination. Consequently, two rules (*ḥukm*) have been laid down: one is that of the religious law and this [lower] world (*sharīʿat wa dunyā*), which concerns man in relation to other men and whose rulers are the prophets – peace be upon all of them; the other rule is that of the Resurrection and the Hereafter (*qiyāmat wa ākhirat*), which concerns God in relation to God, and whose rulers are the truthful imams (*imāmān-i ḥaqq*) – may salutations ensue upon mention of them – those who 'raise up' the Resurrection (*qā'imān-i qiyāmat*).

Now, the age of religious law (*zamān-i sharīʿat*) is a time in which worship (*ʿibādat*) is ordained at specific times, when the practice of external physical behaviour is dictated (*daʿwat bā ẓāhir-i aʿmāl-i jismānī*), and when all acts of worship are completely absorbed in their specific temporal moments. [This age] is called the cycle of concealment (*dawr-i satr*), being particularly characteristic of the prophets – peace be upon them.

[On the other hand], the age of Resurrection (*zamān-i qiyāmat*) [is] when specific times of worship are abrogated, when people are summoned unto God for His own sake, and when all the moments [of life] are completely absorbed in the practice of devotion. [This age] is called the cycle of manifestation (*dawr-i kashf*), which is specifically characteristic of the imam – may salutations ensue upon mention of him.

The Prophet – peace be upon him – appears at the beginning of the cycle of origin (*dawr-i mabda'*). He encompasses it so that through him the lights of the Almighty's Command (*anwār-i amr-i ū taʿālā*), in the form of acts of obedience and worship, collectively prescribed to the generality of humankind, may reach them. As the majority of people in the world are, in the first instance, veiled from accepting and responding to the Divine Command in good faith, and can only perceive what is connected with the senses, fanciful estimation and imagination, the divine providence has decreed that these divine lights – which are absolute intelligible realities (*maʿqulāt-i muṭlaq*) and pure divine graces (*taʾyīdāt-i maḥḍ*) – should become apprehended through the prophets, their family and offspring, and by the senses, estimation and imagination, according to the principle that revelation is [given in proportion to] the degree corresponding to that stage (*al-tanzīl manzilatun mim-tilka al-daraja*). Human beings accepted these things as a result of [their] affinity to the senses, estimation and imagination, and applied themselves to them. These precepts and rules were ordained to control particular realities with the implication of their being consistent with universal realities. For example, the well-being of ordinary people in this world was achieved by [their] adherence to these prescriptions and prohibitions, while the souls of the elect within the community (*millat*) became capable of acquiring [spiritual] perfection by such ways and means, thus [enabling them to] progress from religious practices (*ʿamaliyyāt*) to religious knowledges (*ʿilmiyyāt*), and from that on to purely intelligible realities (*ʿaqliyyāt*).

The imam – may salutations ensue upon mention of him – is situated at the commencement of the cycle of perfection (*dawr-i kamāl*),[1] encompassing both the origin and the perfect fulfilment. The lights of the divine creative volition (*anwār-i amr-i ibdāʿī*), by his command, shine upon those souls who harbour an aptitude to apprehend the perfection of the Divine Command, taking the form of distinctive and true gnosis (*maʿrifat*), love (*maḥabbat*), obedience and devotion. And by the grace of the imam – may salutations ensue upon mention of him and his family and offspring – in accordance with [the saying], 'Spiritual exegesis (*taʾwīl*) is the restoration of things to their origin (*al-taʾwīl radd al-shayʾ ilā awwalihi*)'[2] – these sensible, estimative and imaginal realities become one and the same with the absolute intelligible realities and sheer divine supports (*taʾyīdāt-i maḥḍ*). Say, 'Praise be to God for this, the praise of the thankful.'

However, regarding prophethood, should anyone deny it and claim it to be unnecessary, it may be said to him that man's actions can only be of three types: either all actions are permissible, or all actions are impermissible, or some actions are permissible and some are not. If he says all actions are permissible, he can be killed at once in accordance with his own pronouncement. If he says none are permissible, he should die immediately in accordance with his own pronouncement. However, if he wants neither to be killed nor to die, he must accept that some of these actions are permissible and others not. Now, when the question of legally

1. The *dawr-i kamāl* refers to *zamān-i qiyāmat*, the age of Resurrection.

2. A statement of the classical Ismaili definition of *taʾwīl* as found, for example, in Nāṣir-i Khusraw, *Wajh-i dīn*, ed. Maḥmūd Ghanīzāda and M. Qazvīnī (Berlin, 1924), pp. 51–61. Manuscript 'M' reads, '*al-taʾwīl zāda unsī ilā Allāh*,' meaning '*Taʾwīl* adds to my intimacy with God,' which corresponds more closely to al-Ṭūsī's definition of *tanzīl* above.

permissible and legally forbidden acts is raised, there arises the need for laws and regulations (*ḥudūd wa aḥkām*), which are called the religious law (*sharīʿat*), and such a law requires a founder (*wāḍiʿ*).

Here, he should be asked whether just anyone, whoever he may be, can be the founder [of that law], or nobody can, or some can and others cannot. If he responds to the first two of these questions, the same [rules] as above will apply. Therefore, it will be necessary for him to admit that some can become the founders [of religious law] and some cannot.

Again, he should be asked whether the founder must be appointed by God, [and] assisted and invested with this mission by divine decree, or whether he can be elected by mutual consensus of the community (*ijmāʿ*). If he says that he can be elected by consensus, then if one group obeys him, another group will oppose him, and so the controversy will never be resolved. It follows, therefore, that the founder must be appointed by Almighty God, and must be unique in his claim and mission (*daʿwat*). This is one method of proving the necessity of prophethood.

Another method is as follows: For the sake of their own welfare, the human species in its social life needs the good (*ṣalāḥ*), which is called religion and law (*millat wa sharīʿat*). Here there are two things in view: prevention (*tamānuʿ*) and mutual cooperation (*taʿāwun*). By 'prevention' is meant that a man should be able to retain possession of his property, and by 'co-operation' is meant that individuals cannot procure the welfare of their own interests in isolation [of others]. In all his crafts and business transactions, without which he cannot survive, man cannot do without the assistance of other members of his species in order to acquire what he does not have. Prevention and mutual co-operation must have their prescribed limits and regulations, but nobody can arbitrarily by himself lay down such limits and regulations, because if he did the same conflict as was mentioned above would arise. Therefore, the founder [of these regulations] must be that person whom God has appointed as the executor of His Command (*walī-yi amr*), obedience to whom He has [directly] linked to obedience to Himself: '*Whoever obeys the Prophet obeys God*' [4:80]. This has been another method of establishing the validity of Prophecy.

Further, one may be asked whether the human intellects are all merely potential (*bi-quwwat*) or actual (*bi-fiʿl*). If one responds that all human intellects are all merely potential, it would follow that none of the world's inhabitants are knowing, and that all are deficient and ignorant; and if one were to say that all [human intellects] are actual, it would follow that none of the world's inhabitants are ignorant, and that all are perfect and knowing. The inevitable conclusion is that some intellects are potential and some are actual, and that persons with potential intellects need those whose intellects are actual in order that the latter may actualize the potential intellects of the former.

Moreover, God Almighty has given excellence to certain creatures over others, giving each thing within its own kind a specific limit (*nihāyat*). For example, he made the plant the limit of minerals, the animal the limit of plants, and man the limit of the animal condition. [Similarly], He made the prophetic faculty (*quwwat-i nabawī*) the limit of mankind. In the same way as the creation of these natural kingdoms reached their fulfilment in man who is capable of speech, the creation of man reached its limit or fulfilment in the law-giving (*ṣāḥib-i sharʿ*) Prophet.

The sublime Word (*kalima-yi aʿlā*), the First Intellect (*ʿaql-i awwal*), and the Universal Soul (*nafs-i kullī*), each have a manifestation (*maẓhar*) in this world.[1] The manifestation of the sublime Word is the imam – may salutations ensue upon mention of him – [whose reality] is beyond all human thought and imagination, and above all description, whether it be positive or negative. The manifestation of the First Intellect is the supreme *ḥujjat* (proof) of the imam, who gives perfection its form. The manifestation of the Universal Soul is the Prophet who vouchsafes the souls of men the aptitude to receive, during the initial period (*dawr-i mabdaʾ*) [of religious law], that form which constitutes their ultimate perfection.

When, by the decree of God Almighty, the date and the time arrives that a [new] law-giver should arise and the affairs of the material world should change, and that the religion (*millat*), government, temperaments, languages, ethics, customs and mutual relations of people are on the verge of changing from one kind to another, the celestial figures (*ashkāl-i falakī*) are configured in such a way that a person of prophetic nature (*shakhṣ-i nabawī*) – who is a manifestation (*maẓhar*) of the Universal Soul, both capable of receiving divine inspiration and the bearer of the trust of divine revelation – appears. Due to the harmonious relation and the sensible connection which is formed between him and the community, and reciprocally between the community and him, a sense of exchange in performance and exercise of duties is established between them. He is both a student and a teacher: a student, because he receives his knowledge through revelation (*waḥy*) and inspiration (*ilhām*) from spiritual beings (*rūḥāniyyāt*) and angels; a teacher, because he transmits that knowledge to his community in proportion to that which their minds are capable of understanding.

The reception of revelation and inspiration [by a Prophet] from the transcendental realm (*malaʾ-i aʿlā*) and the supreme angelic dominion (*malakūt-i aʿẓam*) is analogous to the visions we receive in dreams, except that he sees these while he is awake by the swift projection of one thing upon another (*ilqāʾ al-shayʾ ilā al-shayʾ bi-al-surʿa*), meaning that [these things] flash from the Universal Soul, which is the Preserved Tablet (*lawḥ-i maḥfūẓ*), upon his holy soul.[2] It is in this sense that he [the Prophet] says, '*I am a man like you*' [41:6], since he cannot be free from attachment

1. The concept of *maẓhar* (translated in the text as 'locus,' 'manifestation' or 'epiphany') constitutes one of the key features of Nizārī Ismaili thought. Based on the principle of correspondence between the spiritual and material worlds, it defines the imam in his spiritual essence as the *maẓhar* of the Word (*kalima*) or Command (*amr*) of God. The locus is not the imam's physical body which is mortal and changeable, but his inner, spiritual reality which is regarded as eternal and immutable. Al-Ṭūsī comments on this subject further in *taṣawwur* 27, nos. 516–517. See also Henry Corbin, *Cyclical Time and Ismaili Gnosis*, tr. Ralph Manheim and James W. Morris (London, 1983), pp. 103–117.

2. The Pen (*qalam*) and the Preserved Tablet (*lawḥ-i maḥfūẓ*) are Qurʾanic terms (68:1; 85:22), signifying a state of transcendental eternality. Subject to diverse interpretations by commentators, the two terms occur frequently in Ismaili cosmological thought, where they symbolise the Universal Intellect and Soul respectively. This is also the sense conveyed by al-Ṭūsī here, as suggested further in *taṣawwur* 24, no. 332.

to, and consubstantiality and participation with, others, nor from anything connected with their physical affairs. His special distinction is '*It is revealed to me*' [41:6], and since '*It is revealed to me*' cannot be disengaged from '*I am a man like you*,' the descent of revelation and divine inspiration cannot take place in isolation from, and without interference of the imagination (*muʿāriḍa-yi khayāl*). Such interference should be imagined as a fine, transparently clear veil which becomes coarser as it develops, till it reaches the pinnacle of coarseness.

Everyone whose soul has been illuminated by the light of spiritual truths (*nūr-i ḥaqāyiq*) and who has become acquainted with the explanations of the people of spiritual exegesis (*ahl-i taʾwīl*) will see all these things clearly when he reads the Qurʾan. For example, he may find verses in which the exoteric revelation (*tanzīl*) and the esoteric exegesis (*taʾwīl*) are identical, as for example this verse: '*The earth will shine with the Light of its Lord*' [36:69]. [On the other hand], he will also find verses like '*By the [steeds] that run with panting breath*' [100:1], in which there is an immense distance between the [exoteric] revelation and its esoteric exegesis.

Now, the revelation and its spiritual exegesis are analogous to a dream and its interpretation (*taʿbīr*) which a man apprehends when he wakes up. For instance, when he is sound asleep within the walls of his room, his senses at rest, his soul is so entirely absorbed [in the dream] that past, future and present all merge into one in what he dreams. He sees things at that time in his dream which happened a thousand or ten thousand years ago. Clearly he sees this with the sight of the soul (*naẓar-i nafs*) and not with the sight of the eyes. The interpretation of his [dream] depends on how great or small the interference of imagination has been and is according to the strength or weakness of his soul. If the imagination has not interfered, the dream will be true and there will be no need for an interpreter to explain it. But if the imagination has interfered and the dream has become altered by similitudes and mixed with confused reveries and unreal fantasies, an interpreter will be required to explain it. However, if the power of the soul has been strong enough to resist and overcome the imagination and its prattling interference, the interpreter will not need to exert much effort and will be able to penetrate its mystery easily and quickly. In the contrary situation, however, it will be hard and difficult to such a degree that he will be unable to deal effectively with the imagination and uncover the secret [meaning] of the dream. The Prophet's reception of inspiration and the descent of the literal revelation, accompanied by its spiritual exegesis [in the form of] glad tidings (*bishārāt*) or stern admonitions (*indhārāt*), is exactly of this type [of imaginal activity].

The position of the founder of a religious law vis-à-vis his community is like a king who looks about and sees a great many people [before him], some of whom are mad and some of whom are sane, but he puts all of them alike in chains and fetters. Alternatively, he may be compared to a physician who looks about himself and sees innumerable invalids with different diseases as well as a great number of healthy people, yet he prescribes the same drink and the same kind of food and diet for each one of them. Albeit, the king's intention is that madness should depart from the lunatics, and the physician's intention is only just to cure the sick, which is something the healthy do not need. However, if he did not enforce uniform rules on everyone, the principle of his preaching (*da'wat*) and his religion would never become properly arranged, firmly established and securely rooted. You may call the person [who does this] a prophet (*payambar*), the founder of a religion (*wāḍiʿ-i millat*), the giver of a religious law (*ṣāḥib-i sharīʿat*), the Trusted Spirit (*rūḥ al-amīn*), or a manifestation (*maẓhar*) of the Universal Soul, for all these terms have the same meaning.

Let us now discuss the miracle (*muʿjizāt*). Common people have said a lot of things concerning the miracles of prophets, most of which is related [to the realm of] the supernatural (*kharq-i ʿādāt*, lit. 'the breaking of habits'). When someone wants to have rational proofs for their existence, they say that thinking about them is wrong, and that it is useless to try to find the meaning and reality of them. What the adepts of truth (*ahl-i ḥaqq*) say regarding the significance of miracles is that since the prophets – may the peace of God be upon all of them – act as the intermediary link (*wāsiṭa*) between the Divine Command (*amr*) and creation (*khalq*), due to that position (*mathābat*) each manifests a trace of the Divine Light (*anwār-i rubūbiyyat*) according to his innate aptitude and capacity. Thus, it is nothing extraordinary if they are graced by the emanation of divine matter (*mawādd-i ilāhī*) and assisted by spiritual forces (*rūḥāniyyāt*) in order to govern the affairs of the physical realm. Thus, each one of them is specially vouchsafed miracles or marvels as has been narrated regarding the miracles of each Prophet. However, they add, one should not rest with only this outer appearance (*ẓāhir*) but should seek out the spiritual realities (*ḥaqāyiq*) of each [miracle], for appearances correspond to flesh and realities to the spirit.

Concerning miracles and the thaumaturgic powers (*karāmāt*) of the prophets, they [the adepts of truth] also state that, from the point of view of the domain of genus (*ḥayyiz-i jins*), the prophets share with other men – in accordance with '*I am a man like you*' [41:6] – everything that belongs to the physical creation and bodily composition, appearance and form, food, drink, apparel and marriage. However, from the point of view of the domain of differentia (*ḥayyiz-i faṣl*) – in accordance with '*Nor does he speak of his own desire; it is just a revelation sent down to him*' [53:3–4] – the prophets differ from others.

The true miracle is the miracle of knowledge and rational proof (*ʿilm wa ḥujjat*), not the one of action and power. When someone dominates the whole world through power [and brute force], it is possible for a wolf or a lion to overpower him, yet one cannot say that the wolf or lion is superior to him. But in so far as knowledge is concerned, it is possible for someone to furnish an intellectual proof whereby the lips of all rational people in the world are sealed, being rendered incapable of defeating him through argument, unable to utter a single word by way of rebuttal.

In this world, there are both miracles and pseudo-miracles (*shibh-i muʿjiz*), that is to say, sorcery and talismans. Both look alike in the realm of similitudes, yet it is improper to confound the two. One must clearly distinguish between them and the distinction must be made by means of knowledge and intellectual proof, rather than by power and brute force, since the medium of resemblance (*mā bihi al-mushābaha*) must be different from the medium of differentiation (*mā bihi al-mubāyana*). In other words, the medium by which two things resemble each other cannot be the medium of their distinction. Thus, for example, if a resemblance is made [between two things] by means of audition, then the distinction should be made by means of vision; or if a resemblance is made by sensory means, then the distinction should be made by intellectual means. By the same measure, if resemblance pertains to action and force, then the distinction should be by means of knowledge and intellectual proof (*ʿilm wa ḥujjat*).

Therefore such types of miraculous power evaporate here. Undoubtedly, one has to accept that [the sort of prophetic] miracles [discussed here] are a kind of ability or power of which others are incapable. But as long as one does not comprehend the furthest limit of humankind's powers and abilities, how can one know what powers and forces exceed it? Therefore, if someone seeks to know a prophet through the miracles he performs, he should first truly ascertain the limits of each human individual's abilities and powers, and apprehend what constitutes pseudo-miracles such as sorcery, talismans and similar things. Once his knowledge encompasses this, he will be able to apprehend which force and power is superhuman, and which can thus be understood to be a miracle. And it is obvious that this [understanding] is beyond the power of any man, and if it be within someone's power, what need would he have for a prophet? Thus, it is only a prophet who can distinguish [the real] miracle from the pseudo-miracle, and that person who demands a miracle from a person who makes a claim to prophethood is setting up his own reason (*ʿaql*) as the measure, thus weighing himself against the divinity of God and the prophethood of the prophet. Hence, when he comes to have faith in the prophet through a miracle, he is putting his faith in his own intellect and not him. Godspeed to you.

On pseudo-prophets (*mutanabbiyān*). The situation of pseudo-prophets is as follows: When the time is right for a prophet endowed with revelation (*ṣāḥib-i waḥy*) to come into existence, certain heavenly constellations which favour his appearance are configured in harmonious combinations. Although their initial purpose was just to bestow existence on that one individual [prophet], yet at the same moment certain illuminations and effects produced by the movements, constellations and irradiation of stars may come to bear an astrological influence on the horoscope (*ṭāliʿ*) of another person with a horoscope similar to that of the prophet. This astrological influence accordingly affects the natural constitution, physical nature, personality and soul of that other person. However, the [astrological] influence is weak, because, were it strong, all of them would be prophets, or close to the rank of a prophet, and in that case none of the prophets would have succeeded in his prophetic mission. Thus, in proportion to the amount of astrological influence which affects their horoscope, they claim prophethood. But, ultimately their imposture is revealed and recognized by the grace of the will and power of God, which is connected to the prophetic mission of the [true] prophet, so that they are overpowered and humiliated, by the divine favour and bounty of the Almighty's assistance.

(Translated by S. J. Badakhchani)

III

INITIATION, KNOWLEDGE AND MEANING

1

Jaʿfar b. Manṣūr al-Yaman

Abu'l-Qāsim Jaʿfar b. Manṣūr al-Yaman (d. ca. 346/957) was an Ismaili author and *dāʿī* who migrated to the territories of the second Fatimid Imam-Caliph al-Qā'im (r. 322–334/934–946) in Ifrīqiya, now in Tunisia. The *Kitāb al-ʿālim wa'l-ghulām* was probably written before the establishment of the Fatimid caliphate, while the author was still in Yaman. It is a timeless story which presents encounters between seekers of spiritual truth and their guides. Written in a dramatic dialogue form, interwoven with innumerable quotations and references to the Qur'an, it draws the reader to explore complex issues of ethics, faith and metaphysics using the perspective of a range of protagonists from the young seeker to the Knower. The first extract is a moving account of the initiation of a young seeker at the hands of a master who guides him gently through his struggles to find faith and then sends him on his way to spread the message. In the second passage, a religious dignitary, Abū Mālik, discusses the nature of true knowledge and how it might be achieved with a young man named Ṣāliḥ.

Kitāb al-ʿālim wa'l-ghulām
Book of the Master and the Disciple[1]

INITIATION OF THE DISCIPLE BY THE MASTER

[The anonymous narrator continued:] Then they all sat together and talked among themselves late into the night. And when they got up in the morning, they asked permission to see the Shaykh. Now when they entered his room and had finished greeting him, the Shaykh asked them to sit down, and they did so. Then the Shaykh began his speech: 'Praise be to God *Who split* [21:30] with *His light* the dark obscurity of (people's) hearts and Who opened with His justice the locked chambers of what (their hearts) have sought; Who *makes remembrance easy* [54:17, etc.] through *His fashioning (of everything)* [27:88], as a subtle grace for His servants and a loving mercy from Him for all those who are longing for Him. The creatures cannot bear the essence of what He deserves (for all His blessings), yet *He is not pleased for them to be ungrateful* [39:7] for His blessings, so He, in His justice, *imposed upon them* (as their obligation only) *what they were not unable to bear* [2:286, etc.] Thus his

1. Jaʿfar b. Manṣūr al-Yaman, *Kitāb al-ʿālim wa'l-ghulām*, ed. and tr. James W. Morris as *The Master and the Disciple: An Early Islamic Spiritual Dialogue* (London, 2001), pp. 116–122, 138–144.

command was harmoniously balanced between those two points,[1] so that it was called "Justice."

'And out of His bounty, He has given abundantly of His favours, giving (all things) good and beauty, excellence and abundance. Thus no one who prays (to Him) is left disappointed, but neither is the silent person excluded (from His bounty). On the contrary, *His blessings are all-abounding* [31:20] and His favours are marvellous: they are not limited to those who are thankful to them – though (the grateful person's) reward is overwhelming; nor are they removed from those who are ungrateful for them – although their eventual torment is immense! For He has ennobled His blessings above any sort of stinginess, and He has firmly established His arguments beyond any possibility of denial. He has extended *His all-inclusiveness* [4:126] beyond ever being found (in any delimited form), yet He has (so many) signs that He cannot possibly be denied. So He can be found (everywhere), but not delimited; and He can be recognized (in every form), but not described (fully by any of them).

'Praise be to Him Who is so immense – but how subtle He is in His creation! Who is all-powerful – but how merciful and loving He is with His creatures! Who is solitary and supreme – but how just He is in His wise-judgement! Who is infinitely exalted – but *How close He is to humankind* [50:16]! Who is so near – but how infinitely removed He is from (people's) imagining! So worship and serve Him, and be thankful to Him, for *to Him you are all returning* [29:17].'

Then he said: 'As for what comes next, among the marks of honour of (people's) intellects is their use in the seeking (of God), and among the fruits of seeking is finding (Him), and among the distinctive signs of having found (Him) is the sweetness of what is found. For every *fresh, sweet water* [25:53; 35:12] has its outward aspect which can be drunk, and its inner dimension which is hidden. The one who is (truly) seeking it never tires of thinking, and the creatures cannot grasp its ultimate ends; its distinctive signs are true and the duties flowing from the truth are obligatory. That is why it is called 'truth' (*ḥaqq*), because of the necessary verification and realization of its obligatory nature. Therefore, whoever prevents (people) from carrying out the obligations of the truth is unjust. For surely among the obligations (*ḥaqq*) flowing from thinking is the preparatory purification of (our) hearts through the proper modes of behaviour (*ādāb*);[2] and among the obligations of that proper behaviour is the seeking of (spiritual) knowledge (*ṭalab al-ʿilm*); and among the obligations of that knowledge is acting

1. The Arabic here echoes the famous phrase of the Imam Jaʿfar al-Ṣādiq referring to the proper understanding of the subtle balance between divine determination and human freedom and responsibility: 'It is a point between those two points, neither (total divine) determination nor (total) delegation (of freedom to human beings).' See Abū Ḥātim al-Rāzī, *Kitāb aʿlām al-nubuwwa*, ed. Ṣ. al-Ṣāwī and G. R. Aʿwānī (Tehran, 1977), pp. 41–42.

2. *Ādāb* refers here at first to the socially maintained standards and forms of right behaviour, prior to the deeper realization of their true spiritual roots and goals as a result of spiritual awareness or 'knowledge' (*ʿilm*) and the corresponding 'right action' (*ʿamal*) which presupposes that heightened, ongoing spiritual insight. *Ādāb*, in its social and spiritual senses, is one of the central themes of this dialogue.

in accordance with it; and among the obligations of right action in accordance with that knowledge is its purifying it through willing obedience to the *masters of (true) authority* (*ulu'l-'amr*) [4:59]; and among the obligations of that willing obedience is its perfection *both in what is easy and in what is difficult* [94:5–6], (being *tested*) alike in *what is good and in trials and temptations* [21:35]. *So it shall only be granted to those who persevere, and it shall only be granted to the person who has immense good fortune* [41:35].'

[The narrator continued:] Then he turned his gaze toward the young man and said: 'O *brave youth* (*fatā*), you have been honoured by a newly arriving intimate friend, and you have been greeted by a visitor seeking (a soul like yours), so what is your name?'

'*Ubayd Allāh* ('the little servant of God'), son of the servant of God,'[1] he answered.

'That is your description,' replied the Shaykh, 'but we have already been informed about you.'

'I am *Ḥurr* ('freed-man'), son of the servant of God,' the young man replied.

'Then who set you free from being owned, so that you became free?' inquired the Shaykh.

'This Knower set me free,' said the young man, pointing with his hand toward the Knower who had called him (to the way).

'But do you think,' continued the Shaykh, 'that if he is also owned and not your owner, does he have any right to set you free?'

'No, he doesn't,' replied the young man.

'Then what is your name?' repeated the Shaykh.

[The narrator] continued: Then the young man hung his head, bewildered and unable to respond.

'O *brave youth*,' pursued the Shaykh, 'how can we recognize something that has no name, even if it has been born?'

'I have been born to you,'[2] replied the young man, 'so you name me!'

'That is only after the fulfilment of seven days (of waiting),'[3] the Shaykh responded.

'But why must that be postponed until after seven more days?' asked the young man.

'In honour of the new-born infant,' replied the Shaykh.

1. Here the young man begins by punning on the name of his teacher, the Knower of the first half of the dialogue, who had introduced himself initially as 'Abd Allāh. 'Ubayd Allāh is the diminutive form of the same name.

2. This and a number of subsequent passages on the theme of spiritual 'paternity' recall the famous *ḥadīth*: '*I am only like a father* (wālid) *to his son: I am teaching you all...*,' which is found in the collections of Ibn Māja, Nisā'ī, Abū Dā'ūd and Ibn Ḥanbal. See A. J. Wensinck, *Concordance et Indices de la Traditions Musulmane* (Leiden, 1992), vol. 2, p. 131.

3. Here the Shaykh refers explicitly to the parallel of this initiatic ritual with the usual Islamic social custom of waiting seven days before the name-giving celebration for a new-born infant; the language used below also echoes the Qur'anic references to the 'seven days' of creation.

'But what if the new-born should die before the seven days are finished?' the young man continued.

'Nothing will harm him,' replied the Shaykh, 'and after that he will be named.'

'Then will this name by which you'll have named me be my own?' asked the young man.

'In that case *you* would be what is worshipped,' replied the Shaykh.

'But then how should we speak of it?' asked the young man.

'The Name is your owner,' the Shaykh answered, 'and you are owned by it. For you cannot penetrate further than your own (spiritual) rank. Now depart until your period of waiting (is over).'

[The narrator] continued: Then the young man got up quickly, eager to obey, nor did he say anything back, because of his grasp of proper behaviour. So he left, and his spiritual father left with him, until they both returned to their residence.

There the master of the inn greeted the two of them, and he said: 'What is the state of this brother of ours in regard to his need?'

'A promise has been made,' the Knower answered, 'and the one to whom it was given is thirsty, but the appointed time is near.'

[The narrator] continued: So the two of them remained there until the seventh day. Then they asked for permission to see the Shaykh, and when he gave them permission he ordered the young man to perform a complete ablution and to dress in his *finest clothing* [74:4]. So when the young man set about those preparations, his heart was joyful that his need would be fulfilled on that very day, and that this preparation which he had been ordered to undertake was a sign pointing to the good that would come to him subsequently. Therefore when he had completed what he had been ordered to do and the two of them left together, the young man was saying to himself 'What a lucky day, and what an auspicious friend/master (*walī*)!'; and he kept on repeating that many times. Now the only thing that brought him to that state was the abundance of his joy and the intensity of his longing for that knowledge which would bring him closer to (attaining) God's satisfaction.

So when the two of them entered the Shaykh's (room), *they both found him* [18:65] already preparing for the ceremony. Then he greeted them both with blessings of peace, and they returned his greetings.

Next (the Shaykh) ordered the young man to come close to him, *so he approached* and came nearer. Then (the Shaykh) came even closer and began to speak of *what cannot be comprehended by* [18:68] imagination, what pens cannot express, and '*what has not occurred to the heart of any mere mortal* (*bashar*).' This is among those things which must not be mentioned in the schools of sermons and should not be openly expressed in the contents of books, because of its tremendous worth – for it is only unveiled to those who are worthy of it.

Now, when (the Shaykh) had fulfilled his duty and had led (the young man) out of wandering in the wilderness to the end of his guidance, then his way (*madhhab*) became pure, his drinking-place became *sweet*,[1] and '*he came to know his Lord*.' Then *his consecration was accomplished*, through *glorifying what God made sacred* [22:30]. He *held firmly to the solid connection* [with God] [3:103], *circled around the age-old House* [22:29], *fulfilled his devotions through remembrance* (of God) [2:200], and *completed his pilgrimage* [2:196] with *(God's) greatest sign* [53:18; 79:20].

After that, the young man and his spiritual father[2] continued to visit the Shaykh frequently in order to study what he had bestowed. He was always patient with their company, never becoming tired of their questioning, because of his nobility of character, nor ever becoming weary of replying, because of his agreeable nature. So the two of them continued in that state *for a certain period of time* [76:1], until (the Shaykh) knew that (the young man's) *roots* had been well watered and that *his branches had grown tall* [14:24].

Then (the young man) said to the Shaykh, thanking God and him: 'Praise be to God, Who made you worthy of this station, Who then brought religion to life and destroyed ignorance through you, Who *made* you *a refuge and a sanctuary for the people* [2:125]! For you are the gateway for the people *of heaven* [7:40, 15:14] and *the ascending pathway* for the people of the earth [32:5, etc.]. From the light of your glory appear the lights (of right guidance), and from *the abundant rains* [78:14] of your palms flow *the rivers* (of God's grace and blessings) [2:25, etc.]. May you continue thus so that the One Who was pleased with you may gratify you!'

'As for you,' said the Shaykh, 'may God bless you in all that He has bestowed upon you, and may He help grant you success in preserving what He has given you. And may He use you properly to (accomplish) His will and may He make the way easy for you through the light of His right guidance. May *He open up* your *heart* [39:22; 94:1] with the keys of wisdom, and may He ennoble your affair through the path of the (Ismaili) "call" (*al-daʿwa*),[3] and perfect your rank and worthiness by the sincere signs of (proper) responding (to that call). And may He help you to reach in your obedience to Him the most excellent and deserving degree of your *hopes for His satisfaction* [4:114, etc.].

'Now I am bidding you farewell, O my son, and giving you leave to depart. Being separated from you is hard for me, but three things make that necessary for us. First, we are about to travel to another country. Secondly, the great length of this time you have been separated from your family, despite the hardship (for you) in having to

1. In earlier sections of this dialogue, the sweet water of a famous Qur'anic image (25:53) was shown to be a symbol of knowledge of the inner, spiritual dimension (*ʿilm al-bāṭin*), in contrast to the *salty water* of exoteric learning. The Knower stresses there the *two* essential facets of this spiritual knowledge: both its outward aspect 'carried by the *dāʿīs*,' and its inner, 'sealed' spiritual aspect 'flowing down from heaven.' The term *mashrab* (source of water or drinking place), like *madhhab*, often refers specifically to a particular religious school or approach.

2. That is, the Knower of the first half of the dialogue. As already noted several times, the author always uses this specific Arabic term (*wālid*, 'progenitor') to refer to each character's *spiritual* parent, as distinguished from his biological father.

3. The related term *al-daʿwa* is clearly used here in a technical sense to refer to the outward forms of the Ismaili movement.

leave without your (physical) father's permission. For in that is a terrible pain and great sorrow (for him) that can only be removed by your coming back, although I do have hopes for your father (to enter this path) if you are clever and gentle with him. And the third thing is your obligation to pass on what is rightfully required by this (divine) favour which has reached you: for what is obligatory for you is to worship and serve in accordance with it and to call (others) to it.'

'Leaving you is sad for me and not having you there is a great loss for me,' replied the young man, 'but seeking your advice is the better path, obeying you is more obligatory, and (asking) your judgement is more correct. So do give me some parting advice concerning what you judge to be right, and then send me away if you will. And please let my (spiritual) father travel with me to my country, so that I can rely upon him in my work and can look to him for support in all my affairs.'

'I shall do that,' said the Shaykh. 'Now I advise you to be mindful of God *Who created you*, to *uphold* your *trust* [33:72] which you have taken upon yourself, and to safeguard and sustain your (spiritual) father, who *has raised you when you were small* [17:24] and who has worked so hard and long on your behalf, with yourself and with your possessions. So do not dress him up in the garments of pride and do not drag him into situations that would destroy him. Do not allude to him by name and don't try to mention him in your conversation, nor should you visit him in your city, although at the beginning you may have some flexibility (in that regard).'

The young man responded: 'May God reward you with good from an abundant source of blessings, for every thankful person. And may *the Bountiful One* [40:3] compensate you on behalf of those whom you watch over, since their efforts and favours cannot possibly do so. Now I shall observe your parting advice, and please do not stop my share in the blessing of your prayers!'

[The narrator continued:] Then the two of them got up and shook hands with (the Shaykh) and embraced him, while he said goodbye to each of them. Unable to keep himself from crying, he could only speak with gestures. After that the two of them departed, and they travelled until they came near to the young man's city where his father lived.

Then the Knower said to the young man: 'O my son, you already know the Shaykh's parting advice and you can only be rightly guided by his words. Here is your city whose outskirts we have reached, so sit down with us for a moment away from the road. For I want to mention to you some instructions and give you some final advice about how you should act.'

CONVERSATION BETWEEN ṢĀLIḤ AND ABŪ MĀLIK

[The narrator continued:] Then he passed his hand over his face and made the sitting-room ready for them and he ordered his father to present them (to him). Now when they had all come in with him and had greeted him and were seated, *he had* Abū Mālik *come close to him* [12:69, 99] and drew him near to him. And the first thing of which Ṣāliḥ spoke (to Abū Mālik) was that,

He said: 'O Abū Mālik, you have visited us most generously and out of your nobility *you have preceded us to the good* [35:32], for it is I who should have come to visit you, out of respect for your friendship and because of all the obligations to you which I have accumulated in the past.'

'But when has (your) generosity ever stopped, O source of good?' Abū Mālik replied. 'You were lenient and understanding toward us even when you were little, and you have always been generous toward us once you grew up. And (now) you have begun *to call us toward the good* and have become a warner (*nadhīr*) (of God's accustomed ways)[1] [5:19, etc.]. So may your root be nourished, may your branches grow high and may your actions be purified – and *congratulations to you* (*for what you are doing*) [52:19]!'

'Now did you come to accuse me, O glory of the learned,'[2] Ṣāliḥ said to him, 'or to follow me blindly? And what has become of your perfect intellect and that noble practical intelligence which we have been familiar with in you?'

'Your capacity and rank are far above any accusation,' Abū Mālik replied to him, 'and religion is far above any blind obedience.'

'Then how is it,' Ṣāliḥ asked him, 'that you've termed me a "warner," when the warner is a prophet and the prophet is a proof (*ḥujja*) between God and His creatures, both for them and against them? And how can someone be a proof for you who has not (yet) established (the divine) argument against you?'

'You are right,' replied Abū Mālik. 'That is what is necessary (for someone to be a divine proof). Now we are not acting in this situation on the basis of rash words. No, we have come to you *with that which is better* [16:125; 17:53]. And I thought that direct sincerity was more appropriate with someone who has established himself as a guardian for religion and a firm proponent for the truth, who has opened his doors to those who are seeking (the truth). Now that we have recognized the excellence of the search (for truth), we have sought you out and we humbly ask you (to grant us) what we're seeking. So do be attentive to our need!'

'O Abū Mālik,' Ṣāliḥ responded, 'if you have recognized someone's excellence, isn't it also obligatory for you to acknowledge what is their due?'

'Yes,' he answered, 'that is obligatory.'

'So when you recognized the excellence of the search (for truth),' he continued, 'then you also acknowledged what is its due?'

'And what *is* its due?' he asked.

'To understand the ways to (carry out) the search,' Ṣāliḥ explained to him, 'so

1. Along with the complementary task of 'bearing the good news' (of God's loving mercy), the epithet *nadhīr* is one of the most common Qur'anic descriptions of the role of the prophets and messengers; as such, it is not a term that one would ordinarily apply loosely to someone, as Ṣāliḥ immediately points out.

2. The honorary epithet by which Abū Mālik was commonly known. 'Glory of the learned' or 'glory of the rabbis,' alluding to the famous learned Yamanī Jewish convert, Ka'b al-Aḥbar, at the beginning of Islam. In giving Abū Mālik this title here, the author is no doubt ironically pointing to his eventual equally dramatic 'conversion' to the true religion – in this case, to the Ismaili understanding of Islam conveyed by Ṣāliḥ in the following sections.

that you will aim for the way among them that is obligatory for you (in your seeking).'

'Then what are the ways of seeking,' asked Abū Mālik, 'and how many ways are there?'

'There are three ways of seeking,' Ṣāliḥ explained to him. 'There is the seeker who already knows; the seeker who is coming to know; and the seeker who desires (to begin) to know.[1] So which of those three are you?'

'I am in need of coming to know all three of them,' said Abū Mālik, 'so how can I claim a rank that I don't really know?'

'But then how did you claim to be a seeker,' Ṣāliḥ asked him, 'when you didn't even know the ways of seeking?'

'I didn't really know them,' Abū Mālik admitted, 'so make that clear to me.'

'Possessions are the treasures of the people of this lower world,' Ṣāliḥ began, 'and (spiritual) knowledge is the treasure of the people of the other world. Now the search for possessions takes place in three ways: there is the seeker who searches for (more of) what he already has; the seeker who searches *until a determined limit* [11:3]; and the seeker who is searching to obtain charity.

'So likewise there are three ways to seek for religion and the treasures of the other world. There is the seeker who (fully) understands: that is the sanctified knower (*al-'ālim al-rabbānī*)[2] who seeks those who are dead in (their) ignorance in order *to bring them back to life* [2:28] through his knowledge. Then there is the seeker who is coming to understand: that is the person who is seeking to learn, who has already understood some of *the levels of knowledge* [12:76] and who is seeking the final and ultimate (stage) of those levels. And (finally), there is the seeker who is just starting to understand: that is the ignorant person who has at least recognized his own ignorance and that he really knows nothing more than his awareness that he is in need. So he has sought out the (real) knowers so that he can come to learn. Thus those are the three ways (to seek the truth) and the descriptions of those who are seeking.'

'Yes,' replied Abū Mālik, 'those are the ways of seeking both religion and this lower world. Now I am the seeker who is just starting to understand, the one who doesn't understand anything. But I do know that I am in need (of knowledge), so teach me.'

'Do you just "know" that,' he asked, 'or do you really *understand*?'[3]

1. Ṣāliḥ's words here almost literally quote key lines from the Imam 'Alī's famous encounter with Kumayl b. Ziyād, which the Knower had earlier alluded to [in the text].

2. See the explanation of 'Alī's outline of each of these three stages of the spiritual quest (in the encounter with Kumayl recorded in *Nahj al-balāgha*) and its Qur'anic background [in the text].

3. Here Ṣāliḥ begins to develop a key distinction between two Arabic roots for 'knowing,' *'-l-m* and *'-r-f* (translated here as 'real understanding'), which eventually becomes classical in later Islamic thought. Although the two terms in everyday usage were often used synonymously (as Abū Mālik clearly does here), the fact that the unique Qur'anic term for the specifically inspired, divine 'knowing' (*'ilm*) of the prophets and other spiritually accomplished individuals – which is of course the central focus of this entire dialogue – gradually began to be limited to the familiar sort of transmitted, institutionalized formal domains of scholarly learning (typified here by Abū Mālik and his companions), eventually forced

'What's the difference between the two?' asked Abū Mālik.

'Knowledge,' explained Ṣāliḥ, 'is a report,[1] while real understanding is *immediate vision* [102:5–7].'

'Then this is also something that I am in need of knowing,' Abū Mālik admitted.

'As for the "report,"' Ṣāliḥ continued, 'that is (the case of) an ignorant person who doesn't know that he is ignorant until he encounters a knowledgeable person. Then the knower informs him that he is ignorant, so that he knows that he is ignorant and in need of knowledge, according to what that knower told him. So his knowledge that he is ignorant is based on a report.

'As for truly understanding one's ignorance and need, that is when a man knows with his own intellect that he is inquiring after something, although he doesn't know and is ignorant of the (correct) response. So that person's heart becomes constricted because of his ignorance, and his only hope for being released (from that inner tension) is through coming to know whatever it is he is ignorant of. So that person's ignorance is a kind of understanding through his intellect. For ignorance is a need, and that neediness is constricting, and that constriction (of the heart) is an intense need that forces people to seek release, and that release comes from the openness of (really) knowing, since knowledge is a wide-open expanse. So that is what makes you really *understand* that you are in need.'

'I find all that you have described in my own soul,' admitted Abū Mālik. 'Indeed I have truly understood that I was in need, that my neediness was intense. So cure my neediness with your generosity!'

'It seems to me,' Ṣāliḥ replied, 'that you are rushing ahead in your search, before you have found any solid grounding.'

'My neediness forced me to hurry, because of its constriction, so I rushed ahead,' admitted Abū Mālik. 'I recognized the excellence of that open expanse, so I went seeking it.'

'But if your neediness forced you to hurry and you recognized the excellence of that open expanse and sought it,' Ṣāliḥ inquired, 'then how did you come to understand what you were seeking?'

'I became sure of your excellence, so I came straight to you!' Abū Mālik exclaimed. 'You hinted at the real meaning (of religion), so I sought you out.'

'But just how did you become sure that *I*, rather than you, really understood that open expanse (of true knowing), so that you went seeking it?' Ṣāliḥ asked him. 'And how did you know that I was what you were searching for, so that you went seeking me? For no true knower of prophecy has guided you to me, so that you might

Muslims to substitute the *'-r-f* root for the original semantic field of *'ilm*, in ways which are beautifully dramatized in the ensuing discussion here.

1. Or 'piece of (transmitted) information' (*khabar*): that Arabic term is perhaps the most commonly used technical expression for the contents of the actual *ḥadīth*, the transmitted reports about the sayings or actions of the Prophets which had provided the foundation of the predominant later forms of Islamic religious learning, already by the third/ninth century.

come to (truly) know. Nor have you seen in me the confirming signs (of such divine inspiration) so that you might really understand. Don't you see that in your seeking you are really aspiring for the effortlessness of blind imitation (*taqlīd*)? In doing so *you are doing injustice* to wisdom and *to yourself* [65:1, etc.], like the merchant who *measures* [11:84] from the bottom of the barrel: if he doesn't fill up (his measure), he does injustice to his customer; and if he overfills it, he does injustice to himself. The same is true of someone who simply accepts (a piece of) knowledge on the basis of blind imitation: if he puts it into practice, (the person who gave him the knowledge) won't receive any thanks; but if he abandons it, then he's accused of irreligion. But in my opinion you are more intelligent than that.'

'I myself am certainly aware that such a person is like that,' admitted Abū Mālik, 'but I wanted it to be the truth that would confirm itself, so that I could absolve you of having to confirm it. Because disputation gives rise to dissension and controversy, and that gives rise to malice and rancour, as each of the antagonists seeks to overcome his opponent. But once one has perceived the truth, who would persist in defending falsehood?'

'How well you have spoken!' Ṣāliḥ said to him, 'since the truth does confirm itself because of its own excellence and nobility. Whereas disputes, once they have proliferated, will surely distract the hearts (of the disputants) from what is more important than them. Yet there's no getting around what the (true) knowers have set down as the usual rule, when they said that every seed for which the ground has not been properly prepared beforehand will not grow and flourish,[1] and every knowledge for which the hearts (of the learners) have not first been purified by (proper) argument will not flourish.'

'Then mention all the arguments you wish,' replied Abū Mālik. 'For words of wisdom are like a jewel: if you turn it around and scrutinize it, its light sparkles and shimmers, but if you leave it alone, that won't diminish its value at all.'

'You've spoken truly,' Ṣāliḥ answered him, 'but that is only if there isn't any confusion between the jewel and a forged piece of glass; in that case the jewel is quite obvious. But as for when the *false idols* [4:51, etc.] of this lower world multiply their pretensions and disputes about religion until they have deceived (people) by confounding it with other things and have counterfeited and distorted it for those who are seeking (the truth), then there is an obligation for the seeker faced with that situation to have the jewel tested, so that its true value will become clear and so that the counterfeit and its people will be unmasked.'

'You have spoken with justice and have upheld what is required by the truth,' said Abū Mālik, 'and as for the deceptions (undertaken) by such people, we are well aware of them and their shortcomings. That is why we have rejected such deceptions and why we have clung firmly to this opinion (*ra'y*)[2] which you know we have

1. An allusion to the famous Qur'anic passage: ...*That is their likeness* [of the truly faithful] *in the Torah and their likeness in the Gospel: like a seed which sends up its shoot; then He strengthens it and it becomes stronger and rises up on its stalk, pleasing the sowers...* (48:29).

2. The purely consensual, socially based foundations of the term Abū Mālik employs here (*ra'y*,

maintained, and why we have said that *this* position is the genuine jewel. We have supported this opinion, and you and your father have agreed with us about it, and *all together we have held tightly to the cord* [3:103; 2:256] of this opinion. So if you have now found a meaning which is a more precious jewel than this opinion, then – by my life! – some jewels are more valuable than others, and in that case you must show the value of your jewel through a test by which its real value can be known. But as for our jewel, we have already recognized its value, as have you; so say what seems best to you regarding it.'

'As for this "jewel" of you and your companions,' Ṣāliḥ answered him, 'we all used to hold it dear instead of the genuine jewel, until we presented it to the jewellers and experts in gems. But they showed us that it was counterfeit and they wouldn't even accept it from us as a jewel. Instead they said "This is a forgery made of glass," and they showed us its flaws so that it could no longer be considered a jewel. For a jewel is only held in high esteem because of its rarity and preciousness, and because of the opinion that people *of discerning insight* (*baṣīra*)[1] have concerning its value and *their competition* [83:26] regarding it, so that as a result its price can become so lofty. But when the jewellers have rejected it (as a forgery), then who else will acknowledge it (as a gem), or who will accept it after that – except for *the people of delusion* [57:20] who neither buy nor sell? 'So, likewise, (spiritual) knowledge can't be (accepted as genuine) until it has been offered to those who know with (inspired) knowledge from heaven. Then if they accept it, it is genuine knowledge. But if they don't accept it, then it is merely *empty talk* [28:55; etc.], and empty talk cannot be accepted as wisdom, nor will it be accepted by the wise.'

(Translated by James W. Morris)

'opinion' or 'personal judgement') are further highlighted by his repeated literal emphasis ('we...') on the 'collective' aspect of this opinion, which had already been stressed in many earlier passages. We soon learn that the particular doctrine in question is that of the Mu'tazilī theological school, but Ṣāliḥ's counter-arguments are about much more fundamental religious and spiritual issues, not particular disputed points of theological doctrine.

1. Ṣāliḥ's pun here alludes to the Qur'anic meaning of the same term *baṣīra*, where it is applied to the inspired 'spiritual vision' and discernment of the Prophet (12:148), or to other rare signs and forms of guidance having a specifically divine source.

2
Naṣīr al-Dīn al-Ṭūsī

Naṣīr al-Dīn al-Ṭūsī (see Section II, 6) was born to a Twelver Shiʿi family in the town of Ṭūs in Khurāsān. As the passage reproduced in this chapter explains, his family followed and disseminated 'the exoteric sciences,' and his early education was in accordance with this tradition. His father, however, encouraged the young Naṣīr al-Dīn to study more widely, and it was in the course of his intellectual explorations that he became curious about the doctrines of the Ismailis. The *Sayr wa sulūk* is al-Ṭūsī's memoir of his own spiritual journey as he studied various branches of religious knowledge and was left dissatisfied with each. He eventually came to believe in the necessity of a 'truthful instructor' to guide the way to spiritual knowledge, a key Ismaili concept, and was greatly influenced by the sayings of the Imam Ḥasan *ʿalā dhikrihi'l-salām* (d. 561/1166). The passage chosen here describes al-Ṭūsī's increasing desire to become a member of the Ismaili *jamāʿat*, and study with a view to achieving 'inner sight.'

Sayr wa sulūk
Contemplation and Action[1]

AL-ṬŪSĪ'S SEARCH FOR KNOWLEDGE

As a result of predetermined decree and design (*bi ḥukm-i taqdīr wa ittifāq*), I was born and educated among a group of people who were believers in, and followers of, the exoteric aspects of the religious law (*sharīʿat*). The only profession and vocation of my near relatives and kindred was to promulgate the exoteric sciences. From the time that [the faculty] of discrimination began to stir within me, I grew and thrived listening to their opinions about both fundamental principles and derived rulings (*uṣūl wa furūʿ*) [of Islam]. I assumed that, apart from this way, there could be no other religious teaching or method. But my father, a man of the world who had heard the opinions of different kinds of people and had [received] his education from his maternal uncle, who was one of the attendants and students of the chief *dāʿī* (*dāʿī al-duʿāt*), Tāj al-Dīn Shahrastāna,[2] was less enthusiastic about following these regulations. He

1. Naṣīr al-Dīn al-Ṭūsī, *Sayr wa sulūk*, ed. and tr. S. J. Badakhchani as *Contemplation and Action: The Spiritual Autobiography of a Muslim Scholar* (London, 1998), pp. 26–32.

2. Tāj al-Dīn Shahrastāna, more commonly known as Muḥammad b. ʿAbd al-Karīm al-Shahrastānī, the author of *Kitāb al-milal wa'l-niḥal* (*Book of Religions and Doctrinal Schools*), *Kitāb muṣāraʿat al-*

used to encourage me to study [all] the branches of knowledge, and to listen to the opinions of the followers of [various] sects and doctrines.

Then it happened that one of the students of Afḍal al-Dīn Kāshī – may God have mercy on him – came to the region. His name was Kamāl al-Dīn Muḥammad Ḥāsib,[1] who had acquired a first-rate knowledge in a variety of philosophical subjects, especially in the art of mathematics; he had previously been a friend and acquaintance of my father. My father suggested that I should learn from him and frequent his company; so I began to study mathematics with him.

Frequently, in the course of speaking – may God have mercy on him – he would deprecate the exotericists, and explain the unavoidable inconsistency of those who blindly follow the rules of the *sharīʿat*, and I would find his discourse appealing, but whenever I wanted to get to the bottom of what he was saying, he would refuse, remarking: 'That which is the core and essence of the truth cannot yet be mentioned to you, for you are young and do not have experience of the world. If you grow up and are successful, seek for it until you attain it.' Occasionally, as a piece of advice, he would say: 'It is possible that the truth [may be found] among people who are, in the eyes of the group that you know, the most contemptible people,' and he would quote this verse [in which the unbelievers say to Noah]: 'We see not any following thee but the vilest of us, in their apparent opinion' [11:27]. Then he would say: 'You should not pay any attention to whether or not someone has an ugly appearance. If, for example, you find truth with the idolaters, you should listen to them and accept it from them.'

In short, it became clear to me from being in his company that whatever I had heard or seen up to that time [on religious matters] was without foundation. I understood that the truth was in the possession of another group and that I would have to strive hard to attain it.

Not long after this, worldly affairs required him [Kamāl al-Dīn] to move away from the region. [Also at this time] my father departed from this world, and I left my home in search of the truth, intending to acquire the knowledge which guides people to the happiness of the next world. Following the instructions of my father, I studied every subject for which I could find a teacher. But since I was moved by the inclination of my thoughts and the yearning of my soul to discriminate between what was false and what was true in the differing schools of thought and contradictory doctrines, I concentrated my attention on learning the speculative sciences such as theology (*kalām*) and philosophy (*ḥikmat*).

---

falāsifa (*Book of Wrestling with Philosophers*), *Nihāyat al-aqdām fi ʿilm al-kalām* (*Ultimate Footsteps in Theology*), a Qur'anic commentary, *Mafātīḥ al-asrār* (*Keys to the Secrets*), and the famous *Majlis-i maktūb* (*Written Sermon*). For evidence on his leanings towards Nizari Ismailism, see Wilferd F. Madelung, 'Aspects of Ismāʿīlī Theology: The Prophetic Chain and the God Beyond Being,' in *Ismāʿīlī Contributions to Islamic Culture*, ed. S. H. Nasr (Tehran, 1977), p. 59.

1. On Kamāl al-Dīn Ḥāsib there is no reliable report. Afḍal al-Dīn Muḥammad b. Ḥusayn Kāshī or Kāshānī, also known as Bābā Afḍal, is the author of *Anjām-nāma*, *Jāwidān-nāma*, and eloquent quatrains resembling those of ʿUmar-i Khayyām. His works, which are famous as specimens of Persian prose writing, deal mainly with philosophy, ethics and logic. See Jan Rypka, 'Bābā Afḍal,' *EI2*, vol. 1, pp. 838–839, W. Chittick, 'Bābā Afżal-al-Dīn Moḥammad b. Ḥasan Maraqī Kāšānī,' *EIR*; A. Zaryab, 'Bābā Afḍal,' *Encyclopaedia of the World of Islam*, vol. 1, pp. 21–29.

When I first embarked upon [the study of] theology, I found a science which was entirely confined to practices of the exoteric side of the *sharīʿat*. Its practitioners seemed to force the intellect to promote a doctrine in which they blindly imitated their ancestors, cunningly deducing proofs and evidence for its validity, and devising excuses for the absurdities and contradictions which their doctrine necessarily entailed.

In short, I derived some benefit from enquiring into this science, to the extent that I came to know something of the divergence between the sects. I came to understand that [with regard to] the knowledge of truth and the attainment of perfection on which happiness in the hereafter depends, men of intellect agreed in one way or another, summarily but not in detail, on the affirmation of such a truth and a hereafter. However, there was a primary disagreement about whether one could reach the desired objective solely through intellect and reason, or whether, in addition to these, a truthful instructor (*muʿallim-i ṣādiq*) was required. All people are accordingly divided in this respect into two branches: those who believe in reason (*naẓar*), and those who [in addition to reason] believe in instruction (*taʿlīm*). Moreover, those who believe in reason [alone] are divided into different schools – which is in itself a lengthy subject – whereas those who believe in [the necessity of] instruction are a group known as the Ismailis. This was my first acquaintance with the religion of the *jamāʿat*.[1]

As the science of theology proved fruitless, except for an acquaintance [it allowed] with the positions of the adherents to [various] doctrines, I became averse to it, and my enthusiasm to learn [more about it] lost its momentum. Then I started [to study] philosophy. I found this science to be noble and of great benefit. I saw that among the groups [into which] mankind [is divided], the practitioners of this discipline were distinguished by their allocation of a place for the intellect in the recognition of realities, and by their not requiring blind imitation (*taqlīd*) of a particular stand. Rather, in most cases they build the structure of religion in accordance with the intellect, 'except what God wills' [7:188]. However, when the discussion reached the desired objective – that is, the recognition of the True One (*ḥaqq*), the exalted, the most high, and knowledge of the origin and the return (*mabdaʾ wa maʿād*) – I found that they were on shaky foundations in these matters, for the intellect (*ʿaql*) is incapable of encompassing the giver of intellect (*wāhib-i ʿaql*) and the origins (*mabādī*). And because they rely on their own intellect and opinion, they blunder, they speak according to their own conjectures and whims in this field, using the intellect [to arrive] at knowledge of something which is not within its scope.

To sum up, my heart was not satisfied with what they said in these matters, while my desire to attain the truth was not diminished. In my exposition, I shall mention some more aspects of this matter. Many benefits, however, were obtained from this investigation into philosophy, one of them being that I came to know that

1. *Jamāʿat*, literally assembly, congregation or community. In Ismaili literature, from the early Alamūt period, this word is always used for the Ismaili community in particular.

if in any existing thing perfection is potential (*bi al-quwwa*), it cannot change from potentiality into actuality by itself without being affected by something outside itself, because if its essence were sufficient to bring that perfection from potentiality into actuality, the change would not be delayed. Indeed, the attaining of that perfection would have been simultaneous with the existence of the essence. We can take bodies as an example of this: motion is [always] potential in them. Without the effect of something else, that motion is never actualized; otherwise all bodies would be in [perpetual] motion. But when another thing exerts an effect on a body, that potential motion (*ḥarakat*) becomes actual. In this case the other is called the 'mover' (*muḥarrik*) and the body is called the 'moved' (*mutaḥarrik*).

Once this proposition had been established and my soul was satisfied of its truth, my attention was drawn to the point that was made in the science of theology, about the primary disagreement among mankind being whether knowledge of the truth is attainable solely through the intellect and reason, without instruction from any teacher, or whether, in addition to intellect and reason, an instructor is needed. Then I applied the [above] proposition to this situation and found that the truth lay with those who believe in instruction (*taʿlīmiyān*), for knowledge and understanding in man is in itself [merely] potential, and its perfection can only be actualized in men of sound natures, [in whom] intellect and reason are to be found, when something external has exerted an effect on them. Thus, this perfection too can inevitably only be actualized by means of the effect of some other thing. [Accordingly], when that other bestows a perfection, the perfection [here] being knowledge (*ʿilm*), the bestower, in accordance with the previous law, is called the 'instructor' (*muʿallim*) and the one on whom it is bestowed the 'instructed' (*mutaʿallim*), by analogy with the 'mover' (*muḥarrik*) and the 'moved' (*mutaḥarrik*).[1]

It thus becomes clear that without the instruction (*taʿlīm*) of a teacher (*muʿallim*), and the bringing to perfection (*ikmāl*) by an agent of perfection (*mukammil*), the attainment of the truth is not possible; that mankind, with its great number and differences of opinion, is mistaken in its claim that the truth can be reached solely through the intellect and reason; and that the believers in instruction (*taʿlīmiyān*) are therefore correct.

Once this proposition had become clear, I began to investigate the religion (*madhhab*) of this group. But since I did not know anyone who could describe the nature of their doctrine objectively, and could only hear about their beliefs from people hostile to them, and since I knew that I could not rely on a person's prejudices about his enemy, I was unable to get to know [this group] as I should, and out of fear I was unable to disclose my secret.

1. Ḥamīd al-Dīn al-Kirmānī makes a similar comment in the *Rāḥat al-ʿaql*, ed. M. Kāmil Ḥusayn and M. Muṣṭafā Ḥilmī (Leiden, 1953), p. 61: 'It is impossible for the human soul, which is imperfect and in potentiality, to be actualized in the physical world, except through something which is actual in itself, complete in its essence and action. And since, among human beings, no one's soul is actual except those of the Prophets, their legatees and the imams, and those who have been guided by them ... the actualization [of the soul] is impossible except through them.'

In short, I spent [quite] a period of time thinking about this. Then, in the course of my search, I frequently heard from travellers to the [surrounding] countries about the scholarly virtues of the auspicious master, Shihāb al-Dīn[1] – may God be pleased with him – and his deep insight into different fields of knowledge. Then I sought a suitable opportunity and, through the intermediary of a friend who had an association with him, I sent him a letter containing two or three questions about those points in the discourse of the philosophers which I had found to be contradictory and about which I had some observations of my own. Then I was granted the honour of a reply from him – may God be pleased with him – in the handwriting of the master, the chief scribe, Ṣalāḥ al-Dīn Ḥasan[2] – may his glory endure – and in answer to the questions he said: 'For a reason which can only be explained face to face, I am not [in a position] to convey any scholarly communication [in writing].'

Shortly after this, I took the opportunity, while on a journey from Iraq to Khurāsān, to pass through the glorious territory of [Gird] Kūh[3] – may God, the exalted, protect it – and for two or three days [was able to] be in Shihāb al-Dīn's company and hear some of the *da'wat* doctrines from his own mouth. I copied down his words and derived much [benefit] from them. Since the requisites for staying with him and remaining in that place had not been prepared – for several reasons which I need not go into – I journeyed on from there to Khurāsān. A few days later, I happened to see a copy, in mediocre handwriting and antiquated paper, of the *Fuṣūl-i muqaddas* (Sacred Chapters) of [the Imam] *'alā dhikrihi'l-salām*,[4] in the possession of an unworthy person who did not know what it was.

Obtaining [the text] with a ruse, I occupied myself day and night with reading it, and to the extent of my humble understanding and ability, I gained endless benefits

1. Shihāb al-Dīn's full name, as given by Qāḍī Minhāj-i Sirāj in *Ṭabaqāt-i Nāṣirī*, Eng. trans. H. G. Raverty (London, 1881), vol. 2, p. 1197, was Abū'l Fatḥ Shihāb Manṣūr. According to Minhāj, he was the governor of the province of Quhistān until 621/1224, and says: 'At that time the Muḥtasham was Shihāb al-Dīn ... I found him a person of infinite learning, with wisdom, science and philosophy in such wise that a philosopher and sage like unto him there was not in the territory of Khurāsān. He used greatly to cherish poor strangers and travellers ...' He further adds that great men of learning, such as Afḍal al-Dīn Bāmyānī and Shams al-Dīn Khusraw Shāh, attended his court. It was Shihāb al-Dīn who persuaded al-Ṭūsī to write a commentary on Ibn Sīnā's *al-Ishārāt wa al-tanbīhāt*. See al-Ṭūsī's *Sharḥ al-ishārāt wa al-tanbīhāt* (Tehran, 1957), pp. 2–3.

2. Ṣalāḥ al-Dīn Ḥasan, also known as Ḥasan-i Ṣalāḥ-i Munshī, or as he calls himself in the preface to the *Dīwān-i Qā'imiyyāt*, Ḥasan-i Maḥmūd-i Kātib, was the personal scribe to Shihāb al-Dīn. One of his poems is translated in Part Three of this volume.

3. The word *kūh*, meaning mountain, is a suffix that appears in the names of a number of Ismaili fortresses in Iran. It is difficult to say which of the text editors, Qazwīnī or Taqawī, added the word 'Gird' to specify the place where al-Ṭūsī met Shihāb al-Dīn. This, however, was a reasonable assumption on their part because Gird Kūh, or Gunbadān Dizh, about 18 kilometers from Dāmghān on the main route between Khurāsān and western Iran, was the site of one of the main Ismaili fortresses. For further information, see Rashīd al-Dīn, *Jāmi' al-tawārīkh, qismat-i Ismā'īlīyān*, ed. Muḥammad T. Dānishpazhūh and M. Mudarrisī Zanjānī (Tehran, 1959), p. 117, and Marshall G. S. Hodgson, *The Order of Assassins: The Struggle of the Early Nizārī Ismā'īlīs Against the Islamic World* (The Hague, 1955), p. 186.

4. *'Alā dhikrihi'l-salām* or *Li-dhikrihi'l-salām* (lit. 'on his mention be peace') is the honorific title used by Nizārī Ismaili writers for the Imam Ḥasan (d. 561/ 1166) who enunciated the preaching of the *qiyāmat* (resurrection). His sermons known as the *Fuṣūl-i muqaddas wa mubārak* are quoted frequently in the Alamūt and post-Alamūt Nizārī Ismaili literature.

from those sacred words which are the light of hearts and the illuminator of inner thoughts. It opened a little my eye of exploration (*chishm-i taṣarruf*) and my inner sight (*dīda-yi bāṭin*) was unveiled.

Thereafter, my only desire was to introduce myself among the *jamāʿat* when the opportunity presented itself. At that time, in accordance with my inward motivation, I made such strenuous efforts that finally I succeeded. Through the good offices of the exalted royal presence of Nāṣir al-Ḥaqq wa'l-Dīn[1] – may God exalt him – and his compassionate regard for my improvement, I was granted the good fortune of joining the *jamāʿat* and entry among the ranks of the novices (*mustajībān*) of the *daʿwat*, and thus my situation reached the point where it is now.

Nothing can be gained by the illuminated mind in listening to this story except weariness. However, due to the circumstances already mentioned concerning his [Nāṣir al-Dīn's] cordial nature and sympathy for me, its narration seemed to me to be prudent. If God the exalted is willing, it will be covered with the veil of forgiveness and heard with consideration. This [exposition so far] has been a description of the exoteric situation.

From an esoteric perspective, however, when I had reached a position where I could understand – by the proof that has already been cited – that it was the followers of instruction who were correct, I concluded with no additional troublesome thinking that the true instructor can only be he who is the instructor of the followers of the truth.[2] This person, through whose teaching souls move from potentiality to actuality, must therefore be the instructor of the Taʿlīmiyān [i.e., the Ismailis].

Then my mind became preoccupied with considering what particular characteristics would distinguish that instructor from other teachers, and what his instruction would be like. With due submissiveness, I beseeched God the exalted – may His greatness be magnified – to clarify and unveil this question, so that my heart might be appeased. Then I referred [myself] to the intellectual principles which I had already verified and the premises which had been made clear in the *Fuṣūl-i muqaddas*. I combined them, asked questions from here and there, and held discussions and debates with [other] novices (*mubtadīyān*), until gradually, through the stages which I will explain, the scheme of beliefs (*ṣūrat-i iʿtiqādī*) as will be mentioned later on became clear in my mind.

(Translated by S. J. Badakhchani)

1. It was at the request of Nāṣir al-Dīn Muḥtasham (Nāṣir al-Dīn ʿAbd al-Raḥīm b. ʿAlī) that al-Ṭūsī composed and translated a number of writings, including the *Tawallā wa tabarrā* which is translated in Section IV of this part of the volume. Al-Ṭūsī's most important works on ethics, the *Akhlāq-i Nāṣirī* and *Akhlāq-i Muḥtashamī*, are dedicated to Nāṣir al-Dīn.

2. Al-Ṭūsī's deduction is akin to Ḥasan-i Ṣabbāḥ's fourth proposition: 'As the truth is with the first group, therefore, their leader necessarily is the leader of the truthful people.'

3

Abū Yaʿqūb al-Sijistānī

The fortieth and final chapter of al-Sijistānī's *Wellsprings* (see Section I, 2) deals with the way sublime powers influence bodies both in the physical world and in the life of human individuals. It suggests a hierarchy of knowledge where the inspired messenger-prophet is definitely placed above the scholar, given that he can experience the spiritual world and put it to service without having recourse to the material world perceived by the senses.

Kitāb al-yanābīʿ
The Book of Wellsprings[1]

ON THE MANNER OF THE TRANSMISSION OF SPIRITUAL INSPIRATION TO INSPIRED PERSONS IN THE CORPOREAL WORLD

The transmission of spiritual inspiration to the inspired person in the corporeal world is more noble and sublime than the transmission of the powers of the heavenly bodies to the lower, generated kingdoms. We find these latter powers spread by the spheres and the planets throughout the physical kingdoms but without those kingdoms offering a clue as to the manner by which they were transmitted. We do notice that each individual thing receives the influences of astral movements in proportion to the refinement or coarseness of what constitutes it. Subsequently, it produces from those forms the particular properties or natural powers that were secreted in them. In a similar way inspiration from the spiritual world shines in those spiritual substances that are attached to human individuals, but we find no individual of the lower kingdoms other than individual humans that has the ability to make use of this world in order to extract its benefits.

Among the animals we find man alone in extracting the benefits incorporated in the world as the arts. He can put each thing among them into its proper place and cause to appear those wondrous works of art that bring out the perfection of the world and the emergence of its ornamentation. Similarly, we find no one among the individuals of the human race, save those who are messenger-prophets, who can put to service the spiritual world and extract those benefits implicit in it in the

1. Abū Yaʿqūb al-Sijistānī, *Kitāb al-yanābīʿ*, ed. and French trans. Henry Corbin, *Trilogie Ismaélienne* (Tehran and Paris, 1961); English trans. Paul E. Walker as *The Wellsprings of Wisdom* (Salt Lake City, 1994), Wellspring 40, pp. 109–111.

way of arts and can thus put everything in its true place and cause to appear those marvellous regimes through which comes the perfection of the spiritual world and in which is the appearance of its finest ornamentation.

Spiritual inspiration commences when the inspired person becomes able to discover things neither by a route that has the senses as their sources nor by the inference of hidden things from external aspects. He then experiences his soul existing apart from sensible things, forsaking them, and desiring instead the intelligibles that are not attached to material things. The distinction between the scholar and the one inspired is that, for the preservation of his knowledge and wisdom, the scholar requires the material sensibilia whereas the inspired person is independent of these and thus conceives in his mind something the scholar cannot extract by deriving its indicants from sensible signs only. Often, however, when a spiritual thing occurs in the mind of the inspired person – something without an established definition – he expresses it with a sensible sign that allows his people to see what he is describing to them. This is then more firmly fixed in the people's understanding because it resembles a specific, sensible thing. Sometimes also the people witness the contrary of what the inspired person reports to them, and yet the people abandon what they have eyewitness of and accept his report. If the transmission of spiritual inspiration to the inspired person occurred as an aspect of the senses, his report would not have this virtue that raises it above knowledge from sensory evidence.

It has been said that a verbal report is not the equal of an eyewitness. But even though the transmission of spiritual inspiration to the inspired is not by way of the senses – it being purely rational with no admixture of either letters or other verbal composition – he nevertheless subjugates the populace by employing what the people can witness by means of the senses or come to comprehend through speech, which is composed of words and letters. The transmission of spiritual inspiration to the person inspired occurs when he reflects about one particular, individual being, as for example an animal or a tree or some other. His reflecting reveals to him truths pertaining to the knowledge of hidden things and he is thus privy to many secrets concerning invisible matters. Spiritual inspiration thereafter persists in that form.

At times it may happen that a man speaks in front of the inspired person about something the meanings of which that man does not understand. Thereupon a marvellous inspiration is revealed to the inspired person in this other person's words. What is revealed to him becomes a legal source whose use is subsequently incumbent on the populace for the duration of his epoch. Inspiration for the inspired person in the corporeal world is transmitted in this sense also. And in God is success.

(Translated by Paul E. Walker)

4
Ḥamīd al-Dīn al-Kirmānī

In the Sixth Light of *al-Maṣābīḥ fī ithbāt al-imāma* (see Section II, 4 for an introduction), al-Kirmānī employs his wide scholarship and religious authority to explain the need for interpretation of the words of the Qurʾan which might, without knowledgeable elucidation, seem opaque or contradictory.

al-Maṣābīḥ fī ithbāt al-imāma
Lights to Illuminate the Proof of the Imamate[1]

IN PROOF OF THE INTERPRETATION[2] OF THE REVELATION AND THE LAW THAT COMES FROM THE MESSENGERS, WHICH IS KNOWLEDGE, COMPRISING SEVEN DEMONSTRATIONS

The first demonstration: Intellects and souls have no way to comprehend the Return or what is absent from the senses except through sensed representations that the messengers depict for them and by means of their decrees and instruction. The lord of the prophets and their seal, Muḥammad, the Chosen, put to use sensed representations which are extremely wise. Hence, it is necessary that this wisdom have a sure place in the horizon so that it is accepted, and that its stipulations be appropriate so that they are adhered to and its lights so fecund they cannot be cast off. However, what Muḥammad brought as the Qur'an and the law differs in its exterior from the judgments of reason. An example is the statement of God: 'And when your Lord asked the tribe of Adam from those of their loins, their descendants, to have them testify concerning themselves, "Am I not your Lord?" they said, "yes"' [7:172]. It is absurd to bring forth the progeny as if they were atoms, as put forth in the commentaries by those who adhere to the obvious meaning, and to ask them to confirm that God is their Lord despite what exists in the wisdom of God about not accepting the statement of the young, let alone little children, or the statement of little children, let alone atoms, because they are not under the obligation of the law nor under oath. It is also like the statement of the Prophet: 'Between my grave

1. Ḥamīd al-Dīn Aḥmad b. ʿAbd Allāh al-Kirmānī. *al-Maṣābīḥ fī ithbāt al-imāma*, ed. and tr. Paul E. Walker as *Master of the Age: An Islamic Treatise on the Necessity of the Imamate* (London, 2007), Part 1, 'The Sixth Light,' pp. 63–69.

2. In his *al-Risāla al-waḍīʿa fī maʿālim al-dīn*, al-Kirmānī reports: 'We note that our statement given earlier concerning the necessity of interpretation (*taʾwīl*) in our book known as *al-Maṣābīḥ fi'l-imāma* and in our treatise *al-Kāfiya* is quite sufficient in regard to this subject.'

and my *minbar* is one of the gardens of paradise.' The absurdity of this statement, along with the place obviously lacking what is described in it as a garden, requires, in that the Messenger is a wise man to whom the attribute of ignorance is foreign, that it has a meaning that rational minds would accept and agree to, and on the basis of which the revelation's being true and comprised of wisdom is valid. Those meanings are what we call interpretation, the inner sense, the explanation and the elucidation. Hence, the interpretation is necessary.

The second demonstration: We hold that the Prophet summoned to God by means of wisdom, just as he was commanded to do in God's statement: 'Summon to the way of your Lord with wisdom and fine preaching' [16:125]. Anyone who imagines other than this on the part of the Messenger is a heretic. Because it is impermissible to suppose anything other than that; and yet one finds in the outward sense that the Prophet summoned to God and to the worship of Him by certain acts that, if a man were not to perform them in the place he was commanded to do, it would be said that he is mad, playing the jester, or forgetful. The actions of the pilgrimage and its wondrous rites are an example. The external features of these acts, such as addressing the stone, running on the tips of the feet, which is to advance in haste, holding off trimming the nails, cutting the hair of the head and the throwing of pebbles, are not associated with wisdom. Thus, for the Prophet to be summoning by means of wisdom, requires that that to which he summons by these actions has a meaning that is consistent with wisdom and by the understanding of which rational minds are shown what in them is for its salvation and which of them impregnate it with the light of sanctity. These meanings we call interpretation, inner sense, elucidation, significance and explanation. Therefore, the interpretation is necessary.

The third demonstration: In the justice of God, no one is punished for the crime of someone else. He has said: 'No one bears the burden of another,' [6:164]. Yet it is a prescription of the Messenger and of his law to punish the uncle for the crime of his nephew if he kills in error. That is contrary to the justice of God and what He ordered. But it is unthinkable for the Messenger to do what is contrary to His justice and mercy, or that he ordered what would contravene the command of God. Hence, it is necessary that, that and what is like it, have a meaning and a wisdom which, with regard to rational minds, brings it into conformity with the justice of God and His mercy. Those meanings which, with regard to rational minds brings it into conformity with the justice of God and His mercy, are the interpretation that we call the inner sense, the elucidation and the explanation. Therefore, the interpretation is essential.

The fourth demonstration: Those humans that are wise and intelligent appreciate the absurdity of addressing an order to the dead who lack life, have no reward or punishment, no instrument for accepting the commandment to do good and avoid evil, or to respond, let alone to He who is Most High and hallowed, the Lord of the heavens and the earth. Yet the Messenger related of God that He spoke to the heaven and the earth in His statement: 'Then He lifted Himself up to the celestial heaven when it was smoke; He said to it and to the earth, "Come willingly or unwillingly". They replied, "We come willingly"' [41:11]. God is All-knowing and All-wise, and the heaven and the earth are inanimate, lacking a mind and having no tool for speech. Hence, in view of the absurdity of any wise person addressing the inanimate, it is necessary that there is, to His commanding the heavens and the earth and their answering Him, a meaning that makes the statement of God true and which is rationally acceptable as wisdom. That meaning is what we call the interpretation. Hence, the interpretation is necessary.

The fifth demonstration: God has said: 'When He was causing slumber to overcome you as a security from Him and He sent down to you from the skies water with which to purify you, to carry away from you the defilement of Satan, and to strengthen your hearts and firm up your footsteps...' [8:11]. It is known that the defilement of Satan is unbelief, doubt, uncertainty, hypocrisy, ignorance and error and whatever else occurs in the heart, minds and spirits that functions as these do. Given that the defilement of Satan is in hearts and minds, it cannot be supposed that water, which comes down from the sky and is felt and drunk, can purify them, because it is impossible that the matter is like this. And if the water that is mentioned here is natural water, everyone becomes pure, both the believer and the unbeliever. Hence, it is necessary that for this water there is a meaning which, if not for it, an absurdity would have come from God in His saying something that is contrary to it. That meaning we call an interpretation, an explanation, elucidation and an inner sense. Therefore, the interpretation for that and what is like it is necessary.

The sixth demonstration: God made the interpretation of what the Messenger brought obligatory by His saying: 'He it is who revealed to you the Book; of it parts are firmly fixed and they are the mother of the book, but others are ambiguous; those in whose hearts there is deviousness follow what is ambiguous, hoping thereby to spread sedition and the desire for its interpretation, but no one knows its interpretation except God and those firmly grounded in knowledge who say, "We believe in it, all is from our Lord," yet none remember except those with minds' [3:7]. The protest of those who protest is to say that the interpretation is known only to God and that 'those who are firmly grounded in knowledge' is a subject and not predicated on what went before in the statement as a whole. That is false due to the existence of what invalidates their objection in the speech of the Arabs when being brief and concise, as in saying to someone else: 'No one will salute you except so-and-so who will excuse himself; no one knows medicine except so-and-so who argues about it; no one knows grammar except so-and-so who is absorbed in it; no one will come to you except so-and-so who will be riding.' The meaning is that each of the two will offer salutations and one of them will excuse himself; each of them knows medicine but one of the two argues about it; each of them knows grammar and one of the two is absorbed in it; each of them will come and one will be riding. Hence, it is essential that the interpretation be obligatory and that those firmly grounded in knowledge know it. Therefore, the interpretation is essential.

The seventh demonstration: There is no way to comprehend what is unseen and not subject to sensation, other than by means of an expression for it, that is, something that can be seen and sensed. The Messenger reported about what cannot be seen or sensed, such as God, paradise and its felicity, hell and its torments. From this fact it follows that, in his reporting and his expression of what he reported about, he gave an account of what cannot be seen and sensed using what can be seen and sensed. Thus, for example, he reported about paradise, which is the abode of the afterlife and which is neither seen nor subject to sensation, by referring to gardens and streams and trees and fruit and flowing water, and in regard to the manner of being of those in it, [he referred to them] as newborns, cups, pitchers, dark-eyed women, well-kept pearls and all sort of physical benefits that are in their entirety seen and sensed. Another example is his report about hell and its torments, which are neither seen nor sensed, by reference to fire and burning and boiling water and burning thirst and iron chains and fetters and all manner of physical pains that are entirely seen and sensed. If that is a necessary consequence, what he said and did and summoned to in regard to the afterlife, follows the rule of similitudes in forming likenesses. Similitudes require the things that are represented by them and the things that are represented are designated by interpretation. Thus, for what the Messenger brought and summoned to in the revelation and law, there is an interpretation. Hence, the interpretation is necessary.

(Translated by Paul E. Walker)

5

al-Qāḍī al-Nuʿmān

The Fatimid jurist and author al-Qāḍī Abū Ḥanīfa al-Nuʿmān (d. 363/974) served the Fatimids over the reigns of four imams (see Part One, 3), achieving his greatest prominence under the Imam al-Muʿizz (d. 365/975). While best known for his contributions to jurisprudence, al-Nuʿmān was also a poet, a historian and the author of works on esoteric matters. The selection below is from his *Asās al-ta'wīl* (*The Foundation of Spiritual Hermeneutics*). In common with other Ismaili scholars, al-Nuʿmān affirmed that the Qur'an and the Prophetic traditions have an exoteric as well as an esoteric dimension. In this work, he brings out the inner, spiritual meanings of the tales of the prophets, as in the *ta'wīl* of the story of Job (Ayyūb).

Asās al-ta'wīl
The Foundation of Spiritual Hermeneutics[1]

THE STORY OF JOB

Job, upon whom be peace, was one of the Imams of the cycle of Abraham, may God's blessings and peace be upon him. God, may He be exalted and glorified, mentions him in His book:

'And make mention [O Muhammad] of Our bondman Job, when he cried unto his Lord (saying): Lo! the devil (*al-shayṭān*) doth afflict me with distress (*nuṣb*) and torment' [38:41].

By distress (*nuṣb*) he meant evil and by the devil (*al-shayṭān*) he meant the adversary of his time. This was one of the powerful pharaohs who deemed him weak and overcame him. The pharaoh won over those who had accepted Job's *daʿwa*, attracting them away from him and toward himself. He dislodged Job from his position and made him fall in the eyes of the people.

Regarding this God says: 'And Job, when he cried unto his Lord, (saying): Lo! adversity afflicteth me, and Thou art Most Merciful of all who show mercy' [21:83].

The *ḥadīths* relate that Iblīs [the devil] overpowered him, murdered every last one of his children and made off with his wealth, so that he had neither possessions nor

1. al-Qāḍī al-Nuʿmān, 'The Story of Job' from *Kitāb asās al-ta'wīl*, ed. ʿĀrif Tāmir (Beirut, 1960), Chapter 3, pp. 165–167, tr. Shafique N. Virani. The translator would like to acknowledge the assistance of Dr Faquir M. Hunzai and his research assistant, Bassel Rachid, in preparing this translation. The introduction to this chapter is by the translator.

livestock. Then Iblīs caused him bodily affliction that left him in shock. Worms beset him and he was cast upon the dunghill. None but his wife would approach him.

The *ta'wīl* of Iblīs is Job's adversary during his time. His murdering the children is his diversion of those who had accepted Job's *da'wa*. The worms are a symbol of those who responded to Job's *da'wa* and then betrayed him. Their eating of his flesh refers to their consumption of his knowledge, though they were never like him in kind or form.

The *ḥadīth* also relates that he would scoop up the worms that fell from his body, saying to them, 'Eat of the provisions that God has provided for you.' The *ta'wīl* of this is that he conveyed knowledge to them in the hope that they would avail themselves of it, inviting back those among them who had strayed, though they did not follow the path that he had established. His wife, who patiently stood by him, was his *ḥujja* (proof) and the keeper of his secret. The disease that afflicted him is a symbol of his incapacity to sustain his *da'wa* and to appoint *lāḥiq*s and *dā'ī*s. The dunghill is a symbol of his association with the exoteric aspect of the preceding *sharī'a* such that no visitor would approach him, no *mustajīb* (respondent) would draw near to him, nor would anyone be eager to approach him. He was unable to fulfil the duties of his *da'wa* because his adversary had gained the upper hand over him. That was indeed the great tribulation.

When God, may He be exalted and glorified, responded to his prayer, He supported him with knowledge of the truth, by the divine influx with which He inspired him. This was His saying, may He be exalted: 'Strike the ground with thy foot. This (spring) is a cool bath and a refreshing drink' [38:42].

That is: 'Hasten to appoint a member of your hierarchy (*ḥudūd*) to spread this knowledge so that he may wash away all the impurities that the ignorant among the community have mixed in the exoteric aspect of your *da'wa*.' So he did this and the people of his *da'wa* returned to him, joined by others as well. God refers to this as follows: 'And We bestowed on him (once again) his people and therewith the like thereof, a mercy from Us, and a reminder for those who understand' [38:43].

Thus did God comfort him, grant him victory over his enemy and make his *da'wa* firm for him.

The *ḥadīth* narrates that he bathed in the water and his body recovered. God returned to him those of his people, children, cattle and livestock that had died, bringing them back to life. The *ta'wīl* of this is that the people of his *da'wa* returned and that his *da'wa* was set aright for him. The *ḥadīth* also says that he was angry at his wife and had vowed that he would smite her. But when his tribulation disappeared and he came to know of how faithful she had been to him, he regretted this. God, the Exalted, had said: 'And take in thine hand a bundle (*ḍighth*) and smite therewith, and break not thine oath...' [38:44].

The *ta'wīl* of this is that Job had discovered that his *bāb* had innovated something based on his own internal shortcoming. He thus vowed that he would sever their relationship. However, when God relieved him, he regretted the oath he had made, because of his forbearance and wish to protect his *bāb*. [His *bāb*] repented of what he had done, and so it was said to Job:

'Gather your *lāḥiq*s and demote the one about whom you swore an oath to the level of those below him. Do not break your oath, but maintain him at the rank of the *lāḥiq*s. Reduce his rank only in accordance with the error that has been proven against him; rather, be lenient with him and turn to him in forgiveness.' The word *ḍighth* [in the aforementioned verse of the Qur'an] means a bundle of something, like a collection of branches. This is a symbol of his collecting together the *lāḥiq*s.

God continues: 'We found him patient...' [38:44]. This refers to the *bāb* with whom Job was angry. The *bāb* bore this patiently. Regarding this, God, the Exalted, continues: '...how excellent a slave! Indeed, he was ever turning in repentance (to his Lord)' [38:44].

This refers to the *bāb*'s returning to what pleased God, may He be glorified, and disdaining that which displeased Him, may His mention be Exalted. This is what deputation [by God] and repentance truly mean.

(Translated by Shafique N. Virani)

6

Abū Yaʿqūb al-Sijistānī

Chapters 30, 31 and 32 of al-Sijistānī's *Wellsprings* (see Sections I, 2 and III, 3) are particularly rich in religious symbolism. In Wellspring 30, al-Sijistānī offers an exegesis of the words that comprise the profession of faith '*Lā Ilāha Illā Allāh,*' drawing out the meanings hidden in the letters themselves and showing that these words contain the key to Paradise. He goes on in Wellspring 31 to construe the symbolism of the Cross as used by the 'community of Jesus,' or Christians. Wellspring 32 explains how the symbolism of the Cross may be shown to correspond with the exegesis of the Muslim profession of faith.

Kitāb al-yanābīʿ
The Book of Wellsprings[1]

ON THE MEANING OF THE PROFESSION OF FAITH IN THE STATEMENT BY THE PROPHET (THE PRAYER OF GOD BE ON HIM AND HIS FAMILY) THAT '*LĀ ILĀHA ILLĀ ALLĀH* IS THE KEY TO PARADISE'

In this statement, 'paradise' is the Word of God by means of which He originated those things in paradise that have its [form of] being. In nothing is there found the purity of the Word that originates something from nothing. If it existed in anything, that thing could bring about origination from nothing. But this excellence is found in nothing else; [nothing has] the excellence of His Word, exalted and glorious is He, which is thus truly paradise.

The four words in the profession of faith, which are its 'keys,' are the four principles: the two root sources and the two foundations. The Preceder is the key to all existing beings, whether spiritual or corporeal, because every existent is a particular example of what the Preceder combines within its own being since the Originator originated that in it. This is to say, by means of the Preceder all existent beings were 'opened' by the Word. The Follower is, on the measure of its allotment from the Word, the key for all things possessing order and composition, since orderly, composite things cannot be conceived except as they are pictured in the sublime souls prior to their actual appearance as ordered and composed

1. Abū Yaʿqūb al-Sijistānī. *Kitāb al-yanābīʿ*, ed. and French trans. Henry Corbin, *Trilogie Ismaélienne* (Tehran and Paris, 1961); English trans. Paul E. Walker as 'The Book of Wellsprings' in *The Wellsprings of Wisdom* (Salt Lake City, 1994), Wellsprings 30, 31, 32, pp. 91–95.

beings. That is to say, all things ordered and composed were 'opened' by means of the Follower.

The Speaking-prophet is the key to all rational utterances that explain intellectual virtues and psychological compositions indicating the forms of astral beings. Through him – that is, by means of the Speaking-prophet – by the Word, all sacred, legal regimes were 'opened.' The Founder is the key to all that intelligible existences, psychological compositions, and apostolic regimes go back to. He puts everything in its proper place and through him – that is, the Founder – all scientific interpretations were 'opened' by the Word.

The *lā* in the profession of faith is the Founder's tooth [of the key]. It consists of two letters that are half of the letters of the word *Allāh*, which is itself the Preceder's tooth, because *allāh* has four letters. Also it – that is, *lā* – is a word of denial, while *allāh* is a word of affirmation. All this corresponds to the fact that the Founder causes the manifestation of only one half of what flows to the Speaking-prophet from the Preceder and thus he distinguishes the superficial from the true and [the letter] of the law from [its] interpretation. He likewise insists on the denial of doubts in its declaration of the oneness of God. What the Originator reveals in it, the Preceder does not divide but rather produces at the ultimate of perfection. For this reason its word has four letters, since four is the most complete of numbers. It is the Preceder who affirms the Maker whenever it acknowledges the unique Godliness [of the God]. *Ilāh* is the Speaking-prophet's tooth because he is the agent of the Preceder in the corporeal world. In [the word] *ilāh*, one letter is lacking from the word *Allāh*, a *lām*. Accordingly, the Speaking-prophet does not obtain the full completeness of the Preceder, but is nevertheless the master of three levels, namely, apostleship, executorship, and imamate. *Illā* is the Follower's tooth. It is a word of exclusion. Correspondingly, the Follower resembles the Preceder in making corporeal beings appear, but this is not the case for spiritual beings.

These four words indicating the four principles will, if you add them together, 'open' for you all the things in the origination. However, a key will not open a door by itself but rather requires that it have an agent who actually does the opening. In a way similar to this, no one has the preparation to comprehend the ranks of these four principles, which are the keys in the Originator's Word, except through the guiding agency of an imam or Adjunct or Wing. If a single tooth falls off the key, the agent will be unequipped to open the door. Likewise, if the guiding agent fails to acknowledge any rank among these four principles – namely, the Preceder, the Follower, the Speaking-prophet, and the Founder – he will be unequipped to disclose to the seeker any of the signposts of his religion. If he undertakes the disclosure despite this denial, he will only tire himself and his attempted disclosure will add nothing but distress and incomprehensibility. This is exactly what would happen if the master of the key that had lost its tooth wanted to open a door with the same key. He would be unable to do it and would tire himself in trying, although he might destroy the lock through an excessive amount of movement. And it is in this sense that the apostle of God – the prayer of God be on him and his family – declared, '"There is no god but God" is the key to paradise.'

ON THE MEANING OF THE CROSS FOR THE RELIGIOUS COMMUNITY OF JESUS (ON WHOM BE PEACE)

'Cross' is the name for the piece of wood on which a man is crucified so that the whole population may see him, and what is crucified on it is a dead body. Jesus, on whom be peace, informed his community that the master of the day of resurrection, of whom he was the harbinger, will unveil the structural truths of those sacred laws that were constructed of truths and the people will know them and be unable to deny them. This would be like a whole population seeing someone crucified. They would recognize that person and understand his real form, although previous to this most of them were ignorant of him. It is in this sense that he called his day 'the day of unveiling' just as God has said, 'Upon the day when the leg shall be bared, and they shall be summoned to bow themselves' [68:42]. What is crucified on the wood becomes something disclosed, although previously it was something concealed.

Another indication: he also told his community that the master of the resurrection and his deputies will have the facility for producing the explanation of everything even though religion was not imagined to have explanation in it, just as [it was unknown that] the ranks of the hierarchies come together in this lifeless piece of wood.

It was related in one of the Reports that, on the 'night of power,' a light will shine and the walls, trees, and all bodies will bow down to that light. This is a metaphor that was coined to illustrate the power of the messiah, on whom be peace, and his deputies, and their ability to produce the explanation of all things. They investigate things with an instinctive disposition because of a discernment and a deductive proficiency that are inherently a part of their intellects.

The wood Jesus was crucified on was provided for this purpose by a group other than his own and these people were the ones who crucified him on it openly and manifestly. Accordingly, the explanation that the messiah and his deputies, on whom be peace, will reveal concerns the sacred laws of the messenger-prophets who have come before him. The cross thus becomes a clear sign and evidence of all ranks of the hierarchy. [Christian] veneration of it is something required of them, as, similarly, our veneration of the profession of faith is [required by us].

ON THE AGREEMENT OF THE CROSS WITH THE PROFESSION OF FAITH

The profession of faith is built on denial and affirmation, beginning with denial and ending with affirmation. Similarly, the cross is two pieces of wood: a piece that stands on its own and another piece whose placement depends entirely on the placement of the other. The profession of faith is four words. Likewise the cross has four extremities. The end fixed in the ground has the position of the master of interpretation in whom the souls of the seekers attain lasting security. The end opposite this, high in the air, has the position of the master of divine inspiration, in whom the souls of the inspired ones attain lasting security. The two ends in the middle, which are to the left and the right, indicate the Follower and the Speaking-prophet, of whom one is the master of natural composition and the other master of spiritual compilation. One is opposite the other, with the end standing for the Preceder sustaining all of the edges.

The profession of the faith is seven syllables. Similarly, the cross has four angles and three terminations. The four angles and three terminations indicate the seven imams of the era of Jesus in the same way that the seven syllables of the profession of faith indicate the imams of the era of our Speaking-prophet, on whom be peace. Each end of the cross has itself three points, which makes twelve points in all. Likewise the profession of faith has twelve letters. Just as its composition derives from three letters only, not counting repetitions, in a similar way the cross is a compound of planes, lines, and angles. The lines correspond to the *alif*; the planes to the *lām*; and the angles to the *hā'*. Just as the profession of faith is only completed by its being associated with Muḥammad, may the prayer of God be on him and his family, similarly the cross only became venerable after the master of that era was found on it. Let us create graphically here a picture of how the cross corresponds in its sections and parts to the profession of faith [see fig.].

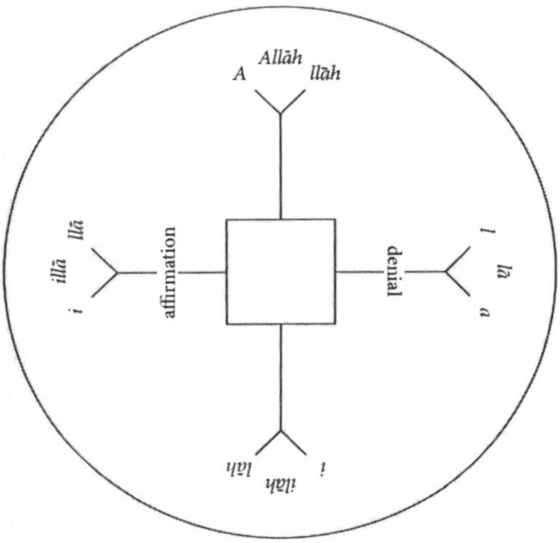

(Translated by Paul E. Walker)

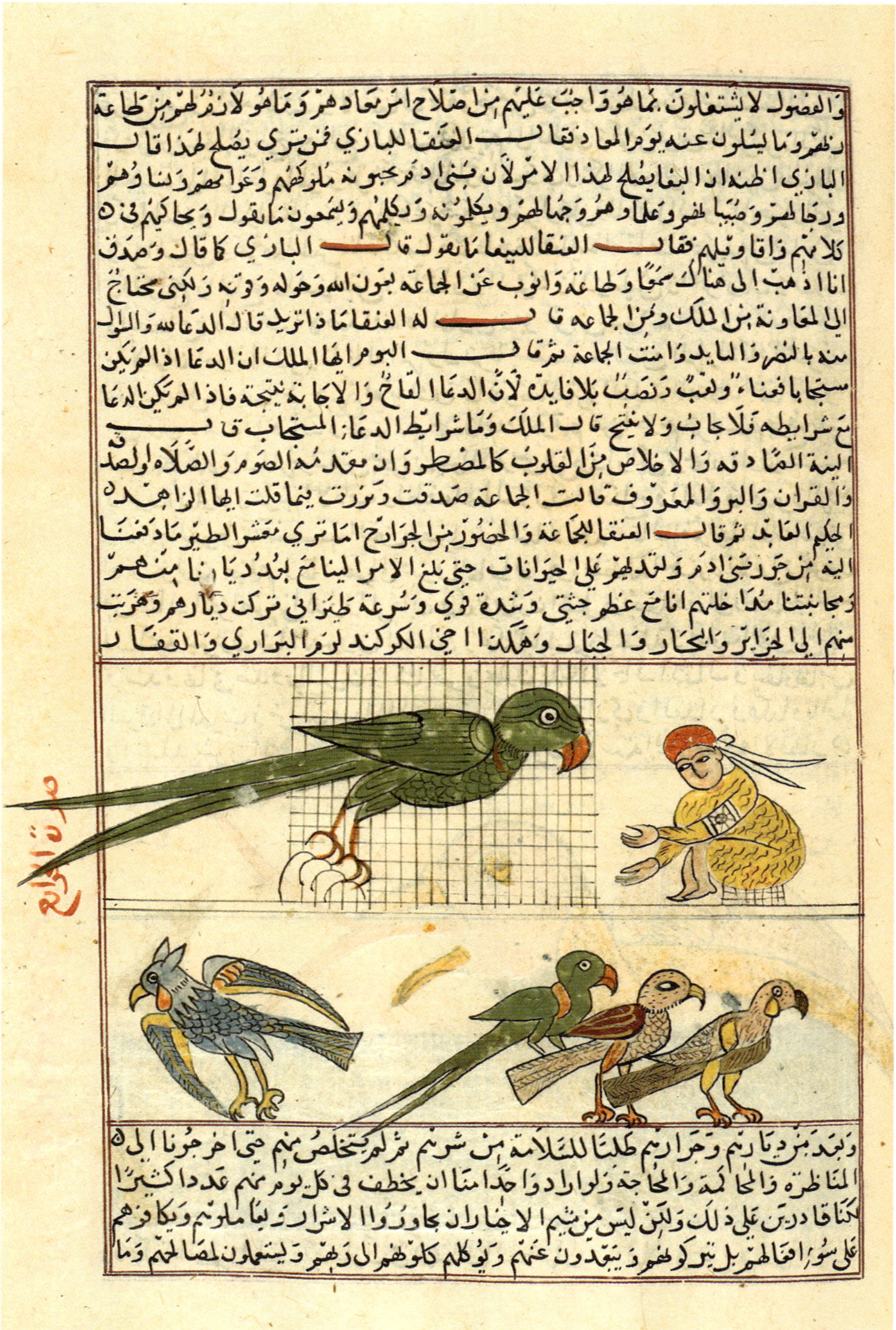

PLATE 4

This image from a 16th-century manuscript of the *Rasā'il Ikhwān al-Ṣafā'* (*Epistles of the Brethren of Purity*) shows a parrot in a cage accompanied by other birds of prey. The parrot was chosen to represent the birds of prey in the great debate with humans before the King of the Jinn.

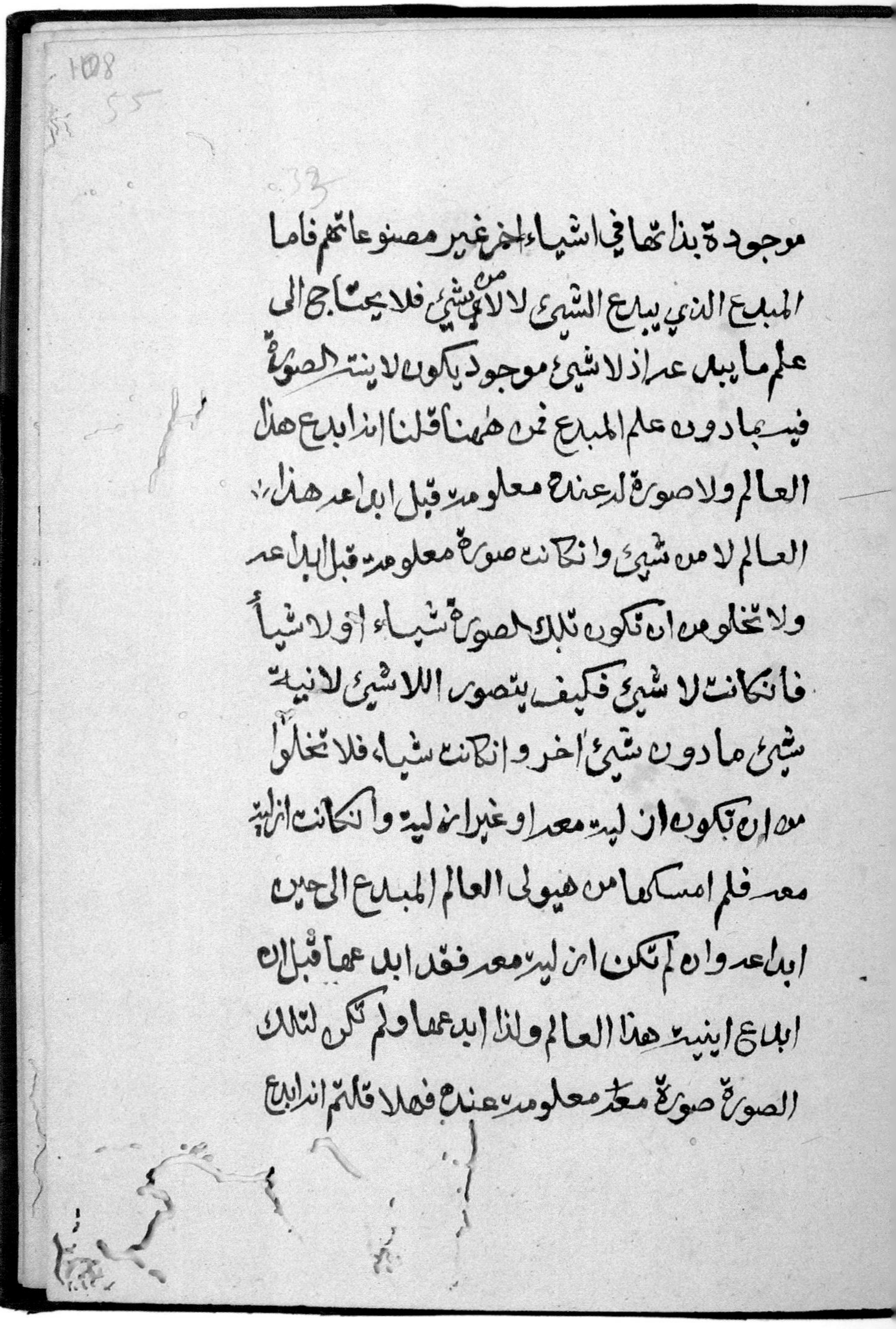

PLATE 5

This diagram of the cross is from Wellspring 32 of Abū Yaʿqūb al-Sijistānī's *Kitāb al-yanābīʿ* (*Book of Wellsprings*), reproduced from a manuscript copied in 1351/1932.

الصليب مع الشهادة بفصولها واقسامها تحت الحس

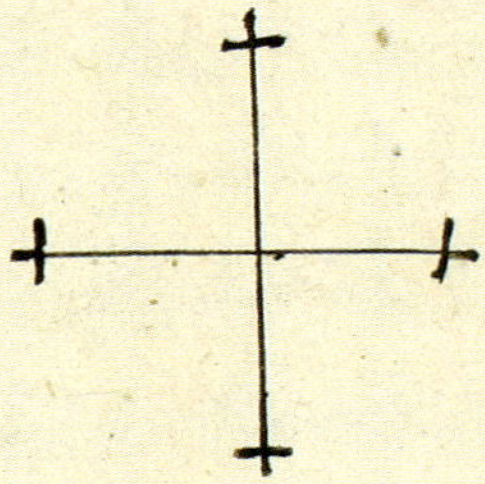

في ان العالم لا صورة له عند المبدع قبل الابداع والذين
قال ان الباري سبحانه ابدع هذا العالم وصورته
معلومة عنده قبل الابداع اذ زعم انه ان لم تكن الصورة
عنده معلومة فقد ابدع ما لم يعلمه لم يعط القياس
حقه وذلك الصورة المعلومة عند الصانعين قبل
اظهارهم الصنعة انما تكون من اجل عجزهم عن
اختراع صناعاتهم لا من شيء فلما كانت صناعاتهم
من شيء ما جاز ان تكون صورها معلومة عندهم

موجودة

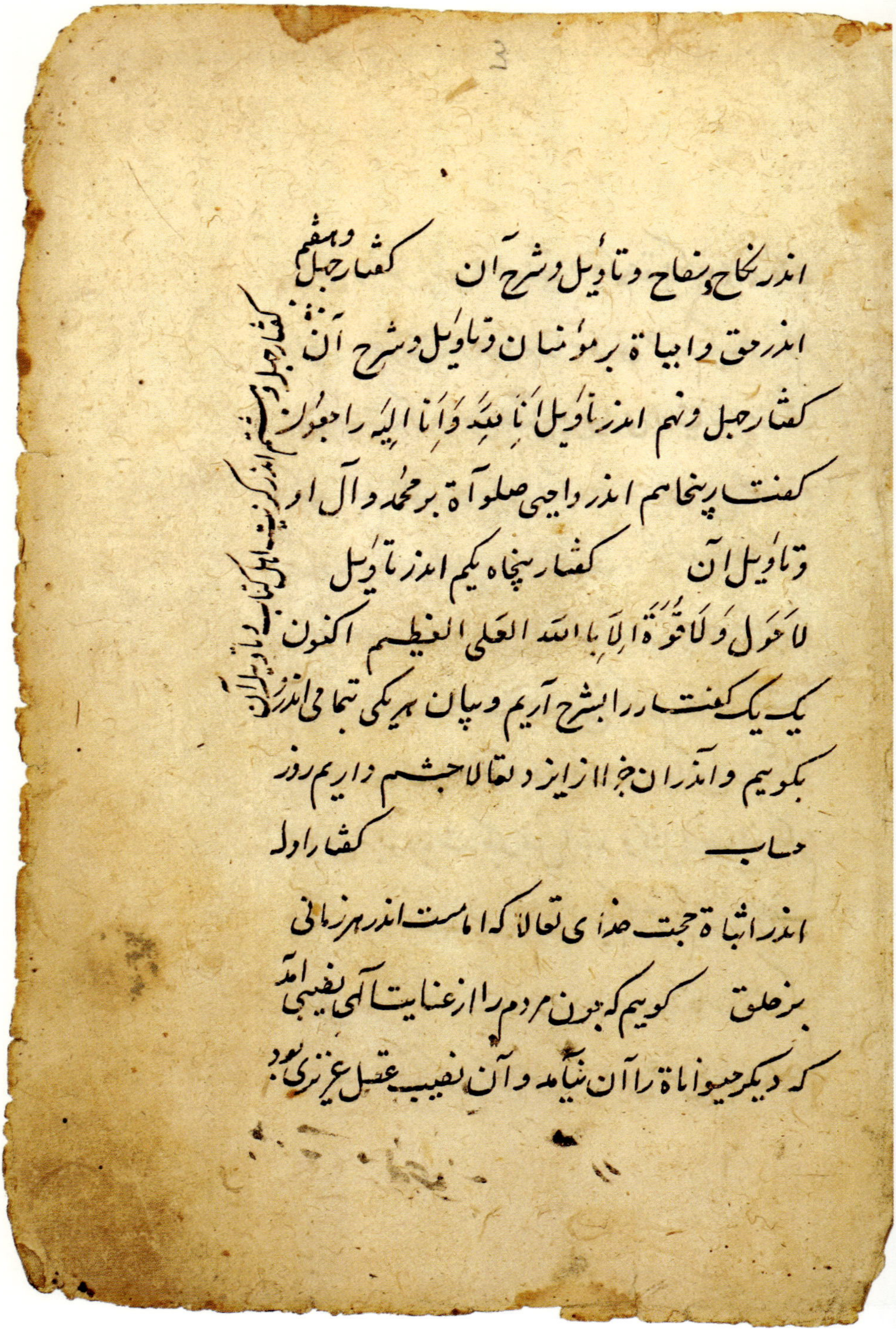
اندر نکاح و سفاح و تاویل و شرح آن گفتار چهل و هفتم
اندر حق و اباحه بر مؤمنان و تاویل و شرح آن
گفتار چهل و نهم اندر تاویل انا لله و انا الیه راجعون
گفتار پنجاهم اندر واجبی صلوات بر محمد و آل او
و تاویل آن گفتار پنجاه یکم اندر تاویل
لا حول و لا قوة الا بالله العلی العظیم اکنون
یک یک گفتار را بشرح آریم و بیان هر یکی تمامی اندر
بگوییم و اندر آن جزا از ایزد تعالی چشم داریم روز
حساب گفتار اول
اندر اثبات حجت خدای تعالی که امامست اندر هر زمانی
بر خلق گوییم که چون مردم را از عنایت الهی نصیبی آمد
که دیگر حیوانات را آن نیامد و آن نصیب عقل غریزی بود

PLATE 6

This is one of the opening pages from an 8th/14th-century manuscript of Nāṣir-i Khusraw's *Wajh-i dīn* (*The Face of Religion*).

7
Nāṣir-i Khusraw

Among Nāṣir-i Khusraw's many works (see above, Part One, 6 and Part Two, I, 3), *Wajh-i dīn* is the most explicit in terms of religious instruction, offering a full explanation of Islamic commandments and duties and their esoteric meaning or *ta'wīl*. This important work is particularly influential among the Nizārī Ismailis of Central Asia, who have preserved and circulated the text. In the first two discourses quoted below, Nāṣir offers an explanation of the nature of knowledge and the spiritual world. In another discourse, he offers an exegesis of the necessity to obey the imam of the time. In the final passage, Nāṣir elaborates on the Qur'anic phrase: 'We belong to Allah and unto Him we are returning' (2:156–57).

Wajh-i dīn
The Face of Religion[1]

ON THE ESTABLISHMENT OF KNOWLEDGE AND DISCOVERING ITS ESSENCE

Believers must first know what knowledge is so that once they have recognized it, they can go in search of it. This is because those who do not recognize what something is can never obtain it. Thus, we say that knowledge means to perceive things as they are. And that which perceives things as they are is the intellect, while knowledge is in the Pearl of Intellect. The Pearl of Intellect is the Word of God, may He be exalted, which subsumes all spiritual and physical existents. It is inappropriate to refer to that which is not subsumed by knowledge as existent. Thus, whatever knowledge encompasses is other than God. As it is unworthy for God to be subsumed by a thing, knowledge being that which subsumes all things, existents and non-existents alike, it is inappropriate for us to say that God is existent or non-existent, for both of these are subsumed by knowledge, whereas God is not.

Hence, we say that pure knowledge[2] is God's Command. Those who have been endowed with greater knowledge are closer to God's Command, have a greater acceptance of it and are more obedient. Those who are wiser are more obedient to

1. Nāṣir-i Khusraw. *Wajh-i dīn*, ed. and tr. Faquir M. Hunzai as *The Face of Religion* (forthcoming), Discourses 3, 4, 36, 39.

2. See Abū Ya'qūb Aḥmad al-Sijistānī, *Kashf al-maḥjūb*, ed. H. Corbin (Tehran and Paris, 1949), pp. 20–21.

God. Those who become completely wise (*dānā-yi tamām*) attain eternal blessing, because the work of the wise results in God's mercy. Human beings are the last of the generated beings[1] [i.e., the three kingdoms of nature: mineral, vegetable and animal] of the world. Their return is to (God's) Command, which is the cause of both worlds. All things return to their origin. O brothers! Strive to seek knowledge in order to draw nearer to God, may He be exalted, for the mercy of the exalted God is knowledge.

[Peace!]

ON THE DESCRIPTION OF THE SUBTLE SPIRITUAL WORLD AND ITS EXISTENCE

We have [already] demonstrated that God's Command, that is, knowledge, was the first thing to come into existence and we have exhibited that the soundness of this statement lies in that all things are subsumed by knowledge. Thus, it necessarily follows that the first thing that came into existence was knowledge. In this discourse we will now demonstrate that the spiritual world first came into existence from the Divine Command and then this world appeared from that one. Further, we say that that world is wise (*dānā*), complete, permanent and subtle. That is, it is entirely soul and knowledge.

Now we will demonstrate that that world was first and was followed by this one. This physical world changes from state to state, and by this change, things such as minerals, plants and animals appear in it. All of these display signs of intending a purpose [by an agent]. That is to say, plants grow upon which the animals depend and humankind appears to look after both of them. Had human beings not existed, all [useful] plants and animals would have been extinct. We therefore know that the purpose of these things does not belong to this world.

If someone were to say that these elements (*ṭabā'i'*) themselves resolve upon the purpose, it is tantamount to saying that this world is both the purposer (*qāṣid*) and what was purposed (*maqṣūd*). This is contradictory. As it is known that the purpose of this world belongs to that world, thus we call that purposer also a world. This is because that purposer can purpose things if there is resemblance between the purposer and the purposed. Based on what we have stated, it follows that that world whose action is this world, resembles this one in some respects. [To elaborate further] since in this world nothing is nobler than knowledge, we say that that world is both receiver and giver of knowledge. In this world the soul receives knowledge and the intellect gives it. Therefore, we say that that world is naught but intellect and soul. This is because only two situations are possible in the world: either the heavens are benefactors while the elements are beneficiaries; or the elements are benefactors while the plants are beneficiaries; or the plants are benefactors while the animals are beneficiaries; or the animals are benefactors while human beings are beneficiaries; or the teacher is the benefactor and the student is the beneficiary; or the Prophet is the benefactor and the community is the beneficiary. Similarly

1 For further elaboration of this point see Nāṣir-i Khusraw, *Wajh-i dīn*, Discourse 9.

among the animals, the male is the benefactor and the female is the beneficiary. Likewise the Creator is the benefactor and the creatures are the beneficiaries.

As this entire world is a beneficiary, containing as it does, plants, animals and minerals that are not in the origin of the elements, we say that that world, which does all this, is the benefactor. At the same time, we say that in itself, that world must also be composed of two parts: the intellect, which is the benefactor and the soul, which is the beneficiary. As we know that this world is the beneficiary, it follows that that world is the benefactor. Since that world is the benefactor, it follows that that world came into existence prior to this world. However, this priority we call antecedence in status or excellence and not antecedence in time. For example, a teacher's precedence over a student is in status or excellence, for at the same time and in the same situation one is a teacher and one is a student, neither before nor after the other.

We will demonstrate that that world is wise because the traces of its wisdom-filled creation are apparent in this world. These include the composition (*tarkīb*) of the celestial spheres in the best and most complete form – a circle; the proportionality of the four elements, each of which is in some respects similar and in other respects different from the others at the same time, such that because of their compatibility these four elements can combine with one another, but because of their differences they do not become a single [substance], thus becoming useless. We have explained this in detail in other books. Since wisdom is apparent in this created world and we have established that that first world is the creator of this world, it is established that that world is wise.

We will demonstrate that that world is complete. To this end we say that we perceive this world to be incomplete. Things appear in this world that are superior to it, such as animals. This is because the world is composed of the four elements [abiding] next to each other, whereas human beings and animals are composed of the four elements, not [abiding] next to each other, but rather combined with each other. If two things next to each other may be called composed, and goodness and well-being lie in [their] composition, then two things combined with each other may be called more composed, and more goodness and well-being may lie in it. With regard to its body, the animal certainly resembles this world as it is composed of the same elements. However, with respect to its feeling and moving soul, it is superior to this world and the world of elements. Hence, it is established that an animal is more complete than the world, for it has a soul while this world does not. When we see something complete in this incomplete world, we affirm that a complete thing does not appear from an incomplete thing save by the providence of something else that is complete. As we established earlier, creation in this world belongs to that world. We say that that world, whose creation is complete, is necessarily complete and that which is complete is permanent.

We will demonstrate that that world is permanent. To this end we say that we see that this world is transitory (*gardanda* = *fānī*) [in its parts] from one state to another, and the reality of transition (*fanā*) is the changing of the state of an existent from the quality called 'existence.' And [if] a thing changes in its parts, inevitably one day [it] changes in its entirety. There are many types of changes in this world: being overpowered by an opponent, when a living thing dies, darkness replacing brightness, stench overcoming fragrance, and so on. All of these are proofs of transition, for transition is the opposite of permanence (*baqā*), just as darkness is the opposite of light and non-existence is the opposite of existence. Thus, these partial transitions indicate the total transition of this world. Since the transition of this created [world] is established, so is the permanence of that world, which is [its] creator. This is because the creator is nobler than the creature, just as permanence is nobler than transition.

Creation in this world is accidental, as is its permanence. Its change of state testifies to its permanence being also accidental. And the quality of an accident does not appear in a thing except from a thing in which it [quality] is substantial, that is to say, essential. [For instance,] heat and light in iron appear accidentally from fire, whereas heat and light in fire are substantial, that is to say, essential. Hence, we have established that the accidental permanence in this world appears from that world. It thus follows that the permanence of that world is substantial, that is to say, essential.

We will demonstrate that that world is subtle. To this end, we say that subtle (*laṭīf*) means something whose traces pass through a body and that body is unable to prevent its passage. An example of this among perceptible things is that a body cannot prevent the power of the subtlety of fire. Do you not see that even if there is a thick, solid [piece of] iron, despite its thickness and solidity, if fire is applied to one side of it, its power penetrates to the other side? When we behold the whales and other animals that have come into existence in the great sea, life having found a way into the wombs of females and the loins of males such that the sperm in the loins of males receives life, begins to move and [after being transferred to the wombs of females] becomes a living creature, we conclude that this is because of the subtlety of that world which is the creator of this world.

We will demonstrate that that world is living. To this end we say that in this world we see that whatever has been endowed with a soul is nobler than that which has no soul. That world, which is the creator, is nobler than this created world, which has no soul. It thus necessarily follows that that world, which is the creator, is entirely soul and knowledge.

Further, as the best thing in this world is the rational animal (*jānwar-i dānā*), that being the human being, we say that since the creator is better than the created, and the best of created things in the world is the rational animal, it follows that this rational animal is closer to the creator as he is better than the other creatures.[1] Since the human being, the rational animal, is superior, and the creature closest to its creator is that which is superior, it is established that that world is alive and knowing. This claim is confirmed by the speech of God, may He be exalted: 'And indeed, the next world is alive, if they but knew' [29:64].

1. See Nāṣir-i Khusraw's *Zād al-musāfirīn*, ed. Badhl al-Raḥmān (Berlin, 1923), p. 179 ff.

We will demonstrate that that world is knowing, seeing, hearing and speaking. To this end, we say that these laudable qualities that appear in human beings are produced by that world. These qualities do not exist in the elements of this created world. It is thus necessary that they be from the creator of this world. As these qualities exist in this world partially, we realize that the totality of knowledge, sight, hearing and speech belongs to that world. All these qualities pertain to the Universal Soul, who receives spiritual help (*ta'yīd*) from the Command of God, may He be exalted, which is the source (*māya*) of both the worlds, through the Universal Intellect.

We say that that world, which is subtle, permanent, powerful, knowing and complete is not a place, nor in a place, nor out of a place. It is the creature of the unique God. Therefore, it is incumbent upon sincere believers to recognize that world and to know that in reality paradise is that world. The souls of those who recognize that world in reality reach that world, even today [*in potentia*], though they are still embodied. If they duly practise the *sharī'at*, they reach that world [*in actu*] and remain there in eternal bliss. May God, may He be exalted, grant success to the believers to do good deeds! *Āmīn*, O Sustainer of the worlds!

Peace!

ON THE NECESSITY OF OBEDIENCE TO THE IMAM OF THE TIME AND ITS *TA'WĪL*

By the grace of God, we say that a human being is a subtle substance embedded in a dense substance, and is constituted of two worlds, the perceptible and the intelligible. While the body is visible and tangible, the soul is invisible and intangible. The visible and tangible human body must be constituted through the mediation of two homogeneous beings, a father and a mother. The third is the child. Similarly, the subtle substance [the soul], which is coupled with the dense substance [the body], cannot be adorned and composed save through the [mediation of] two homogeneous beings, of whom it is the third.

Just as the body attains perfection when, through the mediation of its parents, it acquires the physical pleasures of this world, similarly, the perfection of the soul lies in the mediation of the spiritual father and mother, so that it may attain the pleasures of the spiritual world. It is necessarily established that just as the human body cannot dispense with physical parents, so also the human soul cannot dispense with spiritual parents.

As a person's physical father is the benefactor [in his creation] and his physical mother is the beneficiary, his spiritual father is also the benefactor and his spiritual mother the beneficiary. Thus, we say that the religious father, whose role is to be the father of the believer's soul, is the Prophet, God's blessings be upon him and his progeny, and that the religious mother, whose role is to be the mother of the believer's soul, is his *waṣī*. In comparing the relationship between the spiritual form of the believer's soul and the [the physical creation of] the body, the *nāṭiq*'s *tanzīl* is like the father's sperm and the *waṣī*'s *ta'wīl* is like the mother's ovum. The union of the two physical drops [i.e., the sperm and ovum] creates an adorned form for the physical world, similarly a spiritual form adorned for the spiritual world is created by the union of the two spiritual drops. The soundness of this statement is attested by the Prophet's saying: 'O ʿAlī, I and you are the father and mother of the believers.'[1] This tradition is well substantiated by God's saying: 'The Prophet has more right over the faithful than their own selves, and his wives are their mothers' [33:6]. If the Prophet's wives are the mothers of the believers, the Prophet is their father. The Prophet has said: 'The earth is your mother and it is kind to you.'[2] According to this tradition, it is established that the Prophet is the sky and the father of the believers, and his wives are like the earth and are the mothers of the believers. This is because they possess goodness [and spiritual nourishment] and this issues only from the wise. If it comes [from other than the wise], it is not called goodness.

The sky, by [providing] rain and the radiation of the stars, is the earth's benefactor. The earth receives these and conveys them to the precious stones in the mines, to the plants and to the [various] species of animals. God says: 'And you see the lifeless earth, but when We pour down rain water on it, it is stirred (to life) and increased, and caused to grow every kind of beautiful pair' [22:5]. The *ta'wīl* of this verse is that the constancy and existence of the *ta'wīl* depends on the *tanzīl*. As demonstrated earlier, the *nāṭiq* is like the sky. Thus, the *tanzīl* is like rain. Since the *waṣī* is like the earth, the *ta'wīl* is like those things that grow with heavenly help. Since the *nāṭiq* is the administrator of the entire world of religion, life and not death is attributed to him. God says: 'And We have sent down pure water from the sky, so that We may revive a lifeless land with it' [25:48–49]. That is, 'When We sent down rain water, the earth became alive.' Thus, we say that the *tanzīl* is like the body and the *ta'wīl* is like its soul. The body dies when the soul is separated from it. The *ẓāhir* (exoteric sense) of the *sharīʿat* and its *ta'wīl* as such are also like body and soul. Furthermore, as stated earlier, the earth is like the *ta'wīl* and the sky like the *tanzīl*. This is why death is attributed to the earth and life to the sky.

As it is established that the earth and the sky are essential for the generated things of the physical world, a physical father and mother are necessary for physical procreation. It necessarily follows that there be a spiritual father and mother for the believers in every age. Thus, they must recognize their spiritual father and mother so that they do not remain without lineage. The Prophet has said: 'Whoever dies without recognizing the Imam of his Time, dies as an ignoramus, and

1. Cf. al-Mu'ayyad fi'l-Dīn al-Shīrāzī. *al-Majālis al-Mu'ayyadiyya*, ed. Ḥātim Ḥamīd al-Dīn (Bombay, 1975), vol. 1, p. 381. See also for another version of it in Nāṣir-i Khusraw, *Jāmiʿ al-ḥikmatayn*, ed. H. Corbin and M. Muʿīn (Tehran and Paris, 1953), p. 209; Nāṣir-i Khusraw, *Khwān al-ikhwān*, ed. Yaḥyā al-Khashshāb (Cairo, 1940), p. 258; and Rāghib Iṣfahānī, *Mufradāt*, ed., Nadīm Marʿashlī (Beirut, 1972), p. 3.

2. Cf. al-Shīrāzī, *al-Majālis*, vol. 1, 381; al-Qāḍī al-Nuʿmān, *Da'ā'im al-Islām*, ed. A. A. A. Fyzee (Cairo, 1963), vol. 1, p. 178; Ibn Manẓūr, *Lisān al-ʿarab* (Beirut, n.d.), vol. 4, p. 53.

the place of the ignoramus is the Fire.'[1] Someone who dies as an ignoramus does not have the Prophet. Such a person is in the Fire. Thus, obedience to the imam is incumbent on those who recognize him, if they are in his presence. If they are not, it is enjoined upon them to obey the one who is appointed by the imam in their *jazīra* (island=region).

Not a single group among the [differing] sects and schools rejects the existence of an imam save the Muʿaṭṭilān[2] and Dahriyān[3] who do not have knowledge and who reject it. In fact, they claim that knowledge itself does not exist! Of course, there are people of varying levels of intelligence and ignorance in every school of thought, and the intelligent ones become the imams of the ignorant. However, the point [of contention] is that each group claims that its imam, whom they follow, is the true one. Thus, while all the people agree on the meaning of the imamate, they differ about the name of the imam. It is therefore necessary for the believers to recognize the imam of their time because they must obey him. So let us see whether the imam is needed for religion or for the world or for both.

We say that were an imam to be requisite for the world but not for religion, then the latter would be useless and leaderless. However God, may He be exalted, is far too great to make a useless thing, least of all religion, which is the noblest of all things. Were religion to require an imam but not the world, then the politics of the world would become futile and legal punishment would be useless. It is impossible that God, may He be exalted, would make the imam chief over the nobler thing, but would have withheld from him the baser thing. Therefore, it is evident that the imam is necessary for both religion as well as the world.

Then we considered the execution of the imam's task in religion, that is, whether he is necessary for the unequivocal (*muḥkam*) verses or for the equivocal (*mutashābih*) verses [of the Qur'an]. [It is obvious that] in themselves the unequivocal verses have no need [of explanation], due to their straight and detailed meaning. The imam is therefore necessary for the equivocal verses, for no one can attain knowledge of the equivocal verses by reasoning, except the lord of the *ta'wīl*. We did not find anyone in the community who invites [people] to solve the obscurities of the equivocal verses except a group from the Prophet's family (*ahl-i bayt*). Therefore, we resolved to go to them and found knowledge of the equivocal verses of the Qur'an and the *sharīʿat*. We came to know that they are the lords of the Command of God, may He be exalted, whose obedience He has enjoined upon us by this verse: 'O you who believe! Obey God and obey the Prophet, and obey those who possess the Divine Command (*ulu'l-amr*) amongst you' [4:59].

Thus we say that [the imam] must have seven things in order to possess the imamate. First, the previous imam's indication of entrusting him with the imamate.

1. al-Nuʿmān, *Daʿā'im*, vol. 1, pp. 25, 27; Abū Jaʿfar Muḥammad b. Yaʿqūb al-Kulaynī. *al-Uṣūl min al-kāfī*, ed. and Persian trans. J. Muṣṭafawī (Tehran, n.d), vol. 1, p. 254 ff.

2. On the schools that debated the attributes of God, see C. Gilliot, 'Attributes of God', *EI3*. Also see Richard C. Martin, 'Anthropomorphism' in *Encyclopaedia of the Qur'ān*, vol. 1, p. 103.

3 On Dahriyya (materialists), see I. Goldziher, 'Dahriyya,' *EI*, vol. 2, p. 95.

Second, his noble ancestry, meaning that he should be from the *ahl-i bayt* of the Prophet so that he may share Abraham's prayer. Third, he must have knowledge of religion, by which the rank of imams becomes high. Fourth, he should be righteous, as God says: 'The most honoured of you in the sight of God is the most righteous of you' [49:13]. Fifth, he should wage *jihād* against the infidels with his hand and against the hypocrites with his tongue. Sixth, besides [having] the imamate, he should possess the Prophet's excellent character that he possessed in addition to Prophethood. For this God said to him: 'And you (stand) on an exalted standard of character' [68:4]. Seventh, he should be far from claiming the imamate for himself, because if he claims (it), he will become a claimant and come under the judgement of a judge. Then, if he were the plaintiff, he could not be the judge. Rather, he should have people who would claim [the imamate] on his behalf. In this book we have mentioned the *ta'wīl* of roots and branches, and this much is sufficient for intelligent *mustajīb*s.

Now we will explain the seven pillars of Islam upon which the foundation of religion rests. The seven pillars, which have been mentioned, signify the seven *ḥadd*s. The first is the *shahādat* (confession of faith), which signifies the Precursor [i.e. the Intellect] through whom the *nāṭiq* has received correct *tawḥīd* – that is, that God transcends [being] describable or indescribable, [paired or] unpaired. *Ṣalāt* signifies the Second [i.e., the Universal Soul], who gave the *nāṭiq* his *māddat* (=*ta'yīd*), by which he was able to compile the *sharī'at*, which resembles the *tarkīb* (composition) of the world that proceeded from him (the Universal Soul). *Zakāt* (religious due) signifies the *nāṭiq*, who appointed the *asās* (foundation) to invite to the true knowledge, in which lies the purification of souls from the pollution of polytheism and hypocrisy. *Ḥajj* (pilgrimage) signifies the *asās* with whom the house of religion becomes complete. This is because he is the fourth corner of religion and with four corners a house reaches completion. *Ṣawm* (fasting) of the month of Ramaḍān signifies the imam, for he does not have a known task as the roots of religion have, but he has to preserve the trust. Thus, the imam stands in the rank of *ṣawm*, fasting, that is, to remain silent, because it is not the function of the imam to explain (*bayān*). *Jihād* (struggle) signifies the *ḥadd* of the *ḥujjat* (proof), who does not rest from doing *da'wat* (propagation). Rather, he always wages *jihād* and fears neither reproach nor the one who reproaches. Obedience to the *ulu'l-amr* (possessor of authority) signifies the *dā'ī*, because obedience to the imam becomes incumbent upon believers since the *dā'ī* makes them desire it by showing them the thing which is under the obedience to the imam, for them.

We will now discuss the *ta'wīl* of those things, knowledge of which believers cannot dispense with, so that by seeking knowledge of them, the souls of the seekers on the path may be purified.

Peace!

ON THE *TA'WĪL* OF '*INNĀ LI'LLĀHI WA-INNĀ ILAYHI RĀJI'ŪN*' (WE BELONG TO ALLAH AND UNTO HIM WE RETURN)

We say, by the grace of God, may He be exalted, that it is incumbent upon people to say these words when physical calamities befall them and when they are confronted with difficult tasks. As God, may He be exalted, says: 'Those who say, when a misfortune strikes them: Lo! We belong to Allah and unto Him we are returning' [2:156–57]. The Arabs describe the difficult tasks as the darkness of night, because no task is more difficult than one from which people cannot see a way of escape. That difficult situation is darkness.

Darkness is of two kinds, physical and spiritual. Physical darkness is due to the night and physical calamities (*kārhā-yi bī-sāmān*). Spiritual darkness however, is ignorance and the intractable questions concerning the intelligibles. Dispelling these two darknesses we have described, comes from God through the mediation of two lights. One is the sun that dispels the physical darkness and the other is the imam of the time who, as the sun of insight for spiritual darknesses, unravels difficult knots. When people are overcome by physical darkness and difficulty, they must submit to the decree of God, be pleased with whatever has been decreed and say: 'We belong to Allah and unto Him we are returning.' That is, we belong to Allah, accept what He has decreed and return to Him if any physical calamity befalls us whereby we perish physically.

In *ta'wīl*, when the believers face a difficult question regarding the intelligibles that they cannot solve, they must recite these same words in the sense: 'Our souls belong to the lord of the time, as we have received spiritual life from him and our return during difficulties is unto him,' and know that 'we cannot solve this question and the knowledge of this is with the lord of the time,' so that the door of blessings may open for them. Either they themselves may be able to understand it, or a *ḥadd* (rank) from the *ḥadd*s of religion may open the door of spiritual blessings for them. If those difficulties befall a *ḥadd* from among the *ḥadd*s of religion, he should seek the source (*māddat*) of *ta'yīd* from the lord of the time, peace be upon him. By uttering these words, he may himself strive so that the hidden [knowledge] may become manifest to him. If it does not manifest, he should know that this is due to his own weakness and affirm that the one who knows such spiritual difficulties is worthy of the people returning to him. This is a satisfactory explanation for a sincere believer.

Peace!

(Translated by Faquir M. Hunzai)

IV

FAITH AND ETHICS

1

al-Qāḍī al-Nuʿmān

One of the most important authorities under the early Fatimids, al-Qāḍī al-Nuʿmān (see Part One, 3 and Part Two, III, 5) compiled the *Daʿāʾim al-Islām* around 349/960 under the close supervision of the Imam-Caliph al-Muʿizz. This work became the official compendium of Ismaili law in the Fatimid state. The first volume deals with acts of worship (*ʿibādāt*), the second with temporal matters and transactions (*muʿāmalāt*). The status and longevity of this work can be gauged from the fact that to this day it is used by the Ṭayyibī Ismailis as their legal authority and enjoys the same legal status as other Muslim books of statute on the Indian subcontinent. The extract selected for this chapter explains the distinction between faith (*īmān*) and submission (*islām*).

Daʿāʾim al-Islām
The Pillars of Islam[1]

ON FAITH (*ĪMĀN*)

Jaʿfar b. Muḥammad: Faith consists in professing by the tongue, believing with the heart, and acting in accordance with its [Islamic] tenets.[2] This, and nothing but this, is valid. It is not correct to assert, like the Murjiʾa,[3] that faith consists in profession without action, nor is it correct to say, like a group of the commonalty (*ʿāmma*),[4] that faith consists in 'word and deed' only.

1. al-Qāḍī al-Nuʿmān, *Daʿāʾim al-Islām*, ed. Asaf A. A. Fyzee (Cairo, 1951–1961). English trans. Asaf A. A. Fyzee, revised by Ismail K. Poonawala as *The Pillars of Islam* (New Delhi, 2002–2004), vol. 1, pp. 5–17.

2. Three main elements concur in an act of faith: verbal expression (*qawlun bi'l-lisān*); internal conviction (*taṣdīqun bi'l-janān*); performance of the prescribed acts (*ʿamalun bi'l-arkān*). See Abū Jaʿfar Muḥammad b. Yaʿqūb al-Kulaynī, *al-Uṣūl min al-kāfī*, ed. ʿAlī Akbar al-Ghaffārī (Tehran, 1968), vol. 2, p. 27. Various schools of Islamic law and thought propose varying definitions according to their perspectives. Cf., Louis Gardet, 'Īmān,' *EI2*, vol. 3, p. 1171. Wensinck and Izutsu describe various doctrines concerning *īmān* in detail. A. J. Wensinck, *Concordance et Indices de la Traditions Musulmane* (2nd ed., Leiden, 1992), and Toshihiko Izutsu, *The Concept of Belief in Islamic Theology: A Semantic Analysis of Īmān and Islām* (Tokyo, 1965).

3. The name of a politico-religious movement in early Islam and in later times, that refers to all those who identified faith with belief (or confession of belief), to the exclusion of acts. W. Madelung, 'Murdjiʾa,' *EI2*, vol. 7, p. 606.

4. *ʿĀmma*, as distinguished from *khāṣṣa*, the select community, the truly faithful (*muʾminūn*), refers to the Sunnis.

How can the Murji'ite doctrine that profession without action constitutes faith be correct, while they and the community are unanimous in holding that he who forsakes any obligatory act as laid down by God [in the Qur'an] for His creatures, and disbelieves in it, is an unbeliever (*kāfir*)?[1] [Likewise they assert that] if he persists in such disbelief, it is lawful to put him to death, even though he believes in God and proclaims his belief in His unity and in His Messenger by word of mouth, although he asserts that '[a specific] obligatory act is not one which [the Messenger of God] commanded.' [For instance] God says: *And woe unto the idolaters, who give not the poor-due* [41:6–7]. So God removed them from the faith for their denial of the poor-due. For the same reason, the community agreed to declare the blood of the tribe of Banū Ḥanīfa[2] and the enslavement of their children to be lawful. They were designated as renegades (*ahl al-ridda*) because they refused to pay the alms tax [to the Medinan authority].

Ja'far b. Muḥammad: My father, may God be well pleased with him, said one day to Jābir b. 'Abd Allāh al-Anṣārī,[3] 'O Jābir, has God made the alms tax obligatory upon the idolater?' He said, 'No, He has made it obligatory only on the Muslims.' I [the Imam al-Bāqir] told him, 'I agree with it, but have you not considered the word of God: *And woe unto the idolaters, who give not the poor-due*?' [41:6–7]. Jābir said, 'By God, it was as though I had never read the verse, although it really does occur in the Book of God.' Abū 'Abd Allāh [the Imam] said, 'The verse was revealed in respect of those who apportion the devotion (*walāya*) due the Commander of the Faithful (*amīr al-mu'minīn*)[4] to others beside 'Alī and gave the alms tax due him to the one who set himself up against 'Alī.' But the full details regarding this question are too extensive.

The assertion of the community (*jamā'a*) that faith consists in profession and action without [the conviction of] intent (*niyya*) is impossible; for they are unanimous [in believing] that if a man were to abstain from food and drink for the whole day till night and yet had not [conscientiously] resolved to fast, he has not fasted. Similarly, if a man were to stand [for prayer], bend (*rak'a*), and prostrate himself (*sajada*), and yet had no intent to pray, he has not prayed; if a man were to halt at 'Arafa[5] and his conscious purpose was not to perform the pilgrimage, he has not performed the pilgrimage; and if, without the intent to pay the alms tax, a man were to give away the whole of his wealth in charity, he has not fulfilled the obligation to pay it; and they hold the same regarding the obligatory acts in general. Thus what

---

1. The ethical term *kufr* has two layers of meaning, descriptive and evaluative. For details see Toshihiko Izutsu. *Ethico-Religious Concepts in the Qur'ān* (Montreal, 1966), pp. 21–22, 26, and chapters 7–8.

2. Musaylima, one of the false prophets, who revolted against the authority of Medina, was supported by Banū Ḥanīfa, an ancient Arab tribe with its centre in Yamāma. See W. Montgomery Watt, 'Ḥanīfa b. Ludjaym,' *EI2*, vol. 3, p. 167; 'Musaylima,' *EI2*, vol. 7, p. 665.

3. A respected companion of the Prophet and a devoted supporter of 'Alī [ibn Abī Ṭālib].

4. A title first adopted by 'Umar b. al-Khaṭṭāb when he became caliph and was used exclusively as the protocollary title of a caliph. It is generally applied by the Shi'a to 'Alī b. Abī Ṭālib because they believe the Prophet designated him to command/lead the Muslim community after his death.

5. A hill to the east of Mecca, famous as a place of pilgrimage. On 9th Dhu'l-Ḥijja (the day of 'Arafa) the pilgrims celebrate the prescribed *wuqūf* in the plain of 'Arafa, which lasts from noon to sunset.

the Imam said is proved, namely that faith consists of profession (*qawl*), action (*ʿamal*), and intent (*niyya*). This rule and no other is sound.

The Messenger of God said, 'Verily, actions can be judged only by intentions and every person will [be rewarded or punished] for what he has intended to do. Thus he who abandons his home for the sake of God and His Messenger, his emigration shall be so recognized. But he who emigrates to marry a woman or for worldly considerations, his emigration shall likewise be so recognized.'[1]

Faith consists in testifying that there is no deity other than God alone; that He is without associate,[2] and Muḥammad is His Servant and His Messenger; that Heaven and Hell and the Resurrection are verities; that *The Hour [of Judgement] will [surely] come, there is no doubt thereof* [22:7]; in believing faithfully in the prophets of God and in His messengers and imams; in knowing the imam of the time and accepting him faithfully, obeying his commands; in acting in accordance with what God has rendered obligatory upon His servants and avoiding what has been prohibited, and obeying the imam and accepting what comes from him.

Abū ʿAbd Allāh Jaʿfar b. Muḥammad: Someone asked him about the act, which is most excellent in the eyes of God. [The imam] replied, 'That without which no act is acceptable to God.' The man asked, 'What is it?' [The imam] said, 'Faith in God is of all acts the most exalted; in rank, the most noble; in good fortune, the most sublime.'

The questioner said, 'I asked [the imam], "Tell me about faith. Is it profession with action, or profession without action?" [The imam] said, "Faith consists entirely in action, and profession is part of that action, as there is clear injunction in His Book; its light is manifest, and its proof well founded. The Book bears witness to it, and invites (Man) to it."' The questioner said, '[Please] make this clear, may I be thy ransom [O imam], so that I may understand it (faith).' [The imam] said, 'Verily, faith consists of [actual] states and stages, grades and stations. Faith can be totally complete, or else it may be manifestly lacking, or it may be clearly pre-eminent (or superior).'

The questioner said, 'I asked [the imam], "Can faith achieve perfection, and does it decrease and increase?" [The imam] said, "Yes."[3] I asked, "How so?" He replied, "God, the Blessed and Exalted, has made faith compulsory on each organ of man, and has distributed it in such a manner that to each one of them a duty is allocated which is not allocated to another. For instance, there is the heart that reasons and comprehends. It is the commander of the body, and no organ issues or imports any

1. Both Bukhārī and Muslim transmit this famous tradition. See Wensinck, *Concordance*, '*ʿ-m-l*.'

2. The confession of the oneness of God seems to have served as a token of adherence to the Muslim community from the very beginning. The testimony of the prophethood of Muḥammad was probably added to it very shortly afterwards. M. J. Kister, '*Illā bi-ḥaqqihi* ...: A study of an early *ḥadīth*,' *Jerusalem Studies in Arabic and Islam*, 8 (1986), pp. 61–96, p. 51.

3. The faith can increase and decrease, and it is related to the definition accepted for the act of faith (see note 1 above). The Khawārij, Murjiʾa and Māturīdī-Ḥanafīs consider faith immutable while all other schools accept that it can vary. A. J. Wensinck, *The Muslim Creed: Its Genesis and Historical Development* (Cambridge, 1932), pp. 125 ff., 194 ff.; 'Īmān,' *EI2*.

command without the heart's volition and command. Among the organs are the eyes with which man sees, and the ears with which he hears, and the hands with which he grasps, and the feet with which he walks, and the private parts from which sexuality is derived, and the tongue with which he speaks, and the head wherein is the face. For each of these organs an obligatory duty of faith has been laid down by God in His Book, which is not laid down for any of the others. Thus the heart has duties by which the ear is not bound; the ear has duties by which the tongue is not bound; and the tongue has duties not laid down for the eyes; and what is laid down for the eyes is not for the hands; and the hands are bound by duties which are not for the feet; and the feet are bound by duties which are distinct from those of the private parts; and the duties of the private parts are other than those that are ordained for the countenance.

"Now what is obligatory on the conscience (*qalb*) with respect to faith is the affirmation (*iqrār*), cognition (*maʿrifa*), resolve (*ʿaqd*), and willing submission (*riḍā wa-taslīm*) [to the fact] that God, the Blessed and Exalted, is One; that there is no deity other than God, who is without associate, [He is] God, One, Unique, Everlasting, who has neither spouse nor son; that Muḥammad is His Servant and His Messenger, the blessings of God be upon him and upon his progeny; and acceptance of what comes from God in the form of a Prophet (*nabīy*) or a Book. This is what is obligatory on the conscience concerning affirmation and cognition.

"God says, *Whoso disbelieveth in Allah after his belief – save him who is forced thereto and whose heart is still content with the Faith – but whoso findeth ease in disbelief* [16:106]. He says, *Verily in the remembrance of Allah do hearts find rest!* [13:28]. He says, *Such as say with their mouths: 'We believe,' but their hearts believe not* [5:41]. He says, *If you do good openly or keep it secret* [4:149]; and *whether ye make known what is in your minds, or hide it, Allah will bring you to account for it* [2:284]. The affirmation and cognition, which God has ordained for the heart (conscience), is its function and it is the pinnacle of faith.

"And obligatory on the tongue is the utterance and expression of what is resolved and affirmed by the heart (conscience). God says, *Say (O Muslims): We believe in Allah and that which is revealed unto us and that which was revealed unto Abraham, and Ishmael and Isaac and Jacob, and the tribes, and that which Moses and Jesus received, and that which the Prophets received from their Lord. We make no distinction between any of them, and unto Him we have surrendered* [2:136]. He says, *And speak kindly to mankind* (2:83). He says, *Speak words straight to the point* [33:70]. He says, *Say: (It is) the truth from the Lord of you (all)* [18:29]; and the like of these verses which God has ordered us to say. This then is what God has ordained for the tongue, and that is its function.

"It is ordained for the ear that it should be attentive to what God has commanded and that it should abstain from listening to what God has declared to be unlawful and what is not permissible and is prohibited, and from heeding that which angers God. He [God] says concerning this, *He hath already revealed unto you in the Scripture that, when ye hear the revelations of Allah rejected and derided, (ye) sit not with them (who disbelieve and mock) until they engage in some other conversation. Lo! in that case (if ye stayed) ye would be like unto them* [4:140]. Then, in another place, He excluded (certain persons): *And if the devil cause thee to forget, sit not, after the remembrance, with the congregation of wrongdoers* [6:68]. And he said, *Therefore give good tidings (O Muḥammad) to my bondsmen who hear advice and follow the best thereof. Such are those whom Allah guideth, and such are men of understanding* [39:17–18]. Then He Said, *Successful indeed are the believers who are humble in their prayers, and who shun vain conversation, and who are payers of the poor due* [23:1–4]. He said, *And when they hear vanity they withdraw from it* [28:55]. He said, *When they pass near senseless play, pass by with dignity* [25:72]. This then is what God has ordained for the ear regarding abstention from unlawful things, and this is its [proper] function.

"God has ordered the eye not to look at things which He has declared to be unlawful, and to avert itself from what is illicit. This is its [proper] function and it is part of faith. God says, *Tell the believing men to lower their gaze and be chaste* [24:30]. This signifies that a man should not look at the private parts of others, nor should he expose himself indecently." Then Abū ʿAbd Allāh [the Imam] said, "All the verses in the Qurʾan speaking of protection of the pudenda are parts of [the general regulations of] *zināʾ* (illicit intercourse), except this verse. For, verily, this deals (only) with sight.

"Then God co-ordinated all His commands to the conscience (heart), the tongue, the ear and the eye in one verse, and said, *(O man), follow not that whereof thou hast no knowledge. Lo! the hearing and the sight and the heart – of each of these it will be asked* [17:36]. He says, *Ye did not hide yourselves lest your ears and your skins should testify against you* [41:22]. The meaning of 'skins' is the private parts and thighs. This is the obligatory rule laid down by God for the eyes, which are required to avert their gaze from what is forbidden by God; this is their [proper] function, and it is part of faith.

"God has ordained for the hands that they should not seize what He has forbidden, but should take (only) what He has permitted. He has made obligatory upon them charity, love of kindred, *jihād* in the path of God and ritual purification for prayer. God says, *O ye who believe! When ye rise up for prayer, wash your faces, and your hands up to the elbow, and lightly rub your heads and your feet up to the ankles.*[1] *And if ye are unclean, purify yourselves* [5:6]. In another verse the Almighty says, *O ye who believe! When ye meet those who disbelieve in battle, turn not your backs to them* [8:15]. He said, *Now when ye meet in battle whose who disbelieve, then it is smiting of the necks when ye have routed them, then making fast of bonds; and afterward either grace or ransom* [47:4]. This is also what God has laid down for the hands, for smiting is a treatment prescribed for them. This is part of faith.

"Walking in obedience to God and not on forbidden paths, and going in directions whereby He is well pleased is the duty ordained by God for the feet. God says

1. The Ismailis and the Imāmīs read *wa-arjulikum*, hence the translation is slightly different from Sunni readings.

in this connection, *And walk not in the earth exultant. Lo! Thou canst not rend the earth, nor canst thou stretch to the height of the hills* [17:37]. He says, *Be modest in thy bearing and subdue thy voice. Lo! the harshest of all voices is the voice of the ass* [31:19]. He said, *O ye who believe! When the call is heard for the prayer of the day of congregation, haste unto remembrance of Allah and leave your trading* [62:9]. He said, *Let them go around the ancient House* [the Kaʿba] [22:29]. Concerning what the hands and feet will testify [on the Day of Judgement] regarding themselves, how they and other organs have fulfilled the commands and interdictions of God, God says, *This day We seal up their mouths, and their hands speak out to us and their feet bear witness as to what they used to earn* [36:65]. This too is what God has ordained for the hands and the feet, and this is their [proper] function in regard to faith.

"God has commanded the face to prostrate itself by night and by day at the times of prayer. He says, *O ye who believe! Bow down and prostrate yourselves, and worship your Lord, and do good, that haply ye may prosper* [22:77]. This is a duty common to the face, hands, and feet. In another place He says, *And the places of worship are only for Allah, so pray not unto anyone along with Allah* [72:18]. This is what God has ordained for the organs and members respecting ablutions and prayers.

"God has named prayer 'faith' in His Book, and this is [for the following reason]: when God turned the face of His Prophet in prayer away from Jerusalem towards the Kaʿba and ordered him to pray towards it, the Muslims said to the Prophet: Tell us what you think. How will the prayers we used to say in the direction of the Sacred House (Jerusalem) be considered (by God) and what will be our position? So God revealed the following: *But it was not Allah's purpose that your faith should be in vain, for Allah is full of pity, Merciful towards mankind* [2:143].[1] Thus he called prayer by the name of faith.

"When a man meets God, having protected all his limbs [from illicit actions] and all his limbs having fulfilled the commands of God, he meets his Lord in the perfection of faith and is one of the people of Paradise. But he who has deceived God in the slightest thing, and disobeyed Him, comes to God as one imperfect in faith."'

The questioner said, 'O son of the Messenger of God [that is Imam al-Ṣādiq], I have understood the perfection and the imperfection of faith; but how can faith increase? Can you adduce any proof for it?' Jaʿfar b. Muḥammad said, 'God has revealed an account of this in His Book and has said, *And whenever a sūrah is revealed there are some of them who say: Which one of you hath thus increased in faith? As for those who believe, it hath increased them in faith and they rejoice (therefore). But as for those in whose hearts is disease, it only addeth wickedness to their wickedness, and they die while they are disbelievers* [9:124–5]. He said, *We narrate unto thee their story with truth. Lo! they were young men who believed in their Lord, and We increased them in guidance* [18:13].

1. This refers to the change of *qibla* from Jerusalem to the Kaʿba about eighteen months after the *hijra*. The change to Jerusalem seems to have been effected in Mecca when the Muslims were not allowed to offer their prayers in public.

'Now if faith were a single [unalterable entity], and there were no decrease or increase in it, there would be no excellence in one person or another in respect of it. God's bounties would be distributed equally and the people would all be equal and gradations of excellence would be void. But [in reality] it is by the completeness of faith that the faithful enter paradise: by its preponderance and increase, the faithful excel one another in the eyes of God, and through deficiencies in it, those who fall short enter the Fire.'

The questioner said, 'I asked, "Are there grades and degrees in faith by which the faithful contend for precedence in the eyes of God?" [The imam] said, "Yes."' [The questioner] said, 'Explain to me how this is, so that I may understand it.' [The imam] said, 'Verily, God gives precedence among the faithful in the same way as horses are ranked on the day of racing; then He receives them according to their precedence towards Him. He then gives to each person his proper rank – without diminishing it – according to his desserts. The follower does not precede the leader, nor does the beneficiary come before the benefactor. According to this principle the first of this community takes precedence over the last. It follows [from this reasoning] that ʿAlī b. Abī Ṭālib, the blessings of God be upon him, was the most excellent of the faithful, because he it was who first believed in God among them. If excellence were not determined by priority in the acceptance of faith, then the last to become a Muslim would be equal to the first.

'Yes, indeed, many of the later ones would have precedence over the earlier ones, for we find that among the later faithful ones there are many who perform their religious duties more abundantly than the earlier ones. They surpass the earlier ones in prayer, in fasting, in the performance of the pilgrimage, in waging holy war, and in charity. If priority were not determined by time, we would find many of the later ones outstripping the earlier in the performance of religious duties. But God – glorious be His praise – has denied to the later [believers] the ranks of the earlier ones with respect to faith; or that the one He has placed behind should precede the one He has given precedence, or vice versa.'

[The questioner] said, 'Tell me – [O imam] – how has God assigned priority in faith among the faithful.' [The imam] said, 'God says, *Race one with another for forgiveness from your Lord and a Garden whereof the breadth is as the breadth of the heavens and the earth, which is in store for those who believe in Allah and His messengers* [57:21]. He says, *And the foremost in the race (are) the foremost in the race. Those are they who will be brought nigh* [56:10–11]. He says, *And the first to lead the way of the Muhājirīn (Emigrants)*[1] *and the Anṣār (Helpers),*[2] *and those who followed them in goodness – Allah is well pleased with them and they are well pleased with Him* [9:100]. He said, *And (it is) for the poor fugitives who have been driven out from their homes and their belongings, who seek bounty from Allah and help*

1. A term often applied in the Qurʾan to those Muslims who had migrated from Mecca to Medina with the Prophet.

2. Title of believers of Medina who received and assisted the Prophet after his migration (*hijra*) from Mecca.

Allah and His Messenger. They are the loyal [59:8]. He said, *Those who entered the city and the faith before them love those who flee unto them for refuge, and find in their breasts no need for that which hath been given them, but prefer (the fugitives) above themselves though poverty become their lot. And whoso is saved from his own avarice – such are they who are successful. And those who come (into the faith) after them say: O Lord! Forgive us and our brethren who were before us in the faith, and place not in our hearts any rancour toward those who believe. Our Lord! Thou are Full of Pity, Merciful* [59:9–10].

'Thus God began with the first Emigrants, ranking them in order of priority. He gave the second rank to the Helpers and the third to the Followers (*tābiʿūn*) of them in kindness.[1] He classified each community according to their ranks and stations with Him; and mentioned the seeking of forgiveness by the faithful for those who preceded them so that it would show the superiority of their status; then He mentioned His Friends (*Awliyāʾ*), ranking some of them above others, and the Mighty and Glorious says, *Of those messengers, some of whom We have caused to excel others, and of whom there are some unto whom Allah spake, while some of them He exalted (above others) in degree; and We gave Jesus, son of Mary, clear proofs (of Allah's sovereignty) and We supported him with the holy Spirit* [the Angel Gabriel] [2:253]. He said, *And We preferred some of the Prophets above others* [17:55]; He said, *There are degrees (of grace and reprobation) with Allah* [3:163]; He said, *He giveth His bounty unto every bountiful one* [11:3].

'And He said, *Those who believe, and have left their homes and striven with their wealth and their lives in Allah's way are of much greater worth in Allah's sight. These are they who are triumphant* [9:20]. He said, *Allah hath conferred on those who strive with their wealth and lives a rank above the sedentary. Degrees of rank from Him and forgiveness and mercy* [4:95–6]. He said, *Those who spent and fought before the victory are not upon a level (with the rest of you). Such are greater in rank than those who spent and fought afterwards. Unto each hath Allah promised good* [57:10]. And He said, *Allah will exalt those who believe among you, and those who have knowledge, to high ranks*' [58:11].

These are the ranks of faith, its stations and its aspects, and the states of believers and their varying degrees of virtue resulting from the promptness of their response to the Messenger of God's call.[2] But precedence cannot be of benefit without faith.

1. Admiration of things first and ancient is a major theme in the various branches of Islamic civilization. Traditions idealizing the early period of Islam abound. The generation of the Prophet, the first generation of Muslims, is said to have been the best. Then, a process of irreversible decline set in, hence each successive generation was inferior to that which preceded it. One, therefore, frequently finds that 'whoever is earlier is superior,' or 'virtue belongs to the early one,' in Islamic thought and literature. See also F. Rosenthal, 'Awāʾil,' *EI2*, vol. 1, p. 758.

2. The Qur'an accords early conversion higher religious merit. It states: '*Those who have preceded (others in the faith) shall precede (them to Paradise). These (are) they who shall approach near (unto God, they shall dwell) in the Gardens to Delight.*' (56:10–12). Almost all the translators of the Qur'an into English, except Sale and Yūsuf ʿAlī, have missed this subtle nuance. Those Muslims who joined the Messenger of God only after the conquest of Mecca were particularly reminded by the Qur'an wherein it states: '*Those among you who shall have contributed and fought [in defence of the faith] before the taking*

One who is lacking in faith or has lost it altogether does not profit [merely] by his precedence or priority [in time]. God says, *Whoso denieth the faith, his work is vain and he will be among the losers in the Hereafter* [5:5].

Concerning the word of God, *Whoso denieth the faith, his work is vain* [5:5], Jaʿfar b. Muḥammad said, 'His denial of faith (*kufr*) consists in his abandoning the works which he was commanded to undertake. This likewise confirms what we have said before: that faith consists in word, deed, and belief. There can never be word, deed, and belief without faith and affirmation, for then alone is faith completed. He who asserts, acts, and believes in other than the faith and the truth [we have delineated] cannot be a believer. His works will not benefit him, howsoever he abases himself. God says, *And We shall turn unto the work they did and make it scattered motes* [25:23]. The Mighty and Glorious says, *On that day (many) faces will be downcast, toiling, weary, scorched by burning fire*' [88:2–4]. Numerous are the arguments therefore.'

ON THE DISTINCTION BETWEEN *ĪMĀN* (FAITH) AND *ISLĀM* (SUBMISSION)

God says, *The wandering Arabs say: We believe* (āmannā). *Say (unto them, O Muḥammad): Ye believe not, but rather say 'We submit'* (aslamnā), *for the faith hath not yet entered into your hearts* [49:14]. He says, *They make it a favour unto thee (Muḥammad) that they have surrendered (unto Him). Say: Deem not your Surrender* (islāmakum) *a favour unto me; nay, but Allah doth confer a favour on you, inasmuch as He hath led you to the faith* (īmān), *if ye are earnest* [49:17]. He says, *Then We brought forth such believers* (mu'minīn) *as were there. But We found there but one house of those surrendered* (muslimīn) *(to Allah)* [51:35–6]. The obvious meaning of the Book of God clearly establishes that *īmān* is one thing, and *islām* another. They are not one and the same, as some of the commonalty assert.

Abū ʿAbd Allāh Jaʿfar b. Muḥammad: He said, '*Īmān* subsumes *islām*, but *islām* does not [necessarily] subsume *īmān*. *Islām* is the outward crust [of belief], whereas *īmān* is the inmost and purest [kernel] in the heart.'

[Abū ʿAbd Allāh Jaʿfar b. Muḥammad]: He was asked about *īmān* and *islām*. He replied, '*Īmān* is what is in the hearts; while *islām* regulates marriage, and inheritance, and by it bloodshed is prevented. *Īmān* [necessarily] implies *islām*; while *islām* does not [necessarily] imply *īmān*.'

Abū Jaʿfar Muḥammad b. ʿAlī: He is reported to have repeated this same saying [and explained it as follows]. He drew a circle on his palm and said, 'This circle represents *īmān*.' Then he drew another circle around it, and said, 'This is the circle of *islām*.' He drew the two [concentric] circles like this: ◎. He represented *islām* as the outer circle, and *īmān* as the inner circle, because the latter constitutes

---

of [Mecca], shall not be held equal [with those who shall contribute and fight for the same afterwards]. These shall be superior in degree to those who shall contribute and fight for [the propagation of the faith] after [the above-mentioned success].' (57:10). George Sale, *The Koran: Translated into English from the Original Arabic* (London, n.d.), pp. 517, 521.

[fundamentally] the heart's cognition – as has been explained earlier.[1] Hence *īmān* includes *islām* but *islām* does not [necessarily] include *īmān*. A man may be a *muslim* [outwardly][2] without being a *mu'min* [i.e. without believing with conviction]; but no one can be a *mu'min* without being a *muslim*.[3] This confirms what we said in the preceding chapter, that faith is not complete without the resolve of intent (*niyya*).

The Commander of the Faithful, ʿAlī b. Abī Ṭālib: He was asked 'What is *īmān*, and what is *islām*?' He replied, '*Islām* is affirmation (*iqrār*); while *īmān* is affirmation plus cognition (*maʿrifa*). Whosoever has been given knowledge by God regarding Him, His Prophet and His Imam, and then professes his faith in these three, is a *mu'min*.' He was asked, 'Does the cognition come from God, and the affirmation from the servant?' ʿAlī said, 'Cognizance is a proof (*ḥujja*), a grace, and a bounty from God, while acceptance is a gift which God grants to whomsoever He wills. Cognizance is [something which is] placed by God within the heart, and acceptance is the act of the heart due to God's gift, a protection and a mercy. He to whom God has not given such cognizance, there is no evidence that can be held against him. He should pause and refrain from [speaking and acting concerning] matters of which he has no knowledge. God will not punish him for his ignorance: He will reward him for his obedience and punish him for his disobedience. Nothing happens in these matters except by the ordinance (*qaḍā'*) and decree (*qadar*) of God; by His knowledge and His book without any constraint (*jabr*). For if there were constraints, then man would be deemed to be excused or excusable, although not worthy of approbation. He who is ignorant should turn to us [the imams] for understanding what is difficult for him. God says, *Ask the People of the Reminder (ahl al-dhikr) if ye know not* [21:7].'[4]

ʿAlī [b. Abī Ṭālib]: He was asked, 'O Commander of the Faithful, what is the least [action] by which one may be considered as of the faithful (*mu'min*), or a disbeliever (*kāfir*), or misguided (*ḍall*)?' He said, 'The least by which a man becomes a *mu'min* is that God should grant him true knowledge of His own self so that he may accept obedience [to God]; and that He should grant him knowledge of His

1. Abū Ḥātim al-Rāzī, *Kitāb al-zīna*, fol. 138, gives another illustration on the authority of Jaʿfar al-Ṣādiq. Some of his companions asked him, 'Have you seen the one who has embraced Islam (*dakhala fi'l-islām*) but has not yet embraced the faith (*laysa huwa fi'l-īmān*)?' He [the imam] replied, 'No, rather [it is better to describe him as the one] who has left unbelief (*kufr*) and has been ascribed to faith (*īmān*). I shall give you an example so that you will know the superiority of *īmān* over *islām*. Can you bear witness for a person who enters the Sacred Mosque (*al-masjid al-ḥarām*) that he has [also] entered the Kaʿba?' The inquirer said, 'No.' [The imam] queried, 'Were you to see him in the Kaʿba, can you bear witness that he had entered the Sacred Mosque?' The man responded, 'Yes, because he could not have reached the Kaʿba without having entered the Sacred Mosque.' [The imam] replied, 'You are right, bravo!'

2. One who has embraced Islam without proper understanding and commitment, or the one who conforms to its rituals without conviction.

3. Both the terms *islām* and *īmān* are used in the Qur'an with different connotations. The relation between them is a theological question, which was debated very early in Islam. The various schools of *fiqh* and *kalām* are divided on this issue. For details see L. Gardet, 'Islām,' *EI2*, vol. 4, p. 172.

4. *Ahl al-dhikr* is interpreted by the Shiʿa to mean the imams.

Prophet so that he may obey him; and that He should instruct him concerning His Proof (*ḥujja*)[1] on His earth [the imam] and His Witness *(shāhid)* to mankind so that he may believe in his imamate and affirm his obedience to him.' He was asked, '[What happens] if he is ignorant of other things?' 'Alī said, 'Yes [it is all right], but when commanded, he should obey, and when prohibited he should desist.'

['Alī continued], 'The least thing that will make him an "associator" (*mushrik*, commonly translated as "polytheist") is believing in what God has forbidden and asserting [perversely] that God has so ordained it, then proclaiming it as a creed, and alleging that he worships that which he has been commanded to worship, while that is something or someone other than God the Mighty and Glorious. The least that will cause a man to be misguided is not to recognize the Proof of God on His earth and His Witness to mankind [the imam], so that he could follow [the imam's] example.

(Translated by Asaf A. A. Fyzee and I. K. Poonawala)

1. The term *ḥujja* in Shi'i theology refers to that person through whom the inaccessible God becomes accessible and who serves at any given time as evidence, among mankind, of his will. Thus the Prophet was the *ḥujja* of God, and after him the imam is the *ḥujja*. In the Ismā'īlī hierarchy of the *da'wa*, called *ḥudūd al-da'wa*, the term *ḥujja* is used flexibly for the rank following that of the imam. See L. Gardet and M. G. S. Hodgson, 'Ḥudjdja,' *EI2*, vol. 3, p. 544.

2

Aḥmad b. Ibrāhīm al-Naysābūrī

The *Risāla* by Aḥmad al-Naysābūrī (see Section II, 3), reproduced in this chapter, was of considerable importance and was preserved within later anthologies of Ismaili texts. It is from a period in the early 5th/10th century when the Ismaili *daʿwa* was still developing its institutional structures and offers an invaluable glimpse into how major scholars sought to create its firm foundations. The selection dwells on the qualities of spiritual reflection and temporal leadership that should ideally be found in a *dāʿī*, the cornerstone of the Ismaili *daʿwa*.

al-Risāla al-mūjaza al-kāfiya fī adab al-duʿāt
A Code of Conduct for *dāʿī*s[1]

QUALIFICATIONS FOR THE *DAʿWA*

The qualifications for the *daʿwa* are based on three things: on knowledge, on God-fearing piety, and on governance. Knowledge is divided into two parts, one of which is knowledge of the external and the other of the internal. The external has five divisions. One is the science of legal understanding and rulings on the basis of which people are sustained and religion and the world preserved. It is the foundation of both religion and the *daʿwa*. The second is the science of *ḥadīth*, historical reports, narrative accounts and chains of transmission from the Prophet and the imams. Through it, religion is preserved and the law upheld through the retention of these reports and narrative accounts; they are the basis for legal understanding. The third is the science of the Qurʾan, its interpretation and explanation, knowledge of the fixed and ambiguous in it, that which abrogated and what is abrogated, and the command and the prohibition. The fourth is the science of preaching, of memorials, and of exemplary stories. God the Exalted said to His prophet: 'Summon to the way of your Lord with wisdom and fine exhortation' [16:125]. Exhortation refines the hearts of the people and awakens in them a desire for the afterlife and for religion and withdrawal from this world. The fifth is the science of disputation and discussion by which to counter, in matters of faith, the heretics, deviants, the philosophers, those who uphold the eternity of the world, and the various adherents of false schools of doctrine. Each type of these sciences has various excellences and

1. Aḥmad b. Ibrāhīm al-Naysābūrī, *al-Risāla al-mūjaza al-kāfiya fī adab al-duʿāt*, ed. Verena Klemm and tr. Paul E. Walker as *A Code of Conduct for Dāʿī*s (forthcoming).

they will, if possible, be mentioned at the proper place for it, God willing. The *dāʿī* needs all that because he is consulted for the understanding of religion. If he has not got that, how can he answer? If his understanding of the outward aspect is not good, how is he to have the ability to interpret it? How can he instruct them in religion and summon them to it?

He must be acquainted with the science of the reports coming from the Prophet and of his *ḥadīth*s, and the reports from the imams and what is related from them. He draws on that to determine the accuracy of what he says to novices in order to have them accept it from him. He requires the science of the Qur'an on which he testifies and answers questions about both its literal and figurative meanings. He needs knowledge of preaching, recollection and narration in order to exhort the neophyte. It is as God says: 'Remind, for reminding benefits the believers' [51:55], and He says: 'Remind them, for you are a person who reminds' [88:21], and He says also: 'Ask the people who recall if you do not know' [16:43 and 21:7]. The *dāʿī* requires theological disputation to refute those who oppose, to engage in debate, and to disprove the arguments of opponents with counter-arguments. As God had said: 'Dispute with them with what is best' [16:125].

Inner knowledge breaks down into many types.

Among them is sensate knowledge which involves comprehension of the lower hierarchy and of legal actions, their interpretation and the wisdom in it, and understanding everything that pertains to acts that can be seen or perceived by a person.

A second is cognitive and imagined knowledge, which involves the understanding of the higher hierarchy and the numbers and the comprehension of ideal forms whose reality cannot be seen or sensed by the senses but only apprehended in thoughts and imagination.

Then there is intellected knowledge, which comprises the understanding of things as they truly are, knowledge of their causes, and their beginnings and endings.

These are three stages, the first of which is like mother's milk for the infant. It is for the novice like sensory knowledge in the process of his instruction. The second resembles his becoming educated and associated with imagination and rational knowledge. The third is like the attachment to him of intellect upon the acquisition of which he attains his majority, and he becomes responsible for what he does in respect to his having attained legal maturity which is not subject thereafter to change or alteration.

That which is only sensed is apprehended by the five senses; that which is imagined is apprehended by thoughts; and that which is intellected is the abstract reality itself. A person who apprehends something by the senses moves up to thoughts and he thinks about it until he moves up to intellectual comprehension by which he judges between truth and falsehood and comes to know its reality in the science of religion. They say that sensed knowledge is the science of the law; the imagined is the science of interpretation; and the intellected is the true explanation that never changes. Each one has many branches and a variety of openings for interpretation. Indeed the interpretation of the law is a sea that never drains nor does anyone reach its furthest limit. The science of the Qur'an has no bottom. Knowledge of the higher hierarchy and the spiritual world is not attained by any but the pious person who is keenly intelligent, astute, and diligent. Comprehension of the horizons and souls is a deep ocean and it is the source from which derives the understanding of all other sciences. It is the scale and touchstone to which every other science reverts. What is in accord with it is obviously true; what conflicts with it is false and a lie. Knowledge of the absolute oneness of God is the goal; it is most glorious of the sciences and the most illustrious of the legal impositions. All the acts of worship and knowledge are based on it. The soul's recognition of it is a thing imposed on the human being. By means of it, he attains an understanding of the absolute oneness.

No one attains the comprehension of these ultimate sciences until he combines in himself parts of all the rest: of physics, its causes and the rules that apply to them; of geometry and numbers, and knowledge of philosophy and the roots of the various schools of doctrines and the differences among them. Thus when he reads a book or listens to an argument, he knows what conforms to the truth and what opposes it.

The person of intelligence must reflect on that, for in these times and in this place, discord is due to the lack of being able to discern truth from falsehood. He should distinguish true from the false and not judge of what is true that it is false or of the false that it is true. False judgement leads people from the path of God. For that reason God said to His messenger: 'Do not seek that of which you have no knowledge' [17:36]. Someone might say here that he who knows all is the imam but we say that he does not combine it all completely but rather, most certainly, the root principles behind it. If consulted, he refers the derived problem to its fundamentals. He compares it to its root and refers it to the source of religion to ascertain if it agrees with the source of religion and of nature, otherwise he rejects it by the force of truth and reveals its falsehood. Because he might be asked in his open sessions about something or to speak about an issue in one of these sciences, it is essential that he not be an alien among them and unaware of their discussions.

God-fearing piety is a term combining knowledge and action in conformity with doctrine, upholding the stipulations of the Qur'an, doing what God has commanded, prohibiting what He has forbidden, and that cannot happen without knowledge. A person without sound knowledge is not able to keep God free of association and anthropomorphism. Someone who associates a thing with God or makes comparisons of Him and yet performs all the acts of devotion is not pious and nobody should learn from him. God-fearing piety is the sum of all the virtues and the prohibition of all the vices. For that reason God, glorious is His name, said: 'The most noble of you in the sight of God is the most God-fearing of you' [49:13]; and He said: 'The best of provisions is God-fearing piety' [2:197]; and He said: 'The wearing of God-fearing piety that is best' [7:26], and He said: 'Fear God, O you men of understanding' [5:100 and 65:10]; and He said also: 'Whoever fears God He will make for him a way out' [65:2].

In regard to governance, it has three grades: governance of the individual, governance of the household, and governance of the community.

The *dāʿī* firstly requires governance of the individual, which means to govern his own self. Thus he provides for the welfare of his own soul, governing and controlling it, preventing it from having any of the vices and any bad habits of character, keeping it from reprehensible desire for things that are illicit, bearing itself in conformity with the virtuous, and fulfilling required duties and established regulations. He will censure himself sincerely if he behaves badly, accompanying that with condemnation, regret, reproach and repentance, and he will reward himself if he is good with delight, praise and the urging of more fine actions, and drawing on knowledge in order to direct the novice to it so as to have him adopt his own fine character, follow his words, actions and wise lead. It is as our master al-Ṣādiq Jaʿfar b. Muḥammad, may the blessings of God be upon him, said: 'Be for us silent *dāʿīs*.' They asked: 'How can we summon if we are silent?' He answered: 'Act in accord with what actions we commanded of you and in obedience to God. Make illicit those acts of disobedience that we ordered you to prohibit.' He who succeeds in governing his own self is fit and able to govern others. It is said: Do what is beneficial to yourself and the people will follow you. God said: "O you who believe, guard your own souls; the one who goes astray cannot hurt you if you are guided aright" [5:105].

Governance of the household is the governing by a man of his own family and retainers, controlling them, teaching and educating them, instilling the virtues in them and preventing vices, rewarding those who are good, punishing those who are bad. As God says: 'O you who believe, guard yourselves and your family from the fire' [66:6]; and the Prophet has said: 'A man continues to have the people of his house inherit knowledge and proper comportment until he has entered them all into paradise, losing of them neither the young or the old, the servant or the protégé.' It is as God says: 'Command your family to pray and persevere with them' [20:132]; and He said: 'And he used to command his family to pray and pay the alms tax and he was approved in the sight of his Lord' [19:55]. He who succeeds in governing himself and his family is fit to have charge of governing the rest of the people in matters of faith and he who cannot govern himself and his family is not fit to be a *dāʿī*.

Governance of the community involves supporting the administration of the person who is their leader in matters of the welfare of this life and of their salvation, who educates them on the discipline of communal laws, keeps them from reprehensible and illicit actions, promotes the virtues, rewards those who do good and punishes those who do evil. It is he who is responsible for the wellbeing of their religion. A person who is not good at the governance of the individual, the family, and the community is not fit for the *daʿwa*.

The *dāʿī* must educate the *dāʿī* below him in knowledge, test and try him and arrange his affairs, punishing and rewarding him, each according to his rank. In like manner the *dāʿī* educates a *maʿdhūn* and urges him to rise to the rank that is above him. In the same way he educates the believer and instructs him in knowledge and comportment, raising him thereby to the rank of *ma'dhūn*. It is like that with the novice. He instructs him and arranges his affairs in accord with the degree of his position and on the measure of his aptitude and ability. It is similar with regard to his command of the affairs of the Adherents of Literal Meaning, their governance, the good quality of social relationships with them, contention with them, disputing with them and arguing against them with what is best. Likewise with the masses and the elite and with the protected peoples.[1] He offers to each of them his sincere counsel, a good forecast, and preservation of the welfare of all of them in truth, justice, and fairness. A person lacking these three forms of governance cannot be a *dāʿī*.

QUALIFICATIONS FOR A *DĀʿĪ*

Here now we return to the qualifications for the *daʿwa* and their explanation. We hold that the *dāʿī* must be firmly grounded in the principles of the religion to which he summons with a sincerity and certainty untainted or mixed with another purpose, loyal to the imam for whom he appeals and to the messenger who is the foundation of the religion on whom, to whom, and by whom the *daʿwa* is based. He is one who affirms the absolute oneness of God. A person who does not have sound beliefs, even though he is knowledgeable and a worshipper, but who upholds the literal and the figurative hypocritically and with dissimulation, reveals his own hypocrisy. Those who follow him derive no benefit from his knowledge or his *daʿwa,* which provides, therefore, no blessing. No novice or believer is educated by his hand; no *daʿwa* ever functions properly under him.

He should be God-fearing in his piety and that cannot happen without knowledge of both the exterior and the interior. The origin of piety is to fear God and not to associate anything with Him nor to characterise Him with an attribute of created beings; and, out of fear of God, not to elevate any one in the hierarchy above his proper station nor to degrade any below it and to guard against all forbidden things and be wary of neglecting any of those that are obligatory and of refraining from commanding and prohibiting.

A *dāʿī* should know the exterior and the interior, legally and intellectually. God has said: 'Say: Are those equal, those who know and those who do not know; it is solely those who possess knowledge' [39:9]; and He said: 'Rather these are clear signs in the hearts of those endowed with knowledge' [29:49]; and He said: 'Is then he who guides to the truth more right to be followed; or is he who does not guide unless he is himself guided; how is it with you that you judge in this way?' [10:35]; and the Prophet said: 'There are four items which, should the mount be pressed so hard in going toward, it wears thin in exhaustion, and that would be of little

1. Protected peoples are the Dhimmīs, the people of the book, mainly Christian and Jews, who are afforded the protection of Islam by Qur'anic mandate.

account: Let the servant hope for nothing but his Lord; fear nothing except his own sins; the ignorant be not ashamed of acquiring knowledge; and the learned person, when asked something he does not know, say, "I do not know"'. Our master the Commander of the Believers said: 'Half of knowledge for he who does not know is to say, "God alone knows," and if I came upon a youth belonging to our party who had not tried to acquire knowledge, I would myself see to his instruction.' It is as God says: 'If a group from each party were to remain aside to undertake studies in religion and to admonish their own people when they return to them perhaps they should become able to warn themselves' [9:122]. If a *dāʿī* does not have this sort of knowledge and someone questions him and opponents debate him, they will defeat him and thus cause great harm, discord, disgrace and damage in the teaching. What happened to Jonah in being swallowed by the whale is that he had an opponent who bested him, who drew him out and caused him to fall by breaking him. His being swallowed by him was a result of the paralysis that hit him and the advent of weakness in religion and related matters prior to that.

The *dāʿī* must be chaste and upright. It is as God said: 'To Him rise fine words and the righteous deed He lifts upward' [35:10]; and He said: 'Those who repent, those who worship, those who praise, those who journey, those who bow, those who prostrate themselves, those who command the good and prohibit the reprehensible, and those who maintain the limits set by God and proclaim good tidings for the believers' [9:112]. If they are those who give good tidings, those who oppose them are they that are destined to perish.

He must be kind to the believers, merciful, and forgiving. As God has said: 'We sent you not but as a mercy for the world' [21:108], and He said also: 'They that are merciful among them you will see them bowing and in prostration striving for the grace of God and His approval' [48:29]. The *dāʿī* tries to emulate God in His mercy toward those who serve Him and the Messenger and the imams in their mercy, their compassion, and their solicitude for the community in spite of the community's rebellion and the vileness of their acts and behaviour. It is as God said: 'If God were to punish people according to what they have done, He would not leave on the surface a living being' [35:45]; and as God said to His Prophet: 'Accept forgiveness; command the right; but turn away from those who are ignorant' [7:199].

A *dāʿī* should be humble, not haughty with the believers. God has said: 'That afterlife We grant to those who seek no highhandedness on this earth nor corruption; the good end is for those who fear God' [28:83]. Al-Ṣādiq Jaʿfar b. Muḥammad said as well: 'Do not become scholars who are so tyrannical as to pass your falsehoods as truths of yours'; and the Prophet said: 'Grandeur is a cloak of God who is great and majestic; he who attempts to wrest His cloak from Him God breaks into little pieces.'

A *dāʿī* must be intelligent with a perfect wisdom and knowledge. Knowledge that is not perfect intellectually is unhealthy. As God has said: 'None understand it but the intelligent' [29:43]; and he said: 'It is only those with understanding who perceive' [39:9 and 13:19]; and He said: 'Eat yourselves and pasture your flocks; surely in that there are signs for men of understanding' [20:54].

He must be of noble lineage among his people. Nobility derives from lineage and is greatly esteemed in the eyes of the people. If his lineage is low, whoever sits with him or takes instruction from him, will hold back and the *dāʿī* will humiliate himself in front of him. I have seen many of the people refrain from entering religion because of the low lineage of the *dāʿī* and his descent and his relationship [through his family] to infamous acts and disgraceful occupations. It is for the same reason that they chose for leadership in this world people of nobility and honour. Indeed noble lineage has high importance in the hearts of the populace.

He should be generous and not miserly. Miserliness is reprehensible and unacceptable. As God mentioned: 'Those who are miserly and who command the people to be miserly' [4:37]; and God has also said: 'Those who spend, when they do are not extravagant and not parsimonious, but between those two is proper' [25:67]. If the *dāʿī* is a miser, the novice will follow his lead, learning from him to be miserly and will thus perish. The *daʿwa* should spend on those who deserve it fairly and on those who might not deserve it something to win them over. There are times when it is right to spend an amount because, if it is not spent or is suspended and withheld, the believing families of that region will perish and great harm will result. The Prophet said: 'God fashions the *walī* not otherwise than in accord with generosity'; and he said: 'Generosity is a tree whose base is in paradise; whoever attaches to its branch is brought into paradise; miserliness is a tree whose base is in hellfire; whosoever clings to a branch of it is drawn into hellfire.' He said as well: 'The ignorant person who is generous is better than the knower who is miserly'; and it is said also: 'Generosity is praised by everyone and in all communities.'

A *dāʿī* must be truthful in what he says. If he is not truthful, how will they accept as true what he says? How will they agree to what he says and rely on it? As God has said: 'Fear God and be among those who speak the truth' [9:119], that is, be in the company of those who speak the truth and be followers of the truthful ones who are the imams, may the peace of God be upon them.

The *dāʿī* should be chivalrous; chivalry is an aspect of faith. If he loses his sense of chivalry, he forfeits the respect for him in the eyes of the people, and the novices and the believers will regard him with an eye of contempt.

A *dāʿī* must have modesty; modesty is also a part of faith. Modesty precludes him from many things that dishonour the *daʿwa*. Modesty comprises seeing to the needs of the people, of bearing up patiently, and being affable with the public.

He must be sound of opinion and skilled in administration. The affairs of the *daʿwa* cannot be carried out by bad administration of them. If an error occurs in his administration of the *daʿwa*, it will corrupt it, destroy those who believe in it, and there will be no way or any means to correct it. It is said that four things gives rise to four: the intellect to leadership, sound opinion to governance, knowledge to taking the lead, and clemency to veneration.

A *dāʿī* should do what he says. Religion is the fulfilment of the covenant and the statement. If the believer sees in him a slowness in fulfilling his obligation or a breach of faith, he will do likewise and thereby the religion will become corrupted.

God has praised faithfulness. He said: 'And Abraham who fulfils his engagements' [53:37]; and He said about Ismail: 'He was true to his promise and he was a messenger and a prophet' [19:54].

He must keep secret what is secret. Religion is based on the preservation of secrets that need to be kept from those who are not worthy of them. If the secrets are lost, religion is lost. At times the divulging of a secret connected to a matter of religion has led to the destruction of a nation or the ruin of a province.

A *dāʿī* should be forgiving and merciful to the believers, not malicious, not overly preoccupied with retribution, aggravations, disputes, and contention. Novice believers will always be lacking in knowledge and subject to mistakes and erroneous intentions, which they then regret; but if they are not treated kindly and forgiven for it, they will despair of religion. God has said: 'O My servants who have transgressed against their own souls, do not despair of the mercy of God for He forgives all sins' [39:53]; and He said to Muḥammad His prophet: 'Accept forgiveness; command the right; but turn away from those who are ignorant' [7:199]; and He said also: 'Lower your wing to those of the believers who follow you' [26:215].

A *dāʿī*'s words must be sweet and fine in expression and explanation so as to captivate with his words the souls of the novices, so they will not weary and try to avoid listening to what he says or tire of it. God said: 'A similitude: a good word is like a good tree' [14:24]; and He said: 'Good words go up to Him' [35:10]; and the Prophet said: 'A portion of explanation is enchantment.'

A *dāʿī* ought to be patient and gentle. A variety of people come to him who have minds concerned with different needs and questions. If he is quick to anger and exasperation, the people will try to avoid him. God has said: 'If you were harsh and hard-hearted, they would have broken away from you' [3:159], and He said: 'Be patient for your patience comes from God' [16:127], and He said: 'So be patient just as those of the messengers with firm resolution were patient' [46:35]. There were none more patient than the prophets, the legatees, and the imams despite the evilness of the people of the community and their insubordination. They were patient, put up with their absurdities, and looked upon those who committed sins with the eye of mercy and forbearance in order to save them from hellfire.

A *dāʿī* should also be a statesman. Statesmanship is the foundation of political rule both in religion and in worldly affairs. A person not good at governing cannot achieve perfection in political leadership. It is said that whoever seeks political leadership must suffer the pain of leadership patiently. The *dāʿī* needs to govern individuals in accord with confessional and legal rules and direct souls with knowledgeable governance in order for him to implement the *daʿwa* fully.

A *dāʿī* ought to possess a refinement of soul in addition to knowledge. Knowledge in the absence of refinement of the soul means that it lacks lustre, is unwelcome, its owner deficient in decorum and his knowledge of no benefit to him.

He should have lofty aspirations for he is responsible for great affairs in religion and in the world at large. God grants to the imams of His religion in every era dominion over the earth by means of his *dāʿī*s and *ḥujja*s.

He will have a good social disposition and manner. It is as God has said: 'Live with them with appropriate courtesy' [4:19]; and He said: 'And you are held to the highest of character' [68:4]; and al-Ṣādiq Ja'far b. Muḥammad said: 'Live with the people by their morals and do not call them pigs;' and he also said: 'Endear us to the people and do not make us hateful to them.'

He will be able to take the measure of everyone by observing them and listening to their words. He thus learns about those best suited to religion and those not so, or whose purpose is religious and whose is not religious, who is able to acquire knowledge and who is unable. It is essential that he be good at choosing among them and examining the state of everyone until the position of each becomes clear to him.

He should be well acquainted with the lives of the imams, the arrangement of their *da'was* so that he can follow them, and their example and their traditions.

It is necessary that the *dā'ī* should be able to travel and observe the various regions so that he be acquainted with the nature of the inhabitants of those regions, know what they desire or incline toward of each type of knowledge so as to choose for them the right person to deal with them in debates and disputations.

A *dā'ī* should know the rights of those who immigrate to him, what hardships and trouble they have had to endure, how they might have suffered in leaving behind their family, country, and property. Likewise he ought to recognize the rights of emissaries and visitors and know what fears and troubles have befallen them on the road, and appreciate that each is an honoured person in his own country. Each set out and risked his life and funds enduring those hardships for the sake of religion. He should not esteem them lightly nor look upon them with the eye of contempt, nor think little of their attire or their adornment. He will not regard that person as if he were himself a ruler in his honours and money and the luxury of his lifestyle. He knows that the hearts of kings, princes, commanders, rulers and the believers can be won over and got the better of by kindness to their emissaries. Each sends as his ambassador someone he respects, has confidence in, and has personally chosen for traits of the man that are well known. If he is not acquainted with the person who sent the emissary but concludes from the fine qualities in the emissary that the one who sent that person finds him excellent and is pleased with him, he infers the extent of the sender's status from the stature of the emissary and the letters he brings. The words of the emissary will then carry more weight than the written messages. The rancour of most of the people in a region, and the princes, *dā'ī*s and chiefs, is often the result of scorning and belittling the good offices of their emissaries. This subject is something in which the *dā'ī* must take special care and delight in observing, never becoming impatient with it or slacken from handling it properly. What is expended in matters of this kind is never wasted.

A *dā'ī* should dispatch to the various regions *dā'ī*s who speak the language there. God said: 'We have not sent emissaries except those with the language so that they might present it clearly to them' [14:4], and that means to make the truth clear to them in their language and in information that is most accessible to their understanding. For that reason God granted each prophet a miracle of a type that, in terms of knowledge and eloquence, would appeal to his own community. Since the people of Abraham were worshippers of fire, his miracle was the cooling of the fire. Moses's people made their case based on magic and so his miracle involved the staff. Medicine was the claim of the people of Jesus and his miracle was to do, for the blind and the lepers, what they could not, and in reviving the dead. Since the pride of the Arabs lay in eloquence and bravery, the miracle of the Prophet was the Qur'an and the sword of his legatee which was used to silence and break them. Thereby God defeated them through him and cast them out.

A *dāʿī* must be acquainted with the religious proclivities of the inhabitants of each region, their knowledge and natures, and what they might be inclined to accept and their aptitude for knowledge so that he can overcome them in debate and disputation with them and have them come to accept knowledge from him.

He ought to appreciate the value of the scholars and their position, treat them with deference and honour them, not noticing their poverty and lack of personal adornment, for they are proud and disdainful, not used to humility and being treated lightly. Criticizing the scholars is difficult and is secretly annoying to them; they seize the opportunity and find fault against him in a discussion based on a mistake of language or an error or something that allows for a variety of views. They will expose his fault and strip him of his respect, for the strength of religion lies in the empowerment of the scholars. He who respects learned men respects religion itself, and he who accords them no importance holds himself in contempt. If the people believe in the power of the scholars, they will themselves all desire knowledge and will study to acquire it. The glory of knowledge will but insist on approaching God in true sincerity.

Thus a *dāʿī* should love knowledge and those who have it. People will deduce from his love of the learned that he is one of them and that he is himself a scholar and that he believes and considers true the knowledge that he relates and they therefore accept from him. It is essential that a *dāʿī* hold most of his sessions with the learned because, if he is himself a scholar, he will increase his own knowledge from them and they will also learn from him, and, if he is not, he will learn from them even so. Should he err in some aspect of knowledge, they are better to correct his mistake than his antagonists who will seize on his error and make out of it an argument against him. When his sessions are held with the learned, he takes up with them matters for deliberation and inquiry that need to be studied and have its implications set forth by bringing to bear efforts of thought and study. God [has] said: 'God will raise up in rank those of you who believe and have been given knowledge' [58:11]. This message applies to those of the rank from *mukāsir* to the *bāb*, because all of them are *dāʿī*s to those below them, who are each potentially what they are themselves, and the aim is for the lower to attain the higher rank in actuality. God has said: 'Those of His servants who truly fear God are the learned' [35:28].

A *dāʿī* must also pay honour to the ascetics and the devout among the people of religion and keep their centres close by, so that the people will likewise wish to be devout, have knowledge and be themselves ascetic.

A *dāʿī* ought to stay away from those who cause corruption once he has warned and admonished them so that, perhaps, they may repent. He should not sit with them much, nor like them; he who frequents a given group is one of their number. A man is judged by the company he keeps. God [has] said: 'For whoever is blind to the remembrance of the Most Merciful, to him We assign a satan as companion' [43:36]. Casting out the people of corruption and censuring them induces the people to abstain from corruption, not to wish for it, and allows them more readily to repress and prevent it.

A *dāʿī* must not be ambitious; the origin of every calamity is covetousness. It is related of the Commander of the Believers, ʿAlī, that he was asked, 'What is religion?' and he replied, 'Piety,' whereupon came the question, 'What is the cause of its ruin?' and he answered, 'Greed.' Covetousness prompts the impious *dāʿī* to the taking of bribes and kickbacks in religious matters. The primary result of that is the breaking of the oath of covenant that, in monetary matters or in religion itself, he would not be disloyal to the imam of his time. He who does that is disloyal and he who has broken his oath has left the religion and withdrawn from adherence to the *daʿwa*. Whoever accepts after that an oath from him or discloses anything to him, he is a murderer and a fornicator, someone totally lacking blessedness because his is a family belonging to other than God that has become worse and is debarred.

A *dāʿī* will not necessarily love leadership in this world. That could lead him to falsehood either in seeking a position of leadership by asserting his own credibility or, after he has attained it, of lying out of fear of being deprived of it. It leads him also to disparage whichever of his associates he believes is appropriate for what leadership he himself is appropriate so that that person will not attain the position. It causes him to regard himself as more excellent than his associates; it prompts him to lie, to pursue their faults; and all of this is deceit. Deceit is the root of all reprehensible acts. Deceit results in slander and slander begets hatred, alienation, malice, contention, animosity, warfare, and feuding. Doing that leaves behind religion and the covenant.

It is not essential that the *dāʿī* be voracious and much given to passion, for voracity and excessive longing lead to an affection for the body and forfeiture of the share of the soul and its faculties, prompting him to become miserly, to love riches and that leads to greed and greed leads to treachery. In that there is a departure from religion and the covenant and the abandoning of honour.

It is not right for the *dāʿī* falsely to accuse the believers of a crime or to think ill of them. Thinking ill and lacking trust in the people is a base quality of the soul and one of its lapses. Mistakes of the soul beget a proclivity for contemptible acts. Those deviate from all virtue and from religion.

It is not good for the *dāʿī* to jest too much. Jesting takes away from dignity and engenders animosity and malice in the heart. It is said that joking is the start of mischief because, if the joke is on someone who is lower, it leads to being spread around, thereby removing decorum and inducing impudence toward the subject of the joke. That ends up as animosity. If it was at the expense of someone higher, that person will harbour resentment and enmity between the two will result.

A *dāʿī* should not be obscene in his speech or speak foolishly. For him to be false, untrue or offensive removes his dignity and awe and reduces his status. It is said that any leader who engages in an excess of foolishness and jesting is described as having little intellect and knowledge.

The *dāʿī* should possess gravity, an awe-inspiring manner and be pleasingly attired before his people. His character will be refined, splendid and commanding, and of an appearance such that none who look at him turns away in contempt. Comeliness and good appearance have an influence in hearts, gaining a power and standing that nothing else possesses. For that reason God said: 'And He increased him extensively with knowledge and substance' [2:247].

(Translated by Paul E. Walker)

3

Naṣīr al-Dīn al-Ṭūsī

As we have seen (Section II, 6), *Paradise of Submission* was most probably composed with al-Ṭūsī's concurring assistance during his long sojourn among the Ismailis of Persia. These passages from Chapter 22 are a masterful blend of traditional philosophical and Islamic ethics with the Nizārī Ismaili doctrine of the time.

Rawḍa-yi taslīm
Paradise of Submission[1]

ON THE REFINEMENT OF CHARACTER

When man sets out to acquire perfection of the soul, the first step he takes, by which he becomes prepared for the reception of intellectual matters and gradually reaches the rank of recognition of the imam and thereby the recognition of God, is the refinement of character (*tahdhīb-i akhlāq*). The reason for this is that, to start with, when the human body becomes fit [to receive] the individual soul, and [when] the individual soul assumes the governance of the human body, the soul is extremely weak, and domination falls into the hands of the sensory, imaginative and estimative faculties. As the body becomes stronger, the senses become more dominant, and the onslaught and domination of these faculties increase. Consequently, the soul becomes increasingly veiled from its original function, which is the comprehension of objects of knowledge and roaming freely through the wide expanse of intelligible matters. Thus, as long as one's character has not been refined and the substance of the soul emancipated from enslavement to the powers of nature (*quwā-yi ṭabīʿī*), bestial impurities (*shawāʾib-i bahīmī*), the temptations of habit (*wasāwis-ʿādatī*) and conventional laws (*nawāmīs-i amthila*),[2] neither well-being in this world will be achieved nor can salvation in the Hereafter be expected.

Since in every epoch, all the [sciences of] ethics (*kull-i akhlāq*) and social conduct (*muʿāmalāt*) have been kept in order by the grace of their harmony with the command of the truthful master of that epoch (*amr-i muḥiqq-i waqt*) – may salutations ensue upon mentions of him – and have suffered ill by relinquishing his

1. Naṣīr al-Dīn al-Ṭūsī, *Rawḍa-yi taslīm*, ed. and tr. S. J. Badakhchani as *Paradise of Submission: A Medieval Treatise on Ismaili Thought* (London, 2005), pp. 93–94, 96–103, nos. 265–267, 279–299.

2. See al-Ṭūsī, *Rawḍa-yi taslīm*, no. 190.

command, thus the basis of the refinement of character lies in obedience and utter submission to the command of the truthful master. For one cannot know, in effect, what type of morality every truthful master in each particular epoch prescribes, ordains and considers as appropriate for the people [of his time]. For this reason, if one persists in observing ethical codes and manners permitted and sanctioned by a truthful master, but when another truthful master [of a later epoch] perceives that moral prosperity lies in following a different course which he indicates to be licit, and if one hesitates to follow that [second] command and is troubled with confusion, thus generating objections and scruples within one, such objections will result in the impossibility [of all faith] – may God protect us from that!

Just as man acquired an erect posture in the world of creation (*ʿālam-i khalqī*) and thereby became distinguished from other animals, so must he acquire uprightness of the soul in the world of the Command (*ʿālam-i amrī*) by accepting the true religion, so that by the uprightness he will become distinguished from those human beings who appear to be human but are in reality not. So such uprightness consists of true thoughts (*fikr-i ḥaqq*), truthful words (*qawl-i ṣidq*) and good deeds (*ʿamal-i khayr*). All three must be linked to the command of the imam of the time – may salutations ensue upon mention of him… .

Another of the sayings of the universal teacher (*muʿallim-i kullī*) is that if the disciple fulfils the requisites of 'fear God' (*ittaqū Allāh*) a maxim which can be written on one fingernail, he will acquire all the noble virtues along with all the modes of moral conduct – initially between himself and God, and ultimately between himself and God's creatures – which he need practise, the explanation and analysis of which could otherwise not be contained in a great number of volumes.

For example, if the disciple integrates the fear of God (*Khudatarsī*) into his discipline of reflection (*fikr*), that reflection – being an expression of intellectual irradiation arising from the human rational soul – will put him in harmony with the truth (*ḥaqq*), a harmony which will effect the union of his sol with the true summons (*daʿwat-i ḥaqq*). By the power of its spirituality (*rūḥāniyyat*), an angel will be appointed to guard over his reflection so that it is ever beautified with truth.

And if the disciple integrates the fear of God into his speech (*qawl*), his speech – which is the manifestation of the meanings of what he things – will become an exemplar embodying intellectual knowledge (*mathal-i maʿlūmāt*), an exemplar which becomes the source-spring [of] '*Speak straightforward speech*' [33:70], and from its spiritual power an angel will be appointed to guard over his speech and always keep it adorned with truthfulness.

Once he has attained this, he will have obtained truthful thought (*fikr-i ḥaqq*), righteous speech (*qawl-i ṣidq*) and good actions (*ʿamal-i khayr*), which are the rungs of the ladder (*miʿrāj*) by which he may ascend to the world of the Hereafter. His thoughts will have become an intelligence made up of the Divine Command, his speech will be a spirit made up of that intelligence, and his works will be a body composed of that spirit.

Likewise, in the case of a miserly person: the missionary (*mard-i daʿwat*) will say to him, 'Give so much of the wealth you possess,' but his heart will not be in accordance with this. If they impose it on him and he is not afraid of God, he will resist and will thus forfeit [both] this world and the Hereafter. But if he fears God and considers the matter with pious Godfearing, he will give, even though in the beginning only under duress and with reluctance, but after doing so a few times he will become generous.

Similarly, if envy is dominant, and he considers the matter with pious Godfearing, he will realize that in the whole world no one can attain wealth or honour [merely] by wishing – except by the grace of God Almighty – vouchsafed particularly to him. He should consider that, 'If I envy someone for those blessings and favours that God Almighty has granted him, God will not thereby reduce what He has destined for him just because of my envy. However, since that envy has arisen from my soul and desires to influence the course of his affairs which, of course, it cannot, it will recoil back on my own soul, in accordance with the adage that "Fire devours itself if it finds nothing else to devour."[1] This, that fire [of envy] will consume my own soul, so that I will forfeit [felicity in] both this life and the next, and be overtaken by the wrath of God.' So, in this fashion, he will gradually restrain himself, and abandon reliance on his own might and power, coming to rely instead on the might and power of the Most High. He will put into practice the good thoughts harboured in his conscience and will ultimately reach such a point that if he sees anyone endowed with wealth and prosperity, he will invoke, 'O God, bless him that he may enjoy what he has, and let me likewise have as much as that and much more.' The same applies to the other base characteristics, which would take too long to enumerate.

Likewise, the philosophers state that the reformation of character is similar to the treatment of a patient by a physician. For every human body in which the four humours, namely yellow bile, black bile, blood and phlegm, are in equilibrium will enjoy perfect health and a sound constitution, However, if there be too much or too little of one of these humours in his body, it will be affected with disease and illness in accordance with the increase and decrease in the amount [of that humour]. A physician is therefore needed so that, after acquainting himself with the symptoms and learning the facts, he can undertake – albeit trusting in God and seeking His satisfaction – to treat the body competently and skillfully. He should balance excess [in one humour] by decrease and shortage by increase, and thus bring the body's balance back into a state of healthy equilibrium.

The doctor of the spirit, who is in charge of the refinement of character, is therefore required to examine the state of the moral character, and [as with the physician's practice] to find out which of the four faculties [of the soul], that are comparable to

1. From an Arabic poem alluding to a saying of Imam ʿAlī, cited in [Muḥammad Bāqir] al-Majlisī, *Biḥār al-anwār* (Tehran, 1956), vol. 73, p. 261. With minor variance, the poem reads: 'Be patient with the jealousy of the envious person, because your patience will kill him./Envy is like a fire which devours itself if it does not find anything else to devour.' Al-Ṭūsī quotes the same verse in his *Akhlāq-i Muḥtashamī*, ed., Muḥammad Taqī Dānishpazhūh ([2nd ed.] Tehran, 1960), p. 284.

the four natural temperaments, suffers from imbalance. Thus, he conjoins wilfulness (*ʿazm*) to dryness, gentleness (*narmī*) to humidity, restlessness (*tīzī*) to heat, and calmness (*sākinī*) to coldness. Once he knows this, he should balance each with its opposite. For example, severity with toleration, frivolity with dignity, sexual desire with abstinence, anger with contentment, facetiousness with seriousness, miserliness with generosity, haste with deliberation, and avarice with liberality.

This being so, since all base characteristics arise from sexual desire and anger (*shahwat wa ghaḍab*), some ascetics in Islam have maintained that these two passions should be completely nullified. To this end they try hard to starve themselves of sensual stimuli, retiring into dark hermitages and depriving themselves of all but a small quantity of food. Then people begin to relate with astonishment how a certain ascetic has reached such perfection in asceticism with respect to food that for so many days and nights he has reduced his nourishment to such-and-such a degree, even though [he only eats] such disagreeable food as barley, millets and acorns; and that he constantly and with great passion repeats 'Allāh, Allāh,' and in between collapses and falls into unconsciousness, hinting that at such moments a door to the unveilings from [the realm of the] unseen is opened to him, as if to signify by this conduct that he has been vouchsafed a physical encounter with the presence of the Absolute (*ḥaḍrat-i ṣamadiyyat*). Such a person may generate a huge crowd of followers who attribute to him many marvels and miracles (*muʿjizāt*).

The argument that the adepts of truth (*ahl-i ḥaqq*) have with them on this subject is this: 'Divine wisdom requires that a man's senses be the instrument whereby he acquires perfection of soul – yet you [ascetics] would destroy the soul's instrument of perfection before it reaches that perfection, so that before the eye of reason is opened by the senses, you destroy the eye! You are like someone who mounts a horse and sets out for somewhere, but before reaching that destination, he cuts the horse's heels; since he cannot continue the way on foot, he stops his journey bewildered, so that predators and wild beasts kill him, or he perishes through some other cause. This is because you deprive yourself of the sound nutriment which produces pure and glittering blood. The fine vapour (*bukhār*) generated from this pure blood produces the substance of animal spirit (*rūḥ-i ḥayawānī*), which is the mount upon which the human soul rides, thus keeping the humours in equilibrium. You eat disagreeable food which produces dense and thick blood, and from that dense, thick blood a dark vapour is generated which constitutes the substance of the vital spirit, so that thereby the humours become indisposed, and madness, dejection (*sawdā*) and melancholy (*mālikhūliyā*) overtake you.'

In regard to the attempt to completely eradicate these two forces of anger and sexual desire, it should be understood that one who lacks anger also lacks in moral courage (*ḥamiyyat*), and lacking moral courage, he can be counted neither among the divisions of mankind nor among the divisions of womankind. Should anger ever accidentally overpower his soul, there will be no difference between him and a beast of prey.

[Likewise], one who has no sexual desire or lust must turn his back on generation and reproduction, on which the preservation of the human race and the maintenance of the inhabited world depends. A person who suppresses the power of lust can be counted neither among the divisions of mankind nor among the divisions of womankind. Should lust ever accidentally overpower him, there will be no difference between him and a brute.

However, neither of these attitudes relating to anger and sexual desire mentioned above can be said to be sound or good. Both these methods are objectionable in regard to their approach to [the reality of] this affair, which is to say that there should be neither excess on the one side nor deficiency on the other. Overcoming both of these forces should be accomplished by bringing them to perfection – namely, by bringing both of them under the rule of reason (*ḥukm-i ʿaql*), so that, when they were despotic (*ammāra*) and obstructive, they will now become obedient (*maʾmūr*) and co-operative; where they governed the affairs of reason, now reason should govern their affairs. Thus, the angels will yoke them together – that is, anger in the role of 'male' and lust in the role of 'female' – in a contract of matrimonial union, so that from their marriage will issue forth offspring suitable to their [original] state of being (*ḥāl-i wujūd*):[1] knowledge, wisdom, remembrance (*tadhakkur*), chastity, generosity, courage, truth, veracity, righteousness, meritorious deeds, rectitude, good conduct, love, friendship, concordance, brotherhood, trustworthiness, modesty, patience, tranquillity, dignity, pudency (*ḥayā*), contentment, humility, trust [in God], satisfaction, sincerity, and all else that ensues from such qualities.

If, however – God forbid – the intellect is overpowered by these two forces [of anger and sexual desire], the soul's light and purity will be veiled by their perverse darkness and moral deviation. The devil (*shayṭān*) will bind the marriage contract between them, and that marriage will give birth to offspring which are in contrast to their [original] state of being: ignorance, folly, forgetfulness, hypocrisy, debauchery, miserliness, suspicion, falsity, lying, evil, corruption, error, fault, enmity, hatred, spite, treason, impatience, impudence, shamelessness, malevolence, greed, tyranny, obstinacy, haughtiness, anger, the sowing of dissension, slandering, vanity, conceit, quarrelsomeness, fanaticism, love of wealth, prestige, offspring, flattery and authority, and all that follows from these.

Deny these base characteristics,
so as to uproot them all.
Yes, in a manner befitting each of them,
Let them be controlled by reason and wisdom,
So what is a hindrance becomes a help,
and finds repose in the pacifier.[2]

1. The term '*ḥāl-i wujūd*' is perhaps to be understood in the sense of *fiṭrat*, 'original nature' or 'natural constitution' mentioned in the Qur'an (30:30). Imam ʿAlī b. al-Ḥusayn Zayn al-ʿAbidīn, *al-Ṣaḥīfa al-kāmila al-Sajjādiyya*, prayer 2, verses 9–12, p. 45; tr. W. Chittick as *The Psalms of Islam* (London, 1998), p. 21. The words in brackets appear in manuscript 'T' only in the Persian version of the quote.

2. These lines, although not recorded among al-Ṭūsī's poems, resemble his poetic style. For poems attributed to al-Ṭūsī, see M. Mudarrisī Zanjānī, *Sargudhasht wa ʿaqāʾid-i falsafī-yi Khwāja Naṣīr al-Dīn Ṭūsī* (Tehran, 1956) pp. 153–160, and M. T. Mudarris Raḍawī, *Aḥwāl wa āthār-i Abū Jaʿfar Muḥammad b.*

The truth is that as long as man does not recognize his own errors, sins and shortcomings, his soul will never be able to recollect its own proper realm; [it will] fail to pass through the degrees of meritorious deeds and mount up the steps of perfection. Because of his self-love, it will be difficult, if not impossible, for him to recognize his own faults and shortcomings, and so these will be remain concealed from him. Consequently, conceit will manifest itself, and there is nothing so [morally] detrimental and dangerous as this.

Although the liar is as far as can be from the truth, yet the hypocrite (*murāʾī*) is far worse than the liar, while the conceited (*muʿjib*) person is even worse than the hypocrite. For the liar only tells a lie, while the hypocrite both tells a lie and dissembles in his actions. Because the liar and the hypocrite praise the conceited person, and because the latter, due to his extreme love of flattery and his arrogant conceit (*ʿujb*), finds their words and deeds laudable and pleasing, he neither abstains from this [vanity] nor orders his flatterer to desist [from their praise]. Consequently, every instance of conceited self-admiration which occurs in him inevitably increases his distance from the light of divine guidance, bringing him even closer to the darkness of error and necessarily leads him to the state of '*Verily, they are veiled from their God on that day*' [83:15]. We seek refuge from this in God.

Thus, when one praises, compliments and commends someone for his good deeds, one must first think about what that good actually is, so that one may know who the good man is. Since goodness (*nīkī*) is a concomitant of moral perfection (*kamāl*), it should be understood that one who is in the absolute sense good is [only] one who is perfect and complete in being good [that is, in practising virtue]. And it is obvious unto which of the devotees of the mission (*banda-yi daʿwat*) such a degree can be said to be applied. So when one realizes that one lacks such perfection, and that even [that little of] good which others attribute to one is all a falsehood, one should not be pleased with such falsehood and become confused about one's situation. Rather, one should ask oneself: 'With all these defects of character and shortcomings that engulf me, should I consider myself worthy of such epithets and abase myself by assuming the rank [given by such flattery]?' If so, I would be claiming to be that perfect person. If this idea becomes rooted in my heart, my conceit and stupidity will increase, and each time I regard myself with admiration and self-love, I will descend one more degree into the abyss (*hāwiya*). Therefore, such a man who flatters me and relates so many tales of my supposed goodness is a false worldly friend and, in reality, my [spiritual] enemy regarding the life to come.

Likewise, if one is to call someone evil and reproach him for his wickedness, one should first reflect on what badness is, so as to recognize who the evil-doer is. Since badness is a concomitant of moral deficiency, one who is bad is he whose soul is deficient in every respect. If I am deficient in all respects and have not

---

Muḥammad b. Ḥasan Ṭūsī (Tehran, 1975), p. 627. Some verses of al-Ṭūsī are also quoted in Muḥammad Riḍā b. Khwāja Sulṭān Ḥusayn Ghūriyānī Khayrkhwāh-i Harātī, *Faṣl dar bayān-i shinākht-i imām* ed. W. Ivanow (3rd ed., Tehran, 1960). English trans., *On the Recognition of the Imam*, tr. W. Ivanow (2nd ed., Bombay, 1947).

reached perfection in any respect, and am bad in proportion to that deficiency which belongs to my essence, the wickedness they ascribe to me is thus true and not false, and therefore I should not be offended by the truth and deny it. I should rather be offended by my own deficiency, not by its being pointed out to me. I must oppose this wickedness in myself and not attempt to repudiate his words. Even if he is an enemy and what he says is out of enmity, I must choose from what my enemy and my friend say that which is conducive to the betterment and benefit of my soul in the Hereafter.

Since I am awakened by the words of my enemy but am lulled into the sleep of negligence, nay, the death of ignorance, by the words of my friend, I should be entirely grateful to this enemy of mine. If I were, in effect, to behave in this manner, such a conception would become a cause of my soul's perfection, and with each step that I take in the path of the acquisition of virtuous accomplishments I will gain a further, higher rank. Therefore, the man who reproaches me so much and talks so much about my wickedness is, in the figurative, false and worldly sense of the word, my enemy, but in truth, with regard to the life to come, he is my friend. I should not remain hostile towards this enemy, nor friendly to that friend, but [on the contrary] consider this friend an enemy and that enemy a friend.

In such matters, the firmly established principle on which one can absolutely rely is the fact that, being devotees of the true divine mission (*daʿwat-i ḥaqq*), we know that on the day when '*Their excuse will not profit those who did injustice*' [30:57], we shall be asked: 'If your profession of love for the lord of the age (*imām-i zamān*) be true and sincere, tell us, which one of your friends have you hated for the imam's sake, and which one of your enemies have you loved for his sake?' We shall have to give acceptable answers. There, when all veils are lifted and [the reality of all] affairs divulged, only veracity will be accepted, and no one will be able to resort to sophistry. The acceptable answer will not be that 'So-and-so was the imam's enemy, but since he was my friend I still loved him.' Rather, the acceptable answer will be to say, 'Although so-and-so was my friend, yet, since he was the enemy of the imam I hated him, and since so-and-so was the friend of my lord, I loved him, although he hated me.'

> [In his devotion to You, he attained to such a high degree that] he banished away from himself his intimate associatees because they conceived enmity to You. He brought close to himself those who were far because they responded to Your summons. For Your sake he befriended those who were strangers to him, and for Your sake he held those who were intimate with him as enemies.[1]

Such is the meaning and reality of this [saying]: 'Religion is love for the sake of God and hatred for the sake of God.'[2] Godspeed to you.

(Translated by S. J. Badakhchani)

1. Imam Zayn al-ʿĀbidīn, *al-Ṣaḥīfa*, prayer 2, verses 9–12, p. 45; *Psalms of Islam*, p. 21. The words in brackets appear in manuscript 'T' only in the Persian version of the quote.
2. Attributed to the Imam Jaʿfar al-Ṣādiq, according to al-Barqī, *Kitāb al-maḥāsin*, ed. S. J. Muḥaddith (Qumm, 1952), pp. 262–266.

4

Naṣīr al-Dīn al-Ṭūsī

Among al-Ṭūsī's authentic Ismaili works, the short but closely argued treatise on the key Qur'anic concepts of *tawallā* (Ar. *tawallī*) and *tabarrā* (Ar. *tabarru'*), or solidarity and dissociation, deserves a special place. The text was written around 633/1235 and mentions al-Ṭūsī's patron at the time, Nāṣir al-Dīn 'Abd al-Raḥīm b. Abī Manṣūr (d. 655/1257), the *muḥtasham* or local leader of the Nizārīs of Quhistān, for whom he also wrote his famous works on ethics, including the *Akhlāq-i Nāṣirī* (known in English as the *Nasirean Ethics*).

Tawallā wa tabarrā
Solidarity and Dissociation[1]

For anyone seeking steadfastness in religion, two things are indispensable: one is solidarity (*tawallā*) and the other is dissociation (*tabarrā*). As [Imam 'Alī ibn Abī Ṭālib] has said: 'Religion is love and hate for the sake of God.' To begin with, our brother in faith, Najīb al-Dīn Ḥasan, May God grant him success and fulfil his wishes, beseeched this humble person Muḥammad-i Ṭūsī to write an essay on the subject and there was no alternative but to compose a few words for him, from the sayings of the leaders of religion (*pīshwāyān-i dīn*) and instructors of the people of certainty (*mu'allimān-i ahl-i yaqīn*), especially the present instructor (*mu'allim-i waqt*), exalted king, helper of religion and state, king of Iran 'Abd al-Raḥīm b. Abī Manṣūr,[2] May God exalt his sovereignty and protect his blessed existence.

We begin by saying that mankind possesses two faculties which are subsidiaries and branches of the animal soul (*nafs-i bahīmī*), namely, lust and anger (*shahwat wa ghaḍab*), that is [in Persian], *ārazū* and *khashm*. These two faculties also exist in other animals, and 'to do' and 'not to do' are the outcome of these two faculties. But mankind possesses another soul which does not exist in other animals, namely, the rational soul (*nafs-i nāṭiqa*), and also [a kind] of intelligence which in the Persian language is translated as wisdom (*khirad*).

---

1. Naṣīr al-Dīn al-Ṭūsī, *Tawallā wa tabarrā*, ed. and tr. S. J. Badakhchani (forthcoming). See also Naṣīr al-Dīn al-Ṭūsī, '*Risāla dar tawallā wa-tabarrā*' in *Akhlāq-i Muḥtashamī*, ed. Muḥammad Taqī Dānishpazhūh (2nd ed., Tehran, 1982), pp. 561–570.
2. This was al-Ṭūsī's patron at the time, Nāṣir al-Dīn 'Abd al-Raḥīm b. Abī Manṣūr (d. 655/1257).

It is essential that the animal soul, whose faculties are lust and anger, should be subservient to the human rational soul (*nafs-i gūyāy-i insānī*). The rational soul should be subservient to the intellect and the intellect should abide by the commandment of the truthful commander (*farmāndih-i ḥaqīqat*)[1] who is called the instructor of religion (*muʿallim-i dīn*), so that action is aligned with rectitude (*istiqāmat*). If this were contradicted, action would be diverted and without rectitude. In other words, the intellect would be subservient to the rational soul [and], the rational soul would be subservient to the animal soul, [which would] lead to the pursuit of lust and anger, and consequently, collapse into the blazing fire (*hāwiya*) which is called Hell. We seek refuge in God from this.

Thus, when the animal soul abides by the commandment of the rational soul, lust and anger become more subtle; lust evolves and reaches the rank of yearning (*shawq*), and anger evolves and reaches the rank of aversion (*iʿrāḍ*). Consequently, the one whose rational soul subdues his animal soul would, instead of lust and anger, possess yearning and aversion. When the rational soul falls subservient to the commandment of intellect, yearning and aversion become more refined and perfect and transform into liking (*irādat*) and disliking (*kirāhat*). When intellect falls subservient to the commandment of the truthful commander, liking and disliking transform into solidarity and dissociation (*tawallā wa tabarrā*).

The epitome of solidarity is directing oneself towards someone (*rūy farā kasī kardan ast*), and the epitome of dissociation is abandoning all that is apart from him. One reaches this status when one's lust and anger turns into love and directing oneself towards someone, and animosity and dislike towards all that is apart from him. Otherwise, when the rational soul falls subservient to the animal soul, two other things will be added to lust and anger, namely, love for wealth and love for position. And when intellect falls subservient to the rational soul, two other things will be added to it, namely, greed and arrogance. [All] other base ethics will result from this, and man will be taken to such a position where there is no bad quality in existence that is not present in him. That will end up at eternal ruin. We seek refuge in God from this.

But in the person whose action is straight, when the animal soul drives him towards lust, the rational soul, which is dominant, turns that lust into chastity (*ʿiffat*), the meaning of which is purity of soul. And when his animal soul drives him towards anger, the rational soul turns that anger into forbearance (*ḥilm*), the meaning of which is patience and restraint. When the rational soul drives the person towards love for wealth, intellect turns that into altruism (*īthār*), the meaning of which is giving preference to others over oneself. When the rational soul drives one towards love for position, the intellect turns that into seclusion (*ʿuzlat*) and isolation (*inqiṭāʿ*), that is, avoiding masses. And when the [intellect] drives one towards greed, the commander of the command (*āmir-i amr*) will turn that greed

1. This term, as well as *muʿallim-i dīn* (the instructor of religion) and *āmir-i amr* (the commander of the command) refer to the Nizārī imam.

into contentment (*qināʿat*) and when driving towards arrogance, the latter will turn that into humility (*tawāḍuʿ*). These commendable qualities will act as foundations for other ethics, leading to a situation where all good qualities that are possible in mankind will be attained and the one who possesses them will reach eternal bliss (*saʿādat-i abadī*). May our lord desire that!

Solidarity and dissociation have their respective exoteric and esoteric aspects. The exoteric aspect of solidarity is to face good people and that of dissociation is to detest bad people. The esoteric aspect of solidarity is facing the man of God (*mard-i khudā*), that is, that unique truthful person (*muḥiqq-i yagāna*) who is the foundation of all good things, and that of dissociation is to detest all that which is apart from him.

Two things make solidarity possible, gnosis and affection (*maʿrifat wa maḥabbat*), because they who fail to recognize God and to love Him may not come before Him. Recognition is gnosis and affection is love. Dissociation is also made possible by two things: emigration and endeavour (*hijrat wa jihād*). Emigration is cutting off from everything apart from God and endeavour is making an effort, because unless one cuts off from everything apart from God and strives against His enemies, dissociation will not be complete.

[Of] the above four things, namely, gnosis, love, emigration and endeavour without which solidarity and dissociation are incomplete, each one has an exoteric and an esoteric aspect. The exoteric [aspect] of gnosis is to recognize God; its esoteric [aspect] is to recognize nothing except Him. The exoteric [aspect] of love is to love God; its esoteric is to love nothing except Him. The exoteric [aspect] of emigration is to cut off from His enemies; its esoteric is to cut off from everything other than Him, particularly oneself and one's personal likings.[1] The exoteric [aspect] of endeavour is making an effort against God's enemies to devote in His path one's wealth, position, wife and children; [its esoteric] is to bring down to nothing one's lust and anger, one's love for possession and position, and one's likings and dislikings in His path. Once one accomplishes the above requirements, the conditions of solidarity and dissociation are fulfilled, and what remains is the perfection of religiosity which depends on contentment (*riḍā*) and submission (*taslīm*).

Contentment and submission are realized when solidarity and dissociation become one and the same thing, that is, dissociation is submerged into solidarity. This is similar to when relativity (*iḍāfat*) is submerged into reality (*ḥaqīqat*), the achievable (*mustaʾnif*), into the primordial (*mafrūgh*) and religious law (*sharīʿat*) into resurrection (*qiyāmat*), until absolute solidarity (*tawallā-yi ṣirf*) is attained.[2] Such a solidarity and dissociation would include the solidarity and dissociation that one had in the first instance, and this can only be realized when one's likes and dislikes become one and the same thing. Dislike is submerged into like, resulting in love and gnosis – to become one and the same thing, that is, love is submerged

1. Naṣīr al-Dīn al-Ṭūsī, *Rawḍa-yi taslīm*, ed. and tr. S. J. Badakhchani as *Paradise of Submission: A Medieval Treatise on Ismaili Thought* (London, 2005), no. 235, p. 84.

2. See al-Ṭūsī, *Rawḍa-yi taslīm*, no. 78, p. 40 (tr.).

into gnosis. If one sees no one except Him, from whom is one dissociating oneself? And if one recognizes no one except Him, what should be the object of one's not desiring?

Once things are like this, all one's worldly affairs will be the same and one will be content with whatever happens. No happiness can make one happy and no sadness can cause grief. One will not feel regret for the past nor have [false] hopes for the future. Such being the case, one will have obtained the status of contentment (*riḍā*) which is the same as the status of satisfaction (*khushnūdī*) – meaning that, whatever happens, one will be content and pleased with God, and as such, one can expect God may be pleased with one.[1]

The signs of contentment are three. First, whatever befalls one, be it good or bad, one should not exhibit joy or ill feeling. Second, one should abide by whatever one is commanded to do, whether pleasant or unpleasant, without exhibiting objection or dismay; because it is the commandment of the truthful commander, one should not feel any difference, that is, preferring one side over the other. For example, if one is commanded to make someone happy or harm someone, one should not feel a difference. The third [sign is] that one should not reject any creature and exhibit aversion (*nifrat*); one should not say 'This one is good, that one is bad, this one is a charitable person, that one is an evil doer.' Rather, one should act and do according to whatever one is instructed to say and whatever is revealed to one's heart to do, since it is from the instructor of religion (*muʿallim-i dīn*); [accordingly,] one should learn and should not, under any circumstance, act independently. When one finds these signs in oneself, the status of contentment (*riḍā*) would have been reached.

What remains [is the fulfilment of] submission (*taslīm*). Submission means to surrender (*bāz supurdan bāshad*); the implication of surrender is such that one must dispense with things that cannot accompany one to the Hereafter; one should consider them borrowed and unreal (*majāzī*), for example, eyes, ears, tongue, hand and foot, indeed the whole body, desire, passion, anger, likes, dislikes and internal faculties such as estimation (*wahm*), knowledge and insight (*bīnish*). All these, and all those associated with them such as wealth, position, honour, dignity and so on, even one's life and livelihood (*jān wa zindagānī*), all such things should be considered as borrowed. For example, someone entrusted to take care of someone else's property craves for it to be taken away from him and feels at ease when this happens. One should be happy that a great burden is removed from one's heart and relieved from a great misery when an obligation is fulfilled. Thus, when one reaches such a status when all the [worldly] things around one become worthless and one feels no attachment to them, one has reached the status of submission (*taslīm*).

Once solidarity, dissociation, contentment and submission are acquired, faith is obtained (*īmān ḥāṣil āmada bāshad*). Otherwise, one cannot be called faithful

1. Cf. Qur'an 89:27–28.

(*mu'min*). As it is revealed [in the Qur'an]: *But no, by their Lord, they will not believe until they make thee [the Prophet] the judge regarding the disagreement between them; then they shall find in themselves no impediment touching thy verdict, but shall surrender in full submission* [4:65].[1]

In [the above verse], three conditions have been set for the faithful. The first is authority (*taḥkīm*), meaning accepting [the Prophet's] sovereignty over oneself, which is solidarity, the type which encompasses both solidarity and dissociation. The second and third are contentment and submission. Once one reaches this rank, one becomes a man of faith (*mu'min*). What remains is to reach [the rank of] being certain (*mūqin*). As the relationship of the man of faith with this world is the same as the relationship of the man of certitude with the Hereafter, thus it is revealed [in the Qur'an]: *Those who believe in the unseen* (ghayb) *and have the assurance of the Hereafter* [2:3–4].

Faith means believing and certitude is arriving at certainty. Occasionally, belief may be associated with doubt (*bā ẓann buwad*) but certainty is devoid of doubt. Doubt relates to worldly affairs, while certitude relates to the Hereafter; as has been explained in a number of places in the sacred words.[2] Certitude is such that one knows the Hereafter as if one is looking at it, and this will only happen when one has witnessed the non-existence of the [physical] world and its conditions.

Thus, if one considers this world as [real] existence, one's vision will be reversed, and undoubtedly one will consider the Hereafter as non-existence. If one considers the Hereafter as [real] existence, one will see the world as non-existence, because these two necessitate one another. Thus, the man of certitude is one who sees this world and its affairs as non-existence, and the more he severs his attachment to it, [the more] his certainty of the Hereafter will increase.

Certitude also has three stages: One is *ḥaqq al-yaqīn*, that is, the veracity of certainty; another is *'ilm al-yaqīn*, that is, the realization of certainty; and the third is certainty itself (*'ayn al-yaqīn*), that is, its essence and reality. Veracity of certainty is the position of those men of faith who from this world are facing the Hereafter. Realization of certainty is the rank of those who have attained perfection of the Hereafter. Essence and reality of certainty is the rank of those who surpass the Hereafter. They are called people of Unity (*ahl-i waḥdat*). In this context [the Prophet] said: 'This world is forbidden to the people of the Hereafter, and the Hereafter is forbidden to the people of this world, and both of them are forbidden to the people of God.'[3]

Man can reach the rank of Unity when he abandons both existence and non-existence and his vision surpasses these two ranks. As long as he commutes between existence and non-existence, he can either be a man of the world or a man of the Hereafter. If he desires illusory existence and real non-existence, he is a man of this world and the Hereafter is forbidden to him. If he desires true existence and

1. al-Ṭūsī adds Persian translations of the Qur'anic verses which are not repeated here.
2. This alludes to the words and aphorisms of Imam Ḥasan II *'alā dhikrihi'l-salām* (d. 561/1166).
3. See al-Ṭūsī, *Āghāz wa anjām*, ed. Īraj Afshār (Tehran, 1956), p. 50.

illusory non-existence, he is a man of the Hereafter and this world is forbidden to him. If he desires neither existence nor non-existence, that is, he wants neither self nor selflessness, nor does he know or see any of these two, he will be a man of God and both this world and the Hereafter are forbidden to him.

In other words, if one desires this world or the Hereafter, one will fall from the perfection of that rank [that is, being the man of God] and will be ill-fated, because as long as one yearns for the Hereafter, paradise, reward and bliss, one is seeking one's own perfection. If one desires self-perfection, one loves oneself and not God, and would be the man of multiplicity (*kathrat*) and not unity (*waḥdat*). As [Sanā'ī] says: 'Whatever you see apart from God, it is idol, destroy it!'

Thus, loving anything but God is idol-worshipping. The Hereafter, paradise, contentment and proximity of God (*jawār-i khudā*) are all apart from God. Therefore, the seeker of Unity (*ṭālib-i waḥdat*) should neither indulge nor desire such things or even find himself among those who do so, because the sign of anyone who recognizes God is that one should not want anything except God. Moreover, even seeking gnosis and loving God is in itself multiplicity. Because in [the realm of] Unity there is neither knowing nor known, neither lover nor beloved. All will be God and God alone.

Thus, the one who only sees God and nothing else is the seeker of unity (*ṭālib-i waḥdat*). If God Almighty removes the veils of existence and non-existence from before him, he may reach this rank, and this is a rank that no creature can describe. That which can be described in words cannot be free from denial (*kufr*) and ascribing partners to God (*shirk*). Thus, the seeker (*mujtahid*) should try to remove from before him all that is apart from God, so that he, by his own endeavour, may reach the reality of his own self, God Almighty willing. This is what he [al-Ṭūsī] compiled in his own handwriting.

(Translated by S. J. Badakhchani)

5
Khayrkhwāh-i Harātī

Khwāja Muḥammad Riḍā b. Sulṭān Ḥusayn was a native of the village of Ghūriyān, a dependency of Herat in present-day Afghanistan. He lived in the 10th/16th century and commonly referred to himself as 'Khayrkhwāh,' the 'Well-wisher.' The following is an extract from the beginning of one of his works, entitled simply *The Epistle* (*Risāla*). The passage delves into the importance of spiritual edification, or *taʿlīm*, and the role of the Ismaili hierarchy, the *ḥudūd-i dīn*, in leading the adepts to a recognition of the divine. It also elaborates the existence of three categories among creatures. In the spiritual world, those of the first category testified with knowledge and conviction to God's sovereignty over them; the second category also testified to God's sovereignty, but only in imitation of the first category; and the third category denied the sovereignty of God altogether. The physical world was created so that those of the second category could attain true recognition and certainty. Meanwhile, the first category manifested in the world as the *ḥujjat* or 'proof' of the imam so as to nurture the souls of the second category and to lead them to God by spiritual edification (*taʿlīm*), while the third was manifested to nurture the physical life of the second category.

Risāla
The Epistle[1]

O God, O our Lord.
In the Name of God, the Compassionate, the Merciful.

The goal and purpose of composing these words and penning these expressions is as follows: In our days a veil has been drawn upon the face of truth due to the incapacity and unworthiness of human beings to do without that veil. But now, by his abundant blessings and perfect guidance, Ḥaḍrat-i Mawlānā (i.e., the imam), (may his power and might be exalted) has opened the doors of bounty to his obedient subjects, and has given leave for the veil to be removed from this matter. He appointed this humble

1. Muḥammad Riḍā b. Khwāja Sulṭān Ḥusayn Ghūriyānī Khayrkhwāh-i Harātī, 'Risāla,' ed. Wladimir Ivanow in *Taṣnīfāt-i Khayrkhwāh Harātī* (Tehran, 1961), pp. 1–3; ed. Sayyid Shāhzāda Munīr b. Muḥammad Qāsim-i Badakhshānī, in *Khayrkhwāh-i muwaḥḥid-i waḥdat* (Mumbai, 1915), pp. 1–5; this selection tr. Shafique N. Virani. The Persian text is faulty in places. While the edition of Ivanow is followed here, occasionally Sayyid Shāhzāda Munīr's edition gives a better reading and is used for the translation. The introduction to this chapter is by the translator.

servant to accomplish this service and convey this summons. I therefore considered it obligatory in this task to first raise the awareness and consciousness of the friends (*rafīqān*) of all regions and the respondents (*mustajībān*) of all realms by allusions and indications. Thus, the effect of these words and the influence of this message should be apparent to them. Following this, the aim will be more clearly and unambiguously communicated.

The *pīr* (spiritual master) is the doctor of souls and thus resembles a physical doctor. In some cases, a physical doctor commences treatment by rooting out the source of the illness, not by administering food and drink.[1] Similarly, the spiritual doctor must first address the source of the spiritual illness that afflicts the respondents. That illness is ignorance. In our days, this is held to be the illness of the spirit. Thus, if their ignorance is not pointed out to them right at the outset, they will not be led out of that valley [of believing] that ignorance is not the issue. So long as they do not sincerely accept this and express remorse,[2] nor heave sighs of regret about their past and completely leave that stage behind, they will not enter the stage of seeking wisdom, which is knowledge and gnosis of the lord. What is the use of taking them to that which they do not seek?

It is also apparent that as many of those who now boast of [belonging to] this faith are commoners, explanations suitable to them will be used and we will not begin with proofs based on Arabic expressions. Those who are cast into confusion must seek a proof, so that matters may be clarified for them using both intellectual and scriptural explanations. Why the respondents (*mustajībān*) and teachers (*muʿallimān*) have come [to this world], what their purpose here is, what they must accomplish, what each of them had done aforetime and the word of each should be explained to them.

Right at the outset, it must be known that the goal and purpose of the coming to this world of the respondents and others, who are the manifestation of the second category, is the recognition of the Exalted God (may His name be glorified). In the spiritual world, because they testified [to the sovereignty of God] by mere imitation (*taqlīd*) [rather than conviction, *taḥqīq*], they begged to achieve a status of certainty (*yaqīn*). The Exalted God accepted their prayer. He created this physical world especially so that they could achieve His recognition. It was not created for those of the first or third categories. In the spiritual world, those of the first category testified [to the sovereignty of God] through conviction (*taḥqīq*) and certainty (*yaqīn*), so there was no need for them to come to this world. The members of the third category completely denied [the sovereignty of God], and continue to do so here, [but] they appear in the world because of the claim that those of the second category have over them. The appearance of the first category, which manifests as the *ḥujjat* (proof), is to nurture the souls of the respondents, while the appearance of the third category, which consists of the exotericists, minerals, plants and animals, is to nurture their bodies. This is because the soul cannot attain recognition without the body, and the body cannot survive without these necessities.

1. Read *dafʿ-i mādda-yi maraḍ mī kunad* for *dafʿ-i māda-yi marʿ namī kunad.*
2. Read *muta'assif* in place of *manṣūf* (as per Munīr) or *munṣif* (as per Ivanow).

It must also be known that the *dāʿīs*, *muʿallims*, greater *maʾdhūns*, and lesser *maʾdhūns*, who are members of the spiritual hierarchy (*ḥudūd-i dīn*) below the category of the *ḥujjat*, belong to the second category. As the spirits of the members of the second category are differentiated, some being more noble and powerful than others, they are called the people of ranks (*ahl-i tarattub*). The strong among them are the four aforementioned ranks, and the weak are the respondents (*mustajībān*).

It must also be known that the recognition (of God), which is the purpose of the coming of the second category (to this world), cannot be attained by the intellect alone. There are many scriptural and intellectual proofs that bear this out. Here also lies the difference between this community and other communities. There are others who maintain that [this recognition] can be attained by the intellect on its own. However, this community maintains that both intellect and spiritual edification (*taʿlīm*) are necessary. Nonetheless, it is improper to accept spiritual edification from just anyone. The one who gives this spiritual edification must possess an exclusive trait and miracle in which nobody else shares, that is, his very species establishes the recognition of the Exalted God.[1] This is unattainable by others and is called the miracle of knowledge; in other words, it is a knowledge displayed by nobody else. Everything else in existence shares in mere physical miracles with the perfect ones.

The one who communicates this miracle of knowledge is the *ḥujjat* of the imam. This is because the imam gives this miracle (of knowledge) only to the *ḥujjat*, who then conveys it to others. There can only be one (supreme) *ḥujjat* at a time, and this is why the imam is symbolized by the sun and the *ḥujjat* by the moon. Just as there is but a single sun and moon in this physical world, there is only one imam and *ḥujjat* in the world of religion:

There is a path from the heart of the *ḥujjat* to the imam (*ḥaḍrat*).
He becomes aware by the spiritual support (*taʾyīd*) of his heart.

(Translated by Shafique N. Virani)

1 The *kih* in this sentence must be omitted.

PART THREE

POETRY

Introduction

KUTUB KASSAM

In the vast corpus of poetic literature produced by Muslims over the centuries, the contribution of the Ismailis has been relatively small. This may be partly accounted for by the minority status of the community and the loss of a substantial amount of their literature through the upheavals of history. Nonetheless, what remains is of sufficient quality to warrant increased attention in modern scholarship, which has hitherto been inclined to concentrate on the history and theology of the Ismailis. Although the works of several poets represented in the selection that follows have appeared in edited form, there has been little by way of systematic study and translation of the major Ismaili poets. This neglect is all the more surprising considering that the poetic compositions of the Ismailis enable a valuable and perhaps a unique insight into their religious life, and which is rarely conveyed in their historical and doctrinal traditions.

As we turn to the third part of this Anthology, the reader will sense immediately the change in focus, perspective and tone of the selections. Admittedly, the thematic structure of the poetry is homologous with the discursive and expository writings of the preceding parts in many respects. There is the same engagement with the quest for knowledge, the meditations on *ta'wīl* and *bāṭin* of the Qur'an, the commitment to the Prophet and his progeny, the imperative of recognizing the imam of the time, and so on. But what characterizes Ismaili poetry above all, in contrast to the objectified delivery of the prose narratives, is its self-referential intrinsicality. It offers a mirror reflecting the personality and motivations of the individual poets, exposing the shifting moods, tensions and dispositions of their selfhood. In short, the primary function of these poetic compositions is to disclose the inner, spiritual life of the poets and the communities they represent.

In common with the larger literary traditions of Islamic civilization, Ismaili poetry is the product of diverse cultures, languages and historical epochs, and as such exhibits elements of both heterogeneity and homogeneity. The first section of our selection focuses on poetry in Arabic, produced chiefly during the Fatimid period, and represented by two of its foremost exponents of the poetic art, namely, Ibn Hāniʾ al-Andalusī, the court-poet to the Imam al-Muʿizz, and al-Muʾayyad fi'l-Dīn al-Shīrāzī, the chief *dāʿī* of the Imam al-Mustanṣir. While the former produced verse in all the major modes of classical Arabic poetry including panegyric and amatory, which attained him fame beyond the Fatimid world as the 'Mutanabbī of the Maghrib,' the poetic work of the latter is infused with a pronounced devotional spirit and personal engagement in the cause of his faith that henceforth became characteristic of all subsequent Ismaili poetry.

Al-Mu'ayyad's influence, both as teacher and exemplar, was transmitted most fruitfully to another Fatimid *dā'ī*, the famous theologian, philosopher and poet Nāṣir-i Khusraw, whose verses feature in Section II as he composed all his works in Persian. Arguably the most accomplished Ismaili poet, Nāṣir's poetry abounds with originality of diction, freshness of imagery, intellectual depth and ethical sensibility, together with a passionate commitment to his faith, that is rarely found in the literary genre categorized (often incorrectly) as 'religious poetry.' The Alamūt period is represented by Ḥaṣan-i Maḥmūd, whose collection on the theme of 'Resurrection,' the *Dīwān-i qā'imiyyāt*, has been discovered only recently. He is followed by Nizārī Quhistānī, the most significant poet of the post-Alamūt period. The notable feature of Nizārī's poems is his imaginative synthesis of Ismaili and Sufi ideas, which is also illustrated in the miscellany of other verse from the same period, as well as in the sample of poetry in Persian from the Badakhshān region of Central Asia.

The focus of the third and final section is the *ginān*ic tradition of devotional and mystical poetry from the Indian subcontinent. Consisting of several hundred poems of variable length, the *ginān*s are attributed to a series of preacher-poets, generically called *pīr*s or *sayyid*s, who came to the subcontinent from the 7th/13th century onwards to propagate the Ismaili path of Islam. Proselytizing within a complex milieu of historical, social and cultural contexts at the local level, including the Sufi and *bhakti* movements, the *pīr*s employed a variety of indigenous linguistic, poetic and musical idioms in their compositions. The outcome was a rich and extensive corpus of lyrical, didactic and homiletic verse that was transmitted orally for several centuries and collected in recent times. This tradition constitutes not only an important part of the Ismaili poetic heritage, but also a continuing source of inspiration for Ismailis of South Asian origin to this day.

I

ARABIC POETRY

1

Ibn Hāniʾ al-Andalusī

Muḥammad b. Hāniʾ has been called the first great poet of the Muslim West. Very little is known about his life. He was born in Seville to a father who was also a poet and probably a *dāʿī* working on behalf of the Fatimid caliphate established in 297/909. The young Ibn Hāniʾ was educated in Cordoba and Elvira and soon became well known as a poet throughout Muslim Spain. Spain was then ruled by a branch of the Umayyads and Ibn Hāniʾ's pro-Fatimid stance brought him opposition and persecution. After the accession of the Imam-Caliph al-Muʿizz in 341/952–3, the Fatimid fortunes revived and in 347/958, Ibn Hāniʾ left Spain and joined the Fatimid army then campaigning in Morocco. His panegyric poetry, much of it in praise of al-Muʿizz, was celebrated at the Fatimid court and became widely known throughout Fatimid territories and beyond. His poems are marked by ardent devotion to the Fatimid imams and the Ismaili cause, and valued as the finest examples of Fatimid court poetry. Ibn Hāniʾ died in 362/973 under mysterious circumstances.

O CHILDREN OF FĀṬIMA![1]

O children of Fāṭima![2]
Is there in our resurrection
a means of protection for us,
a sure refuge other than you?

You are the friends of God
and His people,
And His pious *khalīfa*s and proofs,
ever-present on the earth.[3]

You are the people of
prophecy, messengership and guidance,

1. Ibn Hāniʾ al-Andalusī, *Dīwān*, ed. Zāhid ʿAlī (Cairo, 1933), p. 375, no. 24, p. 342–343, no. 22; these selections tr. Faquir M. Hunzai and ed. Kutub Kassam in *Shimmering Light: An Anthology of Ismaili Poetry* (London, 1996), pp. 25, 27–28. The translations have been revised.

2. The 'children of Fāṭima' are the Shiʿi imams descended from the marriage of the Prophet Muḥammad's daughter, Fāṭima, and his cousin, ʿAlī ibn Abi Ṭālib, the first imam.

3. The terms *walī Allāh* (friend of God), *khalīfat Allāh* (vicegerent of God) and *ḥujjat Allāh* (proof of God), are used in Shiʿi theology to designate the Prophet and the imams.

And the pure chiefs
in the light of clear proofs.

You are the people of *tanzīl*
and *ta'wīl*,
of the lawful and the unlawful,
without contradiction or rejection.[1]

If it were asked,
who are the best of the people?
There would be no people to point out
except you.

Indeed, if you were to strike
a rock, a multitude of streams
would burst out of their bounds
and pour forth in sheer abundance!

THE UNITY OF FAITH

I saw the religion,
being united by the Imam;
obedience to him is success,
and disobedience loss.

I count his praise
like the praise of God,
the true submission and praise
by which sin is forgiven.

He is the inheritor
of the world, and to him
belong all human beings
between the two poles.

And that is not acquired
by perspicacity alone,
nor is he compelled
to conjecture in it.

But it is there in

1. In this verse, the imams are seen as custodians of the text of the revelation (*tanzīl*) and as the authoritative sources of its esoteric interpretation (*ta'wīl*).

the knowledge received by
one scholar
from another avid scholar.

It is a treasure of
knowledge divine, which is
truly knowledge, neither physiognomy
nor augury.

(Translated by Faquir M. Hunzai)

2

al-Mu'ayyad fi'l-Dīn al-Shīrāzī

The 62-line poem below was probably written by the future Fatimid *dāʿī al-duʿāt* between 434/1042 and 436–437/1045), when he had been exiled from his homeland in Fārs and was yet to reach Egypt, the site of his greatest achievements. The same period of his life is described in the extract from his memoirs (*Sīra*) in Part One, where his tone is that of an intrepid traveller, braving discomfort and extreme danger as he escapes detection after being rejected by the Būyid ruler of Fārs. This poem has a more melancholy tone and may reflect al-Mu'ayyad's state of mind at this time – a man no longer young, separated from home and family, 'buffeted by the winds of psychological uncertainty and physical danger.' The poem, a panegyric to the Fatimid imams and in particular the contemporary Imam al-Mustanṣir, contains many of the motifs of Fatimid praise poems, but al-Mu'ayyad's distinctive style and voice emerge clearly. He reflects on youth and old age and criticizes the degenerate material world, going on to praise the imams as the noble progeny of the Prophet Muḥammad and ʿAlī. At this time, al-Mu'ayyad had not yet met al-Mustanṣir and his plea for spiritual guidance carries a strong measure of longing. The other poems included in this chapter carry a similar devotional fervour.

O PROGENY OF MUṢṬAFĀ[1]

Old age has effaced the sign of youth
    and the scout of death has drawn near to me:

Frailty of body, laxness of bones, and a colour
    in which yellowness and pallor have appeared.

A beauty and splendour which I have been stripped of,
    by whose stripping, pleasure in life is stripped away!

A blackness, in exchange for which I have been given whiteness –
    [the whiteness] seems pitch-black to the eye.

1. Abū Naṣr Hibat Allāh b. Abī ʿImrān Mūsā al-Mu'ayyad fi'l-Dīn al-Shīrāzī, *Dīwān*, ed. M. Kāmil Ḥusayn (Cairo, 1949), pp. 207–210, no. 3; this selection tr. Tahera Qutbuddin in *al-Mu'ayyad al-Shīrāzī and Fatimid* Daʿwa *Poetry: A Case of Commitment in Classical Arabic Literature* (Leiden, 2005), pp. 200–208. See Qutbuddin's analysis of the poem on pp. 201–218.

All these are clear proofs,
evident, that departure is near.

Do I seem to you the one I was of old
or another? For my affair is strange!

Where – if I am who I was – is my trunk,
fresh, bright, and my succulent branch?

Beauty of stature, word and look,
seizing every heart, plundering.

A hand continually extending powerfully –
how many mishaps have stretched their reins [to gallop] away from it!

A tongue, in the arena of verse and prose,
dallying with every new meaning.

A heart that would confront death fighting,
and face the wrathful lion.

Indeed, all of it has turned away and passed,
what is left to me is flowing tears …

And a heart that burns from grief,
afflicted by the misfortunes of its fate.

It has turned away – no sorcerer will now be of benefit,
It has passed – no physician will now avail.

I am in an abode of exile, it is fitting,
nothing to wonder about, if the stranger is humbled in it.

An abode of strain and trial and tribulation,
its goodness, through all time, is adulterated with harm.

Its beneficence is harshness, its sweetness bitter, obscene
its deed, all its promises false.

Its honour ignominy, its generosity miserliness, hardship
its ease, all its affairs upside down.

An abode of vice – the body is assembled from it,

so [the body], like [the abode], is shame and vice.

The [body's] concern, as long as it remains, is eating and drinking,
and its range carousal and pleasure and perfume.

Aged, it has acquired all kinds of defects
that are disgraceful, which do not age [even] by its aging.

Ambitious desire whose knot is stout, strong,
and cravings whose garments are ever fresh, new.

It persists in its intoxication, while death
is a snare set up for its annihilation.

Alas for the eagerness of desire! Indeed my mind
is oppressed by desire, vanquished.

Alas for myself! For it is my tyranny that is [oppressing] myself,
blame and censure do not bypass me.

Why did I squander my life in error,
when my domain of rectitude was vast?

Why do I become preoccupied with my dark body,
when I am as dusty earth by it?

And [why do] I squander the light through which I am
connected to the noble ones, the ones brought nigh [to God]?!

Is the debaser of a precious pearl, aggrandizer
of a lowly, insignificant shell, intelligent?

[Blame and censure] do not bypass me for what happened. Is there a field
of allegiance fruitful like my field?

What is my excuse, when the True *Daʿwa* is a person
in whose lap I was born and raised?

What is my excuse, when the refuge-giving sanctuary is my house? –
whoever does not take shelter in it faces terror.

The sons of Aḥmad and ʿAlī, with whom [God is] well-pleased,
are my preparation for the Returning when I return.

Masters who are the purest in branch and in root,
all glory is earned from their glory.

Masters who are the revivifiers of decayed bones,
those, by remembering whom, intractable camels become docile.

Masters, to whom from the past ages
and the remaining, all return.

Then they distribute heaven and hellfire among them,
for each [person] has his deserved lot.

They are the refuge when there is no [other] refuge-giver,
and the ones who answer the hapless when there is no [other] answerer.

The trustworthy guides, shelter for followers
whenever a blistering hot day casts its shadow.

The seas, the full moons that have never encountered diminishing
from waning, and that have never been marred by setting.

[It is] from them that the shadow of God's mercy is extended
and the water of right guidance is poured forth.

[They are] Mount Sinai from which we hear the dialogue of God
in ourselves, and the divine secrets become apparent.

[They are] the [paradisiacal] springs of nectar from which we drink,
while the erring one continually drinks boiling water.

O sons of Muṣṭafā, [it is] in you, in you,
that the sorrowful seeks asylum in calamities.

O sons of Muṣṭafā, [it is] from you, from you,
that wishes of our hearts are sought.

You, you are the succour whenever
sins ruin the sinner among us.

You, you are the succour whenever
death approaches and the time comes to depart.

O my masters, how do I praise you,

when the utmost limit of my praise is jumbled speech?!

You have been created from clay, and we have been created from it,
it is apparent however, that we are degrees in it.

Your bodies originate from the clay
from which our souls sprout.

My excuse, if I am not capable of praising [this group of] people,
[is that] this [poem] is a love-prelude to the *Dīwān* of their praise.

May the God of creation [shower] blessings upon them,
as long as the rain-shower pours down from the cloud.

And upon the one who commands their heritage,
and represents the guides from among them.

The Imam who revivifies the one whom he calls –
felicitations to the one who answers him!

[He is] the best shepherd, whatever he guards is safe,
and that which he does not look after is 'looked after' by the wolf.

[He is] the Book that speaks Right and Truth,
through whom the concealed becomes uncovered.

[He is] the Imam Mustanṣir[1] the just, our master,
lamp in the darkness, the one with high lineage and excellent personal qualities.

He is a master for whom [all] masters are slaves,
like bees among whom there is a king-bee;

He explicates the religion of right guidance, and removes
from it the confusion-casting pitch-darkness of doubt.

[His] follower has the winning divining-arrow of [true] religion
like the arrow that hits the mark.

As for his adversary, his religion is pagan,
he does not have any share in the gardens of Eden.

1. The eighth Fatimid Imam-Caliph, Abū Tamīm Ma'add al-Mustanṣir bi'llāh (d. 487/1094).

Hibat Allāh,[1] if the turn of Fate is your enemy
then you are despoiled by it.

And by the sword of harshness, by every scoundrel,
[you are] struck in every condition.

But you are the one who [will] come out dominant, so goodly patience!
[For] indeed the one who is patient in tribulations is noble.

(Translated by Tahera Qutbuddin)

O FRIEND OF ALLAH[2]

I have been guided by Maʿadd[3] to the ways of my return;
to him I have offered my pure love!

My heart is one that sought refuge from itself in (this) loyalty,
which will be my provision on the Day of Judgement.

By God, if my heart turned fleeing away from him,
I will desert my heart openly!

The pure Imam al-Mustanṣir is a lord
who is Allah's proof over the people.

His grandfather is the warner whom God has sent
to humankind as a safeguard to (His) guidance.[4]

Allah has referred to his forefathers when He said:
'And to every people there is a guide.'[5]

O Friend of Allah! May my heart, family and property be sacrificed for you.
Your servant Ibn Mūsā[6] is still a fire blazing amidst groups of
obstinate people,

1. The personal name of the author, Abū Naṣr Hibat Allāh al-Mu'ayyad fi'l-Dīn al-Shīrāzī.

2. al-Mu'ayyad fi'l-Dīn al-Shīrāzī, *Dīwān*, ed. M. Kāmil Ḥusayn (Cairo, 1949), pp. 277, 286, 297, no. 49, vv. 1–9. This and the following poem are from Mohammad Adra's English translation of al-Mu'ayyad's *Dīwān* (forthcoming), nos. 36, 41.

3. See p. 264, n. 1.

4. The Prophet Muḥammad, here conceived as the imam's grandfather, is often referred to in the Qur'an as a warner *(nadhīr)* to the people.

5. See Qur'an 13:7, and the Prophet's *ḥadīth*: 'O 'Alī, I am the warner and you are the guide.'

6. Ibn Mūsā is a patronymic of al-Mu'ayyad.

Plunging myself into mortal throes, offering
my soul generously. O the purest one of the nobles!

Though I am far from my native abode,
all alone, driven away from my old and newly acquired properties,

Maʿadd is my treasure, my family, my property,
my support, as well as my weapons and instruments.

MY REFUGE AND HOPE

My love for Aḥmad and ʿAlī suffices me
as a source of refuge when my death draws nearer (to me).

Then the purest one of the world after the two of them
is Abū Tamīm, Maʿadd, son of ʿAlī!

He is victorious by Allah who aids him;
He is the *qibla* of Truth and the noblest Kaʿba!

He is the lord of the religion of guidance, and a sky of generosity
which enlivens by both its first and later rain.

They are my hope, the only hope
by whom I survive, when my deeds betray me.

(Translated by Mohammad Adra)

THE PURE PROGENY[1]

Peace be upon the pure progeny,
and welcome to their resplendent lights.

In the beginning, peace be upon Adam
from whom came all mankind, whether nomadic or sedentary.

Peace be upon the one by whose flood
the reprobates were made to suffer great misfortune.

Peace be upon the one to whom came
the peace at dawn when he was engulfed by fire.

---

1. al-Mu'ayyad fi'l-Dīn al-Shīrāzī, *Dīwān*, ed. M. Kāmil Ḥusayn, p. 286, no. 41, vv. 1–12, tr. Faquir M. Hunzai and ed. Kutub Kassam, *Shimmering Light*, p. 44. The translation has been revised.

Peace be upon the one who with his staff
overpowered the rebels of the tyrant Pharaohs.

Peace be upon Jesus, the Holy Spirit,
by whose advent Nazareth was honoured.

Peace be upon Aḥmad, the chosen,
the one who intercedes in the hereafter.

Peace be upon Ḥaydar, the chosen,[1]
and his descendants, the radiant stars.

Peace be upon you, O sovereign-lord
of Cairo, and all their gain is with you.

I sacrifice my soul to Mustanṣir,[2]
who is supported by the legions of heaven.

I bear witness that you are God's countenance
by [looking at] which the faces of your followers become resplendent.[3]

You are the custodian of the fountain of life,
and the fountain of your enemies seeps away.

(Translated by Faquir M. Hunzai)

1 Ḥaydar (lion) is one of the names used for Imam ʿAlī, on account of his exceptional courage on the battlefield which was also praised by the Prophet who called him Asad Allāh (the Lion of God).

2 The reign of Abū Tamīm Maʿadd al-Mustanṣir bi'llāh is considered to be one of the longest in Ismaili history and marked the zenith of Fatimid power, prosperity and cultural life.

3 Cf. Qur'an 75:22–23.

II

PERSIAN POETRY

1
Nāṣir-i Khusraw

Perhaps the best-known Ismaili poet in the Persian language, Nāṣir-i Khusraw's (d. after 462/1070) compositions were widely circulated and transmitted and continue to be cherished by Ismailis in Central Asia, Iran and Afghanistan (see Part One, 6 and Part Two, 3). Most of his poems are composed in the *qaṣīda* (ode) form and many have a didactic quality, exhorting moral virtue. Nāṣir encountered intense opposition for his beliefs and writings, leading him to move east, eventually to Yumgān in Badakhshān. The poetry from the latter period of his life is more caustic but highly skilled and eloquent. Although his commitment to the Ismaili message is clearly expressed in his poetry, much of it has wider philosophical and aesthetic appeal.

THAT WHICH IS BEST[1]

Now it is fitting that I change the state of things,
and strive to attain that which is best.

The world in April becomes fresh and green:
through contemplation I'll make my mind like April.

In the gardens and hillsides of my books of prose and verse,
out of verse and prose I'll make hyacinths and basil.

Fruits and flowers will I make from meanings,
and out of pleasing words I shall make trees.

As the cloud makes the desert's face a garden,
I'll make my notebook's face a garden too.

In sessions of debate, upon the wise
I'll scatter flowers of beautiful conceits.

---

1. Ḥakīm Abū Mu'īn Nāṣir-i Khusraw, *Dīwān*, ed., M. Suhaylī (Isfahan, 1956), pp. 303–305, this selection tr. Julie Scott Meisami in her 'Symbolic Structure in a Poem by Nāṣir-i Khusrau,' *Iran: Journal of the British Institute of Persian Studies*, 31 (1993), pp. 103–117. The translator suggests that the structure of this *qaṣīda*, arranged in fifty-six lines (8x7, plus two, final, 'capping' lines) alludes to the numerical foundation of the Ismaili cosmos, ordered by the number of the imams (seven), testifying to the manifestation of the Mahdī (eight), and embodying the esoteric wisdom of the Logos (28) within the exoteric framework of the poem's ethical meaning.

If on these flowers the dust of error settles,
I'll rain thereon clear light of explication.

A palace of my poem I'll make, in which
from its verses I'll form flower beds and verandas.

One spot I'll raise up like a lofty prospect,
another make wide and spacious like a courtyard.

At its gate some rarity of metre
I'll set, trusty and wise, to be its gateman.

Mafʿūlu fāʿilātu mafāʿīlu faʿ[1]
I'll make the foundation of this auspicious building.

Then people of merit from all regions
I'll invite into my palace to feast.

Let no ignorant person enter it, for I
did not build such a mansion for the ignorant.

I shall lay such a feast for the wise man
that from eating I'll render him helpless and amazed.

In the body of discourse, like the intellect itself,
I shall place beautiful and rare meanings as the soul.

If you have not seen discourse in human form,
I'll make for you, in discourse, the form of a man.

For him, from pleasing descriptions and pleasant tales,
I shall form twisting locks and smiling lips.

His meaning I'll make a lovely face, and then,
within the veil of wording I'll conceal it.

When I set my face towards speech, by force
I'll bend its back before me like a polo-stick.

1. This indicates the metre used in the poem.

If my mind, in some part, be dull,
with the hand of thought I'll file it sharp;

And should my soul display the rust of ignorance,
like a mirror I'll make it, through reading Scripture.

The troubles of this evildoing age
I'll ease through renunciation and obedience to God.

I'll wash my hands clean of desire and then,
no longer sleeping, raise my hand above Saturn.

If, in the garment of ignorance, my heart once slept,
now from that garment let me strip it naked.

And as for this unhappy, sleeping body:
let me rise and sacrifice it with the blade of piety.

For it my faults come from my self,
to whom can I cry out against myself?

I shall rise, and by the True God's grace and mercy
lighten Time's heavy load upon my heart,

And make my own person, between good and evil,
poised like the tongue of a balance.

Each moment to it a grain of goodness
I'll add, and diminish its evil,

Until those fetters, collar and chains he placed on me
I'll put back on the hands, feet and neck of Satan.

If the devil doesn't repent what he has done,
I'll make my own soul repent its deeds.

If I'm not able to make my body,
over the demons' train, a Solomon,

the demon within my body and my soul,
in any case, with Reason's blade I'll make a Muslim.

Of speech and deed I'll place on it saddle and bridle,
and make its reins from the wisdom of Luqmān.

Though you may hasten towards the court of Gīlān,
I'm headed for the court of the All-merciful.

Towards the True Guide let me set my face,
and make my self, in conduct, like Salmān:[1]

Go towards the kin of the Apostle, Aḥmad,
and make my body their slave and servant,

So that my name, by glory of the Imam,
I may inscribe upon the book of meanings;

And, from that Sun of Knowledge, make my heart
shine forth as brightly as the Moon in Cancer,

And from the blessed fortune of his sea
make of my heart a casket of pearls and coral.

O you who tell me constantly, advising,
'Throw off this garment, that I may give the word

so that at once, like So-and-so, you may be
introduced into the assembly of the Amīr of Khurāsān:'

Within your head the mists of ignorance are strong;
how can I treat the affliction of ignorance?

How should I throw away my honour like you, fool,
wishing only to fill my pouch with bread?

The Turks were once my slaves and servants:
how should I enslave my body to the Turks?

O you who've given me the bad advice
to do like this or that base fellow:

1. Salmān al-Fārisī, a Persian companion of the Prophet, is highly regarded in Shiʿism for his intimacy with the Prophet. See G. Levi Della Vida, 'Salmān al-Fārisī,' *EI2*, vol. 12, p. 701.

Your world is a cat that devours her kittens;
why should I worship such a one?

Who would be baser than I in this world,
should I pledge my body, like a cat, for bread.

Religion, perfection, knowledge: where should I cast them,
so as to make myself like a desert-wandering ghoul,

And empty of merit, like the ghoul:
how should I be the servant of demons?

It's enough for me to boast, that in both tongues
I order wisdom in both prose and verse.

My soul (to praise the Prophet's family)
I make now a Rūdakī, now a Ḥassān.[1]

My books, with their plentiful beauties of discourse,
are fuller than China, Greece and Iṣfahān.

In treatises, with logical discussion,
I produce proofs as brilliant as the sun;

Over intellectual problems I place sensibilia
in charge, as shepherd and as guardian.

The *Zād al-musāfir* is one of my treasures:
I write prose like that, and poetry like this.

A prison for the believer is this base world;
and so I dwell forever in Yumgān,

Till, on the Day of Judgement, burning fire
for the party of Muʿāwiya I'll kindle.

(Translated by Julie Scott Meisami)

1 Rūdakī was a famous Persian poet of the early 4th/10th century while Ḥassān b. Thābit (d. ca 40/659), an early Arabic poet, was known as the 'poet-laureate' of the Prophet.

THIS OLD HAG[1]

Made off with her own children she did, once more, this old hag – the world.
We became old and she's young again, now isn't that a nice
piece of witchcraft!

Have you ever seen a mother whose son grows old
While his old mamma becomes young over and over?

Really! Someone whose mother becomes youthful while he ages;
Now doesn't that sound like the inverse of sound reasoning?

How can you be fooled by this repulsive old hag's colourful, deceptive garb
When you're well aware of her abominations?

You certainly can't marry this worthless bride.
After all, she's never played the matron for anyone.

When you don't call her, she'll call on you with her endless coaxing,
But when you pursue her, that's when you'll see her true colours!

Day and night, how like a dragon she confronts the wise
While fools she approaches like a cat or weasel.

Chameleon-like she is, her colours ever changing,
Sometimes friend, sometimes foe, like an Indian sword.

This world is like your shadow, always running ahead of you.
Nobody can ever overtake their shadow, so how long will you keep running
after it?

Hoping that a beautiful Turk will serve you,
You've become the slave of a Khān, and dust at the feet of a Turk.

Oh you whom the old world has aged, have you no sense?
How long will you wail over your youth and the springtime of your life?

Anything subject to the course of time, the passage of night and day
Cannot remain changeless. Oh sages, this is where the Manicheans lost
their way.

1. Ḥakīm Abū Muʿīn Nāṣir-i Khusraw, *Dīwān*, ed. M. Mīnuvī and M. Muḥaqqiq (Tehran, 1978), pp. 344–347, no. 164, this selection tr. Faquir M. Hunzai and Shafique N. Virani.

The moment you imagine that it's befriended you single-heartedly,
Take heed! For it will show itself to be two-faced.

If you truly know that He never slumbers,
Then it behoves you not to slumber in obedience to Him.

Follow the path of obedience and hearken to knowledge with the ear
of understanding.
After all, you while away the time listening to every type of music.

Oh you who are occupied in the arts, make the good works of faith
your eternal occupation,
Such that your goodness may find goodness as its reward.

How delighted you are when people speak of the justice of
King Anūshirwān.
So why not be just, so that you really become Anūshirwān yourself?

If you wish to be well-spoken, then listen;
How can you speak well if you don't listen first?

Those who have never approached the learned on their knees
Can never sit with them, knee-to-knee.

When they become pure of conduct, people become strong of heart.
When your conduct is pure and your heart is strong, how secure you
become.

You became well-bred when you ceased coveting from all and sundry,
You became a leader when you became a follower of the wise.

O farmer, this life's your tillage and you're asleep in heedlessness.
Surely, what you sowed today you will reap tomorrow

You must become like wheat that you may be worthy of human beings.
So long as you're tasteless as barley, none save donkeys would relish you.

The only true humans are the folk of God's true faith,
But your ignorance has made you a hermit, isolated from the folk
of faith.

You're such a coward, you fear following the path of lions.
Go – follow those lions! Forsake this deer-like timidity.

Take on the sweetness of a delicious date that human beings may crave you.
Who would like you if you're bitter as a gall-apple?

If you don't exert yourself to the point of exhaustion, you will never learn,
So don't bother seeking equality with the wise.

For no matter how pearl-like a rounded bead may be,
Though it may fool you, a jeweller will know it instantly.

It is through faith that you can make yourself part of the *ahl al-bayt* of Muṣṭafā
If you have faith, don't fret for not having long locks like ʿAlid offspring.

You've heard the tale of Salmān, the words of Muṣṭafā,
That Salmān was of his *ahl al-bayt*, despite his Persian tongue.[1]

If you learn you can lift your crown to the heavens,
Though you be in this dark ditch and fettered in heavy chains.

Ignorance has made you cowardly and lazy so that in weakness
Your soul is incapable of circling the people of strength.

To my mind your cure is knowledge, knowledge of the truth,
Yet day and night from this medicine you fly in terror, fleeing.

All who catch the fragrance of my medicine will doubtless say to you:
'Ah, you're on the path of Nāṣir, son of Khusraw.'

If you desire delightful verse and metres sweet, elegant words brimful with meaning
Read the poetry of *ḥujjat*![2]

(Translated by Faquir M. Hunzai and Shafique N. Virani)

1. For Salmān al-Fārisī, see n. 1, p. 274 above.
2. That is, Nāṣir-i Khusraw himself.

TESTIMONY[1]

The mysteries of God have but one Treasurer,
One Treasurer exalted, with knowledge sublime.
How dare I proclaim the mysteries of God?
Fertile rain cloud of the water of Life is he.
I came to life the moment one drop of rain
Fell from his cloud into my mouth.

THE QUR'AN

God's Good Word is an ocean
Of words,
Brimming with gems of finest worth
And pearls of finest lustre.
Salty, like ocean brine,
Seems its manifest form.
But to those who know and understand,
Inner meaning
Is like a pearl hidden in the depths.
The bottom of the sea lies thick with jewels and pearls,
Why do you keep running along the shore?
Go, seek a diver.

THE NOBILITY OF SPEECH

What is better, what is finer
Than all else in the world?
Not armies or riches, or fields or flocks abounding.
To the wise, the power of speech is sweetest,
Noblest of all that exists in this vain caravanserai.
By this ability to speak were you made lord of all the animals
And they but mere commodities,
Objects to be bought and sold.
Speech, your very voice, is distinguished
From the braying of beasts. Why?
Because it uses consonants and vowels of sound and sense.
Note how meaning reaches the ears of Zayd
From Amr's talk, and how he understands it with his mind.
Look, see with your mind –
Not all seeing happens with the eyes;

1. Nāṣir-i Khusraw, *Dīwān*, ed., M. Mīnuvī and M. Muḥaqqiq, nos. 25, vv. 34–35; 2, vv. 36–38; 225, vv. 1–5, 2; 25, v. 23; 33, vv. 9–10; 74, vv. 37–40; 219, vv. 39–41; 218, vv. 38–43. This and the following poems tr. Alice C. Hunsberger.

With his hands
Does the butcher separate fat from lean.

FAIR MARKET PRICE

If with gold you buy the food
    that feeds your body,
    which can never know,
Then with your life entire must you buy
    the food that feeds your soul,
    whose very essence is knowing.

TREES OF GOD

The world, to God, is like an orchard
And we are all its trees.
Come, O Tree of God!
Let us, now, each of us,
Bring forth a sample of our fruit.

THE WELL-BUILT HOUSE

Our faith is a house built by the Prophet,
That all might find rest inside.
The master of the house does not come in
By the same gate as deliveries of grain.
ʿAlī and his family are the gateway –
Happy who enters this well-built house,
Happy who enters each night
With knowledge and action
For bedding and clothing.

THE HEALING HAND

If you are bent by a thousand misfortunes,
Take hold of the Hand of God and rise,
Up from this deep, dark well.
A wise man knows with his reason
That throughout the land the saving Hand of God of heaven and earth
Is one who descends from Fāṭima.
O sick and suffering one!
Do not foolishly leave the door of this physician,
For, really, you sit at the door of Jesus, son of Mary,
The divine physician.

SEEK KNOWLEDGE

Have you heard at all that the Prophet,
Lord and most noble of apostles,
Told you to 'Seek knowledge,
Even if it be found nowhere but China'?
The Imam is the home of secrets divine,
And Gabriel his trusted companion.
Until you take in your hand the rope of allegiance to him,
The devil will never keep his hands off you.
Where else, but with the Imam, shall knowledge be found?
Where else is the lion,
But in his terrain?
Whoever turns his face toward him,
Shall have Venus and Canopus shine from his brow.
    O Breeze! Pour a thousand praises on him every morning,
From Nāṣir, his devoted servant.

(Translated by Alice C. Hunsberger)

2
Ḥasan-i Maḥmūd-i Kātib

Ḥasan-i Maḥmūd-i Kātib is also known as Ḥasan-i Ṣalāḥ-i Munshī (not to be mistaken for Ra'īs Ḥasan, who lived a generation earlier). There is no reliable information about his early life. He was contemporary with four imams of the Alamūt period, that is, from the Imams Ḥasan *'alā dhikrihi'l-salām* (d. 561/1166) to 'Alā al-Dīn Muḥammad (d. 653/1255). He was also a contemporary of Naṣīr al-Dīn al-Ṭūsī (d. 672/1274) and was instrumental in the compilation of *Rawḍa-yi taslīm*. He was probably born in northwest Iran, in the region of Qazwīn and joined the Ismaili community at a young age. For a long period he acted as a scribe in the court of the Ismaili rulers of Quhistān. He moved to Alamūt, the centre of Nizari Ismaili state in Iran, around 637/1240 and died there in 644/124

SUFFICIENT IT IS, FOR ME[1]

Sufficient it is for me – in both worlds, the blessings of the Imam,
and the invocation on my tongue is always his magnificent name.

Sufficient it is for me – holding fast to the rope of his command and obedience,
since heaven and earth cannot endure in isolation of him.

Sufficient it is for me – and I do not mind if the world
is careless and not mindful of me when the Imam is mindful and caring.

Sufficient it is for me – the Imam of the Time,
the lord of the age, Muḥammad b. Ḥasan,[2] on whose mention be peace.

Sufficient it is for me – his exalted presence, and for the people
of religion and the world, a rank and a sanctuary to enjoy.

Sufficient it is for the rotating stars – about which the angels say:
the dust of his horse-shoe is ample for their prosperity and ease of rotation.

1. Ḥasan-i Maḥmūd-i Kātib, *Dīwān-i qā'imiyyāt*, ed. S. J. Badakhchani (Tehran, 2008), no. 26; this selection tr. S. J. Badakhchani and Daryoush Mohammad Poor. The introduction to this chapter is by the translators.

2. The imam at the time was 'Alā al-Dīn Muḥammad III (d. 653/1255).

Sufficient it is for me – his bounty, justice and caring generosity,
and for this agitated and sinful world today.

Sufficient it is – for the people of earth to arrive at the abode of life
by the lights of his blessings and splendour of his governance.

Sufficient it is – the acceptance of all the three powers
that have been bestowed upon him: rising, resurrection and reward giving.

Sufficient it is – the removal of doubt and darkness from the eyes of
the blind,
that he did rise, proclaimed the Resurrection[1] and bestowed rewards.

Sufficient it is – his rising with good omen as evidence for the Resurrection
and a sign of reward for the entire population of the earth.

Sufficient it is for our hereafter – the distinctions that he manifested
among the ranks of the community and looked upon us distinctively.

Sufficient it is – for the enduring fortune of my life that the jewel
of its ring is engraved with the impression of his obedience.

Sufficient it is for me – to find my way on the Day of Judgement to
the presence of the Almighty with this impression engraved in my soul.

Sufficient it is for Ḥasan – the everlasting honour of obedience,
forever in the world and in religion, the nobility of conviction and belief.

Sufficient it is – and you should say this wholeheartedly,
that the face of his command is perfection for any incomplete soul.

Sufficient it is – the abode of contentment, because treasures and gold
do not deserve by decree of reason to become your deity.

Sufficient is your faith – a gentle breeze which entertains
with sweet fragrance, not the vapours of worldly pleasures and pain.

Sufficient it is for you – to be among the servants of the Imam,
and not to seek affluence, with servants and horses.

Sufficient it is for you – to begin your poems with

1 The reference here is to the proclamation of *qīyāma* (Resurrection) by the Imam Ḥasan *ʿalā dhikrihi'l-salām* in 559/1164 at Alamūt. For details see Daftary, *The Ismāʿīlīs*, 2nd ed., pp. 385–391.

the name of the Imam and be grateful for his blessings and bounty.

Sufficient it is for you – to be praising his friends,
day and night, as recompense for the remembrance of ranks.

Sufficient it is for you – a sip from the goblet of his bounty;
when in such a gathering many goblets of bounty go all around.

Sufficient it is for you – even the scent of a sip,
as you cannot take any more and it is beyond your capacity.

Sufficient it is – and may God bless you to end the poem and say:
Sufficient it is for me in both worlds the blessings of the Imam.

(Translated by S. J. Badakhchani and Daryoush Mohammad Poor)

3

Nizārī Quhistānī

Ḥakīm Nizārī Quhistānī (d. 720/1320) was a celebrated and prolific Persian poet in his own day but has not received much recognition until recently. Little is known about his life, other than what appears in his own works. He was born in Bīrjand, southeastern Khurāsān, to an elite Ismaili family and received a good education. He found employment with the ruler of Sīstān and part of Khurāsān in his twenties, then moved to Herat, where the Kart dynasty administered Afghanistan on behalf of the Mongols. He worked for the Karts as court poet and tax collector, but wearying of the harshness of the administration, resigned his post in 678/1280 and travelled for two years, reaching Ādharbāyjān in northwestern Persia. He then returned to Bīrjand, where he was employed by the local Mihrabānid prince as court poet. Losing favour with court cliques, he was soon forced into exile and retired to the hills of Quhistān, where he wrote several of his works. Nizārī was an original and versatile poet who reinterpreted the classical canon of Persian poetry in compositions spanning a range of poetic genres. Many of his compositions are imbued with Ismaili and Sufi esoteric resonances while others have a distinct ring of social dissent and pessimism. They illustrate how an accomplished Ismaili poet of mystical tendencies found creative expression in the turbulent conditions of the post-Alamūt period. Nizārī's massive *Dīwān* of poetry was recently published in Iran.

THE IMAM OF THE AGE[1]

Vulgar Reason's foot cannot fare the Way of Love.
Intellectuals are all like birds but the Way of Love the snare.

Go and study well all the different sciences, then come to me,
So that I can show you by way of (the) Proof *(ḥujjat)*
That all of that (you've studied) is but half-baked.

1. Ḥakīm Sa'd al-Dīn b. Shams al-Dīn Nizārī Quhistānī, *Dīwān-i Ḥakīm Nizārī Quhistānī*, ed. Maẓāhir Muṣaffā (Tehran, 1992–1994), no. 153, vv. 1527–1533, 1536–1537. This and the following selection tr. Leonard Lewisohn in his 'Sufism and Ismā'īlī Doctrine in the Persian Poetry of Nizārī Quhistānī (645–721/1247–1321),' *Iran: Journal of the British Institute of Persian Studies*, 41 (2003), pp. 229–251; pp. 241, 242. This *ghazal* uses a blend of Ismaili terminology and Persian Sufi imagery. Here, Nizārī avers that all knowledge depends on recognizing the 'Imam of the Age.' These translations have been revised.

Anyone togged up in a turban who stands before you,
You stand behind (in prayer), for 'this is the imam.'

But the world is never devoid, even for a moment, of the Imam of the Age.
Do not be hurt (at this) if you find it offensive; what else can I do?
It is the text of an authoritative tradition (*naṣṣ-i kalām*).[1]

For certain, know that all health and wealth and women are forbidden
For you if you don't know who the Imam of your Age is.

I'd be glad to sell that imamate, for (the price of) the candy of drunkards,
For the turban on his head is in pawn to wine and cup.

Since your imam consists of two (persons), if I ask you
Which one of them is your imam, what will you say in reply to me? …

All the worlds' religious judges will (be sure to) set their signature to the *fatwa*
That 'Nizārī, the drunken sot, is worst among all the masses and the nobles.'

They have no fear of killing me, nor in cremating me (would be touched by any) smoke, but nobody's beard gives me grief, since baby's whiskers are all they wear.

THE TRUTHFUL ADEPT[2]

O youth, go and seek a spiritual master to guide you *(pīr-i rahbar),*
So you make progress forward by following behind him.

Give the reins of yourself over to him, and leave yourself aside,
Having no more concern for your own personal good or ill.

When your surrender to him has been confirmed,
For both the worlds' mystery you'll be a model.

Do not follow the monster of fantasy and fancy;
Don't fall bait for the sham lure of some foolish goose.

---

1. According to Shi'i traditions, the world cannot exist a moment without a *ḥujjat* (proof) or imam of God. See W. Madelung, 'Imāma,' *EI2*, vol. 3, p. 1164.

2. These verses are taken from the *Dastūr-nāma*, a *mathnawī* poem Nizārī wrote towards the end of his life, found in his *Dīwān*, vol. 1, pp. 257–299; vv. 49–57, found on pp. 262–263. Here the reader is exhorted to follow a spiritual guide (*pīr-i rahbar*), revealed to be the Ismaili imam in the final verses.

The one who has personally realized the truth *(muḥaqqiq)* speaks
    otherwise;
Do not, do not rest on what is itself shaky and wobbly.

Do not follow anyone but a man of God;
Your own rationalizations are just a monstrous brigand, not a guide.

At first you will find the truthful adept *(muḥiqq)* through God;
Then you will find God confirmed through the truthful adept.

How fine it is to follow in the Imamate
One who has the pure light of God in his heart.

By that light you will be freed from darkness:
Follow that light, and – farewell!

(Translated by Leonard Lewisohn)

I FOUND THE TREASURE[1]

At the beginning, when I emerged from non-existence to existence,
    I found a hundred different defects in my life.

It was during this perplexity, when I looked at myself, that I found
    the casket containing the hidden treasure.

When I looked carefully at the court of the king of heart, I found
    the intellect as deputy and the soul as gate-keeper.

I wandered much like Alexander in search of the water of life;
    I found it because my fellow-traveller happened to be Khiḍr.[2]

Finally, the Noah of the time led me to the ark of guidance and
    I found myself saved from the billowing deluge.

When I firmly held the rope of God with willing submission,
    I found deliverance from the pit of disappointment.[3]

1. Nizārī Quhistānī, *Dīwān*, pp. 78–81, tr. Faquir M. Hunzai and ed. Kutub Kassam in *Shimmering Light: An Anthology of Ismaili Poetry* (London, 1996), pp. 89–91.
2. Alexander the Great (d. 324 BC), the king of Macedonia who overthrew the Persian Achaemenid empire and invaded India, was the subject of fabulous stories in Arabic and Persian, such as his vain search for the fountain of eternal life. In Muslim tradition, Khiḍr or al-Khaḍir is the name given to the travelling companion and guide of Moses mentioned in the Qur'an (28:60–82).
3. Qur'an 3:103: 'And hold fast all together by the rope of God and be not divided among yourselves.'

Those who search without a guide, in conformity and polytheism,
I found them lifeless like pictures on a wall of stone.

Without the custodian and confidant of secret wisdom, I found
the intellect perplexed in the sea of imagination.

That which mountains, oceans, earth and heaven were unable
to bear, I found in the interior of the human body.[1]

Where once my life was feeble, barren and perplexed, I found
every particle burning bright like the sun.

On the ladders, Gabriel let me pass step by step, until I found
proof to the stations of the friend of God.

Alas! Who would believe me if I said that last night I found
myself sitting with the king, knee to knee?

Now when I travel again within myself, I tell myself: 'Yes, I
found this station because of the king.'

Had it been due to merit, we would be a world apart, but I have
found the path to sit on his threshold.

Whom will I tell what my eyes have seen with certainty, that what
cannot be found here, I found it there fully-formed?

If you trust me, then do not trust yourself, because I too
found this treasure hidden from me at the beginning.

I do not have any capital to meet the expenses of paradise,
although I found his favours beyond the bounds of possibility.

If you are happy with the truth, then paradise is with you;
because from you to paradise, I have found an easy way.

He for whom the sphere has rotated from the beginning of
existence, I found when I turned away from myself.

All things that exist end in their origination; it is only
the ocean of love which I found boundless and fathomless.

1. Qur'an 33:72: 'Verily, We offered the trust to the heavens and the earth and the mountains, but they refused to bear it and were afraid of it, but man undertook it…'

Salvation is in the Imam of the Time; I found the root
of faith in obedience to his commands and prohibitions.

I gave up everything except 'offspring, one from the other'[1]
when I found the permanent Imamate in them.

Turn your back on the desert of time's deviations, because I
found the path to the door of ʿAlī from Salmān's light.[2]

Since he raised Nizārī with the hand of nurture, I found
the foot of his esteem shining to the heights of heaven.

(Translated by Faquir M. Hunzai)

1. Qur'an 3:33–34: 'Verily, Allah chose Adam and Noah and the descendants of Abraham and the descendants of ʿImrān above all creatures, offspring one of the other.'

2. On Salmān al-Fārisī, see n. 1, p. 274 above.

4

Persian Poets of the Post-Alamūt Era

Ismaili traditions of devotional poetry continued to flourish after the Mongol conquests, although much of it has been little known until recently. The period of the Imam Mustanṣir bi'llāh II of Anjudān (d. 885/1480) and his successors saw a flowering of Ismaili devotional poetry, some of which is quoted below. The poet Muḥammad b. Ḥusām b. Shams al-Dīn Muḥammad Khusfī (d. in either 875/1470 or 893/1488) is associated with the village of Khusf in Khurāsān. He became well known for a genre of praise poetry dedicated to the Prophet and Imam ʿAlī, and his poems are found in both Ismaili and non-Ismaili collections.

Among the poets who were followers of the Imam Mustanṣir bi'llāh III, also known as 'Gharīb Mīrzā' (d. 904/1498), was an obscure individual with the pen-name Ḥusayn. His poem, included below, exhorts the renunciation of worldly attachment and affirms devotion to the imam. The poem also indicates that the imam then resided at Anjudān in central Persia, information that is confirmed by contemporary epigraphic evidence.

Dāʿī Anjudānī lived in the last years of the reign of Mustanṣir bi'llāh III and probably survived into the reign of the Safawid Shāh ʿAbbās (r. 995–1038/1587–1629). His brother was also a well-known poet. It is likely that he held a high rank in the Ismaili hierarchy. He was described, in a contemporary register of poets, as a writer of 'many limpid verses, including powerful odes (*qaṣā'id*) and beautiful love lyrics (*ghazaliyyāt*).'

Yet another Ismaili poet of the time wrote under the pen-name Darwīsh. In the poem translated here he calls upon believers to forgo the seductions of the world and arise to serve 'the Lord of the Age,' the Imam Gharīb Mīrzā. Khwāja ʿAbd Allāh-i Anṣārī, a namesake of the 11th-century Sufi, also wrote during the imamate of Mustanṣir bi'llāh III, in whose praise he composed poems such as the one cited here.

Rounding off this selection is a verse from the *Tazyīn al-majālis* or *The Adornment of Assemblies* by Ḥusayn b. Yaʿqūb Shāh b. Ṣūfī, a contemporary of the Imams Khalīl Allāh ʿAlī (d. 1090/1680) and Shāh Nizār (d. 1134/1722). The *Tazyīn* gained great popularity in the Persian-speaking regions of the Ismaili world where it appears that the relevant sections were read on occasions such as the Festival of Breaking the Fast (*ʿĪd al-fiṭr*), the Festival of Sacrifice (*ʿĪd al-aḍḥā'*), the Spring Equinox (*Nawrūz*) and the Winter Solstice (*Shab-i yaldā*).

Ibn Ḥusām Khusfī

THE SEASON OF ORISONS[1]

Brothers, by God, it's the season of orisons,
Seek your desires, for it's the time of needs.

It's the resurrection that manifests every six thousand years,
Now, as it's the seventh, there's the lord of the resurrections.

If you don't recognize the Imam of the Time in truth,
You will head for hellfire, despite your hundred thousand devotions.

All who recognized not their lord
Are certainly plunged in infidelity and darkness.

How can the secret remain hidden between God and his servant?
For God is the knower of mysteries and master of hidden things.

Abandon your caprice and fleshly thoughts, keep your eye steady on the goal,
For naught but nonsense is all in your heart, save him.

All I said from my own imaginings and analogies
Was but a fable and delusion in his presence.

Say the name of Mawlānā with the innermost heart of sincerity,
For he has become manifest, and his summons is the talk of the town.

From east and west the comrades have manifested,
But all of this is bound by a single indication.

In your grace, cast a glance upon your humble slaves,
For among the people there is much discourse.

Give the wine of yearning from the brimful goblet of Mawlānā,
For all of this is due to the mercy of the congregations.

Forgive Ibn Ḥusām, your humble slave,
For he is imprisoned in the well of darkness.

1. Ibn Ḥusām Khūsfī, '*Barādarān ba-ḥaqq mawsim-i munājāt ast*,' in *Majmū'ā-yi Ash'ār-i madhhabī*, ed., Anjuman-i Ta'līm (Mashhad, 1995), n.p., tr. Shafique N. Virani in *The Ismailis in the Middle Ages: A History of Survival, A Search for Salvation* (Oxford, 2007), pp. 136–137.

Ḥusayn

WE CUT OFF OUR HEARTS[1]

We cut off our hearts from attachment to the world,
Regaling our souls by the light of God's mercy.

Having liberated ourselves from the clutches of the demon of ego,
We serve the Imam of the Time with sincerity.

We free our hearts from the fraud of the internal devil,
Sacrificing our lives in the name of the lord of *jinn* and men.

We make the exalted name of the sovereign of faith,
Gharīb Mīrzā, the litany of our tongues.

Sometimes he's a child, sometimes a youth, sometimes an aged man,
'Tis incumbent we make the prophetic tradition our sign.

May my life be sacrificed for ʿAzīzī who has uttered what follows
I present to you a single couplet from his noble discourse:

Without doubt he is ʿAlī himself. In serving him
'Tis not comely to lean an atom towards 'why' or 'wherefore.'

While the folk of the law turn their faces toward the Kaʿba,
We make Anjudān our Kaʿba of reality.

For in the annihilation of the life of this world
Is everlasting life in that one – so hasten to long for life eternal!

By sinning and disobedience all of us have aged,
We become youths once again by the light of obedience to him.

When our spirit is liberated from the insinuation of the body,
We will make our nests in the neighbourhood of divine mercy.

If we remember our origin with probity,
In the manner of lovers, we will turn our faces towards the place of return...

1. Ḥusayn, '*Āmad zamān-i ānki maḥabbat ʿayān kunīm*,' IIS Persian MS 14698, tr. Shafique N. Virani in *The Ismailis in the Middle Ages*, p. 173.

Dā'ī Anjudānī

THE TRUSTED SPIRIT[1]

'Ali of the age, lord of the time, master of the epoch,
From whose pleasure all your desires you find.

Commander of the epoch, the lord at whose court
A hundred kings like Alexander and Caesar you find.

Seated on the throne of '*Whose is the Kingdom,*'[2] by God!
Whatever you seek from the light of his friendship you find.

Shāh Mustanṣir bi'llāh,[3] the bearer of truth (*muḥiqq*) of both the worlds,
In the felicity of whose glance the garden of Ridwān you find.

Treasurer of knowledge divine, king of the throne, by whom
With ease the key to the mysteries of both this world and that you find.

The one signified by the parables of the verses of God's word,
From him the interpretation of the hidden meaning of the Qur'an
you find...

Day and night, by the nobility of his mighty name,
Weeping and composing his glories, the holy spirit you find.

Doubtless, the trusted spirit inspires such that
My heart hastening on the path to the inspirer you find.

From a single hallowed lineage, from 'Alī till present times,
All, over both worlds, the lords of the command you find.

So long as existed the world, 'twas never bereft of one of them,
So long as it shall exist, till the end of time, the very same you find.

Traversing the path of naming the Imams of truth,
Dā'ī! The jewel of your speech is a verity that from the mine you find.

---

1. Dā'ī Anjudānī, '*Qaṣīda-yi dhurriya*,' IIS Persian MS 15030, tr. Shafique N. Virani in *The Ismailis in the Middle Ages*, pp. 174–175.

2. A reference to the famous Qur'anic phrase *liman al-mulk* (40:16). For an Ismaili understanding of this dictum see Naṣīr al-Dīn al-Ṭūsī, *Āghāz wa anjām*, ed. Īraj Afshār (Tehran, 1956), Chapter 2.

3. A reference to either Imam Mustanṣir bi'llāh II (d. 885/1480) or Imam Mustanṣir bi'llāh III (d. 904/1498), known as Gharīb Mīrzā.

Darwīsh

ARISE![1]

O heart, from your home in this shadowy container of dust, arise!
From caring for head, wealth, property and life, like the lovers, arise!

You're trapped in the snare of the world's bait;
Cut away greed, from thoughts of this and that, arise!

Be not seduced by devilish colours
In the cause of servitude to the lord of the age, arise!

Leave to infidels the deceits and blandishments of the world;
In this age of trial, like a chivalrous knight, arise!

Do you desire salvation, O brother of mine?
Then with affection for the king of Anjudān, arise!

Imam of the age, ʿAlī of the time, Shāh Gharīb;
Gird your loins in his service and from your soul, arise!

It's time to decamp from this world, time to depart;
Why do you tarry while your companions have left? O Darwīsh, arise!

Khwāja ʿAbd Allāh-i Anṣārī

WISDOM DIVINE[2]

Those who caught the scent
Of wisdom divine,
With heart and soul,
Became slaves of Mustanṣir bi'llāh.

In love, those who became
Dust at this threshold
Surpass even the portico of the throne
On the basis of their eminence.

I became the slave of a sovereign,

---

1. Darwīsh, '*Dilā az manzil-i īn tīrah khākdān bar khīz*,' IIS Persian MS 14712, tr. Shafique N. Virani in *The Ismailis in the Middle Ages*, pp. 175–176.

2. Khwāja ʿAbd Allāh-i Anṣārī. '*Har ki az ʿilm-i ladunī shammaī āgāh shud*,' collated from IIS Persian MS 15052 and an unnumbered MS, tr. Shafique N. Virani in *The Ismailis in the Middle Ages*, pp. 179–180.

So magnificent and glorious
That all who become his slaves
Become kings of both worlds.

I became a slave so fortunate
That all who beheld me declared:
'What a lucky slave
Is he whose name is 'Abd Allāh, 'the slave of God.'

The longing of this forlorn one
Was but to behold the face of the friend.
Praise be to God,
The heart gained what it desired!

Save for your essence,
In the universe you have no like;
Indeed, those who recognize you
Are peerless.

How wonderful! In every age
He appeared in a different form;
Sometimes he's Mustanṣir,
Sometimes Salām Allāh.

Sometimes an aged man,
A child or a fair youth he becomes;
Sometimes he ascends to the heavens for the ascension,
Or descends into a dark well.

If he appears in a hundred different forms,
Why should those of spiritual insight be anxious?
Those who see with the eye of the heart
Are guided to him aright.

Those who trod not this path
Following your command,
Indeed, though they be familiars of your court,
Are wayward and astray.

By God Almighty!
He who disobeys your order,
Though he may appear an elder of your court,
Is naught but a babe on the path.

O lord!
In this lowly world, you know,
Years and months passed by;
I lived my life in heedlessness.

O lord!
In this world for the sake of that one,
I sowed not a seed;
Now the season's passed.

Then suddenly from the invisible world
An oracle whispered in the inner recesses of my heart:
'Grieve not! For an unexpected felicity
Has been conferred upon you!'

Though I be bereft of worship,
I take joy in the certainty
That all who became beggars at this court
Become lords of majesty.

O lord!
Though I've been mighty impudent,
I shall not grieve,
For your mercy is my companion.

I also ended with your name,
Since in the realms of faith and world,
The beginning of all tasks,
Commences with '*In the Name of God.*'

Ḥusayn b. Yaʿqūb Shāh b. Ṣūfī

THE ADORNMENT OF ASSEMBLIES[1]

I have composed these couplets of poesy
To ornament the assembly of spirits,

That whoever may peruse these verses
May rejoice in the bounty of glad tidings,

That their time be felicitous, their fortune joyous,

1. Ḥusayn b. Yaʿqūb Shāh b. Ṣūfī, '*Tazyīn al-majālis*,' IIS Persian MS no. 7822, tr. Shafique N. Virani.

That their hearts may gain from God what they desire.

By the grace of God, a light shone upon my imagination,
Teaching it lessons about His blessings.

My imagination signalled my tongue:
'I have girded myself to entrust this to you.'

Aided by the lofty aspiration of the Folk of Purity,
I resolved in the world upon writing this treatise.

I have composed it free of intricate words,
And thus prepared it to be easily read

That it may approach the understanding of its listeners
And not be strange to the ears of those who seek its meaning.

I hope that it may become a keepsake of mine,
By which the people of dignity may remember me in their hearts.

My aspiration is that it may be found pleasing
And be close to the hearts of the folk of perfection.

May God's mercy be upon the fortunate souls,
For by His blessings hearts are rejuvenated.

Perchance, I will be included in the aid of His blessings
That my soul may be touched by that joy.

Perhaps, He shall convey glad tidings of healing to this weary one,
Or give hope to the one who seeks it.

I have completed this book, seeking such blessings,
That He may shower His bounties all about – peace!

(Translated by Shafique N. Virani)

5
The Poetry of Central Asia

The Ismailis of Badakhshān have a rich tradition of devotional poetry, much of which is inseparable from the context of its performance. The *maddāḥ* (praise) genre comprises several forms of recited or sung compositions that are preserved within both the literary and oral traditions. Most of the devotional poetry is in Tājik Persian and employs the literary styles of Persian poetry. While some compositions are attributed to classical poets of the Persian tradition such as Ḥāfiz, Rūmī, Saʿdī, and ʿAṭṭār, others are ascribed to the 11th-century Ismaili poet-philosopher Nāṣir-i Khusraw, who is particularly cherished by the Ismailis of Badakhshān. Several poems are unattributed or are the compositions of Badakhshāni poets such as Qudrat-i Shughnānī, Shāh Fiturī, Ghiyās-i Dīn and Shāh Anwarī.

The poems chosen for this section cover a range of devotional genres and themes. One of the most common genres of *maddāḥ* poetry is the *ghazal*, which includes both religious and secular compositions. The first *ghazal* below is attributed to Nāṣir-i Khusraw. *Ḥikāyat*s or versified stories that describe the deeds of Imam ʿAlī are another popular genre of *maddāḥ*, while the *mukhammasāt* or stanzaic poems usually offer praise of ʿAlī and other imams. Finally, the *munājāt* or prayer poems are supplications addressed to God. In the composition offered here, attributed to Ḥasan-i Ṣabbāh, the 11th-century *ḥujja* (proof) of the Ismailis in Persia, the poet begs forgiveness for his sins and longs to be united with the Universal Beloved.

ABODE OF THE SOUL[1]

O you who say that I am a knowing person with sense
Come, if you are a man and make clear to me this difficult story

Come and tell me in clear words: where does the soul from the world of outer appearance remain
When he leaves this house, where does he abide and where is his home?

Is his place in the spheres or in the higher world
Or in the lower world between water, earth and mud?

1. Translated in Gabrielle van den Berg, *Minstrel Poetry from the Pamir Mountains: A Study on the Songs and Poems of the Ismāʿīlīs of Tajik Badakhshan* (Wiesbaden, 2004), pp. 81–82, 229, 278–279, 292–294, 332–333.

If you know this secret then explain it to me now
If not, then go for you are unknowing and a negligent wanderer

My dear, when the soul of a wise man leaves this prison
It will go to the spheres for that house is his achievement

Or he will appear for a moment in human form
But a perfect man like him is fit for prosperity

But the useless and stupid and doubting men:
I shall tell about those suspecting and incapable folk

Two states are possible for the sordid, wandering and defective soul
I will tell both states, prick up your ears and listen carefully

The first is for the ordinary man – when he is brought out of his body
He is chained in jail for many years, that untrue damned one

Again his position is the vegetative state in which he is held
He will remain in the field and he will turn into cow and donkey

O Nāṣir-i Khusraw why do you tell openly such secrets of wise men?
    A sensible man would never tell![1]

THE SEARCHER OF UNITY

O you searcher of Unity, you are all the boasting I am looking for
Listen to my words because I am speaking the words of God

Be the pupil of my heart in the school of learning
If you want me to open the door of secrets for you

If you want to serve in this divine horizon
Then be ready for my command and listen to everything I say

In this treasury of nine roofs there are four porches and six windows
Know the talisman of the treasure of meaning in it
    – it is my world-adorning Being

If you want to see my face, then open the eye of Secret Knowledge
Because the worldly eye does not see a thing except my world-adorning Being

1. [In the tradition of Central Asian Ismailis, this poem is attributed to Nāṣir-i Khusraw.]

Where do you see me in this earthly world with this eye?
Since I am on a place and without a place, I stand above place and abode

If you want to know me then first know yourself
I know every one, I bring knowing and I am knowing

In that sense I have become visible so that you know that I am wise as well as unwise, blind as well as seeing
Become drunk of the cup of longing so that you may learn to know that I am sometimes wine, sometimes the cup and sometimes the cup-bearer

Although everyone is from God on his way to God, I am master of this all
Whatever be the place of highest essence, whatever be the place of lowest essence, I do not need anything and I am free from this all

You will not see anything but me, not at the beginning, nor at the end
In that sense that I am hidden and always visible

For me, there is no change in meaning but in outward appearance I change sometimes and I appear in every form.

PRAISE OF IMAM ʿALĪ

I know there is someone in Mecca
Whose hands may solve all problems

No problem has an obstacle
In his hands lies the salvation of every trouble

He rules over the wild, the birds, the human and the *jinn*
He is the helper of the ones who have fallen into trouble

He is not only the king of mankind and *jinn*
He is also sultan of the fish to the moon

His court is spread from the elevation of the divine throne
The wings of Gabriel are the brooms of his door

That beautiful name has thousands of names
But he is famous these days under the name of ʿAlī

If you have the honour to be in his service
You will reach your heart's desire through his striving

If your prey lies in the paws of a panther
If your mine lies in the mouth of a whale

At any place, be it lands or oceans
He will bring it all to you, in one moment.

THE FIVE HOLY ONES

O heart, now that the tongue is able to speak
Speak always in honour of the five holy bodies
Smash the worth of Aden's pearl into pieces by praising these five
Listen to me with the ear of your soul to their names
There is Muḥammad, ʿAlī, Fāṭima, Ḥasan and Ḥusayn

Know that the origin of all being is these five
The pillars of the house of six dimensions [i.e. the world] are these five
The acceptance of the phrase 'Hasten to prayer' comes from these five
The intercessor of all the people who are saved will be these five
There is Muḥammad, ʿAlī, Fāṭima, Ḥasan and Ḥusayn

When the clay of Adam became visible from water and earth
He opened his eye and looked to the divine throne
He saw these names of the five on the throne, the tablet and the pen
He understood the goal of the creation of his noble essence
There is Muḥammad, ʿAlī, Fāṭima, Ḥasan and Ḥusayn

The saviour of the Prophet Noah in that storm
The one who set Joseph free from the pit and from the jail
Know him as the one who took Jonah out of the whale's belly
The one who cured Job's disease, the one who drove back the worms
There is Muḥammad, ʿAlī, Fāṭima, Ḥasan and Ḥusayn

The protector of Abraham in the burning fire
Surely the one who saved Ismael from being sacrificed
A proof in Seth, Salih, David and Lot
The one who brought Moses across the great sea and the Nile
There is Muḥammad, ʿAlī, Fāṭima, Ḥasan and Ḥusayn...

If you are true of heart, pure and honest
Become the lover of the people of the mantle, refrain from others
Gabriel will be the sixth in the house of five
On the day of Resurrection they will free the people from the fire
There is Muḥammad, ʿAlī, Fāṭima, Ḥasan and Ḥusayn

Someone who separates these five bodies
Do not consider him human if you are human
Consider these five as one and be quiet
Since they are the united light of Truth, intimate with God
There is Muḥammad, ʿAlī, Fāṭima, Ḥasan and Ḥusayn

SUPPLICATIONS

O God you are the Noble Sultan
You are 'In the name of God, the Merciful and Compassionate'
Forgive me, wretched and full of guilt
Forgiver of sins, compassionate, O God in the end
I made a mistake of my own name from the book
From negligence I blackened my own gown
I am drowning in the sea of my guilt
You know the cure of my black fortune
Wash by sighs and laments and miserable crying
The blackness from the letter of my soul
With sighs and laments and sad misery
Through negligence I have remained far from the way of luck
I am unhappy and poor and deprived
I did not serve the master properly
I am ashamed of my own faults
From shame I have bowed my head
Now by the way of excuse and despair
I repent, I repent, I repent
Whatever I entrusted endlessly to fault
I will never turn away from your door
Now I have gone a way different from yours
I do not have another court except your door
Do not throw me from your breast, by your kindness
Do not chase away your own dog from your door
My source (essence) always bears fruit through you
I am like an infant and kindness is my nurse
Since I am a sick child at your door
Do not deprive me from the milk of your kindness
I am less than what is the lowest when I am without you
I am higher than the wheel of heaven when I am with you
Oh God may this bowl full of twists be destroyed
If I should desire anything besides you
On the last moment when the soul is torn from the body
Will you link my soul to the Beloved?
In respect of the pure religion and your convocation

In respect of your emissaries of proof
In respect of the Speaker and the word of your Foundation[1]
In respect of the esteem of your special men
In respect of the gate of that real payment
In respect of the emissaries of the everlasting empire
In respect of Nāṣir and Mustanṣir-i ḥaqq[2]
In respect of the Perpetual and the Absolute Perpetual
In respect of the exalted and sanctified God
In respect of the sinless and holy name
In respect of the right and pure believers
In respect of the clear knowledge of the master
In respect of the Lion of God's men
In respect of the Soul-Sacrifiers
In respect of the feeble and needy
To the humility of the Keepers of the Secret
In respect of the one whose description has no comparison
Your outward appearance has all the time another guise
In respect of the One who is Veiler and Pardoner
Do not take our sins into account
Give me shelter in the shadow of your kindness
Protect me from the temptation of the end of time
Firstly in non-existence I did not exist
I was at rest in that non-being
You wiped from me the dust of non-existence
You opened the door of existence in my face
You made the Seven Fathers my guardians
You made Four Mothers ready to look after me[3]
They brought me from the embrace to the shoulder
You brought me from the Intellect to the ear
By them my sweet life became attainable
Also by them my food and clothing were provided
You gave me body, reason, soul and understanding
You gave me heart and spirit, oh Pure Powerful God
Then you made me one of the prostrating
By your liberality you brought me into existence
You drowned me in your radiance of mercy
The crown of 'Our nobility' you placed on my head
My kernel became adorned by your light

1. [The terms 'Speaker' and 'Foundation' from the Arabic *nāṭiq* and *asās*, refer to the Prophet Muḥammad and 'Alī respectively.]

2. [Mustanṣir-i ḥaqq, the eighth Fatimid Imam-Caliph al-Mustanṣir bi'llāh. The reference to Nāṣir is probably to the Ismaili philosopher-poet Nāṣir-i Khusraw.]

3. [The seven planets and four elements of medieval cosmology.]

Since you made my connection straight to you
For this being of mine happens to be your being
For without your being my being would not have been
Now you have finished me in this manner
Without leaving me at any place
Now it would not be suitable, o my King
If you would leave me hereafter half-way
Be a guide towards yourself, lead the way
Finish my beginning through your kindness
O you who are endless in your own excellence
Bring what concerns poor me to an end
I am one drop of the universal river
Do not leave me in rawness of your kindness
O God make my raw affairs well-cooked
Finish me although I am not finished
Me, without success, fame or name
Joking I have said many crooked excuses
O God accept my crooked excuse
By your kindness, do not throw me out of your hands
God, connect in the end the soul of Sayyidnā[1]
To the dust of the feet of your men
For Sayyidnā calls you in need
Fulfil my needs in return for this supplication
By the rosary, the prayer and the ring of religion
Answer my supplication: Amen.

SWEET BELOVED

Sweet beloved of mine
You took away my heart and soul
Tender silver body
My lily and basil

Desiring your face
I sit beside you
I am your supplicant
My eloquent beloved
Your face became like milk
Your hair like chains
Your love became like an arrow
Your arrow at my soul

1. [This poem is attributed to Ḥasan-i Ṣabbāḥ (d. 518/1124), also known as Bābā Sayyidnā, the founder of the Nizārī Ismaili state in Iran.]

The nightingale in his cage
Complaints like bells
I have no desire except you
My eloquent beloved

Shāh Anwarī,[1] speaking well
Has been writing in this world
Listen to these words
Beloved and friends
Sweetheart of me!

(Translated by Gabrielle van den Berg)

1. Little is known about Anwarī except that he came from a peasant family and died between 1920–1925.

III
THE POETRY OF SOUTH ASIA

1

Pīr Shams

One of the most enigmatic figures of the Satpanth Ismaili *da'wa* in South Asia, Pīr Shams is believed to have been active in Sind between the 7th/13th and the 8th/14th centuries. Although he is primarily associated with Sind, the poetry attributed to him shows a familiarity with other regions, including Badakhshān, Panjāb, Gujarāt and even as remote a region as Bengal. His mausoleum is in Multān, Pakistan. As with many *ginān*s and indeed most poetry that circulated primarily as an oral tradition, some hymns attributed to the Pīr show linguistic characteristics of later times. The poetry attributed to Pīr Shams has a distinctively mystical flavour and draws deeply on South Asian linguistic and cultural forms.

THE NAME OF THE ETERNAL[1]

You are my Swāmī, O Everlasting (*qā'im*) and Eternal (*dā'im*)!
But only a few, yes, only a few,
    know your Name (*nām*).

Indeed the promise (*kol*) of the trustworthy one is certain;
The true servant (*bando*) was Muḥammad himself,
    yes, Muḥammad himself.

The Pīr will take reckoning of the servant;
So follow humbly, yes, follow humbly,
    the sayings of the Guru.

Keeping company of the pious (*sādhu*),
    the servant becomes pure;
Whereas the heedless one (*gāfal*) sits there
    weeping, yes, weeping.

Life is but a hundred odd years long;
O Devotee! Finally death too comes,
    yes, it comes.

---

1. Pīr Shams, '*Kāyama dāyama tuṃ moro sāmī tere nāme bī koī koī*', in *100 Ginān nī chopaḍī* (3rd ed., Mumbai, 1919), vol. 2, no. 82; tr. Tazim R. Kassam in *Songs of Wisdom and Circles of Dance: Hymns of the Satpanth Ismā'īlī Muslim Saint, Pīr Shams* (Albany, NY, 1995), p. 183.

Pīr Shams, the ocean-hearted and moonlike, said:
What the Creator (*kirtār*) intends,
that occurs, yes, it occurs.

THE GOLDEN-MANED LION[1]

The golden-maned lion forgot his own true form;
Keeping the company of sheep, he became as a lamb.
Under such a delusion, he left behind his own life.
O Brother! Banish all your delusions and repeat, "'Alī, 'Alī.'

Refrain:
'Alī is present, and 'Alī will always be!
Hold fast to this assurance in your heart.
Yes indeed! Hold fast to this pledge in your heart!
O Brother! Banish all your delusions and repeat, "'Alī, 'Alī.'

If he crushed his illusion, the lion would come to his senses;
His heart would be rid of its sheeplike qualities,
And never again would he slumber under such an illusion.
O Brother! Banish all your delusions and repeat, "'Alī, 'Alī.' [*Refrain*]

All souls (*jīv*) have come and fallen into ignorance (*avidyā*);
In their egoism, they have lost the Beloved by their own doing;
They came [into the world] by accident, yet they act arrogantly.
O Brother! Banish all your delusions and repeat, "'Alī, 'Alī.' [*Refrain*]

If you keep the company of the Perfect Man (*murshid al-kāmil*),
When ignorance approaches, it will be dispelled;
Then will you realize matters concerning the heart.
O Brother! Banish all your delusions and repeat, "'Alī, 'Alī.' [*Refrain*]

If you conquer delusion you will recognize the Beloved (*saiyān*);
O Believer (*mu'min*), recognize your true self by yourself!
Pir Shams says you should practice this.
O Brother! Banish all your delusions and repeat, "'Alī, 'Alī.' [*Refrain*]

(Translated by Tazim R. Kassam)

---

1. Pīr Shams, '*Kesarī sīṃha sarūpa bhulāyo*,' in *Mahān Ismāilī sant Pīr Shams rachit ginâno no saṃgrah* (Gujarātī), vol. 2 (Mumbai, 1952), pp. 63–64, no. 59, vv. 1–5; tr. Tazim R. Kassam in her *Songs of Wisdom and Circles of Dance*, pp. 277–278.

PLATE 7

This famous poem from an early 20th-century manuscript of the *Dīwān* of the Fatimid poet Ibn Hānī' al-Andalusī celebrates the Fatimid conquest of Egypt.

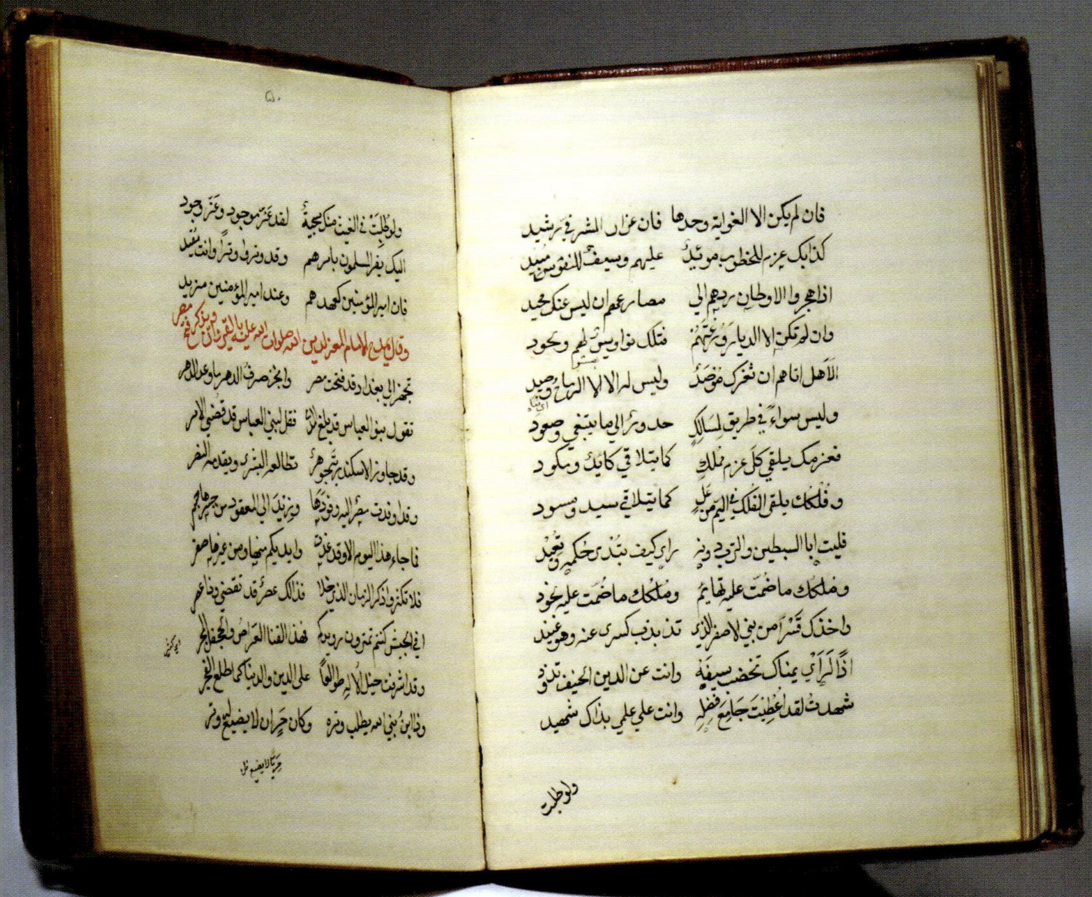

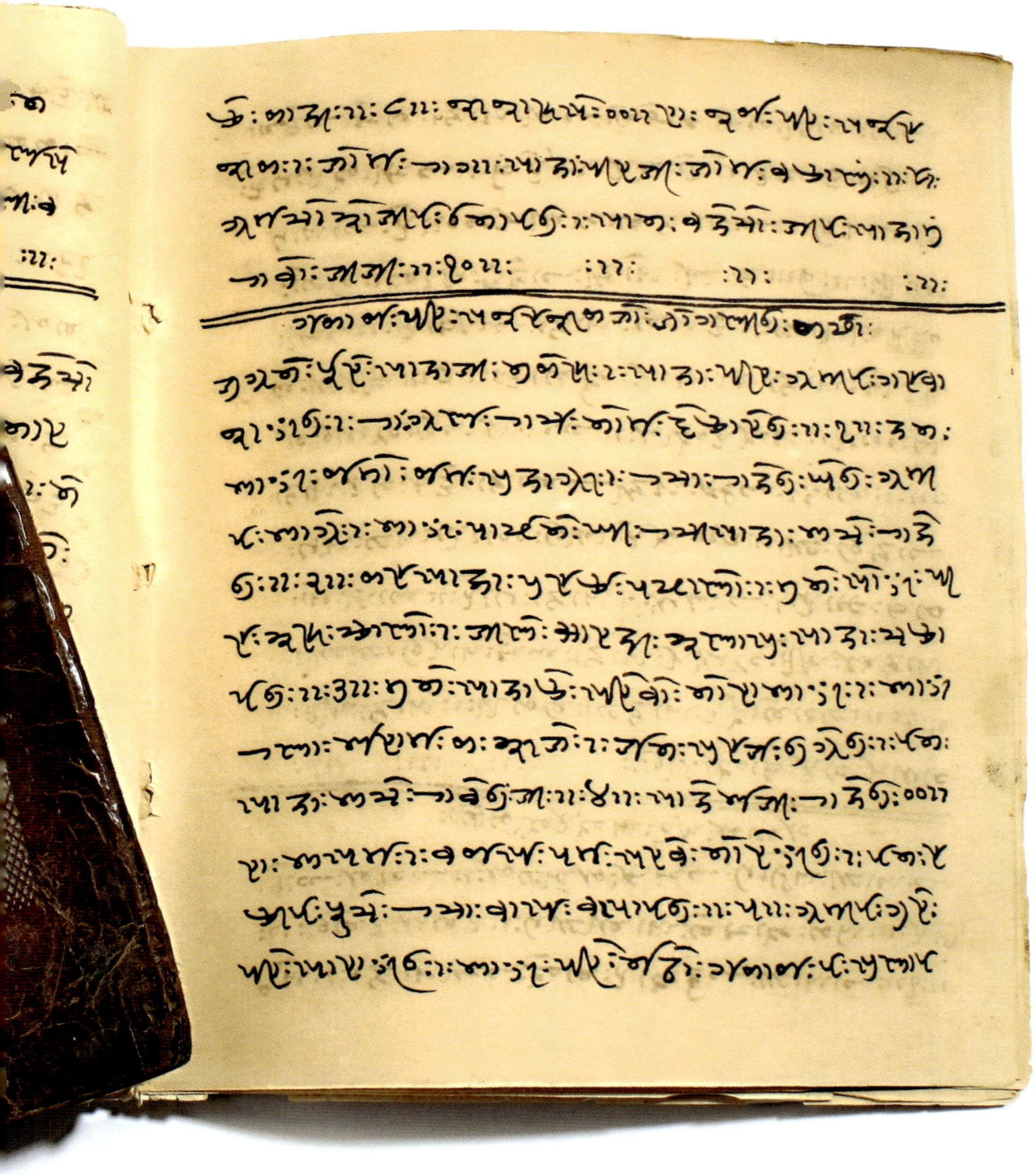

PLATE 8
This 19th-century manuscript, bound in blind-tooled leather, contains *ginān*s written in the Khojkī script. The page reproduced here shows a *ginān* attributed to Pīr Ṣadr al-Dīn, *'Jugame phire shāhājī munerī'* (The imam's herald travels the world).

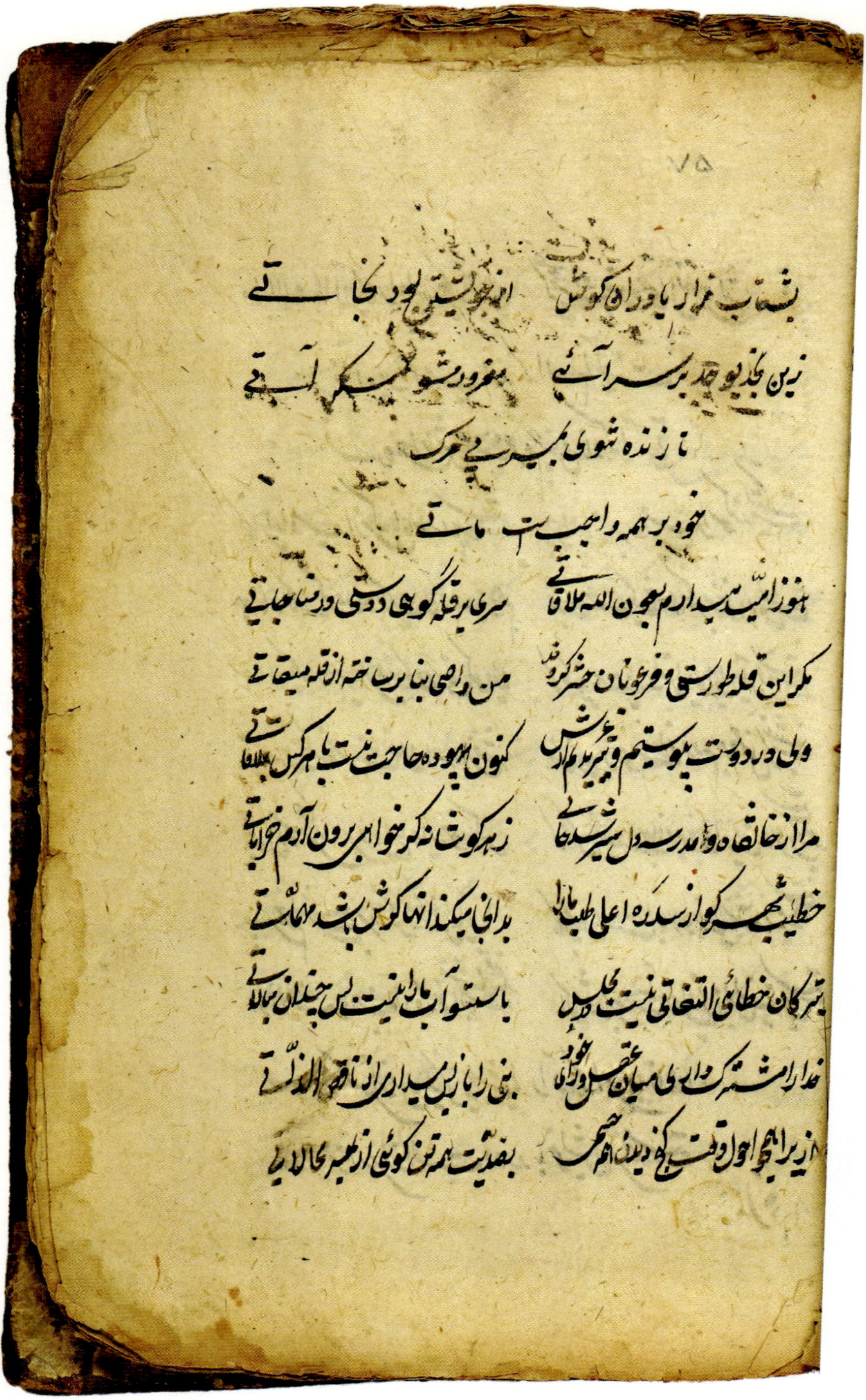

PLATE 9

A poem on the ever-renewed presence of the imam from a 19th-century manuscript of the *Dīwān* of the Persian poet Nizārī Quhistānī.

2
Pīr Ṣadr al-Dīn

Pīr Ṣadr al-Dīn (Sadardīn in Indic languages) played a key role in systematizing and consolidating the Nizārī *daʿwa* in South Asia from the late 8th/14th century. He is chiefly associated with Uchch in southern Sind, where he is believed to have converted a number of Hindus from the Lohāṇā caste, who acquired the title Khojā after entering the Ismaili fold. His shrine is in Jetpur, near Uchch. Compositions attributed to Pīr Ṣadr al-Dīn represent the largest corpus in the *ginān* tradition, although as with other compositions in South Asian devotional literature, it is unlikely that the Pīr was the sole author of all the works attributed to him. These works continue to have great importance for Ismailis of South Asian origin.

SELECTIONS[1]

I

The First, Incomparable Creator-King,
Allah –
He is the very One
In our hearts.

O Allah!
The heart full of your worship
Is the pure translucent heart.

II

You are the First,
You are the Last,
You,
You alone
Are my Lord.

1. Pīr Ṣadr al-Dīn, '*Alaf nirāle khālak rājā*,' in *100 Ginān nī chopaḍī* (Mumbai, n.d.), vol. 4, no. 62, pp. 118–119, vv. 1, 2; and in *Mahān Ismāili sant Pīr Sadardīn rachit ginān no saṃgrah* (Mumbai, 1952), vol. 1, no. 41, p. 49; '*Avala tūṃhī ākhara tūṃhī*,' in *Mahān Ismāili sant Pīr Sadardīn rachit ginān no saṃgrah*, vol. 1, no. 128, p. 133; *Saloko moṭo tathā nāno* (Mumbai, 1934), v. 58 and v. 94; these extracts tr. Aziz Esmail in *A Scent of Sandalwood: Indo-Ismaili Religious Lyrics* (London, 2002), pp. 93, 101, 167, 174.

You
Are the Apparent,
You
Are the Hidden
You,
Such as You are,
You alone
Are my Lord in truth.

III

The entire world says,
Beloved, beloved.
But the beloved
Is had by none.
The lips relate but one story,
While of the beloved's mystery,
None knows a thing.

IV

Love does not
grow in fields;
Nor is love
sold in shops;
Love arises
in the heart,
and the heart
it corrodes,
through and through.

(Translated by Aziz Esmail)

THE IMAM'S HERALD[1]

The Imam's herald travels throughout the world
Blessings be upon the Imam, the Pīr and the community
For the Imam has appeared in the fortress of Alamūt

Brother, we are perpetually blissful
By God, he has arrived, the community enjoys its fortune
Hail the advent of the lord 'Alī in the West!

1. Pīr Ṣadr al-Dīn, '*Jugame phīre shāhājī munerī*,' in *102 Ginānajī chopaḍī* (3rd ed., Mumbai, 1912), vol. 4, no. 3, vv. 1–4; tr. Shafique N. Virani in *The Ismailis in the Middle Ages: A History of Survival, A Search for Salvation* (Oxford, 2007), p. 43.

Recognize the Supreme Man, lord of Light
Friends, know the Pīr to be he
Who has led you to the lord of Twelve Splendours[1]

Serve none other than that very lord, my brother
Friend, never doubt in this
Hail the advent of the lord
As glorious as the risen sun!

THE TRUE GUIDE[2]

Friend! None but a few know of the exalted station. Indeed, they alone recognize it who have found the true guide.

Friend! Within the heart, at the confluence of the three spiritual rivers, there is an imperishable light. There – a shimmering effulgence, pearls are showered.

Friend! I completely lost consciousness of my physical self when my meditation mounted the empyrean, bursting forth.

Friend! I beheld the place of the lofty throne, I saw the seven islands, the nine continents.

Friend! The religious scriptures and books cannot fathom this, for there is neither day there, nor night, neither sun, nor shade.

Friend! My lord is not such that he can be spoken of. He is to be seen – for he is indescribable, and nameless.

Friend! How sweet is that lord, indescribable, nameless.
Says Pīr Ṣadr al-Dīn, truly,
with my own eyes, I have seen him!

(Translated by Shafique N. Virani)

1. The twelve splendours (*bār kaḷā*) refer to the sun, perhaps because it passes through twelve signs of the zodiac on its celestial rounds.

2. Pīr Ṣadr al-Dīn, '*Sakhī māhā pad kerī*,' in *100 Ginān nī chopaḍī*, (5th ed., Mumbai, 1935), vol. 3, no. 30, vv. 1, 4, 9–13; tr. Shafique N. Virani in *The Ismailis in the Middle Ages*, p. 181.

FOR THE LOVE OF THE BELOVED[1]

Whenever the love kindles within the self for the Beloved,
That love will wipe out your ego.

Night and day he (the lover) is awake and cannot sleep;
Continuously his eyes weep.

It is as if the heart is set afire
With the flame which the lover himself turns into fire.

The soul feels (such cries) as if it were a bird
That it would have flown away to catch a glimpse of the Beloved.

For the love of the Beloved, I would sacrifice myself.
O (how I yearn) to go and embrace Him!

My Beloved has pierced me so with His love,
That out of separation I am groping about like a person insane.

Without the Lord, life is nothing.
For the sake of my Beloved I have cried every day.

The one who is wounded in the heart,
How can he sleep in peace?

Day and night I cannot sleep;
Every day tears flow from my eyes.

I am dying, my Beloved, because of You,
and do You not feel pity (for me)?

(Translated by Ali S. Asani)

1. Pīr Ṣadr al-Dīn, *Būjh nirañjan* (Karachi, 1976), pp. 60–62; tr. Ali S. Asani in *Ecstasy and Enlightenment: The Ismaili Devotional Literature of South Asia* (London, 2002), p. 161.

3

Pīr Ḥasan Kabīr al-Dīn

Ḥasan Kabīr al-Dīn (d. ca. 1470) was the son of Pīr Ṣadr al-Dīn who inherited his father's title of Pīr and extended the *daʿwa* beyond Uchch, and perhaps even beyond Sind. He is buried in Uchch where his tomb is now revered as that of a Sufi saint called Ḥasan Darya. He is credited with a large number of *ginān* compositions.

A HIGH AND LOFTY FORTRESS[1]

A high and lofty fortress,
Beneath which flows a river.
I am a tiny fish adrift in the river.
O my Lord, come and rescue me.

Refrain:
I am tormented without the vision of You,
O my Beloved, O my Husband, come home!
(Although) this devotee forgot to worship You,
Yet, my Beloved, show me Your face.

I am in a (fragrant) little room of incense and sandalwood,
Whose doors are built with good deeds,
(But) closed shut with the locks of love,
O my Lord, come and open them. [*Refrain*]

Alas, I am imprisoned in the cage of family (worldly) attachments;
Only a few can truly understand
The agony of my body;
O Lord, come and soothe my anguish. [*Refrain*]

Please do not be so angry;
My Lord grant me your vision.
This is the humble plea of Pīr Ḥasan Shāh:
O my Lord, come and rescue me. [*Refrain*]

(Translated by Ali S. Asani)

---

1. Pīr Ḥasan Kabīr al-Dīn, '*Ūṃchā re koṭ bahu vechana*,' in *Ginān-e-Sharīf: Our Wonderful Tradition* (Vancouver, 1977), pp. 89–90; tr. Ali S. Asani in *Ecstasy and Enlightenment*, pp. 165–166.

ENTREATY[1]

From the beginning of time, God the transcendent has existed,
 without qualities or form, by Himself.
It is you, O Master, who are our real origin, though our forms have
 become separate.

Refrain:
Be gracious, my Lord, for the weak have You as their refuge.

Countless ages have passed for us, coming in various forms.
Many births have befallen us as we have entreated You, O Lord,
 to unite us with You.

In the time of the Void, O Master, You performed endless marvellous deeds,
 and sported in Your transcendent form.
O Yogi of ancient days, why do you delay? How long, O Master,
 will You remain thus?

In the sixteen primal elements, O Master, You sported: how can I praise
 that sport?
We have been entreating You since that day, so lend us your ear, O Master.

In the Darkness in Your transcendent form, You were sunk in contemplation,
 O Master.
It is to the group which recognized You that the believers whom
 You wed belong.

In the great cycles of time, crores have been saved, as the Invisible One
 has made himself manifest.
Thirty-three crores of divine beings have meditated upon You in awareness.

Throughout the ages I have waited in hope, but You have not wed me.
Now I am in the prime of my youth, so preserve my honour,
 O Lord of the three worlds.

I have come, O Master, with the pots filled with water on my head.[2]
Take down my pots. For fear that You may return my pots,
 I plead for Your forgiveness of my sins.

1. Pīr Ḥasan Kabīr al-Dīn, '*Venati*' in *Elam sār: saṃgrah rāg mālā*, ed., Lālajī Devarāj (Mumbai, 1905), pp. 111–112, vv. 1–13; tr. Christopher Shackle and Zawahir Moir in *Ismaili Hymns from South Asia: An Introduction to the Ginans* (2nd ed., Richmond, 2000), pp. 96–99.

2. ['Pots of water' is a South Asian motif for the sins that weigh down the soul.]

Cast a veil to cover me, O Master, for I am full of faults.
I am weak and dependent, and my honour lies with You, O Lord.

I have waited in hope for endless ages: hear me, O Lord of the three worlds.
The prime of youth has come upon me, and now I shall be put to shame.

In the four ages I have wandered in countless forms, but no marriage
has taken place.
Have the wedding performed, O my Master. Be gracious,
O miraculous Lord.

O Master, how long can I remain alone, while my days pass in lack of love?
Banish this lack of love, O Master, and turn it into married bliss.
May the Lord of the fourteen worlds preserve my honour.

No parents, sisters or relatives look after me. I have come to You for protection.
My honour is in Your hands, O Lord.

(Translated by Christopher Shackle and Zawahir Moir)

4

Nūr Muḥammad Shāh

The son of Sayyid Imām Shāh, an Ismaili poet and preacher who settled in Gujarāt in the mid 15th century, Nūr (or Nar) Muḥammad Shāh (d. ca. 940/1534) was a prolific versifier. Among the compositions attributed to him is the *Satveṇī moṭī*, a mystical treatise of over 200 cantos. Many passages of this poem, including those translated here, caution believers from becoming attached to the ephemeral world and urge them to work towards the everlasting life of the next world. Fāṭima, the daughter of the Prophet, is praised as a paragon of resignation and spiritual love.

THE PERISHABLE BODY[1]

Like a shadow cast at noon
When not a mote remains steady

Why waste your life chasing after
What constantly moves, like the shade of a tree?

How exquisite the first buds appear
But on the appointed day, all of them will rustle, falling to the ground

Indeed, to whom will this not happen?
Just as the leaves have fallen from the *pīpal* tree

Though one wearies saying 'mine, mine'
All the blind are enmeshed in this

None but you my true lord, my beloved, none but you

Having seen the play of the tender buds
Never be fooled
When the appointed day arrives
All of them will rustle and fall to the ground

1. Nūr Muḥammad Shāh, '*Satveṇī moṭī*,' nos. 10–12, nos. 41–42, tr. Shafique N. Virani. An earlier version appeared in his 'The Voice of Truth: Life and Works of Sayyid Nūr Muḥammad Shāh, a 15th/16th Century Ismā'īlī Mystic.' Unpublished MA thesis (McGill, 1995), pp. 66–67; 87–89. The introduction is by the translator.

Seeing this fleeting world
How can you love the morrow?

None who came to this world remained
They were just like bubbles upon the water

First the beloved created Adam
You beheld his coming, yet thought not of his departure

He was made king over both the worlds
Yet, in the end, even he was not allowed to stay

Whoever has come has gone as well
From amongst them I see not a soul who remained

None but you my true lord, my beloved, none but you

Bind not your heart to a home
In which you cannot live
Just as a foreigner is but a guest
Who tarries, yet whose thoughts are elsewhere

While the field is verdant and flourishing
Why not take heed immediately?

People and family are naught but poor millet
For whom the harvest of truth is lost

When the beloved's elixir takes effect
All false actions are put to flight

All this coarse millet remains not standing
Yet you bear so much pain and suffering for it

All have come for the sake of the elixir
And shall flee these parched, arid fields

None but you my true lord, my beloved, none but you

Take heed
While the field is fertile
Know that people, family and relations
Are naught but poor millet.

THE POVERTY OF FĀṬIMA

If there is any lady it is Fāṭima
Who lived like a foreigner in this world

She longed for the house of ʿAlī
Yet did not incline toward the spinning wheel

Then the Prophet advised her
'Why don't you take the spinning wheel in your hand

You will get sustenance from the hand of your lord
Why not dedicate your life to this spinning wheel?'

Muḥammad was true at heart
Such was the wisdom he gave to his daughter

None but you my true lord, my beloved, none but you

Friendship is a game of tribulation
That most cannot play
Only those whom the sustainer exalted
Were given a meeting with him

The next day Fāṭima set out for home
She walked along, seeing naught but her faith

Without faith nothing but loss could be seen
Then she covered her head with an old shawl

When the friends were afflicted by the world
They abandoned it

This is how they met the lord
Only then they went and played the game of love

She who is engrossed in affection is in married bliss
Intoxicated, she burns herself in love

None but you my true lord, my beloved, none but you

Those most thirsty for love
Play the game of love

The Prophet showed the way of meditation
To unite us with the Lord.

(Translated by Shafique N. Virani)

Glossary

Listings in the glossary are selected terms and names, chiefly of Arabic and Persian origin, frequently appearing in the text. In this glossary, pl. is the abbreviated form for 'plural,' sing. for 'singular' and q.v. (*quod vide*) is used for cross-reference.

adab (pl. *ādāb*)	Refinement, culture; rules of behaviour, code of conduct
ahl al-bayt	People of the house; members of the household of the Prophet Muḥammad, including especially, besides him, ʿAlī, Fāṭima, al-Ḥasan, al-Ḥusayn and their progeny. The Prophet's family is also designated as *āl Muḥammad.*
ʿālim (pl. *ʿulamāʾ*)	A learned man; specifically a scholar in Islamic religious sciences.
amīr (pl. *umarāʾ*)	Military commander, prince; many independent rulers also held this title in the Islamic world.
amr	Command; specifically the divine command or volition.
anṣār	Helpers; the Medinans who supported the Prophet after his emigration (*hijra*) from Mecca to Medina, as distinct from the *muhājirūn* (q.v.).
ʿaql	Intellect, intelligence, reason.
asās	Foundation; successor to a speaking prophet, *nāṭiq* (q.v.).
ʿawāmm (or *ʿāmma*)	The common people, the masses, as distinct from the *khawāṣṣ* (q.v.).
bāb	Gate; the Ismaili religious term for the administrative head of the *daʿwa* (q.v.) under the Fatimids, sometimes also called *bāb al-abwāb*; the highest rank after the imam in the *daʿwa* hierarchy of the Fatimid Ismailis; the equivalent of *dāʿī al-duʿāt* (q.v.), mentioned especially in non-Ismaili sources; also a chapter or short treatise.
bāṭin	The inward, hidden or esoteric meaning behind the literal wording of sacred texts and religious prescriptions, as distinct from the *ẓāhir* (q.v.); hence Bāṭinīs, Bāṭiniyya, the groups associated with such ideas. Most of these groups were Shiʿi, particularly Ismaili.

bayʿa (or *bayʿat*)	Formal recognition of authority, especially the act of swearing allegiance to a new sovereign or spiritual leader.
bhakti	A Sanskrit word for devotion.
dāʿī (pl. *duʿāt*)	He who summons; a religious propagator or missionary, especially amongst the Ismailis and other Shiʿi groups; a high rank in the *daʿwa* (q.v.) hierarchy of the Ismailis.
dāʿī al-duʿāt	Chief *dāʿī*; see *bāb* (q.v.).
daʿwa	Lit. 'summons,' 'mission' or invitation to Islam; it also refers to the entire organization developed for this purpose, especially amongst the Ismailis. The Ismailis often referred to their movement as *al-daʿwa*, or more formally as *al-daʿwa al-hādiya*, 'the rightly guiding mission.'
dawr (pl. *adwār*)	Period, era, cycle of history; the Ismailis held that the history of mankind consisted of seven *adwār*, each inaugurated by a speaking prophet or *nāṭiq* (q.v.) six of whom brought a revealed message in the form of a religious law whereas the seventh, identified with the *mahdī* (q.v.) or *qāʾim* (q.v.), would unveil the 'inner truths' (*ḥaqāʾiq*, q.v.) of all.
dīwān	A public financial register; a government department; the collected works of a poet.
farmān	Royal decree; written edict. For the Nizārī Ismailis any pronouncement, order or ruling made by their imam.
fiqh	Technical term for Islamic jurisprudence; the science of law in Islam; the discipline of elucidating the *sharīʿa* (q.v.).
ghayba	Absence; the word has been used in a technical sense for the condition of anyone who has been withdrawn by God from the eyes of men and whose life during that period of occultation (called his *ghayba*) may be miraculously prolonged. In this sense, a number of Shiʿi groups have recognized the *ghayba* of one or another imam (q.v.) with the implication that no further imam was to succeed him and he was to return at a foreordained time before the Day of Resurrection, *qiyāma* (q.v.), as the Mahdī (q.v.).
ghulāt (pl. of *ghālī*)	Exaggerator, extremist; a term of disapproval for individuals accused of exaggeration (*ghuluww*) in religion and in respect to the imams (q.v.); it was particularly applied to those Shiʿi personalities and groups – as well as to certain Sufis – whose doctrines were offensive to the majority.
ginān (or *gnān*)	Derived from Sanskrit, meaning meditative or contemplative knowledge; a term used for a poetic composition

in an Indian language ascribed to one of the *pīr*s who founded and led the Ismaili community in South Asia. Composed in a number of Indic languages, the hymn-like *ginān*s are recorded mainly in the Khojkī script.

ḥadīth — A report, sometimes translated as Tradition, used for the speech and practice of the Prophet Muḥammad and for the Shiʿis, also for those of the imams (q.v.).

ḥaqā'iq (sing. *ḥaqīqa*) — Truths; as a technical term it denotes the gnostic system of thought of the Ismailis. In this sense the *ḥaqā'iq* are the unchangeable truths contained in the *bāṭin* (q.v.); while the law changes with every law-announcing prophet or *nāṭiq* (q.v.), the *ḥaqā'iq* remain eternal.

ḥaqq (pl. *ḥuqūq*) — Truth, the real, (frequently applied to God). Also meaning legal right.

ḥudūd (sing. *ḥadd*) — Limits, terms, legal punishments; a technical term denoting the various ranks in the *daʿwa* (q.v.) hierarchy of the Ismailis, also called *ḥudūd al-dīn*.

ḥujja (or *ḥujjat*) — Proof or the representation of proof. In Shiʿi Islam, it designates prophets and imams as 'proofs' of God's presence or will. In the pre-Fatimid and Fatimid periods, *ḥujja* referred to a dignitary in their religious hierarchy. In the Nizārī Ismaili *daʿwa*, the term generally denoted the chief representative of the imam, sometimes also called *pīr* (q.v.).

ʿilm — Knowledge, more specifically religious knowledge. Most of the Shiʿa hold that every true imam (q.v.) possesses a special knowledge, *ʿilm*, divinely inspired and transmitted through the *naṣṣ* (q.v.) of the preceding imam.

imām (pl. *a'imma*) — Leader of a group of Muslims in prayer. The Shiʿa normally restrict the term to leaders descended from ʿAlī b. Abī Ṭālib and the Prophet's daughter, Fāṭima. The office of imam is called imamate (Arabic, *imāma*).

jamāʿa (or *jamāʿat*) — Assembly, religious congregation; community of the believers; used by Nizārī Ismailis since the Alamūt period in reference to their individual communities.

jazīra (pl. *jazā'ir*) — An island; a term denoting a particular region of the *daʿwa* (q.v.) region. The Fatimid Ismailis categorised the world into twelve geographical regions for their activities.

kashf — Manifestation, unveiling; in Ismaili doctrine, it is used specifically in reference to a period, called *dawr al-kashf*, when the imams (q.v.) were manifest, or when the *ḥaqā'iq* (q.v.) would no longer be concealed in the *bāṭin* (q.v.), in distinction from *satr* (q.v.).

khawāṣṣ (or *khāṣṣa*)	The elite, the privileged people, as distinct from the *ʿawāmm* (q.v.).
khudāwand	Lord, master; used in reference to the central rulers of the Nizārī state in Persia and the Nizārī imams of the post-Alamūt era.
lāḥiq	The conjoint one. A rank in the *daʿwa* hierarchy of the Ismailis.
maddāḥ	Genre of performance of devotional Ismaili poetry, practised by the Ismailis of Badakhshān.
madhhab (pl. *madhāhib*)	Doctrine, movement, creed; a system or school of religious law in Islam.
maʾdhūn	Licentiate; a rank in the *daʿwa* (q.v.) hierarchy of the Ismailis below that of the *dāʿī*.
mahdī	The rightly guided one; name applied to the restorer of true religion who, according to a widely-held Muslim belief, will appear and restore justice before the end of the world. In Imāmī and Ismaili usage the term *qāʾim* frequently replaced that of *mahdī*.
mawlā (pl. *mawālī*)	Friend, lord, master; freed slave; client of an Arab tribe. Title applied to the imams.
muʿallim	Teacher, specifically religious teacher; a rank in the *daʿwa* (q.v.) hierarchy of the post-Alamūt Nizārī Ismailis.
mubdaʿ/ibdaʿ	Directly originated. Used in Ismaili thought to refer to the Prime Intellect and other timeless beings of the spiritual world. *Ibdaʿ* refers to direct origination.
mubdiʿ	Originator. See also *mubdaʿ/ibdaʿ*.
muhājirūn	Emigrants; collective name of the Prophet's Meccan followers who accompanied him in his emigration (*hijra*) from Mecca to Medina, as distinct from the *anṣār* (q.v.).
muḥtasham	A title used commonly in reference to the leader of the Nizārī Ismailis of Quhistān in eastern Persia during the Alamūt period.
mustajīb	Respondent; a term denoting an ordinary Ismaili initiate or neophyte.
nabī (pl. *anbiyāʾ*)	Prophet.
nafs	Soul.
naṣṣ	'Text,' specifically of an explicit ruling; used in Shiʿi Islam to refer to the Prophet Muḥammad's designation of ʿAlī as his successor and, by analogy, of an imam by his immediate predecessor.
nāṭiq (pl. *nuṭaqāʾ*)	Speaker, one gifted with speech; in Ismaili thought, a 'speaking-' or law-announcing prophet who brings a new religious law (*sharīʿa*), abrogating the previous law and,

	hence, initiating a new *dawr* (q.v.) in the religious history of mankind.
pīr	'Elder,' spiritual guide, Sufi master; used loosely in reference to the imam and the holders of the highest ranks in the *daʿwa* (q.v.) hierarchy of the post-Alamūt Nizārī Ismailis; a chief Nizārī *dāʿī* in a certain territory, used by South Asian Nizārīs in reference to the administrative heads of the *daʿwa* in South Asia. See *shaykh*.
qāḍī (pl. *quḍāt*,)	A religious judge administering Islamic law, the *sharīʿa*.
qāʾim	'Riser'; the eschatological Mahdī (q.v.).
qaṣīda	Ode; a poetic genre, normally eulogistic.
qibla	The direction to which believers face during prayer. Among early Muslims, the *qibla* was Jerusalem before being fixed toward the Kaʿba in Mecca.
qiyāma	Resurrection and the Last Day; in Ismaili thought, it also came to be used in reference to the end of any partial cycle in the history of mankind, with the implication that the entire history of mankind consisted of many such partial cycles and partial *qiyāma*s, leading to the final *qiyāma*, sometimes called *qiyāmat al-qiyāmāt*.
risāla (pl. *rasāʾil*)	Treatise, letter, epistle. Also used in the sense of prophetic message.
ṣāmit	Silent one; successor to a speaking prophet, *nāṭiq* (q.v.).
satr	Concealment, veiling; in Ismaili thought, it is used specifically in reference to a period, called *dawr al-satr*, when the imams (q.v.) are considered to be hidden from the eyes of their followers, or when the *ḥaqāʾiq* (q.v.) are concealed in the *bāṭin* (q.v.), as distinct from *kashf* (q.v.).
shaykh	Old man, elder; the chief of a tribe; any religious dignitary; in particular, a Sufi master or spiritual guide, qualified to lead aspirants on the Sufi path, *ṭarīqa* (q.v.); in this sense called *pīr* in Persian.
sunna	Custom, practice; particularly that associated with the exemplary life of the Prophet, comprising his deeds, utterances and his unspoken approval or disapproval; it is embodied in *ḥadīth* (q.v.). Commonly used by Sunnis as distinguishing mark of their tradition, hence the name Sunni.
tafsīr	Explanation, commentary; particularly the commentaries on the Qurʾan; the external, philological exegesis of the Qurʾan, in distinction from *taʾwīl* (q.v.).
taʿlīm	Teaching, instruction; in Shiʿism, authoritative teaching in religion derived from the imams (q.v.) .

tanzīl	To send down (a revelation to a prophet); specifically the exoteric (*ẓāhir*) aspect of revelation
taqiyya	Precautionary dissimulation of one's true religious beliefs, especially in time of danger; used especially by the Twelver (Ithnāʿasharī) and Ismaili Shiʿis.
taqlīd	To imitate, copy; following another's authority.
ṭarīqa	Way, path; the spiritual path followed by Sufis (q.v.); any of the organized Sufi orders. It is also used by Nizārī Ismailis in reference to their interpretation of Islam.
tashbīh	Likening; specifically, ascription of human characteristics to God, anthropomorphism.
taslīm	Submission, acceptance
ta'wīl	The educing of inner meaning from the apparent; as a technical term among the Shiʿis, particularly the Ismailis, it denotes the method used for the allegorical, symbolic or esoteric interpretation of the Qur'an, the *sharīʿa*, historical events and the world of nature. Translated also as spiritual hermeneutics, *ta'wīl* may be distinguished from *tafsīr* (q.v.).
ta'yīd	Inspiration, spiritual support.
ʿulamā'	See *ʿālim*.
umma	Community, any people as followers of a particular religion or prophet; in particular, the Muslims as forming a religious community.
walāya/walī	Closeness; carries the basic meanings of friendship, assistance, allegiance, kinship, authority, or the devotion due to the one in authority. In Shiʿism, the *walī* par excellence is ʿAlī b. Abī Ṭālib or the imam more generally. In Sufism, *walī* (pl. *awliyā'*) may be applied to any great *shaykh* with credible spiritual powers, hence it is frequently translated as 'saint' or 'friend' of God.
waṣī (pl. *awṣiyā'*)	Legatee, executor of a will; refers in Ismaili usage to the successor to a prophet, also called *asās* (q.v).
ẓāhir	The outward, literal, or exoteric meaning of sacred texts and religious prescriptions, notably the Qur'an and the *sharīʿa* as distinct from the *bāṭin* (q.v.).

Bibliography

Abū Isḥāq Quhistānī. *Haft bāb,* ed. and tr. W. Ivanow. Bombay, 1959.

Abu'l-Fawāris Aḥmad b. Ya'qūb. *al-Risāla fi'l-imāma,* ed. and tr. Sami N. Makarem as *The Political Doctrine of the Ismā'īlīs (The Imamate).* Delmar, NY, 1977.

Aga Khan III (Sulṭān Muḥammad Shāh). *The Memoirs of Aga Khan: World Enough and Time.* London, 1954.

Ājurlū, Laylā. *Kitābshināsī-yi jāmi'-i Ḥakīm Nāṣir-i Khusraw Qubādiyānī,* ed. R. Musalmāniyān Qubādiyānī. Tehran, 1384 Sh./2005.

Amir-Moezzi, Mohammad Ali. *The Divine Guide in Early Shi'ism: The Sources of Esotericism in Islam,* tr. D. Streight. Albany, NY, 1994.

An Anthology of Philosophy in Persia: Volume II, Ismā'īlī and Hermetico-Pythagorean Philosophy, ed. S. Hossein Nasr with M. Aminrazavi. Oxford, 2001.

Asani, Ali S. 'The *Ginān* Literature of the Ismailis of Indo-Pakistan: Its Origins, Characteristics, and Themes,' in D. L. Eck and F. Mallison, ed., *Devotion Divine: Bhakti Traditions from the Regions of India.* Groningen, 1991, pp. 1–18.

__ 'The Ismaili *ginān*s as Devotional Literature,' in R. S. McGregor, ed., *Devotional Literature in South Asia: Current Research, 1985–1988.* Cambridge, 1992, pp. 101–112.

__ *Ecstasy and Enlightenment: The Ismaili Devotional Literature of South Asia.* London, 2002.

Badakhshānī, Sayyid Suhrāb Valī. *Sī va shish ṣaḥīfa,* ed. H. Ujāqī. Tehran, 1961.

Bayburdi, Chingiz G. A. *Zhizn i tvorchestvo Nizārī-Persidskogo poeta XIII-XIV vv.* Moscow, 1966. Persian trans., *Zindagī va āthār-i Nizārī,* tr. M. Ṣadrī. Tehran, 1370 Sh./1991.

Bertel's, Andrey E. *Nasir-i Khosrov i ismailizm.* Moscow, 1959. Persian trans., *Nāṣir-i Khusraw va Ismā'īliyān,* tr. Y. Āriyanpūr. Tehran, 1346 Sh./1967.

__ and M. Bakoev. *Alphabetic Catalogue of Manuscripts found by 1959–1963 Expedition in Gorno-Badakhshan Autonomous Region,* ed. B. G. Gafurov and A. M. Mirzoev. Moscow, 1967.

Bosworth, C. Edmund. *The New Islamic Dynasties: A Chronological and Genealogical Manual.* Edinburgh, 1996.

Brett, Michael. *The Rise of the Fatimids: The World of the Mediterranean and the Middle East in the Fourth Century of the Hijra, Tenth Century CE.* Leiden, 2001.

Brockelmann, Carl. *Geschichte der arabischen Litteratur.* Weimar, 1898–1902; 2nd ed., Leiden, 1943–1949. *Supplementbände.* Leiden, 1937–1942.

Browne, Edward G. *A Literary History of Persia.* London and Cambridge, 1902–1924.

The Cambridge History of Iran: Volume 4, *The Period from the Arab Invasion to the Saljuqs,* ed. Richard N. Frye. Cambridge, 1975.

The Cambridge History of Iran: Volume 5, *The Saljuq and Mongol Periods*, ed. John A. Boyle. Cambridge, 1968.

The Cambridge History of Iran: Volume 6, *The Timurid and Safavid Periods*, ed. Peter Jackson and L. Lockhart. Cambridge, 1986.

Chittick, William C. 'Baba Afżal-al-Dīn Moḥammad b. Ḥasan Maraqī Kāšānī,' *EIR*, vol. 3, pp. 285–291.

Corbin, Henry. *En Islam Iranien. Aspects spirituels et philosophiques*. Paris, 1971–1972.

__ 'Nāṣir-i Khusrau and Iranian Ismāʿīlism,' in *The Cambridge History of Iran*: Volume 4, pp. 520–542, 689–690.

__ *Temps cyclique et gnose Ismaélienne*. Paris, 1982. English trans., *Cyclical Time and Ismaili Gnosis*, tr. Ralph Manheim and James W. Morris. London, 1983.

Cortese, Delia. *Ismaili and Other Arabic Manuscripts: A Descriptive Catalogue of Manuscripts in the Library of The Institute of Ismaili Studies*. London, 2000.

__ *Arabic Ismaili Manuscripts: The Zāhid ʿAlī Collection in the Library of The Institute of Ismaili Studies*. London, 2003.

Cortese, Delia and Simonetta Calderini. *Women and the Fatimids in the World of Islam*. Edinburgh, 2006.

Dachraoui, Farhat. *Le califat Fatimide au Maghreb (296–365 H./909–975 Jc.): histoire politique et institutions*. Tunis, 1981.

Daftary, Farhad. 'Persian Historiography of the Early Nizārī Ismāʿīlīs,' *Iran*: *Journal of the British Institute of Persian Studies*, 30 (1992), pp. 91–97.

__ *The Assassin Legends: Myths of the Ismaʿilis*. London, 1994.

__ (ed.) *Mediaeval Ismaʿili History and Thought*. Cambridge, 1996.

__ *A Short History of the Ismailis: Traditions of a Muslim Community*. Edinburgh, 1998. French trans., *Les Ismaéliens*, tr. Z. Rajan-Badouraly. Paris, 2003. Persian trans., *Mukhtaṣarī dar taʾrīkh-i Ismāʿīliyya*, tr. F. Badraʾī. Tehran, 1378 Sh./1999.

__ 'The Ismaili *Daʿwa* outside the Fatimid *Dawla*,' in Marianne Barrucand, ed., *L'Égypte Fatimide, son art et son histoire*. Paris, 1999, pp. 29–43.

__ 'Intellectual Life among the Ismailis: An Overview,' in F. Daftary, ed., *Intellectual Traditions in Islam*. London, 2000, pp. 87–111.

__ 'Naṣīr al-Dīn al-Ṭūsī and the Ismailis of the Alamūt Period,' in N. Pourjavady and Ž. Vesel, ed., *Naṣīr al-Dīn Ṭūsī, philosophe et savant du XIIIe siècle*. Tehran, 2000, pp. 59–67.

__ *Ismaili Literature: A Bibliography of Sources and Studies*. London, 2004.

__ *Ismailis in Medieval Muslim Societies*. London, 2005.

__ *The Ismāʿīlīs: Their History and Doctrines*. 2nd ed., Cambridge, 2007.

__ 'Rāshid al-Dīn Sinān,' *EI2*, vol. 8, pp. 442–443.

__ 'Satr,' *EI2*, vol. 12, Supplement, pp. 712–713.

__ 'Ismaʿilism. iii. Ismaʿili History,' *EIR*, vol. 14, pp. 178–195.

De Smet, Daniel. *La Quiétude de l'intellect: Néoplatonisme et gnose ismaélienne dans l'œuvre de Ḥamîd ad-Dîn al-Kirmânî (Xe/XIes)*. Louvain, 1995.

Encyclopaedia Iranica, ed. E. Yarshater. London and New York, 1982—.

The Encyclopaedia of Islam, ed. M. Th. Houtsma et al. 1st ed., Leiden and London, 1913–1938; reprinted, Leiden, 1987.

The Encyclopaedia of Islam, ed. H. A. R. Gibb et al. New ed., Leiden, 1960–2004.

The Encylopaedia of Islam, Three, ed. Gudrun Krämer et al. Leiden, 2007–.

Encyclopedia of Religion, ed. M. Eliade. London and New York, 1987.

Encylopedia of Religion, ed. Lindsay Jones. 2nd ed., Detroit, 2005.

Esmail, Aziz. *A Scent of Sandalwood: Indo-Ismaili Religious Lyrics (Ginans).* Richmond, Surrey, 2002.

Fidā'ī Khurāsānī, Muḥammad b. Zayn al-ʿĀbidīn. *Kitāb hidāyat al-mu'minīn al-ṭālibīn,* ed. Aleksandr A. Semenov. Moscow, 1959.

Fyzee, Asaf A. A. 'The Study of the Literature of the Fatimid *Daʿwa,*' in G. Makdisi, ed., *Arabic and Islamic Studies in Honor of Hamilton A. R. Gibb.* Leiden, 1965, pp. 232–249.

__ *Compendium of Fatimid Law.* Simla, 1969.

Gacek, Adam. *Catalogue of Arabic Manuscripts in the Library of The Institute of Ismaili Studies.* London, 1984–1985.

Gnosis-Texte der Ismailiten, ed. Rudolf Strothmann. Göttingen, 1943.

The Great Islamic Encyclopaedia (Dā'irat al-Maʿārif-i Buzurg-i Islāmī), ed. K. Mūsavī Bujnūrdī. Tehran, 1367 Sh.—/1989—

The Great Ismaili Heroes, ed. A. R. Kanji. Karachi, 1973.

Ḥāfiẓ-i Abrū, ʿAbd Allāh b. Luṭf ʿAllāh al-Bihdādīnī. *Majmaʿ al-tawārīkh al-sulṭāniyya: qismat-i khulafā'-i ʿAlawiyya-yi Maghrib va Miṣr va Nizāriyān va rafīqān,* ed. M. Mudarrisī Zanjānī. Tehran, 1364 Sh./1985.

Haft bāb-i Bābā Sayyidnā, ed. W. Ivanow, in his *Two Early Ismaili Treatises.* Bombay, 1933, pp. 4–44. English trans. M. G. S. Hodgson, in his *Order of Assassins,* pp. 279–324.

Halm, Heinz. *Kosmologie und Heilslehre der frühen Ismāʿīlīya. Eine Studie zur islamschen Gnosis.* Wiesbaden, 1978.

__ *Die islamische Gnosis : Die extreme Schia und die ʿAlawiten.* Zürich and Munich, 1982.

__ *The Empire of the Mahdi: The Rise of the Fatimids*, tr. M. Bonner. Leiden, 1996.

__ 'The Ismaʿili Oath of Allegiance (*ʿahd*) and the "Sessions of Wisdom" (*majālis al-ḥikma*) in Fatimid Times,' in *MIHT*, pp. 91–115.

__ *The Fatimids and their Traditions of Learning*. London, 1997.

__ *Die Kalifen von Kairo. Die Fatimiden in Ägypten 973–1074*. Munich, 2003.

__ *Shiʿism*, tr. J. Watson and M. Hill. 2nd ed., Edinburgh, 2004.

Hamdani, Abbas. *The Beginnings of the Ismāʿīlī Daʿwa in Northern India.* Cairo, 1956.

__ 'The Fatimid Daʿi al-Mu'ayyad: His Life and Work,' in *Great Ismaili Heroes*, ed. Kanji, pp. 41–47.

al-Ḥāmidī, Ibrāhīm b. al-Ḥusayn. *Kitāb kanz al-walad,* ed. M. Ghālib. Wiesbaden, 1971.

Ḥasan Kabīr al-Dīn, Pīr. '*Venati*', in Lālajī Devarāj, ed., *Elam sār: saṃgrah rāg mālā.* Mumbai, 1905, pp. 111–112.

__ '*Ūṃchā re koṭ bahu vechana*', in *Ginān-e-Sharīf: Our Wonderful Tradition*. Vancouver, 1977, pp. 89–90.

Hillenbrand, Carole. 'The Power Struggle between the Saljuqs and the Ismaʿilis of Alamūt, 487–518/1094–1124: The Saljuq Perspective,' in *MIHT*, pp. 205–220.

Hodgson, Marshall G. S. *The Order of Assassins: The Struggle of the Early Nizārī Ismāʿīlīs against the Islamic World*. The Hague, 1955; repr., Philadelphia, 2005.
__ 'The Ismāʿīlī State,' in *The Cambridge History of Iran:* Volume 5, pp. 422–482.
__ *The Venture of Islam: Conscience and History in a World Civilization*. Chicago, 1974.
Hunsberger, Alice C. *Nasir Khusraw, The Ruby of Badakhshan: A Portrait of the Persian Poet, Traveller and Philosopher*. London, 2000.
Hunzai, Faquir. M. and Kutub Kassam (ed. and tr.), *Shimmering Light: An Anthology of Ismaili Poetry*. London, 1996.
Ibn al-Haytham, Abū ʿAbd Allāh Jaʿfar b. Aḥmad al-Aswad. *Kitāb al-munāẓarāt*, ed. and tr. Wilferd Madelung and Paul E. Walker as *The Advent of the Fatimids: A Contemporary Shiʿi Witness*. London, 2000.
Ibn ʿIdhārī, Abu'l-ʿAbbās Aḥmad b. Muḥammad al-Marrākushī. *al-Bayān al-mughrib fī akhbār al-Andalus wa'l-Maghrib*, vol. 1, ed. G. S. Colin and E. Lévi Provençal. Beirut, 1956.
Ibn al-Walīd, ʿAlī b. Muḥammad. *Dāmigh al-bāṭil wa-hatf al-munāḍil*, ed. M. Ghālib. Beirut, 1403/1982.
__ *Tāj al-ʿaqāʾid wa-maʿdin al-fawāʾid*, ed. ʿĀrif Tāmir. Beirut, 1967. Summary English trans. W. Ivanow as *A Creed of the Fatimids*. Bombay, 1936.
Ibn al-Walīd, al-Ḥusayn b. ʿAlī. *Risālat al-mabdaʾ wa'l-maʿād*, ed. and French trans. H. Corbin, in *Trilogie Ismaélienne*, text pp. 99–130, translation as *Cosmogonie et eschatologie*, pp. 129–200.
Idrīs ʿImād al-Dīn b. al-Ḥasan. *Kitab zahr al-maʿānī*, ed. M. Ghālib. Beirut, 1411/1991. Selection, ed. and tr. W. Ivanow, in his *Ismaili Tradition*, text pp. 47–80, translation pp. 232–274.
__ *ʿUyūn al-akhbār wa-funūn al-āthār*, vols. 1–7, ed. M. al-Sagherji et al. Damascus and London, 2007–2008.
__ *ʿUyūn al-akhbār wa-funūn al-āthār*, vol. 5 and part of vol. 6, ed. Muḥammad al-Yaʿlāwī as *Taʾrīkh al-khulafāʾ al-Fāṭimiyyīn bi'l-Maghrib: al-qism al-khāṣṣ min Kitāb ʿuyūn al-akhbār*. Beirut, 1985.
__ *ʿUyūn al-akhbār wa-funūn al-āthār*, vol. 7, ed. Ayman F. Sayyid, with summary English trans. by Paul E. Walker and Maurice A. Pomerantz as *The Fatimids and their Successors in Yaman: The History of an Islamic Community*. London, 2002.
Ikhwān al-Ṣafā. *Rasāʾil Ikhwān al-Ṣafāʾ*, partial ed. and tr. Lenn Evan Goodman as *The Case of the Animals versus Man before the King of the Jinn: A Tenth-century Ecological Fable of the Pure Brethren of Baṣra*. Boston, 1978.
Ivanow, Wladimir. *Ismaili Tradition Concerning the Rise of the Fatimids*. London, etc., 1942.
__ *Studies in Early Persian Ismailism*. 2nd ed., Bombay, 1955.
__ *Problems in Nasir-i Khusraw's Biography*. Bombay, 1956.
__ *Ismaili Literature: A Bibliographical Survey*. Tehran, 1963.
Izutsu, Toshihiko. *The Concept of Belief in Islamic Theology: A Semantic Analysis of Īmān and Islām*. Tokyo, 1965.
__ *Ethico-Religious Concepts in the Qurʾān*. Montreal, 1966.
Jaʿfar b. Manṣūr al-Yaman, Abu'l-Qāsim. *Kitāb al-ʿālim wa'l-ghulām*, ed. and tr. James

W. Morris as *The Master and the Disciple: An Early Islamic Spiritual Dialogue*. London, 2001.

__ *Kitāb al-kashf*, ed. R. Strothmann. London, etc., 1952.

Jafri, S. Husain M. *Origins and Early Development of Shīʿa Islam*. London, 1979.

Jamal, Nadia Eboo. *Surviving the Mongols: Nizārī Quhistānī and the Continuity of Ismaili Tradition in Persia*. London, 2002.

Jambet, Christian. *La grande résurrection d'Alamût. Les formes de la liberté dans le Shîʿisme Ismaélien*. Lagrasse, 1990.

al-Jawdharī, Abū ʿAlī Manṣūr al-ʿAzīzī. *Sīrat al-ustādh Jawdhar*, ed. M. Kāmil Ḥusayn and M. ʿAbd al-Hādī Shaʿīra. Cairo, 1954. French trans., *Vie de l'ustadh Jaudhar*, tr. M. Canard. Algiers, 1958.

Juwaynī, ʿAlā al-Dīn ʿAṭā-Malik. *Tārīkh-i jahān-gushāy*, ed. M. Qazwīnī. London, 1912–1937; tr. J. A. Boyle as *The History of the World-Conqueror*. Manchester, 1958.

Kāshānī, Abū al-Qāsim. *Zubdat al-tawārīkh: bakhsh-i Fāṭimiyān wa Nizāriyān*, ed. M. T. Dānishpazhūh. 2nd ed., Tehran, 1366 Sh./1987.

Kassam, Tazim R. *Songs of Wisdom and Circles of Dance: Hymns of the Satpanth Ismāʿīlī Muslim Saint, Pīr Shams*. Albany, NY, 1995.

Khākī Khurāsānī, Imām Qulī. *Dīwān*, ed. W. Ivanow. Bombay, 1933.

Khams rasāʾil Ismāʿīliyya, ed. ʿĀrif Tāmir. Salamiyya, 1375/1956.

Khayrkhwāh-i Harātī, Muḥammad Riḍā b. Khwāja Sulṭān Ḥusayn Ghūriyānī. *Faṣl dar bayān-i shinākht-i imām*, ed. W. Ivanow. 3rd ed., Tehran, 1960. English trans., *On the Recognition of the Imam*, tr. W. Ivanow. 2nd ed., Bombay, 1947.

__ 'Risāla,' in *Khayrkhwāh-i muwaḥḥid-i waḥdat*, ed. Sayyid Shāhzāda Munīr b. Muḥammad Qāsim Badakhshānī. Mumbai, [1333/1915], pp. 1–98; in *Taṣnīfāt-i Khayrkhwāh Harātī*, ed. Wladimir Ivanow. Tehran, 1961, pp. 1–75.

al-Kindī, Abū Yūsuf Yaʿqūb b. Isḥāq. 'Essay on the Prostration of the Outermost Sphere and its Obedience to God,' in M. A. Abū Riḍā, ed., *Rasāʾil al-Kindī al-falsafiyya*. Cairo, 1950–1953.

al-Kirmānī, Ḥamīd al-Dīn Aḥmad b. ʿAbd Allāh. *Majmūʿat rasāʾil al-Kirmānī*, ed. M. Ghālib. Beirut, 1403/1983.

__ *al-Maṣābīḥ fī ithbāt al-imāma*, ed. and tr. Paul E. Walker as *Master of the Age: An Islamic Treatise on the Necessity of the Imamate*. London, 2007.

__ *Rāḥat al-ʿaql*, ed. Muḥammad Kāmil Ḥusayn and M. Muṣṭafā Ḥilmī. Leiden, 1953.

__ *al-Risāla al-durriyya fī maʿnā al-tawḥīd waʾl-muwaḥḥid*, ed. M. Kāmil Ḥusayn, Cairo, 1952; tr. Faquir M. Hunzai as '*al-Risālat al-durriyah*,' in *APP*, vol. 2, pp. 192–200.

Kister, M. J. '*Illā bi-ḥaqqihi* … A Study of an Early *ḥadīth*,' *Jerusalem Studies in Arabic and Islam*, 8 (1986), pp. 61–96.

Klemm, Verena. *Memoirs of a Mission: The Ismaili Scholar, Statesman and Poet al-Muʾayyad fiʾl-Dīn al-Shīrāzī*. London, 2003.

al-Kulaynī, Abū Jaʿfar Muḥammad b. Yaʿqūb. *al-Uṣūl min al-kāfī*, ed. ʿAlī Akbar al-Ghaffārī. Tehran, 1388/1968; ed. J. Muṣṭafawī, Tehran, n.d.

Lalani, Arzina R. 'Aḥmad b. Ibrāhīm al-Naysābūrī,' in Oliver Leaman, ed., *Biographical Dictionary of Islamic Philosophy*. London and New York, 2006, vol. 2, pp. 158–160.

__ 'Naṣṣ,' in *The Qurʾan: an Encyclopaedia*, ed. Oliver Leaman. London and New York, 2006, pp. 488–451.

Landolt, Hermann. 'Khwāja Naṣīr al-Dīn al-Ṭūsī (597/1201–672/1274), Ismāʿīlism and Ishrāqī Philosophy,' in N. Pourjavady and Ž. Vesel, ed., *Naṣīr al-Dīn Ṭūsī, philosophe et savant du XIIIe siècle*. Tehran, 2000, pp. 13–30; reprinted in his *Recherches en spiritualité iranienne. Recueil d'articles*. Tehran, 2005, pp. 3–23.

__ 'Jāmiʿ al-Ḥikmatayn, 2: Sharḥ-i Nāṣir-i Khusraw bar qaṣīda-yi Jurjānī,' in *Encyclopaedia of the World of Islam*, ed. G.-A. Haddad-Adel. Tehran, 2005, vol. 9, pp. 328–329.

__ 'Walāyah,' in *Encyclopedia of Religion*, 2nd ed., vol. 14, pp. 9656–9662.

__ 'Suhrawardī between philosophy, Sufism and Ismailism: a reappraisal,' in *Dâneshnâmeh*, ed. G.-R- Aavani. Tehran, 2003, vol. 1, pp. 13–29; reprinted in his *Recherches en spiritualité iranienne*, pp. 107–118.

____"Aṭṭār, Sufism and Ismailism,' in Leonard Lewisohn and Christopher Shackle, ed., *'Aṭṭār and the Persian Sufi Tradition: The Art of Spiritual Flight*. London, 2006, pp. 3–26.

Lawson, Todd (ed.) *Reason and Inspiration in Islam: Theology, Philosophy and Mysticism in Muslim Thought, Essays in Honour of Hermann Landolt*. London, 2005.

Lewisohn, Leonard. 'Sufism and Ismāʿīlī Doctrine in the Persian Poetry of Nizārī Quhistānī (645–721/1247–1321),' *Iran: Journal of the British Institute of Persian Studies*, 41 (2003), pp. 229–251.

Madelung, Wilferd. 'The Sources of Ismāʿīlī Law,' in *Journal of Near Eastern Studies*, 35 (1976), pp. 29–40; reprinted in his *Religious Schools*, article XVIII.

__ 'Aspects of Ismāʿīlī Theology: The Prophetic Chain and the God Beyond Being,' in S. H. Nasr, ed., *Ismāʿīlī Contributions to Islamic Culture*. Tehran, 1977, pp. 51–65; reprinted in his *Religious Schools and Sects in Medieval Islam*. London, 1985, article XVII.

__ 'Naṣīr ad-Dīn Ṭūsī's Ethics Between Philosophy, Shiʿism, and Sufism,' in Richard G. Hovannisian, ed., *Ethics in Islam*. Malibu, CA, 1985, pp. 85–101.

__ 'Ismāʿīliyya,' *EI2*, vol. 4, pp. 198–206.

__ 'Shīʿa,' *EI2*, vol. 9, pp. 420–424.

al-Majdūʿ, Ismāʿīl b. ʿAbd al-Rasūl. *Fahrasat al-kutub wa'l-rasā'il*, ed. ʿAlī Naqī Munzavī. Tehran, 1966.

al-Majlisī, Muḥammad Bāqir. *Biḥār al-anwār*. Tehran, 1376/1956.

al-Malījī, Abu'l-Qāsim ʿAbd al-Ḥākim b. Wahb. *al-Majālis al-Mustanṣiriyya*, ed. M. Kāmil Ḥusayn. Cairo, [1947].

Mallison, Françoise. 'Hinduism as Seen by the Nizārī Ismāʿīlī Missionaries of Western India: The Evidence of the *Ginān*,' in Günther D. Sontheimer and H. Kulke, ed., *Hinduism Reconsidered*. New Delhi, 1989, pp. 93–103.

al-Maqrīzī, Taqī al-Dīn Aḥmad b. ʿAlī. *Ittiʿāẓ al-ḥunafā' bi-akhbār al-a'imma al-Fāṭimiyyīn al-khulafā'*, ed. Jamāl al-Dīn al-Shayyāl and Muḥammad Ḥilmī M. Aḥmad. Cairo, 1387–1393/1967–1973.

Marquet, Yves. *La philosophie des Iḫwān al-Ṣafā'*. Algiers, 1975.

__ 'Ikhwān al-Ṣafā',' *EI2*, vol. 3, pp. 1071–1076.

Meisami, Julie Scott. 'Symbolic Structure in a Poem by Nāṣir-i Khusrau,' *Iran: Journal of the British Institute of Persian Studies*, 31 (1993), pp. 103–117.

Minhāj-i Sirāj, ʿUthmāṇ b. Sirāj al-Dīn. *Ṭabaqāt-i Nāṣirī*, ed. ʿAbd al-Ḥayy Ḥabībī. 2nd ed., Kabul, 1342–1343 Sh./1963–1964; tr. H. G. Raverty as *Ṭabaqāt-i Nāṣirī: A General*

History of the Muhammadan Dynasties of Asia. New Delhi, 1970.
Mirza, Nasseh Ahmad. *Syrian Ismailism: The Ever Living Line of the Imamate, AD 1100–1260*. Richmond, Surrey, 1997.
Moir, Zawahir. 'The Life and Legends of Pir Shams as Reflected in the Ismaili Ginans: A Critical Review,' in Françoise Mallison, ed., *Constructions hagiographiques dans le monde Indien. Entre mythe et histoire*. Paris, 2001, pp. 365–384.
al-Mu'ayyad fi'l-Dīn al-Shīrāzī, Abū Naṣr Hibat Allāh b. Abī 'Imrān Mūsā. *Dīwān*, ed. M. Kāmil Ḥusayn. Cairo, 1949.
__ *al-Majālis al-Mu'ayyadiyya*, vols. 1 and 3, ed. M. Ghālib. Beirut, 1974–1984; vols. 1–3, ed. Ḥātim Hamīd al-Dīn. Bombay and Oxford, 1395–1426/1975–2005.
__ *Sīrat al-Mu'ayyad fi'l-Dīn dā'ī al-du'āt*, ed. M. Kāmil Ḥusayn. Cairo, 1949; part tr. Joseph E. Lowry as 'The Autobiography of al-Mu'ayyad fī al-Dīn Hibat Allāh al-Shīrāzī (ca. 1000-1077),' in Dwight F. Reynolds, ed., *Interpreting the Self: Autobiography in the Arabic Literary Tradition*. Los Angeles and London, 2001, pp. 132-144.
Mudarris Raḍawī, Muḥammad Taqī. *Aḥwāl wa āthār-i Abū Ja'far Muḥammad b. Muḥammad b. Ḥasan Ṭūsī*. Tehran, 1354 Sh./1975.
Mudarrisī Zanjānī, M. *Sargudhasht wa 'aqā'id-i falsafī-yi Khwāja Naṣīr al-Dīn Ṭūsī*. Tehran, 1335 Sh./1956.
Muntakhabāt Ismā'īliyya, ed. 'Ādil al-'Awwā. Damascus, 1378/1958.
al-Mustanṣir bi'llāh, Abū Tamīm Ma'add. *al-Sijillāt al-Mustanṣiriyya*, ed. 'Abd al-Mun'im Mājid. Cairo, 1954.
Mustanṣir bi'llāh (II). *Pandiyāt-i jawānmardī*, ed. and tr. W. Ivanow. Leiden, 1953.
Nanji, Azim. 'An Ismā'īlī Theory of *Walāyah* in the *Da'ā'im al-Islām* of Qāḍī al-Nu'mān,' in Donald P. Little, ed., *Essays on Islamic Civilization Presented to Niyazi Berkes*. Leiden, 1976, pp. 260–273.
__ *The Nizārī Ismā'īlī Tradition in the Indo-Pakistan Subcontinent*. Delmar, NY, 1978.
__ 'Towards a Hermeneutic of Qur'ānic and Other Narratives in Isma'ili Thought,' in Richard C. Martin, ed., *Approaches to Islam in Religious Studies*. Tucson, AZ, 1985, pp. 164–173.
__ '*Sharī'at* and *Ḥaqīqat*: Continuity and Synthesis in the Nizārī Ismā'īlī Muslim Tradition,' in Katherine P. Ewing, ed., *Sharī'at and Ambiguity in South Asian Islam*. Berkeley, 1988, pp. 63–76.
__ 'Ismā'īlī Philosophy,' in S. Hossein Nasr and O. Leaman, ed., *History of Islamic Philosophy*. London, 1996, vol. 1, pp. 144–154.
Nāṣir-i Khusraw, Ḥakīm Abū Mu'īn. *Dīwān*, ed. Naṣr Allāh Taqavī et al. Tehran, 1304–1307 Sh./1925–1928; ed. M. Suhaylī. Isfahan, 1956; ed. M. Mīnuvī and M. Muḥaqqiq. Tehran, 1353 Sh./1974; ed. Ja'far Shi'ār and Kāmil Aḥmad-Nizhād. Tehran, 1378 Sh./1999. Partial English trans., *Forty Poems from the Divan*, tr. Peter L. Wilson and G. R. Aavani. Tehran, 1977. Partial English trans., *Make a Shield from Wisdom: Selected Verses from Nāṣir-i Khusraw's Dīvān*, tr. Annemarie Schimmel. London, 1993; reprinted, London, 2001.
__ *Gushāyish wa rahāyish*, ed. Sa'īd Nafīsī. Leiden, 1950; ed. and tr. Faquir M. Hunzai as *Knowledge and Liberation: A Treatise on Philosophical Theology*. London, 1998.
__ *Jāmi' al-ḥikmatayn*, ed. H. Corbin and M. Mu'īn. Tehran and Paris, 1953; French trans., *Le livre réunissant les deux sagesses*, tr. Isabelle de Gastines. Paris, 1990; partial translation into English by Latimah Parvin Peerwani, in *APP*, pp. 293–311.

__ *Khwān al-ikhwān*, ed. Yaḥyā al-Khashshāb, Cairo, 1940; ed. ʿAlī Qavīm. Tehran, 1338 Sh./1959.
__ *Safar-nāma*, ed. and French trans. Charles Schefer as *Sefer Nameh, relation du voyage de Nassiri Khosrau*. Paris, 1881; repr., Amsterdam, 1970; ed. Maḥmūd Ghanīzāda. Berlin, 1341/1922; ed. Muḥammad Dabīr Siyāqī. 5th ed., Tehran, 1356 Sh./1977. English trans., *Nasir-i Khusraw's Book of Travels (Safarnama)*, rev. tr. Wheeler M. Thackston. Costa Mesa, CA, 2001.
__ *Shish faṣl*, ed. and tr. W. Ivanow. Leiden, 1949.
__ *Wajh-i dīn*, ed. Maḥmūd Ghanīzāda and M. Qazvīnī. Berlin, 1343/1924; ed. Gholam Reza Aavani. Tehran, 1977.
__ *Zād al-musāfirīn*, ed. Muḥammad Badhl al-Raḥmān. Berlin, 1341/1923; ed. S. I. ʿImādī Ḥāʾirī. Tehran, 1384 Sh./2005.
Nasr, S. Hossein (ed.) *Ismāʿīlī Contributions to Islamic Culture*. Tehran, 1977.
__ 'Afḍal al-Dīn Kāshānī and the Philosophical World of Khwājah Naṣīr al-Dīn Ṭūsī,' in M. Marmura, ed., *Islamic Theology and Philosophy: Studies in Honor of George F. Hourani*. Albany, NY, 1984, pp. 249–264.
al-Naysābūrī, Aḥmad b. Ibrāhīm. *Ithbāt al-imāma*, ed. M. Ghālib. Beirut, 1404/1984.
__ *Istitār al-imām*, ed. W. Ivanow, in *Bulletin of the Faculty of Arts, University of Egypt*, 4, part 2 (1936), pp. 93–107. English trans. W. Ivanow, in his *Ismaili Tradition*, pp. 157–183.
__ *al-Risāla al-mūjaza al-kāfiya fī adab al-duʿāt*, facsimile ed., in V. Klemm, *Die Mission des fāṭimidischen Agenten al-Muʾayyad fī d-dīn in Šīrāz*. Frankfurt am Main, 1989, pp. 205–277.
Nizārī Quhistānī, Ḥakīm Saʿd al-Dīn b. Shams al-Dīn. *Dīwān-i Ḥakīm Nizārī Quhistānī*, ed. Maẓāhir Muṣaffā. Tehran, 1371–1373 Sh./1992–1994.
Nomoto, Shin. 'An Early Ismaili View of Other Religions: A Chapter from the *Kitāb al-Iṣlāḥ* of Abū Ḥātim al-Rāzī (d. ca. 322/934),' in Lawson, ed., *Reason and Inspiration*, pp. 142–156.
al-Nuʿmān b. Muḥammad, al-Qāḍī Abū Ḥanīfa. *Asās al-taʾwīl*, ed. ʿĀrif Tāmir. Beirut, 1960.
__ *Daʿāʾim al-Islām*, ed. Asaf A. A. Fyzee. Cairo, 1951–1961. English trans., Asaf A. A. Fyzee, completely revised by Ismail K. Poonawala as *The Pillars of Islam*. New Delhi, 2002–2004.
__ *Iftitāḥ al-daʿwa wa ibtidāʾ al-dawla*, ed. Wadād al-Qāḍī. Beirut, 1970; ed. Farhat Dachraoui. Tunis, 1975. English trans., *Founding the Fatimid State: The Rise of an Early Islamic Empire*, tr. Hamid Haji. London, 2006.
__ *Kitāb al-himma fī ādāb atbāʿ al-aʾimma*, ed. Muḥammad Kāmil Ḥusayn. Cairo, [1948]. Abridged English trans., Jawad Muscati and A. M. Moulvi as *Selections from Qazi Noaman's Kitab-ul-Himma; or, Code of Conduct for the Followers of Imam*. Karachi, 1950.
__ *Kitāb al-majālis waʾl-musāyarāt*, ed. al-Ḥabīb al-Faqī et al. Tunis, 1978.
__ *Taʾwīl al-daʿāʾim*, ed. Muḥammad Ḥasan al-Aʿẓamī. Cairo, 1967–1972.
__ *al-Urjūza al-mukhtāra*, ed. Ismail K. Poonawala. Montreal, 1970.
Nūr Muḥammad Shāh. *Satveṇī moṭī*. Mumbai, n.d., nos. 10–12 and 41–42.

Panj risāla dar bayān-i āfāq va anfus, ed. Andrey E. Bertel's. Moscow, 1970.
Poonawala, Ismail K. 'al-Qāḍī al-Nu'mān's Works and the Sources,' *BSOAS*, 36 (1973), pp. 109–115.
__ 'A Reconsideration of al-Qāḍī al-Nu'mān's *Madhhab*,' *BSOAS*, 37 (1974), pp. 572–579.
__ *Biobibliography of Ismā'īlī Literature*. Malibu, CA, 1977.
__ 'Ismā'īlī *ta'wīl* of the Qur'ān,' in A. Rippin, ed., *Approaches to the History of the Interpretation of the Qur'ān*. Oxford, 1988, pp. 199–222.
__ 'al-Qāḍī al-Nu'mān and Isma'ili Jurisprudence,' in *MIHT*, pp. 117–143.
__ 'The Beginning of the Ismaili *Da'wa* and the Establishment of the Fatimid Dynasty as Commemorated by al-Qāḍī al-Nu'mān,' in F. Daftary and Josef W. Meri, ed., *Culture and Memory in Medieval Islam: Essays in Honour of Wilferd Madelung*. London, 2003, pp. 338–363.
__ 'Hadith, iii. Hadith in Isma'ilism,' *EIR*, vol. 11, pp. 449–451.
al-Qurṭubī, Abū 'Abd Allāh Muḥammad b. Aḥmad. *al-Jāmi' li-aḥkām al-Qur'ān*. Beirut, [1952]-1967.
Qutbuddin, Tahera. *al-Mu'ayyad al-Shīrāzī and Fatimid* Da'wa *Poetry: A Case of Commitment in Classical Arabic Literature*. Leiden, 2005.
al-Rāzī, Abū Ḥātim Aḥmad b. Ḥamdān. *A'lām al-nubuwwa*, ed. Ṣalāḥ al-Ṣāwī and G. R. A'wānī. Tehran, 1977. English trans., excerpt, as *Science of Prophecy*, tr. E. K. Rowson, in *APP*, pp. 140–172.
__ *Kitāb al-iṣlāḥ*, ed., Ḥasan Mīnūchihr and Mahdī Mohaghegh. Tehran, 1377 Sh./1998.
Rashīd al-Dīn Faḍl Allāh Hamadānī. *Jāmi' al-tawārīkh: qismat-i Ismā'īliyān wa Fāṭimiyān wa Nizāriyān wa dā'īyān wa rafīqān*, ed. M. T. Dānishpazhūh and M. Mudarrisī Zanjānī. Tehran, 1338 Sh./1959.
Rypka, Jan. *History of Iranian Literature*, ed. K. Jahn. Dordrecht, 1968.
Sabzālī Ramzānalī, Pīr. '*Ālījāh Mishanarī Sabajā-alī-bhāī nī musāfarī: Madhya Eshiyā nī rasik vigato*,' *The Ismaili*, Mumbai (24 April 1924), p. 4 and (19 October 1924), p. 2.
Ṣadr al-Dīn, Pīr. '*Alaf nirāle khālak rājā*,' in *100 Ginān nī chopaḍī*, Mumbai, n.d., vol. 4, no. 62, pp. 118–119; and in *Mahān Ismāili sant Pīr Sadardīn rachit ginān no saṃgrah*. Mumbai, 1952, vol. 1, no. 41, p. 49.
__ '*Avala tūṃhī ākhara tūṃhī*,' in *Mahān Ismāili sant Pīr Sadardīn rachit ginān no saṃgrah*, vol. 1, no. 128, p. 133.
__ *Būjh nirañjan*. Karachi, 1976.
__ '*Dhan dhan ājano dāḍalore ame harīvar pāyājī*', in *100 Ginān nī chopaḍī*. 4th ed., Mumbai, 1934, vol. 5, no. 42.
__ '*Jugame phīre shāhājī munerī*', in *102 Ginānajī: chopaḍī*. 3rd ed., Mumbai, 1912, vol. 4, no. 3.
__ '*Sakhī māhā pad kerī*', in *100 Ginān nī chopaḍī*. 5th ed., Mumbai, 1935, vol. 3, no. 30.
__ *Saloko moṭo tathā nāno*. Mumbai, 1934, vv. 58, 94.
Salisbury, E. E. 'Translation of Two Unpublished Arabic Documents Relating to the Doctrines of the Ismā'īlīs and Other Bāṭinian Sects,' *JAOS*, 2 (1851), pp. 257–324.

Shams, Pīr, '*Kāyama dāyama tuṃ moro sāmī tere nāme bī koī koī*', in *100 Ginān nī chopaḍī*. 3rd ed., Mumbai, 1919, vol. 2, no. 82.

__ '*Kesarī sīṃha sarūpa bhulāyo*', in *Mahān Ismāilī sant Pīr Shams rachit gināno no saṃgrah*. Mumbai, 1952, vol. 2, pp. 63–64, no. 59.

Shackle, Christopher and Zawahir Moir. *Ismaili Hymns from South Asia: An Introduction to the Ginans*. 2nd ed., Richmond, 2000.

al-Shahrastānī, Abu'l-Fatḥ Muḥammad b. 'Abd al-Karīm. *Kitāb al-milal wa'l-niḥal*, ed. W. Cureton. London, 1842–1846; ed. A. Fahmi Muhammad. Cairo, 1948; ed. M. S. Kaylani, Beirut, 1965; ed. 'Abd al-'Azīz Muḥammad al-Wakīl. Cairo, 1387/1968. German trans., *Religionspartheien und Philosophenschulen*, tr. Th. Haarbrücker. Halle, 1850–1851; repr., Wiesbaden 1969; Partial English trans., *Muslim Sects and Divisions*, tr. A. K. Kazi and J. G. Flynn. London, 1984. French trans., D. Gimaret et al. as *Livre des religions et des sectes*. Louvain and Paris, 1986–1993.

Sheikh, Samira. 'Religious Traditions and Early Ismā'īlī History in Western India: Some Historical Perspectives on Satpanthī Literature and the Gināns,' in Tazim R. Kassam and Françoise Mallison, ed., *Gināns, Texts and Contexts: Essays on Ismaili Hymns from South Asia in Honour of Zawahir Moir* (New Delhi, 2007), pp. 149–167.

Shihāb al-Dīn Shāh al-Ḥusaynī. *Khiṭābāt-i 'āliya*, ed. H. Ujāqī. Bombay, 1963.

__ *Risāla dar ḥaqīqat-i dīn*, ed. W. Ivanow. Bombay, 1947. English trans., *True Meaning of Religion*, tr. W. Ivanow. 2nd ed., Bombay, 1947.

al-Sijistānī, Abū Ya'qūb Isḥāq b. Aḥmad. *Ithbāt al-nubū'āt (al-nubuwwāt)*, ed. 'Ārif Tāmir. Beirut, 1966.

__ *Kashf al-maḥjūb*, ed. H. Corbin. Tehran and Paris, 1949. French trans., *Le dévoilement des choses cachées*, tr. H. Corbin. Lagrasse, 1988. Partial English trans., *Unveiling of the Hidden*, tr. H. Landolt, in *APP*, pp. 71–124.

__ *Kitāb al-yanābī'*, ed. and tr. Henry Corbin, in *Trilogie Ismaélienne*, text pp. 1–97, partial translation as *Le livre des sources* pp. 5–127, ed. Muṣṭafā Ghālib. Beirut, 1965. English trans. Paul E. Walker as 'The Book of Wellsprings' in his *The Wellsprings of Wisdom*. Salt Lake City, 1994, pp. 37–111.

Smoor, Pieter. 'al-Mahdī's Tears: Impressions of Faṭimid Court Poetry,' in U. Vermeulen and D. de Smet, ed., *Egypt and Syria in the Fatimid, Ayyubid and Mamluk Eras II*. Leuven, 1998, pp. 131–170.

Steigerwald, Diane. *La pensée philosophique et théologique de Shahrastânî (m. 548/1153)*. Saint-Nicolas, Québec, 1997.

Stern, Samuel M. *Studies in Early Ismā'īlism*. Jerusalem and Leiden, 1983.

Stroeva, Luydmila V. *Gosudarstvo ismailitov v Irane v XI-XIII vv*. Moscow, 1978. Persian trans., *Ta'rīkh-i Ismā'īliyān dar Īrān*, tr. Parvīn Munzavī. Tehran, 1371 Sh./1992.

al-Ṣūrī, Muḥammad b. 'Alī. *al-Qaṣīda al-Ṣūriyya*, ed. 'Ārif Tāmir. Damascus, 1955.

al-Ṭabrisī, al-Faḍl b. al-Ḥasan. *Majma' al-bayān fī tafsīr al-Qur'ān*, ed. Hāshim al-Rasūlī and Faḍl Allāh al-Ṭabāṭabā'ī. Tehran, 1379/1959.

Thalāth rasā'il Ismā'īliyya, ed. 'Ārif Tāmir. Beirut, 1403/1983.

Trilogie Ismaélienne, ed. and tr. Henry Corbin. Tehran and Paris, 1961.

al-Ṭūsī, Naṣīr al-Dīn. *Akhlāq-i Muḥtashamī*, ed. Muḥammad Taqī Dānishpazhūh. 2nd ed., Tehran, 1361 Sh./1982.

__ *Majmūʿa-yi rasāʾil*, ed. M. T. Mudarris Raḍawī. Tehran, 1335 Sh./1956.
__ *Rawḍat al-taslīm yā taṣawwurāt*, ed. and tr. W. Ivanow. Leiden, 1950; *Rawḍa-yi taslīm*, ed. and tr. S. Jalal Badakhchani as *Paradise of Submission: A Medieval Treatise on Ismaili Thought*. London, 2005.
__ '*Risāla dar tawallā wa-tabarrā*,' in *Akhlāq-i Muḥtashamī*, ed. Muḥammad Taqī Dānishpazhūh. 2nd ed., Tehran, 1361 Sh./1982, pp. 561–570.
__ *Sayr wa sulūk*, ed. and tr. S. Jalal Badakhchani as *Contemplation and Action: The Spiritual Autobiography of a Muslim Scholar*. London, 1998.
van den Berg, Gabrielle R. *Minstrel Poetry from the Pamir Mountains: A Study on the Songs and Poems of the Ismāʿīlīs of Tajik Badakhshan*. Wiesbaden, 2004.
Virani, Shafique N. *The Ismailis in the Middle Ages: A History of Survival, A Search for Salvation*. Oxford, 2007.
Walker, Paul E. *Early Philosophical Shiism: The Ismaili Neoplatonism of Abū Yaʿqūb al-Sijistānī*. Cambridge, 1993.
__ *Abū Yaʿqūb al-Sijistānī: Intellectual Missionary*. London, 1996.
__ *Ḥamīd al-Dīn al-Kirmānī: Ismaili Thought in the Age of al-Ḥākim*. London, 1999.
__ *Exploring an Islamic Empire: Fatimid History and its Sources*. London, 2002.
Wensinck, Arent Jan, ed. *al-Muʿjam al-mufahras li-alfāẓ al-ḥadīth al-nabawī*. Leiden, 1943.
__ *Concordance et Indices de la Traditions Musulmane*. 2nd ed., Leiden, 1992.
__ *The Muslim Creed: its Genesis and Historical Development*. Cambridge, 1932.
al-Yamānī, Muḥammad b. Muḥammad. *Sīrat al-ḥājib Jaʿfar b. ʿAlī*, ed. W. Ivanow, in *Bulletin of the Faculty of Arts, University of Egypt*, 4 (1936), pp. 107–133; tr. W. Ivanow, in his *Ismaili Tradition Concerning the Rise of the Fatimids*. London, etc., 1942, pp. 184–223; French tr. Marius Canard, 'L'autobiographie d'un chambellan du Mahdî 'Obeidallâh le Fâṭimide,' *Hespéris*, 39 (1952), pp. 279–329, reprinted in his *Miscellanea Orientalia*, London, 1973, article V.
Zayn al-ʿĀbidīn, ʿAlī b. al-Ḥusayn. *al-Ṣaḥīfa al-kāmila al-Sajjādiyya*, ed. Fayḍ al-Islām. Tehran, 1375/1955; tr. W. Chittick as *The Psalms of Islam*. London, 1988.

Index

muḥtasham, leader of Nizārīs of Quhistān 17, 241, 325
al-Muʿizz li-dīn Allāh, Fatimid caliph 6, 7, 8, 34, 49, 59, 60, 61, 62, 63, 64, 66, 211, 253, 257
al-Mujbira (Predestinarians) 143
mujtahid 155, 246
mukhammasāt 298
Multān, in Sind 7, 27, 309
Multānī 24
Mumbai 77, 80
muʾmin (believer) 26, 38, 40, 41, 42, 49, 50, 51, 52, 53, 60, 63, 65, 93, 94, 95, 96, 132, 134, 147, 180, 183, 203, 204, 205, 206, 207, 215, 217, 218, 219, 220, 223, 227, 228, 229, 230, 232, 290, 303, 316, 318, 324, 326
Muʾminābād 17
munājāt (prayer poems) 298
Murjiʾa 211, 212
mushrik 221
mustajīb (respondent) 193, 206, 248–249, 325
al-Mustaʿlī, Fatimid caliph 11, 12, 15
Mustaʿlians (Mustaʿliyya) 1, 2, 7, 11, 12, *see also* Bohras, Dāʾūdīs, Ṭayyibīs
al-Mustanṣir, Fatimid caliph 9, 10, 11, 15, 17, 18, 71, 102, 253, 260, 265
Mustanṣir biʾllāh II, Nizārī imam 290
Mustanṣir biʾllāh III, Nizārī imam, *see* Gharīb Mirzā
Muʿtazila 143
muwaḥḥid (unifier) 89–96 *passim*

nabī, *anbiyāʾ*, *see* prophets
nadhīr (warner) 147, 175, 265
nafs (soul) 7, 9, 85, 89, 91, 98, 99–101, 105–110, 111, 112, 115, 122, 132, 136, 140, 148, 153, 154, 155, 156, 162, 181, 183, 187, 200, 201, 202, 203, 204, 224, 225, 229, 232, 234–240 *passim*, 241, 242, 248, 266, 267, 272, 273, 275, 278, 280, 283, 287, 294, 297, 298, 302, 303, 304, 305, 314, 319, 325; animal soul (*nafs-i bahīmī*) 241, 242; universal soul (*nafs-i kullī*) 103, 111, 115, 153, 161, 163, 164, 171, 177, 202, 206
Nafūsa, in North Africa 44
Najīb al-Dīn Ḥasan 241
Nāṣir al-Dīn ʿAbd al-Raḥīm b. Abī Manṣūr, Nizārī *muḥtasham* in Quhistān 241
Nasirean Ethics, see *Akhlāq-i Nāṣirī*
Nāṣir-i Khusraw, Ismaili *dāʿī* and author 1, 4, 10, 11, 22, 33, 34, 71, 77, 80, 85, 102, 199, 254, 271, 298, 299
naṣṣ (designation) 63, 286, 324, 325
nāṭiq, *nuṭaqāʾ* (speaking or law-announcing prophets) 121, 138, 148, 196, 198, 203, 204, 206, 322, 323, 324, 326
al-Naysābūrī, Aḥmad b. Ibrāhīm, Ismaili *dāʿī* and author 5, 135–141
Nazareth 267
Near East 71
Neoplatonism 4, 7, 9, 85
Nile 72, 73, 74, 301
Nīshāpūr (Nisābūr), in Khurāsān 73, 74
Nizārī Quhistānī, Ḥakīm Saʿd al-Dīn b. Shams al-Dīn, Nizārī poet 21, 24, 33, 254, 285
Nizārīs 1, 2, 11, 12–29, 149, 241, 326
Noah (Nūḥ) 38, 40, 54, 181, 287, 301
North Africa 2, 4, 5, 6, 33, 35, 44, *see also* Ifrīqiya, Maghrib, Morocco, Tunisia
nubuwwa, *see* prophecy
al-Nuʿmān b. Muḥammad, al-Qāḍī Abū Ḥanīfa, Ismaili jurist and author 3, 4, 5, 8, 14, 33, 34, 49–58, 59, 61, 62–66, 86, 192–194, 211–221
Nūr al-Dīn Muḥammad, Nizārī imam and lord of Alamūt 17–18
Nūr (Nar) Muḥammad Shāh, Ismaili author 318–321

oath of allegiance, *see ʿahd*, *baʿya*
occultation, *see ghayba*
ontology 102
Originator, *see Mubdiʿ*

Pakistan 1, 11, 23, 29, 77
Pāmīrs 34
Pandiyāt-i jawānmardī, of Imam Mustanṣir biʾllāh (II) 25, 26